THE
UPSET

*Jack Fleck's Incredible Victory over
Ben Hogan at the U.S. Open*

AL BARKOW

CHICAGO
REVIEW
PRESS

Copyright © 2012 by Al Barkow

All rights reserved

First edition

Published by Chicago Review Press, Incorporated

814 North Franklin Street

Chicago, Illinois 60610

ISBN 978-1-61374-075-0

Interior design: Jonathan Hahn

Library of Congress Cataloging-in-Publication Data

Barkow, Al.

   The upset : Jack Fleck's incredible victory over Ben Hogan at the U.S. Open / Al Barkow.

   p. cm.

   Summary: "A thrilling play-by-play, shot-by-shot recounting of one of the most famous golf games of all time, this book brings back to life the look and feel of the entire three days of regular play and the fourth-day playoff of the 1955 U.S. Open at the Olympic Golf Club in San Francisco. Jack Fleck had the slimmest of resumes as a professional tournament golfer: he had never even come close to winning on the PGA Tour. Yet Fleck got himself into a playoff with Ben Hogan—one of the greatest players in golf history—for the game's most prestigious title; and when Fleck defeated Hogan, it was not just surprising, it was incredible. Relying on firsthand sources, this insightful study of a poignant moment in golf history reveals the players' mental processes as they strategized their game and handled their emotions and offers a fascinating look at two different approaches to competing for a golf championship: Hogan, who employed a stoic, no-nonsense approach to the game and Fleck, a practitioner of hatha yoga. The book presents a critical view of Hogan's inexplicable defeat and a convincing explanation for Fleck's mind-boggling victory, which was considered at the time and remains to this day one of the most unexpected outcomes in all sports history"— Provided by publisher.

   ISBN 978-1-61374-075-0 (hardback)

   1. U.S. Open (Golf tournament) (1955 : San Francisco, Calif.) 2. Fleck, Jack. 3. Hogan, Ben, 1912-1997. 4. Golfers—United States. I. Title.

   GV970.3.U69B37 2012

   796.352'068—dc23

Printed in the United States of America

5 4 3 2 1

"Relax? How can anybody relax and play golf? You have to grip the club, don't you?" —BEN HOGAN

"In yoga, relaxation is taught as an art, breathing as a science, and mental control of the physical as a means of harmonizing the body, mind, and spirit."
— INDRA DEVI, *Forever Young, Forever Healthy*

CONTENTS

AUTHOR'S NOTE

W HEN WRITING, historians routinely speculate on the inner thoughts, language, and actions of the principal people in their story. It is essential to enriching the narrative, making it come alive. These suppositions or interpretations are made on the basis of the writer's knowledge of the subject and the character of the individuals involved. In my case, I have been writing on every aspect of golf for over a half century, especially the history of the game. Over those years, I have had personal dealings with both Ben Hogan and Jack Fleck, not to mention virtually everyone else who appears in this tale. I feel quite confident interpreting and expanding on the details of one of the most remarkable events in sports history: the historic U.S. Open match between Jack Fleck and Ben Hogan.

I have made a point to describe the basic playing of every hole exactly as it happened. I gleaned information from newspaper coverage and other on-the-scene reporting, Fleck's well-detailed description of the play in his books, and my conversations with him. I also viewed some film of shots played, although there is precious little of that, and got a few bits of information from people who were present at the match. Unfortunately Hogan never wrote about the match.

The play-by-play is based on what I know of how they played the game—their habits, tics, way of going about their business. I watched Hogan play a lot of golf, and I've seen Fleck play enough for those descriptions to be authentic.

ACKNOWLEDGMENTS

MUCH THANKS TO BILL CALLAN, archivist of the Olympic Country Club, who was extremely helpful in the research for this book, and Jessica Smith, also of the Olympic Club.

Also, an appreciation of my colleagues and good friends Bill Fields and Mike Bartlett, who gave this book a professional read and whose insights contributed to the final version. And a special thanks to Yuval Taylor, a very good editor.

Finally, thanks to John Monteleone, my agent, and his partner in crime, Laurie Fox, for finding a good place for this book.

PROLOGUE

Two Characters in Search of a Championship

JACK FLECK KNELT IN THE SAND on Ocean Beach, at the far west side of San Francisco. Wave spray from the Pacific Ocean lightly coated his thin, jut-jawed face. He was praying for good luck or divine intervention or good karma—he wasn't quite sure—in the great task he had ahead of him that afternoon. He would be competing against Ben Hogan on the Lake course of the Olympic Country Club in a playoff for the 1955 U.S. Open championship. *Ben Hogan! Well, of all things!* Fleck wasn't sure the prayers would help, but they couldn't hurt. They could reinforce the voice he was sure he heard while shaving the previous morning. It came through the mirror. Someone, or something, delivered the message—twice—that he was a man of destiny and was going to win the U.S. Open.

At the same time, Ben Hogan was in his room at the Saint Francis Hotel, in downtown San Francisco, finishing the burdensome but absolutely essential task of encasing his right leg from mid-thigh to mid-shin in a cottony elastic wrapping, making sure it was not too tight or too loose. This followed sitting in a warm Epsom salt bath for fifteen minutes. He did this before every round of golf, and it had become as routine as breakfast, lunch, and dinner. It began after he recovered, more or less, from the highway accident he suffered six years earlier that nearly killed him and, among other things, left his legs forever fragile and vulnerable to stress—such as walking a golf course and especially making his vigorous golf swing.

Hogan's wife, Valerie, with her long, sad face, watched her husband do the wrapping. It was not a difficult job to run the bath or apply the wrap, and she would have liked to help. She used to offer, but he always said no, no, he could do it himself, and she no longer applied to assist. Her husband needed to be the sole manager of his life. He liked to think he didn't need anyone else, that all he had accomplished was entirely of his own doing. That was not true, of course, but it was how he wanted to understand himself and the world to understand him.

In strictly golf-accomplishment terms, Fleck had no business being part of the upcoming confrontation. As a professional golfer he was in the "qualifier" class. By common consensus that is to golf what an "opponent" is to prizefighting: a pug with no chance of beating anyone of consequence and who serves as fodder to build up the record of contenders, those with real potential. A qualifier is a player who manages to get into the field of a golf championship but only gives it numerical legitimacy.

Fleck had played twenty tournaments on the 1955 pro tournament circuit, starting in January, and earned a mere $2,500 in prize money. He was just about breaking even financially, but only because he didn't drink or smoke and was otherwise very close with a buck. He got that way as a boy growing up during the Great Depression. His father had been a truck farmer but failed during a misbegotten land rush and from then supported his wife and five children with the sketchy and uncertain living of a salesman. There were three boys and two girls. Jack was the third born, the middle child, the one who gets ignored and ends up doing something special or different.

Fleck's wife, Lynn, was back home in Davenport, Iowa, with their four-year-old son, Craig. She looked after the two public golf courses at which her husband was the professional/manager. She had encouraged Jack to try the tournament circuit full-time this year. In past years he had gone out from November through March to play the winter tour and then returned home to his day jobs. But now, at thirty-two, it was time to give big-time tournament golf a complete, all-year effort and once and for all determine if he had the goods.

"Give it a try, dear," Lynn Fleck had said to her husband, "and see if you can do it." Based on his overall performance over the last year and a half, it seemed clear he couldn't "do it." And yet, because he was an accurate driver of the ball, Fleck was not discouraged when he arrived at the Olympic Country Club for his practice rounds. He had a feeling before the tournament began that he might be able to finish in the top ten. That was his goal. It would get him into the next year's championship without having to qualify.

Ben Hogan had somewhat loftier expectations going in. It was not just a matter of winning this particular edition of the National Open, as it was commonly called. He had already won it four times.

But a fifth one would make it truly special. No one had won that many. Hogan ordinarily liked to project himself as unconcerned with such statistics, as if he was just out to excel and earn the first-prize check. But in this championship he made no bones about wanting to set a new record. He felt it would cement his place in golf history, a feeling that reflected the insecurity not uncommon among highly accomplished individuals, athletes in particular, who are forever fearful they are about to lose their unique edge or run out of luck. If he could have stepped back and viewed himself objectively, Hogan would have realized he didn't need any reassurance of his place in the annals of the game. He was already cast in bronze, properly recognized as one of the greatest golfers the game had ever had.

There was another incentive for Hogan, one that was more immediate and very real. At the age of forty-two, this could be his last opportunity. Every time he entered a championship he felt, or his body told him, that his capacity to play at the highest level was getting closer and closer to being over. He had played only six tournaments all year leading up to this mid-June date and had said more than a few times during the practice-round days at Olympic that he was working harder to prepare for this Open than any other before and that it was getting to be too much for him.

The general details of the head-on collision of Hogan's Cadillac with a bus that was wrongly passing traffic on a fogbound two-lane highway in west Texas, in February 1949, were well documented in newspaper and magazine articles and in a feature movie, *Follow the Sun,* that appeared in 1951. If he hadn't, at the last second, leaned over to protect Valerie from the oncoming bus, he would have been speared to death by the steering wheel of his car. As it was, he sustained tremendous injuries: a fractured collarbone and ankle, a double fracture of the pelvis, a chipped rib. He also developed blood clots that required a unique surgery that saved his life and allowed him to eventually, heroically, almost incomprehensibly win more major championships than he had won before the accident.

That said, Hogan was never wholly relieved from circulation problems in his legs. Few knew the day-to-day toll he was paying to continue competing. He didn't volunteer that information. He was an extremely private man when it came to all aspects of his personal life and had an exceptionally intimidating manner that daunted any effort to break in where no one was wanted. So tight was he in this regard that even Valerie did not know until some five years into their marriage that Hogan's father had committed suicide. And that her husband, a young boy at the time, was in the house and perhaps at the scene when the fatal shot was fired. Even then, Valerie learned of it by accident, overhearing her sister-in-law mention it in a conversation with an aunt.

No guessing was necessary to know Hogan's legs were a problem. He limped noticeably wherever he played, and on the Lake it seemed even worse. The course is not roly-poly hilly in its overall topography, but there are some substantial rises and a very steep stairway up to the clubhouse from the course. And the grass was almost always wet from the mist and fog that were endemic to the site. Even though the fairways were closely mown, it was a heavy walk. Hogan often rubbed his knees as he climbed the "Olympian" hills. When he was not shaking hands with a fellow player, chatting with the press, or otherwise in presentation mode, his face in repose had a hauntingly gaunt expression. A teenager who sneaked onto the course to see Hogan play a practice round was amazed to learn that Hogan and his father were the same age: "He didn't look like forty-two at all; more like fifty-two to me, maybe sixty."

Hogan had another issue weighing on him. In the fall of 1953 he went into business as a golf-equipment manufacturer. The Ben Hogan Co. opened its doors in Fort Worth, Texas, where Hogan had lived ever since he was a teenager. Most of the money for the start-up came from two close friends—Pollard Simon, who made his fortune in the construction business, and Marvin Leonard, a Fort Worth department store magnate. The first production run of Ben Hogan irons came out in the summer of 1954, and the clubs were well received. Hogan billed his clubs as being for the "better player," and they had both the look and playability that Hogan felt represented the motto. Many better players, including tournament pros, felt the same. But there were serious problems with the second run, which prompted a strong disagreement with Pollard Simon and led to the dissolution of their partnership. A lot of money was involved.

When Jack Fleck arrived in San Francisco six days before the start of play, he drove around the working-class town of Daly City, which was close to the Olympic Club, and found a decent room in the El Camino Motel on Mission Street. It was only a ten-minute drive to the course. Fleck asked if the furniture in his room could be rearranged so he had space for his hatha yoga exercises. He also asked for the bed to be situated so he could sleep with his head toward the north. He had read up on magnetism while at sea as a sailor in World War II and came across a theory that humans sleep most soundly when they are parallel to the magnetic lines of force that encircle the earth from north to south. The concept is also iterated in Hindu scripture, suggesting, among other things, that people who sleep in an east-west position have more dreams than north-south sleepers. That didn't come up in his study of Hindu-based hatha yoga, but in any case, Jack Fleck wasn't much interested in having dreams that week. For golfers they are usually troublesome, bordering on nightmares. The proprietor of the El Camino Motel was accommodating. The bed was reset on a north-south line.

Fleck took most of his meals during the week at the small, narrow Beacon Diner, directly across the street from the motel. There were eight revolving stools before a Formica counter and three small tables along the wall. He could get the kind of food he ate, at a good price. He did not eat meat or anything white—white flour, sugar. He ate a lot of fruit. He referred to himself as a fruitaholic.

After his exercises he ate breakfast at the Beacon—a bowl of dry cereal, orange juice, a banana, a slice of whole-wheat toast, and a cup of tea—ingesting the food in a kind of meditative state. As he chewed and swallowed he stared past the buxom waitress and through the wide front window out onto the street. After paying the check and leaving a half-dollar tip, a little higher than usual, but, win or lose, he was in for a good-sized check—more than he had won that year to date—he drove to Ocean Beach. There, along the shoreline, he walked a bit, then knelt to pray. That done, he got into his one-year-old four-door Buick and drove off to the Olympic Country Club, only five minutes away, to make his date with Ben Hogan and play for the National Open championship. Tee off time was 2:00 PM.

As Fleck was slowly eating his breakfast, Ben Hogan, his right knee now bound for the day, had a room-service breakfast of scrambled eggs, toast, a cup of coffee, and a glass of ginger ale. He ate slowly but with a conscious purpose. He had once watched

Walter Hagen, the great champion a generation before him, reach for a glass of water in something close to slow motion. Hogan's friend and swing mentor, Henry Picard, said Hagen's manner was a way of slowing his metabolism against a tendency to do things too quickly with his hands. Such quickness was detrimental to the golf swing, in which speed kills . . . except at the moment of impact.

This was one of a number of means by which Hogan sought to slow his internal tempo and subsequently that of his quick-paced swing. He would play as many practice rounds as possible with players such as George Fazio, who wielded his clubs like a maestro conducting *La Mer*. Another of Hogan's tactics for slowing himself down was to drive under the speed limit to the golf course. He wasn't driving this week—the Olympic Club was providing complimentary car service to the players. But every day Hogan asked the fellow driving the car to keep under the thirty-five mile-per-hour speed limit. As for the ginger ale, he was told once that ginger had blood-thinning properties, and while there was little more than a trace of the spice in a glassful of Canada Dry, he felt it slimmed his hands a bit and gave him a more sensitive feel for the clubhead.

Valerie Hogan stayed back to pack their bags, attend church, and have some private time before heading out to the course. She was hoping it would be the last time she would have to go through the whole experience, this National Open business. But she knew, with an internal sigh, that it wouldn't be.

STAGE SET

O F ALL THE DISTINCTIONS GOLF HAS in the world of sports, none is more telling and potentially compelling than the diversity of its venues. All football fields are the same length and width, as are tennis courts and basketball courts, not to mention the height of the net and dimensions of the baskets. A baseball field can be tweaked a bit to affect play—the distance from the plate to the outfield fences, the depth of the infield grass—but the pitcher pitches from sixty feet, six inches, and it's ninety feet between the bases everywhere in the world.

No such rigid standardizing of its field of play exists in golf, which is one of the game's enduring charms—and selling points. As those who claim golf is the toughest game say in the vernacular, "There ain't any sand traps between first and second base and no creek ten yards from the end zone." Except for the standardized diameter of the hole where the ball ends up, each and every golf course has its own dimensions, arrangement of hazards, undulations of terrain, peculiarities of turf, and configuration of holes. No two holes on a golf course are ever exactly alike in their form. All the more fascinating is that the challenges—the width and angle of the fairways, the incorporation of water hazards, the positioning of and contouring of the greens . . . in short, the difficulties of a golf course—are man-made. Even on the Scottish links, where the game was born, the golfers would route the holes so that the sand-filled mounds—the bunkers—formed by sheep digging in for shelter against the incessant winds became obstacles to the golfers.

In the United States, with terrain far more varied than in Scotland, more ingenuity was needed to produce golf courses deemed sufficiently demanding of players. Courses built on perfectly flat ground in Florida or the Midwest, where there are no natural obstacles already in place, are invariably turned into layouts featuring deep man-made pits Americans have come to call *traps*, cunningly placed ponds, oddly banked greens, and very often roller-coaster fairways. If no stands of trees are extant, thousands are planted to hem in fairways. If native trees are on the property, fairways are placed to bring them into play. It is generally accepted that a dead-flat course with no bunkers or water or trees will not attract golfers, because the game is too easy, or seems to be. In fact, the harder a course is to play, the more praise it receives, or at least the more of a reputation it engenders.

Which is to say, given the problems inherent to hitting just one solid golf shot, let alone two in a row, those who crow about building "the hardest golf course in the world" are at heart sadists. Sadomasochists, really, because if they play the courses they demand be built, then they are inflicting pain on themselves as well as their fellow man. And when an important contest such as the U.S. Open is to be held on one of these hard courses, it is further *manipulated*, as critics of the United States Golf Association would have it, to make it even more difficult.

The USGA sets the gold standard in making courses as trying as possible, and especially when it comes to the U.S. Open.
The association demurs at the many harsh and sometimes profane
adjectives it hears regarding the preparation of courses it uses for
the championship. Its most memorable rationalization for fairways
through which a foursome must walk single file, play out of rough
as high as an elephant's eye, and putt on greens as slippery as mer-
cury is, "Our objective is not to humiliate the best players in the
world, it's to identify them."

Be that as it may, when average golfers happen onto a U.S.
Open course in the days before the grandstands, scoreboards, and
gallery are in place, they will immediately sense that something
special is afoot. The definition of the fairways is the most distin-
guishing characteristic, their unusual narrowness sharply defined
by the deep and darker grass that borders them. The courses exude
a tone of magnitude, significance, and consequence. Except for its
overall length, which can't be seen at a glance, the Lake course of
the Olympic Club had that air about it even before the USGA and
the members of the club got their hands on it. But, of course, that
was not enough.

The Olympic Club was founded in 1860. It was the first of its
kind in the nation, its central purposes to provide a facility for its
members to get into or stay in good physical condition through
exercise and athletics of one sort or another and to have a place
to hang out. It was also meant to develop high-level competitive
amateur athletic talent. The Olympic Club formed teams to vie
in national and international competitions in many sports—basketball, football, rugby, swimming, boxing. One club member was
James J. "Gentleman Jim" Corbett, the heavyweight champion
who defeated the legendary John L. Sullivan for the title. Corbett

taught boxing at the Olympic Club for many years. In 1909 an Olympic Club member, Ralph Rose, set the world record for the shot put. In 1915 the club's basketball team won a national amateur championship, and in 1941 the fabled basketball player Hank Luisetti, an Olympic Club member, introduced the one-hand jump shot to the game and led the club's basketball team to the AAU (Amateur Athletic Union) championship. In 1918 golf was added to the mix.

Golf was steadily gaining attention in the United States after Francis Ouimet's remarkable playoff victory over Harry Vardon and Ted Ray in the 1913 U.S. Open. The game was "officially" only in its second decade in the United States when Ouimet took the title at the Country Club, in Brookline, Massachusetts. He was a twenty-year-old amateur golfer who had done nothing of competitive note nationally and not much locally. But he managed to defeat the #1 and #2 players in the world head-on. That Vardon and Ray were Englishmen made Ouimet's achievement all the more satisfying to an American audience. It generated a wave of new New World golfers.

Following the trend, in 1918, when the one-year-old Lakeside Golf Club ran into financial problems, the Olympic Club bought it. (In a neat turn, a notable member of the Olympic Club in 1955 was Ed Lowery, who caddied for Ouimet in that historic 1913 playoff.) It didn't take long for golf to catch on in a big way among the Olympic members, and the club eventually outgrew Lakeside. In 1924 it purchased considerable land adjacent to the Lakeside course, eliminated that course, and built two new ones. Both were the work of Willie Watson, a noted Scots-born course designer, and Sam Whiting, who was in charge of constructing the layouts. Whiting also contributed to the design of the course, especially when he was appointed the club's maintenance supervisor or greenkeeper.

One course was named Ocean, as it was more open to the nearby Pacific Ocean. The other was named the Lake, or Lakeside, for its proximity to inland Lake Merced. At the outset the Ocean course was the more highly regarded of the two, largely due to a few visually dramatic holes in the dunes-like area about a quarter-mile west of the Skyline Highway entrance to the club's grounds. When a powerful storm caused landslides that buried those holes, Whiting was assigned to restore them. Given considerable leverage, Whiting put all eighteen holes of the Ocean course east of the Skyline Highway. And he made some significant additions to the Lake, especially the planting of thousands of trees on what was a treeless piece of land. They would become imposing, dramatic-looking trees—eucalyptus, pines, green cedars, and the particularly distinctive California cypress. The Ocean remained an excellent test of the game, especially in having to deal with the wind, but Whiting's trees gave the Lake such a formidable aspect that it came to define the club.

The general chairman of the 1955 U.S. Open was Bob Roos, a longtime member of the Olympic Club and for many years a force in Northern California golf. He was an excellent player who qualified for two U.S. Opens and eleven U.S. Amateur championships, played in six British Amateur championships, and once defeated a young Ken Venturi in a U.S. Amateur match. He was the club champion many times over. A short man, he wore horn-rimmed glasses through which came the clever look of a shrewd businessman. Roos headed up Roos Brothers, a chain of retail clothing stores with its flagship store in downtown San Francisco. And he was as calculating a golfer as he was a retailer. He made up for his lack of distance with the driver by becoming a wizard at chipping and putting.

It was Roos who first proposed the idea of holding a national championship, in particular the National Open, at the Olympic Club. He was encouraged by the membership. In 1953 Roos began a campaign to achieve that goal. He knew that the USGA's general practice was to try out a potential Open course by first putting its second-biggest championship—the U.S. Amateur—on it. In a letter to Joseph P. Dey, the executive secretary of the USGA, Roos pointed out that the Lake course would make an excellent venue for that event. Roos reminded Dey that the Lake had been previously tested by the game's top players. In 1930, 1932, and 1939 it hosted the National Match-Play tournament, in which all the top professionals of the era competed. In 1930 Leo Diegel, a PGA champion, defeated Al Espinosa in the final. In the 1932 final Dick Metz defeated Horton Smith, the first and third winner of the Masters. And in 1946 the San Francisco Open was played on the Lake course, with Byron Nelson, who was then at the very peak of his world-class game, coming away the winner with a three-over-par 283. Ben Hogan, only two years away from winning his first U.S. Open, finished third, ten shots off Nelson's pace. Nelson's winning score made it clear that Olympic's Lake course had a very sturdy character.

Dey was impressed by the course's past history, but he was also cognizant of a feeling held by many in golf that the USGA, head-quartered in New York City, was eastern-seaboard oriented and did not sufficiently recognize the abundance of superb national championship golf courses elsewhere in the country, especially on the West Coast. Of the fifty-four U.S. Opens played to date only one had been held in California. That was in 1948, when Ben

Hogan won it at the Riviera Country Club in Los Angeles. Putting those two elements together, Dey simply told Roos, "Let's skip the Amateur and play the 1955 National Open at Olympic." Roos and the club members couldn't have been happier.

Roos immediately began the process of amending the Lake course. Robert Trent Jones Sr., the preeminent golf course architect in the country, was hired to suggest changes and oversee making them. In the previous four or five years Jones had become the "doctor" of U.S. Open courses. Some, including Ben Hogan, would say he was guilty of malpractice after Jones doctored the Oakland Hills Country Club layout in Birmingham, Michigan, for the 1951 U.S. Open. Oakland Hills' South course was formidable in the buff, so to speak, but Jones determined that it needed an upgrade in its fairway bunkering.

The course was opened for play in 1918, and based on the distance the pros were getting on average with their drivers, Jones relocated existing fairway bunkers and added new ones so they would come into play. The idea was to put an added premium on accuracy off the tee. Either because the players were leaving their drivers in the bag and laying back off the tee to stay short of the bunkers—thus having to play longer approach shots—or because they were taking a chance and finding the sand, there were only two rounds in the 60s in the 1951 championship. One was by Hogan, a dogged, brilliant three-under-par 67 in the last round that gave him a two-shot victory over Clayton Heafner, who, also in the last round, shot a 69. Detroit's golf reporters had been calling the revised Oakland Hills South course a "monster," and in his victory speech Hogan referred to that description, saying he had tamed it. He did not coin the term for the course, but it became associated with him.

There was nothing new in the readjusting of golf courses for the game's best players. Ever since the invention of the three-piece rubber-core golf ball at the turn of the twentieth century by two Ohioans, Coburn Haskell and Bertram Work, golf courses were regularly being lengthened to "protect" them from super sub-par rounds by the game's best players. The Haskell ball (a generic term; eventually, various manufacturers put their own brand name to it) was also dubbed the "Bounding Billie" for the distance it rolled after landing. It was much livelier than the solid gutta-percha ball that had been used for almost a half-century. And, as ball makers gradually made improvements on the Haskell, making balls that could be hit farther and farther, courses kept getting longer. So would the Lake.

It was Jones's charge in his Olympic Club assignment to bring the Lake course "up to modern standards." Before Jones made the revisions, the Lake played to 6,373 yards from the backmost tees. It was indeed too short for the Open, and Jones set a number of tees farther back. The 18th, in particular, was lengthened by close to forty yards. Even though the 17th, originally a short par-5 at 485 yards, was turned into a 460-yard par-4, overall the course was lengthened by 327 yards to 6,760 yards, and the par for the course dropped from 71 to 70. But it would play a good bit longer, owing to the weather conditions. For one thing, the dew and fog moistened the fairways, which did not give a lot of roll. Also, the cool, damp air and the low altitude (the site is only a few feet above sea level) impeded the distance a ball would travel. These factors put some 150 unmeasured yards on the course as a whole. It would play at around 6,900 yards.

An unusual feature of the hitherto untouched Lake course was that it had no fairway bunkers. A few were scattered randomly left and right on some holes, vestiges of the day when the course had no trees. They had become sequestered in among Sam Whiting's trees and were effectively not in play for the U.S. Open. As to adding any, however, Jones was kept well in check. Most people felt that few, if any, were really needed. Whiting's trees had grown to maturity over the past thirty years and closed in the fairways. So only three fairway bunkers were added. Two of them, not in play off the tee, were on the right side of the fairway, some fifty yards short of the first green. They would be factors for second shots and mainly only those played from the rough—or, if a bold player thought he could carry them, in trying for the green from the fairway. The other one was truer to its designation, being placed some 245 yards from the tee on the left side of the 6th fairway—within driving distance. A number of existing greenside bunkers were deepened or expanded to tighten the approach shots, but that was it in respect to the bunkering of the course. Except for a ploy Bob Roos tried but in the end didn't get away with: the dreaded Oakmont Furrows.

When the Oakmont Country Club, just outside Pittsburgh, was opened for play in 1905, Henry Fownes, who founded the club and who evidently had a mean streak as wide as his course, was bound and determined to make it the most difficult in the world. Aside from building the fastest greens known to man, he devised a rake with two-inch-long tines set about a quarter-inch apart that was used to create deep furrows in all the sand traps. The sizing of the tines was perfect. A golf ball fit snugly within the furrows. Adding to the difficulty, the sand was raked so the furrows were perpendicular to the line of play. Unless a misdirected ball happened to end up atop a furrow, the odds of which were very long, it was just about impossible to hit a decent recovery shot. The furrows took a skill shot out of the game and effectively made the bunkers as punishing as water hazards. Finally, after the 1953 U.S. Open at Oakmont, there was so much complaining about the furrows that the USGA banned the feature. Bob Roos claimed he did not know of the ban and outfitted the Olympic Club grounds crew with the damned rake. A likely story. When the USGA saw the furrowed bunkers Roos was told to rake the sand in the customary way.

But no matter how the bunkers were raked, it was the rough that got everyone's attention—and for good reason. The USGA set down parameters for its length. The first six feet or so off the fairway, called the "collar" (now known as the "first cut"), was to be in the range of four inches deep. From that point back it could be grown to eight inches or higher. To this Bob Roos added another element that was not a part of the USGA's specifications—the density of the grass.

In the spring of 1955 Roos and the club's greenkeeper, Elmer Border, overseeded the Italian rye grass and heavily fertilized it. They then refertilized it ten days before the championship to give it a truly wrist-wrenching consistency. The grass itself was thick bladed, so overall the rough was matted and exceptionally resistant to golf clubs trying to pass through it. Furthermore, Roos went above the USGA specs by growing the collar at close to six inches high.

When the players began taking their practice licks, the complaints about the rough came quickly and in waves. Everyone barked that lengthy shots to the greens were practically impossible. They had no choice but to use a lofted club just to get their ball back onto the fairway. The rough was playing like one course-length lateral water hazard. Ed "Porky" Oliver played only six holes in his first look at the course because, he claimed, the rough had by then worn him out. He added a bit of hyperbole, noting that he lost half a dozen balls in those few holes he played. But in truth, all the players were having trouble finding balls in what they called the cabbage, broccoli, trash, cooked linguini, and myriad other metaphors.

When Joe Dey arrived at Olympic a week before the start of play and heard the torrent of tirades about the rough—and saw it for himself—he ordered the collars taken down two inches. Ironically, many players said it didn't help; it actually made things worse. With the longer rough, the matted grass might keep the ball close to the top, a position from which they had something of a chance to hit it. At the lower height balls sank down to the ground, leaving little to no chance of making contact without getting a fistful of grass between it and the clubface. Either way, thin-wristed golfers were in danger of serious sprains.

As Sam Snead put it, when asked what he thought of the rough, "If I told you what I think you couldn't publish it. The strongest man in the world can't hit the thing ten feet out of some of this grass."

Roos added another couple of wrinkles, one that was undetectable by newcomers and couldn't have been barred in any case, once it was discovered. The 7th hole, at 266 yards, was obviously a potentially very easy birdie hole. Because most of the players could carry a driver, on average, 220 yards in the air, Roos let the rough grow from the tee to 220 yards out. With the hole playing into the prevailing westerly wind, the tee shot would require a powerhouse drive with great accuracy to reach the forty-six-yard-long fairway. And of course a layup was out of the question. However, Joe Dey commanded that the rough be cut back to 185 yards in length from the tee. Still, Roos saw to it that even if the second shot was with a wedge or 9 iron out of the fairway, it would be no bargain.

The 7th green was completely surrounded by sand traps—it was, in effect, an island green—but with the approach shot being so short, Roos felt it needed some exploitation. He added a mound in the middle of the green. It wasn't a high one, it wasn't all that obvious to the naked eye, but it was there and it made a difference. He added the mound a couple of months before play began, and so it seemed a preexisting, intrinsic component of the course. It hadn't been there in the original design and was gone soon after the Open concluded. The members would not stand for it. The mound could careen well-struck approach shots off the green or at least to its outer perimeter, and it definitely complicated the putting. It was a nasty little trick.

What was Roos up to with all his evil machinations? One might think he would have some sympathy for the players, based on his extensive personal experience in U.S. Open play. He himself had been victimized, so to say, by the USGA's course-altering policies. But another factor was at work. Members of golf clubs hosting the game's best players in a tournament are like strict fathers protecting their nubile young daughter's purity. They do not like anyone taking advantage of their babies. It is called course pride, expressed as an article of faith with words like, "Those hotshot pros are not going to cut up *our* course."

This attitude has some history to it. For example, in the early days of the pro tour—the 1930s—the members of private clubs, or owners of public courses hosting a tournament, would one day water the fronts of the greens, cut the holes in the back half, and keep that portion rock hard. Anyone coming up short with an approach would be left with a sixty-foot putt. If the approach carried to the back half, the ball would bound over the green and leave a delicate chip shot back to the hole. The next day, the order would be reversed. The front half would go unwatered, and the hole would be cut there.

Only a day or so into Open week the headlines screeched that the Lake was the toughest course ever used for a national championship, that the winning score would be the highest in years, that the pros should fear for their lives, that it was a Herculean task just to play nine holes. The club defended Bob Roos, saying he was following USGA specifications to the letter and that the preparation of the course was entirely under the association's purview. Not quite, but that indeed became a fact when, after the 1955 U.S. Open, the USGA put it in writing that it would take over *all* aspects of course conditions and preparations for all its championships.

Another component in the makeup of the stage set was something over which Bob Roos and the USGA had no control: the weather. During the month of June in the rest of the United States there is a conventional early hint of the coming summer heat; sometimes it has already arrived. More than a few U.S. Opens, always held in June, had been played in muggy weather. Mark Twain is erroneously credited with saying that the worst winter he ever spent was a summer in San Francisco. He never said it, but the witticism has some validity. The chill in the air at the Olympic Club "goes right to my bones," Sam Snead said. It feels wet even if the rainy season is over. A gray mist or an actual fog is often the city's roof. It's called the marine layer. All the more at Olympic, which is so close to the ocean that creates it. Toney Penna, who played the tour for years before becoming the club designer for the MacGregor Golf Company, reminded all the players coming to Olympic to bring a lot of sweaters and corduroy trousers.

Surprisingly, based on Hogan's expressed dislike for the work Robert Trent Jones Sr. did in revamping, upgrading, or bastardizing U.S. Open courses, he had nothing but good things to say about the Lake course. He said it was tough but very fair and the right sort of test for the national championship. Was Hogan trying to soften his image as a hard case, a steel-cut golfing machine, in order to gain favor in the public eye for his new line of golf clubs?

A local sportswriter, Joe Williams, thought he smelled something of the kind. After noting the complaints about the course by
Claude Harmon and others, Williams wrote: "Hogan's reaction to
the rough took a different turn. His fulsome and repetitious praise
of the course would have interested Freudian cultists. There was
a surface sheen to his remarks that smacked more of the mannerly
house guest than an uninhibited analyst or forthright critic." It
seemed unimaginable that the cold-eyed little Texan was doing
public relations. But there you have it.

Others who read or heard Hogan's remarks about the course
had another take. They thought he might be pulling a con on the
field. If Hogan thought it was not such a tough track, the rest of the
guys would not work so hard. That would make it a little easier for
Hogan to come away with the winner's trophy. Some among this
cohort also suggested that all of Hogan's limping was another of his
gamesmanship ploys. Getting everybody to think he was not up to
the task because he was too sore and achy might also get everyone
to ease back. A specious notion, and not really the case. Hogan was
not a totally well man physically, but everyone also knew that it was
no bar to his playing outstanding golf over the long haul.

Jack Fleck had no qualms about any of it—the weather, the
rough, the narrow fairways, the greens that many players felt were
too small for the length of shots that had to be hit into them. Fleck
was simply happy to have managed to qualify for the championship. It could be played in the Mojave Desert, the jungles of New
Guinea, or Normandy Beach, and he'd tee it up with no complaints at all. He was in excellent physical condition and was ready
to get it on.

REHEARSALS

ACCIDENTS OF TIME AND PLACE, in retrospect, can be thought of as predestined. And so it was in the unlikely case of Jack Fleck and Ben Hogan going head-to-head on golf's main stage.

Fleck got into golf in his early teens as a caddie, and for the reason most kids from his financial background did during the Great Depression: to make money and help with the family finances. During those hard times Jack and his brothers helped plant vegetables for the family larder, topped onions, and slipped cardboard into their shoes against the holes in the soles. The family raised chickens every year for the eggs, to supplement their protein intake. The boys took any odd job that came along—delivering newspapers, raking leaves, weeding gardens, shoveling snow, mopping out the high school restroom. Jack's older brothers knew about making some money caddying at the local country club—at forty-five cents per round—and that spurred young Jack's original interest in the game.

But it was when the 1936 Western Open, a major championship at the time, came to the Davenport Country Club that Fleck's interest in golf really began to flower. He worked as a forecaddie during the event and was struck by the ability of the professionals and their purposeful manner. An impressionable fourteen-year-old looking for a way to separate himself from his working-class milieu, he made a firm, unequivocal decision to become a golf professional. Not that he showed any special talent for the game at the time. He played on his high school team, but with little distinction. He worked at it, though. During the winter months when a junior and senior in high school, he worked at the winter golf school operated by Tom Cunningham in the Blackhawk Hotel, in downtown Davenport, which allowed him to hit balls into a net. He became so intent on his aim to be a professional golfer that he did not enter amateur tournaments as a teenager. A shortage of money had something to do with it, but with unfettered resolution he declared himself a pro even before he was one in fact.

After Fleck graduated high school in 1939 he got a job cleaning clubs at the Davenport Country Club. But his boss, the head professional, would not let him play the course after his work was done, so he quit. He took the night shift at a number of factory jobs so he could play at the public courses around town. One job was as a pattern maker for the Bettendorf Company, a manufacturer of train cars and other heavy equipment. He was getting thirty-nine cents an hour, good pay at the time. But late in December he quit that job and traveled south to San Antonio, Texas. He wanted to see for himself what the pro tour was like. He saw the Texas Open, the Tucson Open, and the New Orleans Open and, while hanging around, made contacts with two Iowa club professionals who were trying their luck on the winter tour. Through these connections Fleck got a post as assistant professional at the Des Moines Golf & Country Club. He worked there for two summers, and, in 1942, with the United States at war, he joined the navy.

On D-Day at Normandy, Fleck served on a ship that lobbed rockets into the German defenses as American troops waded through the water to reach Utah Beach. He saw the gray water of the English Channel turn to red with the blood of American soldiers. He did similar duty in the Mediterranean theater, before being sent home to be with his mother when she was dying. He arrived two hours before she passed away. He was then assigned to the Pacific theater of operations, but halfway to Pearl Harbor the war ended and he was discharged in San Diego. He took a long bus ride home to Bettendorf.

In December 1945 he traveled west to California with two pro friends who were going to play the winter tour, starting in San Diego. He hit balls for the first time in four years, then played his first round of golf in all that time. He shot 93. But he kept practicing and playing. He failed to qualify for the Los Angeles Open and the San Francisco Open, which was played at the Olympic Club, but the next week he played in the Richmond Open, across the bay, and made the cut. However, a 77 in the last round put him out of the money. Nonetheless, in two short months Fleck had shown marked improvement. Ben Hogan played just ahead of him in that last round and missed an eagle putt on the last hole that would have brought him a tie with Toney Penna for the victory. But Fleck and Hogan did not connect in any way in Richmond.

Fleck returned to his job as assistant professional at the Des Moines Country Club in the spring of 1946. When the clubhouse burned down, he sought other employment and in 1947 was hired by the Davenport Park Board as professional at the city's two municipal golf courses—Duck Island and Credit Island. He was twenty-six and didn't yet know how to drive a car, but he had a position that allowed him to make a living and work as hard as he wanted to on his golf game. He played in regional tournaments, and in his first regular tour event, the 1949 Cedar Rapids Open, he shot a first-round 67 and eventually finished fourth. It earned him a check for five hundred dollars.

Fleck played the 1949 Florida winter tour beginning in October but returned home in December to marry Lynn Burnsdale, a Chicagoan he had met when she came into his shop to get a club repaired. They took their honeymoon in California, where Jack continued playing the tour, starting in San Diego. He failed to get into the money in any of the eleven events in which he played from California through Florida and returned to his job in Iowa. He did qualify for the 1950 U.S. Open but missed the cut. This was the Open in which Ben Hogan made his fabled comeback from his highway accident, winning in a playoff over George Fazio and Lloyd Mangrum.

Near the end of 1950 Jack and Lynn Fleck had a child. The father wanted to name him Snead Hogan Fleck. The mother would not hear of it. They settled on Craig Wood Fleck. The baby's namesake, Craig Wood, was a star of the pro tour in the 1930s and 1940s and winner of a Masters and U.S. Open, among other tournaments. After the birth Jack went out with Lynn to play the winter tour, leaving baby Craig with his grandparents.

From then on Jack followed the itinerary of many club professionals from the snowbound states who wanted to test their talent on the tournament circuit. From the end of October through March they played tournaments starting in Florida, jumped to California at the start of the new year, and made their way back through the South to Florida before heading home to their day jobs. Jack Fleck followed that pattern, finishing in the money here and there and barely making expenses. Then, in late 1953, Jack and Lynn made the decision that he would give the tour a full-time shot—two years, from January through November—to find out once and for all if he could make the grade "out there" and, if not, at least get it out of his system. Lynn was the one who proposed the idea.

Jack Fleck did not have great length off the tee, even in his twenties, and one winter he visited a pro in South Carolina named Melvin Hemphill, who helped him with this part of his game. Hemphill made a difference. He had Fleck kink his right knee to the left in the address position, which helped him drive his legs to the left in the downswing and generate more clubhead speed. He was better able to get off his right side, as the pros put it. Hemphill also got Fleck to keep his chin up at address so there was room for his left shoulder to make a full turn on his backswing. In all, Fleck picked up some twenty yards on his tee shots. Distance off the tee is an important component to success in big-time golf, especially if a golfer is not too adept with the putter, and Fleck had trouble with the so-called flat stick.

All well and good, but the bigger issue for Jack Fleck was his temperament. It was destructive, and he would have to do something about it if he was to have any chance at all of becoming a successful tournament pro.

Ben Hogan didn't play in the 1936 Western Open, the tournament in which Jack Fleck forecaddied and where his interest in playing tournament golf grabbed his soul. Hogan was still struggling to cure the disastrous hook he hit with his driver when under pressure. It was the chink in his armor that kept him from the success many thought was before him. By 1940, though, he had conquered the problem and was becoming one of the big stars of the tournament circuit. When at home Fleck took notice of him via newspaper photos and Movietone newsreels at the local movie house. And he watched Hogan play and practice when out on the tour.

What he saw had an intrinsic appeal. Fleck was himself a quiet, reserved person and carried himself much like Hogan did—little show of emotion, an understated style of dress featuring grays and tans and single-toned shoes. More significantly, he picked up on Hogan's basic swing shape, a backswing designated as flat, in which the club wraps more around the body than taking a vertical line. Fleck's swing was not quite as flat as Hogan's, if only because he was much taller: he stood six feet one to Hogan's five feet eight. Fleck also had a long, high follow-through that was in good balance but with something of a dancer's flair. Hogan's conclusion to his swing was tighter, the club continuing around his body past impact and held fairly close to it. It reflected someone who sought absolute control of his actions, while Fleck projected a somewhat looser figure.

Fleck's relationship with Hogan became far more immediate—and consequential—in early 1955 when he was on the winter tournament circuit. He visited the pro shop of one-time touring pro Stewart "Skip" Alexander in St. Petersburg, Florida, and noticed a box with a set of new Hogan irons. They were being sent back to the Hogan plant, in Fort Worth. Fleck asked Alexander if he could have a look at them and, of course, was obliged. All the pros were very much interested in what the great golf technician on the course would produce in a factory.

For a number of years Hogan had been, like many of the best players in the game, under contract to play equipment made by the MacGregor Golf Company. The company had a long history in American golf and was noted for making first-class woods and irons. But the MacGregor ball was not up to the same standard.

Once Hogan became a superstar he refused to play the ball, preferring the Spalding and Titleist brands. Henry Cowan, the president of MacGregor, had been giving Hogan some slack in this respect. But in 1953, feeling it had finally been brought to the level of other brands, Cowan insisted that all MacGregor contract players, including Hogan, play it in competition. Hogan still didn't think the ball was good enough, refused the order, and was fired. He didn't mind.

Many in golf thought Hogan forced the ball issue with MacGregor so he would be free to start up his own equipment company, something he'd had in mind for a year or two. That may have been part of his motivation, but, despite Henry Cowan's proclamation, his ball was not a good one by comparison with the top-of-the-line balls—Titleist, Wilson, Dunlop, and Spalding. More than a few professionals who honored their contract and continued to play the MacGregor Tourney—Mike Souchak and Jack Burke Jr., to name but two—would say in subsequent years that their loyalty to the company's ball cost them victories.

In any case, everyone was curious to see what Hogan had come up with in the way of a club design, and they liked what they saw. A central feature was how the irons were set, which was a few degrees more open than conventional clubs. That is, when the club was placed behind the ball, the face aimed slightly to the right of the intended target. It was one of Hogan's answers to defeating the hook, the overly right-to-left trajectory that has been the bane of all high-level golfers since the game was invented. No matter what brand of iron was in hand—Wilson, Spalding, MacGregor— the tour pros, almost to the man, laid the blade open at address. They could then release the clubhead with speed and power at impact and create a mild right-to-left draw as opposed to a sharply turning hook. Hogan's irons were meant to save them the trouble of laying open the clubface.

Fleck also admired the irons because they were not offset, the leading edge of the blade slightly behind the left side of the shaft. The Wilson Sporting Goods Company exaggerated this feature so much that it was called a gooseneck. Its purpose was also to prevent hooks. After waggling the Hogan irons and otherwise giving them a good look, Fleck wondered aloud if Hogan would make a set for him. If he wanted a set for nothing, he was discouraged by a fellow tour pro and friend, Mike Krak, who was with him in Alexander's shop. Hogan was not known to be very generous, for one thing. And for another, although Krak would not say it to his friend's face, he was sure Hogan was not likely to give his goods away to a low-end pro with not much of a record as a player. Fleck had made no dent on the collective consciousness of the tour in 1954. He missed many cuts, and when he made one he picked up a small check. Krak was wrong. People in golf didn't know, yet, that Hogan had a commercial side.

Alexander advised Fleck that if he wanted to pursue the idea he should contact Charley Newman, the general manager of the Ben Hogan Company. Fleck wrote a letter, and a week later he received one back from Newman saying Mr. Hogan would be glad to make him a set at no cost to Fleck, and that he should send in his specs—length, swing weight, shaft flex, etc.

Hogan knew very well that getting tournament players to use a company's equipment gave the brand exposure, the recognition that leads to sales. However, it generally works only if the clubs are in the hands of those who win tournaments, often come close to winning, and regularly finish in the money. All the players at that level were currently contracted to play equipment made by Wilson, MacGregor, and Spalding, the big-three equipment makers at the time. But even if he could get a Middlecoff or Demaret to switch over and play his clubs, Hogan couldn't afford to pay them. Thus, Ben Hogan providing clubs for a player with Fleck's record was to some extent the act of a desperate businessman looking for any port in a storm.

To compound this expression of Hogan's business posture, Newman told Fleck that if he happened to be invited to play in the Colonial National Invitational tournament, held in Fort Worth in May, he could pick up his clubs then. There actually was no *if* about it. Ben Hogan "owned" the Colonial Invitational. He had won the tournament four times. He was a super-honorary member of the Colonial Country Club, site of the event, and hung around the club and played the course often. If Ben Hogan wanted someone invited to play in the Invitational, it was fait accompli, a done deal. He had an invitation sent to Fleck, even though his record that year, and overall, hardly justified it.

The tournament was meant as a showcase of the best thirty-five or so players on the tour. The sponsor's exemption, as it was called, was reserved for a player or two who had not quite reached that level yet but showed signs of becoming an elite golfer, who had either won that year on the circuit or seriously contended more than once. It was usually a rookie, but if not, a veteran who had been struggling but refound his game during the first five months of the year. The other special invitee was Dow Finsterwald, clearly a comer in his first year on the circuit. But never mind such credentials. Jack Fleck would be using Hogan irons in the Colonial Invitational.

It was Hogan's way with men he didn't know well to refer to them as "fella." He might start using the fella's first name if he came to like him or respected his game. This could take some time, for Hogan was not a social animal, and he had very high standards when it came to a golfer's ability. Nonetheless, when on the Monday of the week of the Colonial Invitational Fleck went to Hogan's factory on Pafford Street to pick up his clubs, Hogan came out of his office and with a fine smile and handshake greeted Fleck with a "Hi, Jack, nice to meet you." It was the first time Fleck ever met Hogan in the flesh.

Although close to two months had gone by since Hogan made the offer, Fleck's irons were not yet ready. Neither were the woods, but the delay of the irons was at the heart of Hogan's business problem. Labor costs had been high in producing the first run. They required a great deal of individual handwork; the grinding to the final shape of each head and the subsequent polishing was labor intensive. The main problem, though, was that the hole in the hosel has to be drilled perfectly straight and to just the right length and diameter for the shaft to be properly aligned when inserted. If it was off by just the slightest bit, the club would not function at maximum efficiency.

Johnny Bulla, a fine tour player and an inveterate golf insider, recalled that for the second production run Hogan wanted to reduce the cost of drilling the holes in the hosels, each one having been done with a hand-operated drill. A new drill for the purpose had been developed and would lower labor costs, but Hogan was advised that it was not reliable and might not do the work correctly. He decided to go ahead with it anyway. As predicted, the drill did not work well, and most if not all the holes were poorly drilled. The clubs were not suitable for the market, and Hogan decided to scrap them. One of his financial backers, Pollard Simon, suggested they sell the clubs to driving ranges in Japan and the United

States as a way to recoup some of the financial loss. Hogan would not have that and declared that some $150,000 worth of golf clubs would be ditched like banana skins, buried behind the factory or chopped up and melted down (no one knew for sure which). Pollard was terrifically unhappy over Hogan's decision to junk the clubs, and said so. At that, Hogan borrowed $400,000 from a local bank and bought out one of his few close friends, and, until then, a loyal supporter.

The part of the story that made news and quickly became a stanza in the Hogan reputation was his decision to throw out the defective clubs. It fit the image of Hogan the perfectionist and added a personification of him as a highly ethical industrialist. It was to his credit that he would not market a faulty piece of equipment, even if it would be hard to discover, but few people knew it was his fault in the first place. That didn't match the Hogan legend being nurtured, that of him being a paradigm of the scientific method.

Hogan's other financial backer, Marvin Leonard, was talking with Bing Crosby and others about guaranteeing Hogan's bank loan and taking his name off it. That had not yet come to pass when Hogan greeted Fleck outside his office. Nor was it resolved when Hogan was in San Francisco making his run at the 1955 U.S. Open.

Hogan told Fleck on that Monday morning that his sticks weren't quite ready. The irons would be in two days, except for the wedges. He promised he would try to get those two vital clubs to him as soon as possible, and if Fleck qualified for the U.S. Open, he would hand-deliver the wedges at the Olympic Country Club.

Why should it have taken so long to make the clubs? It may have been in part because time was needed to go back to the original manufacturing method—hand-drilling those holes in the hosels. But the fact was that Hogan had simply forgotten about the offer.

In the first round of the Colonial Invitational, Fleck used his old irons and woods, as he had not used the new ones long enough to put them in play. He shot a good round of 70. But then, as the old adage adapted to golf has it—"It's not the arrows but the archer" that makes good shots—Fleck used Hogan's clubs starting with the second round and shot 72-75-79 to finish twenty-seventh and out of the money. Finsterwald, by the way, finished second.

Concerned about the results he got with the new clubs, Fleck reflected on his performance with them and concluded that in many instances he was hitting the clubs farther than his usual distance—another five or so yards with the irons—which was confounding his club selection. He wondered why, and the day after the Colonial ended Fleck went back to the Hogan factory to examine the structural details of the clubs more thoroughly—and to adjust other elements.

He found some interesting things that were departures from the norm. First, each club was a half-inch longer in length than the standard. And the lofts were stronger than conventional. That is, where a 5 iron length was commonly thirty-five and one-half inches and the loft was universally thirty-two degrees, the Hogan 5 iron was thirty-six inches long with twenty-eight degrees of loft. The increments were small in themselves, but it doesn't take much to make a difference in respect to golf shots. Both the longer length of the clubs, which gave a bit more length to the swing, and the reduced loft created more distance. Hogan was breaking with standards that had been set in stone for at least a half-century (and presaged what would happen in club manufacture in the years to come).

More specifically to his particular needs and preferences in the club's specs, Fleck found that the lie angle on the clubs was not correct; they were not going through the ground squarely when he made contact with the ball. An adjustment was needed to accommodate his height and how he addressed the ball. Also, the shaft flex was stiff, whereas he liked his shafts to have a bit more flex—medium-stiff was what he used. It gave him a better feel for the clubhead and a kind of musical quality to his swing. For him, hitting the ball was like a Glenn Miller orchestral arrangement of "String of Pearls" or "Moonlight Serenade"—the music he and his buddies liked so much while in World War II. Fleck was not a "hitter" of the ball as much as he was a "conductor" of it. That the lie angle and shaft flex were not correct indicated the clubs had not really been built to his specs; they were off-the-rack standard goods.

Fleck had the adjustments made that morning in Hogan's factory. That he was given access to the factory floor was in itself unusual. Hogan was very secretive about his manufacturing processes. Even such friends as Jimmy Demaret and Jack Burke didn't get in. While the shafts were changed and the lie angle corrected on his irons, Fleck noticed a couple of barrels filled to overflowing with brand new irons that somehow didn't appear to be destined for pro-shop sales racks. When Fleck asked about them, the repairman told him that those were going to Japan. So perhaps Pollard Simon got a bit of his way.

It didn't take Fleck long to adjust to the new irons, and he began hitting them well. And, as promised, Hogan did deliver the two wedges to Fleck. Like a good deliveryman, he presented them to Fleck in the locker room on Monday morning of U.S. Open week.

Ben Hogan and his wife, Valerie, flew first-class into San Francisco from Fort Worth nine days before the first round of the 1955 U.S.

Open. It had become his standard operating procedure to arrive that early to prepare for this championship, the one he prized the most and for which, by virtue of both his game and personality, he had an almost eerie capacity to either win or seriously contend. He could come early because he was no longer a touring pro, playing the circuit's weekly events. The condition of his legs didn't allow that anymore. And he had his young and uncertain golf equipment company to look after.

Ben Hogan came from a financially strapped background, just as Jack Fleck did. Hogan's father, a blacksmith, did not do well at his trade. When he took his own life his wife was left to raise the three children—her eldest son, Royal; her daughter, Princess; and the youngest, William, who always went by his middle name, Benjamin, and finally just plain Ben. The Hogan boys sold newspapers, worked as delivery boys, and caddied, among other pick-up jobs, to help out at home. Royal Hogan became a pretty good golfer, but he was more interested in making money and went into business. His little brother, who was not nearly as loquacious, made up his mind very early on—in his mid-teens—that the game of golf was going to be his way in the world. Like so many men physically smaller than his contemporaries, Ben brought along a Napoleonic determination to succeed.

It was a struggle, because he didn't have special athletic gifts. He did have strength, though, and not only of will. A Chicago doctor who examined him for a minor problem once when he was out on the tour observed that Hogan was one of the strongest people he had ever seen. It helped, too, that Hogan grew up in a golf-centric locale, so to speak. Although the winter months could get fairly chilly around Fort Worth, the weather overall was such that he could play year-round. And in the Fort Worth–Dallas area was also a cohort of golfers who liked to perform well and appreciated others who did. Club pros like Ted Longworth helped young fellows with some talent get jobs in the game and a place to play and practice. And the good players in the milieu set a high standard. Byron Nelson, the same age as Hogan, set the bar the highest. Nelson and Hogan were fellow caddies at the same private club and would compete hard against each other then and for the rest of their competitive lives.

When Hogan traveled to Houston he met Jimmy Demaret, a brilliant golfer and personality, who was connected to the pro golf elite in that city. Jack Burke Sr., whose son Jackie Jr. would become an outstanding tour player, was a legendary teacher of golf. Every pro of note, and some amateurs as well, sat at Burke Sr.'s dinner table and talked golf swing and how to play. When they fanned out into the world at large, they looked after one another by finding club jobs where they could make some money and work on their games. Hogan became part of what was a kind of Texas golf mafia. When he couldn't solve the hook problem, Henry Picard, a highly accomplished professional who had won a PGA Championship and a Masters tournament and then became an outstanding teacher of the game, helped Hogan. At one point he promised him financial aid if he went broke out on the tour, but more importantly he gave him the instruction that cured the hook and turned him into a star.

By the time World War II came along, Hogan was a celebrity tournament player, and his military service involved playing golf stateside with higher-up officers. After the war, he slid right back into tour life, where he and his contemporaries knew he belonged. He was an intense man who didn't make many friends on tour. That seemed to be immaterial to him. Because he was such a good player he gained the utmost respect of his fellow pros. But warm affection was something else.

In the days leading up to the first round of play in the 1955 U.S. Open, Hogan cased the joint the way Willie Sutton checked out banks he was going to rob. He left out no detail. Every practice round over the Lake course brought Hogan to decisions on how to play each hole, always leaving room for change depending on the strength of the wind and its direction, how the ball was sitting on the grass, how he was hitting the ball that day, and many other considerations. He made note of what clubs he used from certain points: A 6 iron downwind from the eucalyptus tree in the right-hand rough, the one with the bark hanging loose. A 4 iron into the wind from the front edge of the fairway bunker on the left at the 6th.

He didn't go by yardage, however. He played by sight, which informed his body how much force he needed to put into the shot. He once played a round of golf with a young fellow who kept asking Hogan what club he hit for every shot to the green. From the center of the fairway in the middle of the round he had 160 yards into the green. After hitting the shot, the question came once again. At that, Hogan dropped eight balls and hit each one onto the green with every iron in his bag, from 2 iron to 9 iron. He then told the young man to never ask him again what club he hit. He needn't have bothered. The fellow would never again be invited to join him in a round of golf.

Hogan was especially alert to the nature of the greens that would receive the shots. Did they bank from left to right, right to left, back to front? That information didn't have much to do with how it would affect his putting. It determined the trajectory on which he would send the approach shot and how the ball would react after it landed. Would it bounce to the right, left, straight ahead? He didn't always hit the renowned "Hogan fade," where the ball fell gently to the right at the end of its flight. He would hit a light draw when necessary. His goal with approach shots was to land the ball on the green, have it take one short bounce, and stop more or less in its tracks. Ideally, it stopped where he would be left with as level a putt as possible, or at worst an uphill one. He might make note of what was behind each green—a bunker, heavy grass—but he didn't consider that a major issue; he was almost never long with his approach shots.

Hogan was a conservative golfer on the course, just as he was a conservative person off it. His golf reflected his approach to the world. He played a percentage game. He almost never went for a "sucker" pin, one in which the hole is tucked into a corner of the green behind a bunker. If that was the situation, he would play the ball to the wide part of the green and perhaps curve it toward the hole if he had a good lie to play from or if the green was soft. If the hole was cut in the front portion of the green, a favorite placement in the U.S. Open because it can confuse depth perception, he almost invariably played past it. He made note if the flagsticks were longer than conventional, a little trick of the eye the USGA sometimes played to further tease perception.

All the pros examined a golf course in the same broad way— noting the grain on the greens, the prevailing wind, clubs used from certain locations, and so on—but Hogan was a cut above the rest. A case in point was his first practice round at the Merion Golf Club in 1950, where he made his phenomenal comeback to win the U.S. Open only eighteen months after the devastating highway collision that wrecked his body. He was getting his first look at

Merion and was being shown around by a member of the club, Frank Sullivan, a low-handicap golfer and a Philadelphia lawyer who had handled a suit Hogan brought against a local publishing firm. When they reached the 18th hole, which presents a blind tee shot (a hill some thirty yards in front of the tee hides the fairway from view), Sullivan told Hogan the line was the flagpole, a very tall one, directly behind the green some 410 yards distant. Hogan dutifully hit his drive dead on line with it. The next day when they arrived at the 18th tee, Sullivan reminded Hogan of the line. Hogan said no, it was seven yards to the right. Seven yards. And that's where he hit his ball. The difference? Seven yards to the right would give him a flat lie on a fairway that tilted slightly down to the left from the line to the flagpole. His approach shot would be lengthened by four or five yards, but that was inconsequential. It was the level lie he was after. And that's where he hit his tee shot for the first four rounds of the championship.

Also at Merion that year he took the 5 iron out of his bag and replaced it with a 4 wood. The 5 iron is one of the most used clubs in a set, its loft producing a yardage very often needed on any golf course. But after two practice rounds Hogan determined he would have a number of shots for a 4 wood but none for a 5 iron. The 4 wood went in; the 5 iron was out.

Hogan could be so acute in his assessment of a golf course because of the extraordinary control he had over the trajectory and distance of the shots he hit. He was especially accurate with the driver, the longest club in the bag and the one the great majority of golfers, including professionals, have trouble controlling. If there is a secret to winning the U.S. Open it is to put most if not all your drives in the fairway. That means fewer shots to play out of punishing rough, from which it is so difficult to make solid contact with the ball. Tellingly, it was his lack of control with the driver that held Hogan back for so long. But he had forged a compact, flat-plane swing that lent itself to control. Seeing it from a distance, one knew the ball he hit would not be off line—not by very much, anyway. His swing was not the graceful, free-flowing motion of a Sam Snead or the simple single-plane action of Gene Littler. Hogan's was a more complicated action, different body parts moving at slightly different times. But he repeated it metronomically. It was all that practice, for which he was famous and which his swing needed to keep in the groove.

Hogan didn't give up distance for accuracy, though, which surprised casual observers who saw only his physical size. He stood five feet eight and weighed 160 pounds, but he had exceptional strength, some of it inherited but more coming from the hours upon hours upon years and years of hitting practice balls.

However, in his early practice rounds on the Lake course Hogan's distance off the tee was noticeably shorter than was customary. He was giving up as many as twenty yards to the other players in his groups. Was it his age creeping up on him and the chronic physical problems lingering long after his recovery from the accident? His age might have had something to do with it. And the troublesome legs and perpetually aching left shoulder were surely factors. He was losing range of motion and strength. There was that, but more than anything there was his strategy. It was clear to see he had shortened the length of his backswing and was not as aggressive through impact. He did it because the rough on the Lake course was much more severe than common, and he was willing to give up yardage for an even more controlled driver. He wanted to play his approach shots as often as possible from the fairways; every time would suit him just fine. He would have to play longer shots into the greens, but he was confident of his ability to do that and felt the overall strategy would provide him a better chance of winning.

Hogan did not spend a great deal of his preparation time on his putting. He obviously understood how important it is to the game, but he felt that because Olympic's greens were relatively small, he would not need to spend much time developing a feel for putts of length—more than thirty or thirty-five feet. He didn't plan on any of his approach shots being farther than that from the hole. And, the greens being fairly flat, figuring out the undulations was not especially complicated. Like all the courses of the time, most of the greens were higher at the back than at the front, the slope intended to provide drainage that ran water off the front of the green. Thus if one's approach was on one side or the other of the hole, a putt would break left or right to some degree or other. Hogan knew which way was west, of course, and that in the afternoon the blades of grass that create grain would turn toward the setting sun. Grain affects the speed of putts and the amount of curve they have.

He did hit practice putts from various parts of the greens to the holes where they were cut in the practice rounds and also to places where they were expected to be during the tournament. But he considered all of it a necessary evil. Hogan didn't like putting. He didn't think it was golf. *Golf* was *hitting shots*. That is, with a driver, fairways woods, and irons, making full or modified full swings and sending the ball out on a certain trajectory—a little right-to-left or a lot, low to get under a strong headwind, etc. *Golf* was hitting shots the required distance and in such a way that the ball would land, take one bounce, and stop—or run forward if necessary. Hitting shots took precise, well-trained physical coordination of the various body parts involved in the swing, while staying

in good balance. All of that was the great technical, physical challenge of the game and gave the greatest satisfaction when it came
off well. A finely struck golf shot was for Hogan equivalent to a
complicated but ingenious machine turning out a fine tool. It was
the art of the game and its purest expression of ability, hard work,
talent, and skill.

Putting didn't come close to any of that, in his estimation. It
required no strength, no intricate synchronization. It was the work
of pissants, golfers who didn't hit the ball especially well from tee
to green but saved holes and rounds and won tournaments with
outstanding putting. He had little respect for the likes of these.
Hogan rarely talked about putting to anyone, including the few
pros he did speak with about technique. He was certainly a good
enough putter to win all the championships and tournaments on
his record, but in his heart of hearts, making them was more accident than design.

In non-tournament rounds of golf with fellow pros at tournament sites or at home—they could never be called casual rounds,
for when it came to golf, nothing about it was casual to Hogan—
he always set up one of the gambling games based on points for
shot-making. If one hit the fairway with a driver it was worth three
points, hit the fairway with a 3 wood or long iron from the tee, two
points. Miss in either case, minus two points. Hit the green with
anything over a 6 iron, three points, an extra point if the shot was
closer to the hole than everyone else's; two points for hitting the
green with a 6 iron and less, two points for closest to the hole. Miss
the green, minus two points. Five bucks a point. Nobody putted if
they didn't want to; putts weren't worth anything.

Yet he couldn't help but realize that the quality of his putting
had deteriorated over the past year and that this could very well

have stood in the way of winning any of the few tournaments he played. It was partly due to his attitude, but something else was happening. From time to time he found himself in a kind of stall mode. He would stand over the ball and have the damnedest time starting the stroke. It was especially the case on putts from ten feet or less. He was missing more and more from that length, the length that is so often critical to saving pars when greens are missed in regulation. He was famous for his cold, penetrating stare into golf space—prompting the epithet "the Hawk"—but his actual vision may have been diminishing, especially in his right eye. It was another consequence of the accident. He would never say anything about this to anyone, but it occurred to him that it might be hampering his ability to see the line of his putts, which led to his freezing over the ball.

He was not so foolish as to not investigate ways out of the putting dilemma. Someone suggested he try hypnosis, and he had one session in Fort Worth. But he didn't like the feeling of being out of control that is the hypnotic state. He didn't go back. He occasionally would experiment with a different putter, but in his mind it didn't make much difference what sort was in hand. He always went back to the one he had been using for years. He was comfortable with the look of it and stuck with it. He didn't consult anyone about his putting; Jackie Burke Jr., a putting meister, might have helped. But he determined to work out the putting by himself, as—in his mind—he did everything else in his life.

Hogan played his first practice round over the Lake course with Sam Snead, Byron Nelson, and Cary Middlecoff. With the exception of Middlecoff, this was the triumvirate of American golfers from the 1930s through the 1950s. Middlecoff was a superb player, one of the best ever, but being a bit younger didn't quite make the pantheon. Nelson had announced his retirement from competitive golf in 1946, a year after his phenomenal streak of eleven straight victories and eighteen in all for the year. But he did come out on occasion, averaging around five events per year for the past nine years. This would be his first appearance in the U.S. Open since 1946, his entry more sentimental than anything else. He had won the San Francisco Victory Open on the Lake and the San Francisco Open in 1944 and 1946. He had to pre-qualify for this Open, but San Francisco was a city where he had a good playing history. And he felt like playing.

Hogan and Snead were not friendly off the course. Their lives traveled on entirely different arcs. Snead was a notorious womanizer, an outstanding hunter and fisherman, and a teller of incredibly obscene jokes in any company. Hogan played golf, practiced golf, made golf clubs, watched the news on television, went to the occasional movie, and socialized with only a few people in Fort Worth, mainly for Valerie's sake. But Hogan and Snead each had tremendous respect for the other's game. No matter Snead's chronic problems with the U.S. Open, which he had yet to win, Hogan always wanted to know how Sam was doing, at least until he was clearly out of the running. Hogan was also using Sam in playing that practice round with him. He wanted to ingest some of Snead's rhythmic swing tempo.

Hogan played the rest of his practice rounds with a mix of other top players, and every one with Claude Harmon. Harmon had a brassy personality that somehow appealed to Hogan, who also admired the way Harmon could move the ball around a golf course. Harmon was a career club professional who, remarkably, was able to periodically leave his pro-shop duties and lesson tee and play exceptionally well in major events. He won the

1948 Masters by five shots over Middlecoff and ten over Hogan. Harmon was a master bunker player and otherwise had a knack for strategizing and playing problem shots, which Hogan appreciated. During the winter months Harmon was the head professional at the Seminole Golf Club, in south Florida, where Hogan spent every December getting his game in shape for the upcoming season. He was as close to a really good friend among golf pros as Hogan had.

After playing six practice rounds on the Lake, Hogan determined that par for the course was 72, two more than the official card par. He concluded that the 17th, although shortened enough to be a regulation par-4, albeit a very long one, would still play like a par-5. It would require a very long second shot from a sloped fairway to reach the green in two, and he didn't think even he could manage that all four times. He rated two other holes as par-4.5—the 457-yard 5th and the 429-yard 11th. From those calculations he judged that a score of one under his par, 287, no more than 288, would be good enough to win. That was the number he would play for; all his strategic decisions would be based on it until such time, no doubt very late in the proceedings, when it was clear a lower number was required. Then he would make adjustments in his strategy and perhaps even in his swing.

His last two practice rounds, with only Harmon along, were on the Ocean course, where he tested his swing and the flight of the ball in the windier conditions that prevailed on that course. He also dropped a bag of shag balls on the tee of the 11th hole of the Ocean and, all alone, hit shots under left-to-right wind conditions. It was a situation he expected to face fairly often, and he wanted to be well prepared for it. As he liked to say, "Never hit a shot during a round that you haven't practiced beforehand." He was as methodical as an accountant or a civil engineer (or bank robber) in his preparations. He did not smell the roses along the way.

Jack Fleck had played a tour event in Fort Wayne, Indiana, two weeks before arriving in San Francisco for the Open. He earned $230 for a sixteenth-place finish, then drove home to Davenport to spend a week with his family and check on how things were going at the two public courses that he, Lynn, and Lynn's brother-in-law and sister managed. Were the maintenance guys cutting the greens properly? How many sleeves of balls and bags of tees were sold? He then drove 185 miles east to Crete, Illinois, just south of Chicago, to try to qualify for the Open. He shot rounds of 73 and 72 over the Lincolnshire Country Club course. He didn't think it would be good enough when he finished play, but it was; he had the third-lowest score and made it into the field. Among the other qualifiers was one regular tour pro, the well-known and accomplished Ed "Porky" Oliver, who would encourage Fleck in his play. Fleck drove back to Davenport, spent two days there, then made the drive to San Francisco, just under two thousand miles, in forty-nine hours.

All the other times when Fleck drove west from home or from Florida, it was in late December to play in the California portion of the circuit. It always began with the Los Angeles Open in the first week of January—the tour's opening day. He would leave Davenport and drive down through Kansas, then across the Oklahoma and Texas Panhandles, New Mexico, Arizona, and California's eastern desert and scrubland. From Florida it was a similar route, except for Kansas and the Panhandles. For the most part it was a drive through a dry, dingy, brown, seemingly lifeless semidesert.

This trip, though, in early summer on the two-lane Lincoln Highway from beginning to end, was different. The terrain was flat much of the way, especially in the early going, but green and rich gold with maturing stands of corn and wheat. Cattle grazed in pastures, which was not enough word for the expanse of their fields. The sun set stunningly in front or to the left of him. Then there was the magical rise of the Rocky Mountains suddenly punctuating the horizon—so grand and snowcapped in June. The steady hum of the tires on the roadway, the whish of wind through the open window, the expanse of the land, and the big sky had a tranquilizing effect on him. He had been getting free of the distress of so many ordinary golf shots, mediocre rounds in the low and high seventies, and the painful self-doubt about the trajectory of his experiment as a full-time tour player, and this drive helped the transition. The broad but entrancing landscape he was passing through reduced the anxiety and pressure of golf. He didn't say it in so many words, but he got from this June passage through the midriff of the American West a Zen-like release from common caring. It coalesced with the fine, soft state of being that had been inching its way into him in the past year in a kind of subliminal way; he thought the hatha yoga he had been practicing might also be a part of it.

Beneath a benign exterior Jack Fleck had long had a problem with his temper on the golf course. It wasn't expressed in the most common way—throwing clubs, burying them in the turf, or banging them into or against his bag after a shot didn't work out. Neither did he curse. He would just quit playing. Sometimes in the middle of a round that was going poorly he would pick up his ball and walk in. If it was during a tournament he would be a wd-er, as those who withdrew from a tournament were called. But after he withdrew he did not go on to the next stop on the tour and practice and cool off, which is what most of the wd-er pros did. He would just head home to Iowa, where he would stew and fidget for a few days or more, before going back out there. It had gotten to the point that Lynn Fleck told him she was tired of this behavior and was becoming less and less inclined to support him and to encourage his effort to become an accomplished tournament golfer.

Lynn Fleck's first real taste of her husband's temperament at golf came on their honeymoon, at the 1950 Phoenix Open. After thirty-six holes Fleck was in the top ten, but he had three-putted a number of greens and was so upset that he withdrew. Lynn couldn't understand the decision. For all the poor putting, he was still in position to make a check. But Jack would not change his mind. Two days later they were back in snowy Davenport. Lynn was not pleased. In 1954 she told him that if he continued this behavior and didn't show true grit and determination, she was not going to be getting up at 5:30 every morning to work in the pro shop, not to mention take care of their youngster. He'd have to come back to his day job permanently.

It was not just a matter of walking off golf courses in fits of anger. There was an edge to Jack Fleck, a blurting obstinacy. He spoke his mind when peeved, without considering the circumstances. He had a few run-ins with tour officials over rules calls, starting times, and course conditions that turned them against him. In a Fort Wayne Open he took a legal drop from casual water, but an official, who didn't see the entire sequence, questioned Fleck about it. He thought it was an illegal drop. Rather than explain the situation to the official, Fleck brushed him off with, "You tend to your job, I'll tend to mine." The official then passed it around to other players that Fleck had cheated. Fleck heard about it and got confrontational with the official. He was three strokes off the lead after thirty-six holes but withdrew.

Fleck was not antisocial in the strictest sense of the term, but there was a distance he created between himself and the rest of the world in which he lived. He was different for his milieu. He ate "oddball" food—yogurt, whole wheat bread. He stood on his head for minutes at a time. The other pros shook their heads at this. Who was this character? He didn't sit around the locker room and toss the bullshit with the guys. He didn't hang out in bars and look for women. He went to the movies alone when on the road. He had a few tour-playing friends—Walker Inman Jr., Mike Krak— but there was about him a distinct self-absorption. It actually made him a good candidate for success in a game that was by its nature a most singular enterprise. Golf appeals to those not especially interested in social connection—to loners—and there was a lot of that in Fleck. He had only himself to satisfy with his golf, but he wasn't doing so.

Lynn Fleck was not the only one getting on his case. An Iowa pro named Bob Crouch, who was some years older than Fleck, told him in no uncertain terms that he had a poor temperament for the game and if he didn't do something about it he should quit playing in tournaments. Fleck held Crouch in high regard and was moved by his evaluation.

He was restless with failure, an attitude that does not go well in the game of golf, which takes enormous patience and the fortitude to work through the bad patches of play that everyone suffers. It is not a game for those who seek instant gratification, or maybe even long-term. You can get angry, and there hasn't ever been a golfer who didn't. But the ones who eventually succeed have a broader perspective and let the anger dissipate as quickly as it rises up in the system. Or they suppress it and use its energy to excel. It's a hard game, and poor swings and bad bounces come with the territory. Gene Sarazen, a great champion with a pithy but wise assessment of the game, often said golf was a game of good misses. "Miss 'em good," he said. You are not going to hit many perfect shots in a round, and the ones that are imperfect have to be as close to good as possible. Walter Hagen said it in a different way. He expected to hit, at best, five really good shots in a round. For the rest of the day it was a matter of limiting the damage. Fleck, for a long time, had trouble with that approach.

Playing professional tournament golf was all he had ever wanted to do since he was a teenager, but perhaps he wanted it too much and was unable to bear not getting to where he thought he should be as a player. Anger arises out of a feeling of not having control of yourself and what is important to you; you feel helpless and strike out at the thing you want so badly.

But anger is multifaceted. He grew up in an insecure world, a man from the other side of the social tracks who was hypersensitive to slights, real and perceived, and in his search for self-esteem through golf had trouble dealing with failure. He may also have been responding to a feeling of guilt. He had gone against his parents' wishes in taking up golf as his life's work. After graduating high school his job as a pattern maker with the Bettendorf Company had long-term promise. He had a little artistic talent—his father had once been a professional photographer. The work took skill, a certain artisanship, and he became adept at it quickly. He could count on it for steady employment. In the hard times of the Depression a job that paid reasonably well, or anything at all, was manna from heaven.

His mother and father were disappointed that he left the job in the first place, but to replace it with a career in golf seemed especially foolish. What could be more economically unpromising than a game for the wealthy when even the rich people were having difficulty? And to consider making a living playing in tournaments was beyond comprehension. Fleck loved his mother and father and was always appreciative of how they scrimped and did whatever they could on limited means to have food on the table and decent clothes for their children. Now here he was struggling along spending money traveling around the country making the occasional two or three hundred dollars a week, and many weeks nothing at all. Was that any way to get ahead in the world? If golf it was to be, he should at least stay home at his job running the city golf courses and saving money for a rainy day. So, when he missed another short putt in Florida or scored too high to earn even fifty dollars on the week in Ohio, did his anger and quitting arise out of a feeling that he was disappointing his parents?

Fleck was well aware that his bad humor affected his performance in tournaments—and important personal relationships. He was trying to deal with the problem, which is why he was alert to what he saw in a bookstore window in Santa Monica, California, two years before the 1955 U.S. Open. He was taking a walk after dinner when he noticed a book written by Indra Devi titled *Forever Young, Forever Healthy: Secrets of the Ancients Adapted for Modern Living*. The title was a mouthful but spoke to Jack Fleck's deep interest in healthy foods and exercise. It was a book on yoga, which offered specific exercises and an intriguing sidebar, a corollary—meditation that conveys tranquility. Fleck was also drawn to the book upon learning of Devi's background.

Indra Devi was born in Latvia in 1899 as Eugenie Peterson. Her father was a Swedish bank director. Her mother was a Russian noblewoman. Indra attended drama school in Moscow as a girl and with her mother escaped to Berlin at the outset of the Communist revolution in 1917. At age fifteen she read a book by the famed Indian poet Rabindranath Tagore, then books on yoga, and sailed to India to pursue this interest. She became an actress and took a stage name, Indra Devi, and sought to take yoga lessons from a famed guru. She was refused at first, because she was a Westerner and a woman. But she persisted and became the first Westerner and woman to study yoga with a recognized guru. She eventually moved to Southern California and introduced yoga discipline to many Hollywood stars, including Gloria Swanson. Devi died in 2002, at 102 years of age.

The book did not cost much, and Fleck bought it. The dual value appealed to his sense of thrift. For a couple of bucks he could learn new ways to build up his strength and flexibility and at the same time do something about his emotions, his temperament. It was a purchase that would have an enormous influence on his future. Gradually, ordinary mishaps stopped getting to him as they had in the past. If his car didn't start right away, if it took a few turns of the ignition and feeding the gas a little more, he didn't get jumpy the way he had. If a waitress brought him white bread instead of the whole wheat he had ordered, he didn't snap at her. And when he hung a six-foot putt on the lip he just tapped the ball in, lifted it out of the cup, and went on to the next tee. Sometimes he found himself in the middle of a round and not knowing what hole he was on. It always happened when he was playing especially well. He was always surprised by this but enjoyed the realization that he had gotten himself into another space, one much better than the usual.

Fleck's on-site preparation for the Open was in itself unusual, compared to the rest of the players. He did not spend a lot of time and energy on the practice range. He hit some balls before a round to loosen up, to get a feel for the clubhead. But he wasn't a range rat, someone who, like Hogan and almost all the other pros, would spend an hour or so every day on the practice range hitting a hundred or more balls. Fleck found that when he had been a ball beater, as the saying went, he would end up simply hitting and raking—hit a ball and pull another one over from the pile and have a go at it almost before the previous one landed. Over and over, hit and rake. It was for him dangerously mindless repetitiveness. He felt it led to getting too immersed in swing mechanics. Fleck understood swing technique but played golf mostly by instinct or feel.

He wasn't entirely intuitive in his approach to the game. After all, he was from Iowa, a farming state with small towns and cities where being practical is a first principle of life. All the more so when the family economy is in tough straits. When his father moved the family onto a property with two ramshackle houses, he and his brothers helped tear them down, save the best pieces of wood, and straighten the used nails for another use. All of which teaches one to be careful, precise.

When he got into tournament golf Fleck understood how important it was to know the yardages for approach shots. Everybody stepped off the distance from bunkers to greens, for example, but he wanted to have it just right. So one winter in Iowa he took steps in the snow and measured their length from toe to toe. If the step didn't come off at exactly thirty-six inches—one yard—he adjusted his stride to come to that distance. Then, on a golf course, when he stepped off distances from the tee to a fairway bunker or from the bunker to the front of a green, he had the yardage perfectly measured.

But how long did it take to get the yardages? Once around was enough. They didn't change, and after his first trip around the Lake course he just played it. He played forty-four holes every day from Saturday through Tuesday—two complete eighteen-hole rounds, then the first eight holes again, as the eighth green was located just below the hilltop clubhouse. On Wednesday, the day before the competition began, he played only thirty-six holes. It was a lot of golf on a course that took a toll on the body. He played one round each day with his tour pals, Walker Inman Jr. and Mike Krak. They then went off to the practice tee. They thought Fleck would wear himself out with the extra twenty-six holes each day. So Fleck played those by himself. When he was assigned his caddie, John Schroeder, a forty-two-year-old, Fleck was not sure Schroeder was up to this practice routine. He thought Schroeder might be too old. He also thought he might be a drinker and carouser, which wouldn't do. But Schroeder assured Fleck he was up to the task and was otherwise a straight arrow.

That Fleck could play so much golf over such a trying piece of ground attested to the fine physical condition he was already in. Walking all those holes made him even more fit. But there was more to it than that. He was infusing the course into his bones and marrow. It was easy for him to adopt this regimen, because he just liked the course. He liked it from the moment he stepped onto it. The way the holes looked from the tees fit his eye. Where Ben Hogan saw the Lake course as a tablet on which he chalked his

calculations, Jack Fleck saw himself as the tablet and the chalk. He
was comfortable in its embrace, into which he melded like the dye
infused in a piece of silk. The ambience appealed to him. The haze
hanging over those wind-shaped cypress trees and the whistle of
the wind blowing through, around, and over them sang of ghosts
and goblins, of strange, eerie vibrations, of other worlds. It was
enchanting. It matched up with the mood that had been coming
over him and that had been reinforced by the long and ultimately
spiritual drive he made from Iowa to San Francisco.

Every evening before the tournament began the Hogans had dinner in the hotel dining room, usually along with Claude Harmon.
In a worldly city known for excellent restaurants and a variety of
cuisines, Ben Hogan was a Texas steak-and-potato man, with an
iceberg lettuce salad on the side coated with French dressing. He
and Harmon talked about the golf swing, the Lake course, the golf
business, business in general. Hogan had his own business, but he
was being steered by friends into some valuable oil-well leases and
other investments. He was never going to be poor again.

Valerie sat quietly at her place, saying very little. None of the
subjects interested her, including golf. Or especially golf. For all
the years she had been so close to the game and one of its greatest
players, she knew very little about it and never had much inclina-
tion to learn. She had tried to play it once or twice but quickly gave
it up. Her husband never encouraged her. She had gone to Texas
Christian University for a year, where she studied journalism. She
aimed to write for the society page. A restrained woman, in ways
as private as her husband, her career goal may have been her way
to lose her innate shyness. But then along came Ben. Valerie had
been living a very lonely existence since her husband had become

a great success. It was worst of all on the road, when she couldn't visit with her sister and friends in Fort Worth.

When they were first married, in the depths of the Depression, and Ben was struggling to find his game, he and Valerie had a common bond. It was based on mutual striving, with Ben the striver and Valerie the support person. She had no trouble with her role. Even if her husband had already been a successful man she would have taken the same position. That was what women of her time and place did. And that is what the men of that time and place expected—perhaps even more so among Texas-bred men.

The couple did make decisions together about certain aspects of their lives: what neighborhood in which to build their home, what its architecture would be—although it was Ben's decision to have only one bedroom in a seven-room house. Valerie prevailed when it came to furniture style and decorations. After he became a champion Ben thought about living in Southern California. He liked the weather . . . and the turf on the golf courses. Valerie won that one, though, opting for Fort Worth, where she had family and friends.

However, when it came down to the one really big decision between them, it was Ben's call all the way. Occasionally there was mention in the press that the Hogans were childless. The reason Ben Hogan gave was in a tone of ethical or moral consideration. "It wouldn't be fair to the child, my having to be away so much," said Ben. What he really meant was, a child and the responsibilities he would have to take on would stand in the way of his career as a professional golfer. And that came first and last. If there was any reflection on what a life without children would mean for Valerie, it was never mentioned. Even if Valerie had gotten up the nerve to repeal the statute, her husband gave her little opportunity for a "accident" to happen. Valerie Hogan accepted her lot, so it appeared. But during an interview with Margarette Curtis—writing for *Golf Digest*—during the week of the Open, the wife of another tournament pro, Ralph Hutchison, happened by and made mention that she had only one child. To which Valerie Hogan, then forty-four years old, softly said, "One is better than none."

Dinner over, it was to the room and, for Ben, some television news. Then to bed to rest his legs. He seemed on the surface to be cool about the upcoming days, but Valerie knew differently. He was grinding his teeth while asleep, as he always did when he was going into competition.

On Wednesday night of Open week Jack Fleck had a small meal at the diner across the street from his motel. He then went back to his room and listened to his Mario Lanza records, called Lynn in Davenport, and chatted briefly with her and Craig. He turned off Lanza to do his yoga exercises and then hit the sack with his head to the north. As he lay waiting for the sleep to come, a thought arose, a familiar one that seemed to arise increasingly more often on the night before the start of a tournament. He recalled the days when he was at Utah Beach, on D-Day. He knew he was relatively safe from enemy fire but was still scared. It was the noise, especially—the amount of it, the consistency of it, and the incredibly hard quality of it—that frightened him. This was truly deadly dangerous. It was not a movie with John Wayne duking it out with some bad guys. Fleck saw soldiers fall on that beach who did not get up again. How does that compare with teeing up a golf ball in a competition? There is no comparison. He slept well, deeply.

SUPPORTING CAST

T HE U.S. OPEN WAS ALMOST ENTIRELY TRUE to its designation. Any *male* golfer could try to qualify—amateur, professional, private club member, or public fee golfer. (It wasn't until the 1980s that *male* was removed from the entry form.) Between 1919, when the championship was resumed after being suspended for two years due to World War I, and 1955, the quality of American golf flowered. The pro tournament circuit, an American innovation, was developing a range of excellent players, and only four of the thirty-one winners of the Open could be considered dark horses— Cyril Walker, Johnny Goodman, Sam Parks, and Tony Manero. Some observers thought Ed Furgol, who won it in 1954, might be in that category, but he'd been playing the tour with some success for over a decade when he took the title. Still, of the 1,522 men who tried for the 1955 championship and the 162 who did make into the starting field, only between ten and fifteen could be deemed potential winners.

Aside from the rigors of an Open course, the very designation of the event adds psychological weight to it. Some will say it is just another tournament. The course may be a little harder, but the same players who compete week after week on the tour are going at one another again with the same equipment. Yet it is still different because of what it's called—the *United States* Open. *National* Open, as it was long referred to, was just as potent a psychological designation.

In the previous five years Ben Hogan was invariably the favorite to win, and for good reason: he won in three of them—1950, 1951, and 1953 (he had also won in 1948). Still, there was always speculation about who else might take the title, perhaps even more this time because Hogan was seen as getting a bit long in the tooth.

Harry Hayward, covering golf for the *San Francisco Chronicle,* listed his ten top favorites, with a bit of commentary *à la* the horserace handicapper. His morning line, as it were, went as follows.

1. **Sam Snead** . . . *the Slammer is on his game.*
2. **Cary Middlecoff** . . . *a repeat of his Masters job would be good enough.* [Middlecoff won the 1955 Masters earlier in the year.]
3. **Ed Furgol** . . . *the defending champ is sharp.*
4. **Ben Hogan** . . . *determined to snare a record fifth Open title.*
5. **Gene Littler** . . . *heir apparent if the old guard falters.*
6. **Harvie Ward** . . . *could be the first amateur winner since Johnny Goodman.*
7. **Dick Mayer** . . . *his practice round 66 proves him ready.*
8. **Mike Souchak** . . . *has the strength to beat the course.*
9. **Byron Nelson** . . . *1939 champ is returning to form.*
10. **Bobby Rosburg** . . . *local boy consistently in the money.*

Those who included number odds had Sam Snead the favorite at 3-to-1. It was a generous and perhaps heartfelt assessment given Snead's history in the championship. Snead had been bedeviled by this one and only competition. For all his marvelous talent and capacity to win tournaments—a record seventy-five, including eight major titles—he could not get the U.S. Open under his belt. Close, but no cigar.

What was Snead's problem? In his very first Open, in 1937, he set a new seventy-two-hole scoring record, 283, at the imposing Oakland Hills Country Club, in Birmingham, Michigan. However, in the late afternoon a tall, stoop-shouldered Texan, Ralph Guldahl, dashed home with a 69 to defeat Snead by two shots. The consensus was that it was just one of those things and that Snead was going to win the title more than once. The winner of three tournaments on his first swing of the national tournament circuit, in 1937 he was clearly a rising star. He had stunning power coupled with one of the most graceful golf swings to come down the pike since MacDonald Smith.

Snead had a poor Open in 1938, but in 1939 it appeared he had it locked up. All he needed was a par-5 on the 72nd hole, and the championship was his. The trouble was, he didn't know it. There were no scoreboards scattered around the course in those days, and believing he needed a birdie, he made a poor decision. He tried to reach the green in two with a brassie (2 wood) from a sketchy lie in the rough. He half topped the ball, and it caught a bunker. He took a couple of shots to get out of it and ended up three-putting for an 8. He finished fifth, two strokes out of a playoff with Byron Nelson, Craig Wood, and Denny Shute.

This was the loss that, it came to be assumed, sat on his psyche like a bag of awful and shaped his U.S. Open history. The thought was that he could never get over that disastrous triple bogey. From then on, when he did get himself into close contention, and he did more than once, he seemed to find ways to fail. He lost a playoff in 1947 when he missed a putt of less than three feet, tied for second in 1949, and was second in 1953. In three of those close finishes he made a poor decision or just didn't hit the shot he needed—often a putt—which gave him a reputation as a poor clutch putter. It wasn't really true, but the U.S. Open has a way of exaggerating reality.

One way or the other, it was widely perceived that the Open had become a psychological hitch in Snead's game. And yet, although now forty-three years old, he was such an exceptionally powerful player that he was still considered a serious threat. And he was coming off a tour victory, the Palm Beach Round Robin, played in New York two weeks earlier.

Snead, as an indication of his cerebral problem with the Open, was covering himself with excuses, should he once again fail in this major of majors. Aside from noting that the Lake was the hardest Open course ever, he complained that the chilly air was penetrating. He also noted to reporters that so much sand had been spread on all the tees that "a man can't get a grip on the earth with his feet. It gives the feeling of hitting out of a sand trap. On those tee shots we like to feel we're really digging in—toes and all. The ground has to be firm." In this Snead would be quite prophetic, although not in regard to his own fate.

Julius Boros, a onetime accountant who didn't turn pro until he was twenty-nine years old—he was now thirty-five—began making his mark in U.S. Open golf in 1950, when he finished ninth. He followed that with a tie for fourth in 1951. He then won the title in 1952, finishing four shots ahead of Ed Oliver and five ahead

of Hogan. Boros had one of the most important requirements for playing well in this championship. He was a very accurate driver. And he was deceptively long off the tee with his loose-looking and even-cadenced swing. An added ingredient was an excellent touch for the short game, which he executed without hesitation. He went after clutch, final-hole chips and putts for titles with the easy dispatch of someone nipping at dandelions during a walk in the park. He was also a superb greenside bunker player.

Cary Middlecoff had practiced dentistry in Memphis, Tennessee, but decided tournament golf would be his career after winning the prestigious North & South Open in 1945, while still an amateur. After turning pro he established himself as a compelling force in the game with twenty-eight victories leading up to the 1955 U.S. Open, including the 1949 U.S. Open and the 1955 Masters. A tall man who distinctively dipped his body into impact with the ball, his most idiosyncratic swing action was a pause at the top of his backswing. All golfers try to hold the club for a brief moment in what is called the transition to the downswing. Some old pros put it as "letting it gather," *it* being the force to be generated for impact. Middlecoff exaggerated the *it*. It was especially interesting that he could manage that longish pause, because he was a nervous person. He walked with a quick, somewhat jerky stride and, once over the ball in the address position, waggled his club and looked up at the target numerous times before finally beginning the swing. He was one of the slower players on the circuit—*deliberate*, as the euphemism goes.

The defending champion, Ed Furgol, disproved the time-honored instruction that golfers must keep their left arm straight. He was a phenomenon in that his left arm was permanently bent some thirty degrees and was ten inches shorter than his right arm. When

he was a boy, his elbow was shattered in a playground fall and, as a result of poor treatment, remained crooked. The upper portion of the arm was extremely thin. But he had powerful hands and created a unique swing, which he practiced endlessly. In the days before the golf glove was commonly used, Furgol, who didn't wear one, would periodically take scissors and cut off the ridge of black calluses that developed on his left hand from all the ball beating. His career had been hampered by a violent temper, but he seemed to have gotten it under control.

A curious piece of trivia is attached to Furgol's U.S. Open victory. He was the only winner to take the title playing on two courses—sort of. In the lead playing the last hole, a par-5, he hooked his drive badly into a thick stand of trees and had no clear path back to his fairway. He did have a clear route to the adjoining 18th fairway of Baltusrol Golf Club's Upper Course, and after asking if it was permissible to play his second shot out onto it and being told it was, he did just that. He then hit a short-iron third shot onto the green and two-putted for his par. When Gene Littler, playing in the group behind, failed to birdie the 18th, Furgol had his victory.

Winning two U.S. Opens in succession is a rare accomplishment. Only five golfers had done it coming into 1955, the last being the quintessential U.S. Open player, Hogan, in 1950 and 1951. Still, Furgol was in his prime age-wise and was coming off a victory in the Canada Cup championship, an international two-man team event. Furgol won the individual side and, with partner Melvin "Chick" Harbert, won the team title as well.

Gene Littler was the choice of many observers and fellow professionals to win the 1955 Open. Like Middlecoff, Littler's first victory against professional competition came while he was still

an amateur—in his case it was the 1954 San Diego Open. He then turned pro and, in June of that same year, made his first big run at the Open, finishing second to Ed Furgol. Littler was known as Gene the Machine for how he was able to repeat his finely shaped swing time after time, and with a tempo that echoed his calm demeanor. He seemed unflappable under pressure.

Although he had won only once as a professional, at the 1954 Miami Open, Bob Rosburg was a pick for this championship because he had been a junior member of the Olympic Club since the age of eleven. At twelve he defeated retired baseball legend Ty Cobb for the First Flight club championship. Cobb was needled so much afterward that he was rarely seen around the club in the following years.

As it happened, Rosburg had been an outstanding baseball player at Stanford University, from which he graduated, and had signing offers from major-league teams. Although his loose-jointed swing didn't evince championship-caliber golf, it consistently produced a left-to-right flight pattern that is always an advantage playing on narrow fairways. But above all, Rosburg was a superb putter. He had a way of walking with his chin on his chest and a facial expression suggestive of someone experiencing a bad odor. He also complained often about his game, even when it was going well. But beneath the seemingly downbeat exterior was the heart of a fierce competitor. His familiarity with the Lake course and his growing prowess on the pro tour caused him to be listed as a favorite.

Another local consideration, although he wasn't a native San Franciscan, was North Carolinian E. Harvie Ward Jr. Ward was not only one of the best amateur golfers in the world, but many around the game thought he was one of the best golfers in the game, period.

The last amateur to win the Open was Johnny Goodman, who had done it in 1933 at the North Shore Country Club in Glenview, Illinois, and none had come close since. But Ward was special. He had a well-formed golf swing, was a brilliant putter, and just had a knack for the game. He broke through competitively in 1948, winning the esteemed North & South Amateur, was the NCAA individual champion playing for the University of North Carolina, and in 1952 won the British Amateur. His play in the Masters was impressive. He tied for fourteenth in 1954 and was the low amateur at Augusta National in 1955, when he tied for eighth place.

Ward had moved to the Bay Area and was selling cars for Eddie Lowery, who claimed his Van Ness Motors was the biggest Lincoln-Ford car dealer in the world. Lowery made it possible for golfers of Ward's ability to play often. Ken Venturi was another of Lowery's sales force. Ward would appear on the sales floor in the morning and in the afternoon tee it up at the Olympic Club, the San Francisco Golf Club, and other good venues in the area. Often Lowery, a low-handicap golfer, was in the foursome. Ward had considerable experience with the Lake and was so highly thought of by one local newspaper handicapper that he went to the gate at 6-to-1.

Listing Byron Nelson as a possible winner was more sentimental than realistic. Nelson hadn't played in a U.S. Open since 1946, when he lost in a three-way playoff to Lloyd Mangrum. Nelson had more or less retired from competitive golf in 1945. He cited his nerves as the reason for leaving the competitive scene at the age of thirty-four. He did make regular appearances in the Masters, though, and teed it up in a few regular tour events every year, though he hadn't performed at a very high level. Because only the previous five U.S. Open winners were exempted into the field,

Nelson had to go through qualifying. He just made it in, in San Francisco, with rounds of 75 and 72. He was given some odds—20-to-1—but no one expected him to be a real factor in the outcome. It wasn't his age so much as that he hadn't been playing enough competitive golf. His presence, though, added a ring of eminence to the championship.

Dick Mayer—a slender, solemn touring pro who addressed everyone as "Blue"—had a classic swing and game. He had the Hogan look, with the same flat white cap and wasp-waist physique. He had won only twice on the pro tour but had tied for fourth in the 1954 U.S. Open, which led to him getting a bit of notice. (Two years later he would win the Open in a playoff with Middlecoff.)

Jackie Burke Jr. was a smallish man with a wry Texas wit who said he didn't have thick enough wrists to play out of U.S. Open rough. But he was as smart as a whip at golf and otherwise. He was a charter member of what was noted earlier as the American golf mafia led by his father, who himself was a fine player; he tied for second in the 1920 U.S. Open. A congenial man, he hosted the aforementioned round-table discussions at his dinner table with just about everyone of note in American golf's first half-century. Jackie Jr. grew up in that environment, sat at a table with all those stars, and drank in all the golf wisdom that was spouted. Jimmy Demaret, thirteen years older, was Jackie's "babysitter" when he first went out on the tour. An outstanding putter, Burke could just flat-out *play*. In 1952 he won four straight tournaments on the winter tour, the longest streak of victories after Nelson's eleven in a row.

Tommy Bolt was a wonderful shot-maker, but he had a temperament that kept him from maximizing his promise. Although he turned pro rather late, in his early thirties, from 1951 through June

1955 he won nine tournaments. They included semi-majors—the Los Angeles and North & South Opens. Because he won twice on the 1955 winter tour Bolt was reckoned to be one of the hottest players in the field and a legitimate contender.

Mike Souchak stirred a lot of interest with his first PGA Tour victory, the 1955 Texas Open. He shot a first-round 60 that tied the single-round record but set a new record with a 27 for the first nine. He continued the outstanding play and in the end set a tour record of 27 under par for seventy-two holes. A burly man who played football for Duke University, he looked like someone with the strength to handle the Lake course's thick rough. The look was not deceiving.

Another who was considered capable of making a run at the title was Porky Oliver, who was the medalist in the qualifier in Crete, Illinois, where Jack Fleck also qualified. Oliver first came to notice in 1940, when he tied Lawson Little and Gene Sarazen for the U.S. Open, at 287. But his final round was nullified because he (and five others) teed off fifteen minutes before he was scheduled. They were trying to get the final round in before a threatened rainstorm hit. The 240-pound, five-feet-nine Oliver won seven events on the pro tour from 1940 through 1953 and lost to Ben Hogan in the finals of the 1946 PGA Championship. He also was second to Hogan in the 1952 U.S. Open and the 1953 Masters. He had some pretty good golf chops, which plays on his other nickname: Porkchops.

Also in the field was a twenty-five-year-old newcomer to professional golf who showed some promise. His name was Arnold Palmer, and he had made a mark by winning the 1954 U.S. Amateur the year before he went out to play for pay. People were impressed with his powerful game; he was a ball banger making a powerful thrust with every club in the bag. The ground seemed to shake under the force of his contact with ball and turf.

Gene Sarazen thought Gene Littler had the best chance of winning. He called Littler one of the Trailer Boys, so called because he was one of a number of younger tour pros who traveled the circuit pulling a house trailer. Palmer was another one.

Sarazen also said that Open courses with such punishing rough as at the Olympic Club often bred an upset winner.

Another entrant in the 1955 Open assessed the course and his chances in the championship, but his views didn't reach the newspapers prior to the playing of the championship. Nobody was interested. However, for good reason, they emerged in the aftermath and are more than a little poignant, considering the source. A letter sent via airmail (for six cents) on June 12, 1955, from San Francisco to John O'Donnell, the legendary sports editor of the *Davenport (Iowa) Democrat* contained the details.

Hi Coach,

Well, I would play you $5.00 a hole on this course! It's a great one! You sure would have a great time covering this tournament. If at all possible, you should fly out and watch and cover this one! You love golf and you only live once.

Had a long trip out, but am getting back to normal. Will play this one for keeps, not that I don't do it in all tournaments, but the Open is the big one.

This golf course, the Olympic Club, will gain national recognition as one of the greats. They really fixed it up big. I think seven to nine over par will win, a 287 or 289. Par is 280. Although if the weather is very good for three days it could be 284 or 285. Was talking to Middlecoff. He thinks it will be higher than most people are guessing. Snead, Hogan, Middlecoff, Nelson, have been playing for a week. No one has broken par, only one 70. They were the only touring pros and contestant here when I arrived Friday. Dick Mayer came in then also, and a few came in today. I'll make a prediction, the old guard will win! Snead, Hogan or Middlecoff. My guess at the first ten finishers: Snead, Hogan, Middlecoff, Jack Burke, Bolt, Furgol, Littler, Nelson, Boros, Souchak. And yours truly may sneak in there.

If you can't make it, watch it on TV. Yours truly,

Jack Fleck

ACT I

B EN HOGAN WAS UP AT 6:00 AM to begin his first round. His tee-off time was 10:00 AM—"Bobby Jones time," as it's said, the time when the elite golfers get to start their play. It's when the body has woken sufficiently and the blood is running on pace, when breakfast has been well digested and there is no rush to get to the practice tee and hurry one's warm-up. It's also when the gallery has arrived in numbers to see the stars. The last element was the tournament's business but not Hogan's. Once asked if he ever considered himself an entertainer, his response was a curt, absolute "No."

He looked out the window, which faced west, and liked what he saw out where he would be spending the day. The sun wasn't out quite yet, but it was coming. There was much blue for so early in the day, and the sky was streaked with thin clouds. He called down to the hotel desk to find out the temperature and the wind velocity expected for the day. The fellow at the other end of the line didn't know about the wind but said the temperature was predicted to be in the mid-to-high sixties. Warm for San Francisco in June. But there would still be a chill to it, especially out there.

And all of it could change in an hour in this land of microclimates, where subtle and sometimes not so subtle changes in temperature, moisture, and wind direction can occur from one block to the next, or so it seems. He would wear the serge slacks, which were a touch heavier, a woolen golf shirt, and a V-neck sweater. He did not dress himself thoughtlessly. He was pragmatic but was also conscious of style and shade.

He ran his bath, added the Epsom salt to the warm water, and stirred to dissolve it with his right hand. As the tub filled he stood before the toilet for his morning pee, which was slow coming. *Now what?* he asked himself. *Prostate?*

He lit his first cigarette of the day, which he fixed into the black cigarette holder he had begun to use, but only in private. He didn't want to affect his trademark public image as a hardworking, blue-collar toiler, the reality of which he had been quietly shedding when the money started getting good. No one could tell at a glance that his sweaters were fine cashmere, that his slacks were custom made, that his shoes were handmade in England. A cigarette holder, though, spoke of salons and chandeliers. Hogan was never going to be a salons-and-chandeliers kind of guy, but he did like quality clothes, and he was more aware of images and perceptions than he would ever let on. Especially now that he had a business to build up.

The cigarette would be the first of at least forty he would smoke during the day. His body odor often had the acrid scent of burnt nicotine. The bath took some of that away. Splashes of Aqua Velva after his shave helped bury it. Mouthwash did some more of the work. He had preordered room-service breakfast to be delivered at 7:00 PM, making sure ginger ale was included with the scrambled eggs, toast, and coffee. Staff people were unaccustomed to including ginger ale in breakfast orders. Hogan's hands were feeling puffy. He pushed down his pajama bottom, unbuttoned the upper, and eased out of it, making sure he didn't turn his left shoulder in some odd way. He entered the tub left foot first so there would be less pressure on the right leg and also holding onto the shower bar above. At the same time, he pressed his right hand against the wall to further assure he didn't slip. He then slid carefully down into the bliss of warm water. The cigarette holder remained locked between his teeth. With the holder he could smoke the Chesterfield down to the very end and then easily set it aside.

As he soaked he worked up his swing key for the day, the one thought that would precede every shot. Yes, he believed in the automatic response of arms, legs, hips, etc. to take desired positions during the swing that comes from relentless practice—muscle memory, it is called—but he didn't want to take any chances. By concentrating on one of those moves, or some segment within, the others would fall into place. This day it was eyes on the ball. *How did Runyan put it, way back when? "See the ball being hit." Yes.*

Valerie was staying in town. She wanted to do a bit of shopping, read a magazine, and walk a few of the picturesque but less hilly of the city's streets.

Jack Fleck began his Thursday with his exercises. His tee time was 10:40 AM, a good one. Somehow he got lucky, so he had plenty of time. He was up at 6:00 AM and wanted to be at the course by 8:30 AM to loosen up with twenty or twenty-five practice shots and then hit a lot of putts on the putting clock.

He sat on the floor with his back straight and his legs crossed in front of him—a classic yoga position—and held it for two minutes. He then lay down on his back and spread his right leg laterally as far as it would go, held it there, then did the same with the left leg. Ten repetitions of each. The Hip Opening Pose. Next were Inversions. Staying on his back, he raised his lower body to where his hips were as vertical as his legs; he held his hands at his hips. Then came Side Bending. Standing, he raised his arms and clasped his hands together and bent at the waist—to the left and hold, to the right and hold. He handled the postures easily. He had been doing them for over two years and was so flexible he was holding the positions longer and longer. Afterward, he called home. Lynn said little Craig was fine and missed him, that all was well at the courses. She wished him good luck and said they better ring off; the calls were costly.

Fleck then shaved, dressed, and walked across Mission Street to the Beacon Diner, looking both ways to see if a streetcar was coming. He had orange juice, a bowl of oatmeal with a banana, a slice of toasted whole wheat bread, and a glass of water. He drove north to the Olympic Country Club, parked in one of the spots reserved for contestants, and went about his pre-round routine.

The press run-up to a golf championship is fraught with speculation, predictions, and many assorted facts and anecdotes that sometimes turn out to be prescient. Or simply trivial. It's a matter of filling the space and generating interest for the next day's issue, until the real thing comes along.

Newspaper readers learned in the Monday through early Thursday editions that Bob Rosburg had just come through a bout with the measles and that Gene Littler, who was staying with the Rosburgs (no trailer that week), was safe from being infected.

Sam Snead told a newsman that he might have ague, and it was reported that Hogan whistled and hummed "Davy Crockett" throughout a practice round (the movie was playing in town). A seventeen-year-old amateur from Maryland named Deane Beman was thought to be the youngest qualifier in U.S. Open history. He got in as first alternate when Harry Bassler decided not to play. Toney Penna, referencing the effect the climate would have on the event, was reported to have said, "The fog can fool you. If the weather's bad the scores may hit the low ceiling."

Vern Callison, one of the better amateur golfers in Northern California, said he played a practice round with a "hacker by the name of Fleck," and Callison wondered how he (Fleck) ever managed to qualify. (Callison shot rounds of 89 and 80, then departed the scene.)

Ed Furgol thought the course was much easier than the layout on which he had won the 1954 title. (He then said, after a first-round 79, that it was the hardest Open course he ever played.)

Sam Snead was brimming with confidence after a final practice round of 68. In fact, for the three practice rounds previous to that one he shot scores of 70, 71, and 71, and on the eve of the championship's first round he was quoted as saying, "Man, just let me keep those four rounds for the Open right now. Ah'd just sit on the veranda and watch the other guys try to do better."

After his first practice round on the Lake, in which he reportedly shot an 83, Gene Littler said the course was eight times tougher than the one on which he had finished second the previous year. After they cut down the rough he said, "OK, now it's only four times harder."

Some quotes from baseball players were noted: "Golf helps most baseball players because a swing is a swing. I like for my pitchers to play golf during the baseball season" (Al Lopez, manager of the Cleveland Indians). "Golf makes you watch the ball until the last second, and that's what we have to do in baseball"

(Gil McDougal, Yankee infielder). "Playing golf helps a baseball player hit a low pitch, the timing and coordination of both swings are the same. Lefty O'Doul could hardly foul a low ball until he began playing golf" (Paul Waner, Hall-of-Fame outfielder). "I had to quit playing golf because it caused me to upper cut with my baseball swing" (Al Rosen, Cleveland Indian third baseman).

Some of the newspaper writing had a lively flair, while at the same time getting down to specifics. For example, *San Francisco Chronicle* sports columnist Art Rosenbaum wrote in Wednesday's edition what the first hole would play like.

> There will be the usual dramatic introduction [of the player's teeing off], and then the golfers will hit their drives down a fairway thickly roughed on the sides. . . .
>
> A big hitter will debate his second shot. He will prance around the top of the knoll and wish he hadn't eaten that second order of ham for breakfast as his stomach rumbles with excitement. His target is a tiny, heavily trapped green. . . . He is facing a ticklish decision . . . that could spell success or failure, for he knows he can carry the green with a two-wood. However, if he [doesn't] he's in trouble. . . . [If] he deliberately plays short . . . an easy pitch will get him home. This golfer is wise to some of the secrets of the Olympic Club's Lake course.

Reports also stated that ten miles of rope would be supported by 2,400 stakes to control the expected 10,000 to 12,000 fans coming out every day to watch the tournament. It was the second year that galleries were no longer allowed to walk on the fairways to follow play.

Then, finally, there was the golf.

Off the first tee, Ben Hogan, the cuffs of his trousers folded up one width against the moist turf, hit his driver on a slightly right-to-left trajectory that finished in the left corner of the fairway. With a clear view of the green but too far back to reach it with his second shot, he played a 4 wood just short of the bunkers fifty yards from the green. He then hit a wedge shot onto the green about fourteen feet from the hole. (Did he read Art Rosenbaum's column, or did Rosenbaum read Hogan's mind?) His first putt was on line but came up short by a foot. He tapped in for a par-5 and was off but not running. He was on form. Hogan was not a golfer who dashed to the rail right out of the gate and into the lead. Like most great champions, he played a waiting game; he played steady, solid golf and waited for the front-runners to back up.

The caddie assigned to Hogan when he had arrived at the Olympic Club was a seventeen-year-old high school boy. Hogan said he was too young and that he wanted an older man. Tony Zitelli—a man in his late twenties—took the bag. It was a surprising request, because Hogan wanted nothing more from a caddie than to keep up with him and keep the clubs clean. Sam Snead, by contrast, was dependent on a caddie who could judge what club he should hit for approach shots. Oddly, for so superb a golfer, Snead had trouble clubbing himself. Hogan had no such problem.

Chain-smoking and sitting whenever he found a bench on a tee and had some time before it was his turn to play, Hogan's first round was a mixed bag. The ball-striking was excellent, the quality of a great player. But his putting put him in the weekend-golfer class. At the long second hole his second shot finished in a bunker beside the green. He made a fine recovery, blasting the ball to within five feet of the hole, but he missed the putt to bogey the hole; the putt didn't even touch the cup. At the par-3 3rd and par-4 6th he had birdie chances from fifteen and twenty feet and didn't come close to making them. At the 8th he had a six-footer for birdie that came up short. And he three-putted the 9th green after drilling his first putt six feet past the hole and missing the one coming back. However, by methodically hitting fifteen out of eighteen greens in regulation, he managed a 72. He made only one birdie on the round and took a total of thirty-five putts, a very high number for a contender. His score was two over the card par but even par by his own reckoning. And that's exactly how he characterized it.

A headline in the *San Francisco Chronicle* read, "Hogan Calls His 72 'Par in My Book.'" He told newspapermen gathered around him in the locker room that he played "darned good." What he meant was that he had hit a lot of sound shots from the tees and fairways.

Jack Fleck was off to a shaky start, bogeying the par-5 first hole. Bogeying a par-5, no matter how long or difficult it may be, is like giving up a stroke to the field. They are the holes where the birdies must come. He also made bogeys on the 3rd and 6th holes, playing loose approach shots. But he got one of the bogeys back on the short par-4 7th, where he hit a crisp wedge approach to within four feet of the hole and made the putt. He turned the front nine in a two-over-par 37.

On the back nine it was a bit worse. He bogeyed four holes and had no birdies to make up any of them. He felt confident, though. The mistakes were merely mechanical. They had nothing to do with his thinking, his strategy, or—most important—his emotions.

He ended up with a round of 76 and yet found himself in a reasonably good position vis-à-vis the field.

He was tied with eighteen others for the eighth-lowest score of the day. Behind Fleck by a shot or more were such stalwarts as Middlecoff, Boros, Littler, Furgol, Rosburg, and Nelson. And Sam Snead was way back. He made a twelve-foot putt on the 18th hole for par to just barely break 80. Fleck did not feel he was out of the competition, not by any means, and was particularly satisfied with his mind-set. It was not a great score, but as that Air Force guy he met said all the time, "Negative perspiration."

Snead's round of 79 was the biggest surprise of the day, except to those convinced he just did not have whatever headwork it took to win the U.S. Open. His driving is what caused him so much grief. Close Snead observers thought he didn't do well in the U.S. Open because he wouldn't revise his game for the setup, that is, the narrower fairways. If it was a par-5 hole he played a driver off the tee, when a judicious 2 iron or 3 wood was a better play to an especially slim landing area or short dogleg. On this day his driving was not good. He hit a number of drivers through the doglegs and into deep rough.

Clearly, the course played as difficult as predicted. Of the 162 starters, 73 shot from 80 to 89, and there were five rounds in the 90s.

The leader by three strokes after round one was Tommy Bolt, who had a "sizzling" 67—a boon to the newspaper guys, who were stuck with reporting so many high scores. Bolt was good copy, because he was a character famous for his explosive temperament and one-liners. With a prominent chin that—when in a red-faced snit—he raised à la Franklin D. Roosevelt, over the years his irritability prompted some not especially inventive but alliterative nicknames: Tempestuous Tommy, Terrible-Tempered Tommy, and the inevitable Thunder Bolt.

He was always good for colorful anecdotes and quotes. He once advised golfers who threw their clubs in anger to always throw them forward so they could just "pick 'em up on the way." When Bolt withdrew from tournaments, he did it with a certain panache. Once, in the middle of a rainy fourth round of a Houston Open in which he was not doing well, he was waiting in the fairway to play his approach shot. It was a longish wait, and finally he said, "I'm standing out here ruining clothes that cost more than I can win in this tournament. I'm going in." And he did. Bolt was a very snappy dresser—and withdrawer.

Bolt had worked as a carpenter around Houston, did some hustling on local municipal courses, and didn't turn pro until he was in his early thirties. But he became a fine shot-maker in the big time, with a long and elastic swing, and when he made some putts, he could win—and did. In his first round over the Lake course he had twelve one-putt greens and a total of only twenty-five on the day. That didn't happen too often, the temper thing often getting in the way. But after his first round he was all smiles and didn't have much to say to the newsmen except to remark that those who called him Terrible-Tempered Tommy were themselves "terrible-tempered newspaper guys."

In second place, with a round of 70, was Walker Inman Jr., a friend of Jack Fleck's but even less known in the golf world. He and Fleck, who were paired for the first round, played a lot of practice rounds together and sometimes shared driving from one town to the next. Inman was out of Augusta, Georgia, and was making his first run at the tour after being discharged from the military earlier in the year. He had won just over $200 so far. He was in that category that pops up in the U.S. Open from time to time, a totally unheard-of player who has a very good opening round and more often than not falls by the wayside as the tournament progresses into the second round.

In third, alone, with a 71 was Jack Burke Jr., who didn't find enough rough during the day that his thin wrists couldn't handle.

Next came Hogan, Babe Lichardus—a colorful New Jersey player—and Mike Souchak, with 73s. There were five players at 74, including Doug Ford and Harvie Ward Jr. It was not the most stellar list on the first page of the leaderboard, but it was only the first round. There was a lot of golf to be played.

After his round Hogan repaired to the practice range to hit balls for an hour. This was becoming routine among all the tournament players. No matter how many championships one has played, and even won, the one on the table takes a toll on the nerves. Banging out balls at the end of the day has a cathartic effect. But Hogan also worked on a couple of shots he had not hit well that day because his driving had been a bit erratic and he found the rough on a couple of holes. And he hit thirty or so pitch shots, which he knew would be increasingly important if he began to miss greens with second shots from the rough.

As always, Hogan drew a gathering to watch him practice. Often he would find a location where no one could get to him, but at Olympic there was no longer such a place. The Ocean course was being used as a parking lot. Watching Hogan practice had become a must-do among tour players as well as spectators. Everyone was mesmerized by his concentration, for one thing, but more so by his accuracy. People chuckled in awe at how little the shagger had to move to recover each ball. He would just step a few yards back as Hogan went to a longer club. Otherwise, he could catch them with the shag bag itself.

But what was the secret to his remarkable accuracy? What was he doing that was different from everyone else? What piece of swing business had he worked out that made him so damn good? Hogan's secret! It had taken on a mystery of biblical proportions. People wondered if, like Moses, Hogan actually met with God and received from Him the Golf Commandments. Or did he make them up himself in a glorious moment of monumental creativity? Everyone had for some time noted Hogan's weakened left-hand grip, in which he turned his hand more to the left on the handle than was conventional. It was meant to keep his hands and wrists from turning too much to the left at impact and putting the dreaded hook spin on the ball. Everyone saw how his right foot was not flared out to the right, as was common, but was set perpendicular to the line of flight. This helped prevent a lateral slide of the body to the right in the backswing and created a taut springboard for going into the downswing. But those things were too obvious; there must be something else.

Many tour pros, generally from the middle to lower ranks, would watch Hogan's moves and try to discern what he was doing; they were looking for something special. Well-established, successful golfers such as Middlecoff or Burke or Snead or Heafner may have been curious about Hogan's action and especially liked the flight pattern of his shots, but they weren't about to incorporate any of his swing points into their own games. A few of the most experienced pros dismissed the whole "secret" thing with casual disdain. Jimmy Demaret was asked once what he thought Hogan's secret was. He sniggered and scoffed and said, "Oh, Christ. He just drops it in there." Meaning the right elbow was tucked into his right side as he began his downswing, which prevented the clubhead coming to the ball from outside to inside the target line. This was perhaps the most conventional swing technique ever conceived. There was more to Hogan's swing than that, though; it did look like there might be something special going on.

Hogan enjoyed the notion that he had a secret, and he was about to cash in on the presumption everyone had that there was one. Word was out that he was going to reveal it in an upcoming August issue of *Life* magazine. It was said he was getting anywhere from $10,000 to $25,000 for it. Either way, it was a lot of dough for a golf tip. There were some hints leaking out as to what the secret was. The noted golf writer Herbert Warren Wind helped Hogan write the article and let slip the words *pronation* and *supination*, which sent everyone to the dictionary to find out what they meant.

The secret revealed in *Life* magazine was described as a cupping of the left wrist at the very top of the backswing and an instant before beginning the downswing. Cupping means that the left hand is more or less tilted inward, creating a slight bend (or cup) at the conjunction of the wrist and back of the hand. When the tour pros read the article there was a widespread opinion that the Hawk was putting everybody on. No one had ever seen this cupping action. And when two years later Hogan's celebrated instruction book, *Five Lessons: The Modern Fundamentals of Golf*, written with Herbert Warren Wind, appeared, there was no mention whatsoever of the secret that he gave to *Life* magazine. Indeed, in one place, when discussing the backswing, he writes, in capital letters, "THE ACTION OF THE ARMS IS MOTIVATED BY THE MOVEMENT OF THE BODY, AND THE HANDS CONSCIOUSLY DO NOTHING BUT MAINTAIN A FIRM GRIP ON THE CLUB."

His practice session finished, Hogan walked slowly to the locker room to change shoes and get a car back to the St. Francis. He did not stop to do any putting on the way in.

He and Valerie ordered a room-service dinner and ate while watching the news on television. There were too many golf fans in the hotel who would stare and bother him for autographs if he ate in the dining room. After dinner Valerie picked up her romance novel. Ben made a call to his plant manager's home to see how things were going.

Following his round, Jack Fleck spent twenty minutes or so on the practice putting green, where he hit putts of various distances. He checked the scoreboard, which was almost complete by this point, and was satisfied where he stood in the field. A lot of well-established players had higher scores, some quite a bit higher. He, Walker Inman, and Mike Krak went out for dinner. Afterward, Fleck called home, listened to Mario Lanza, and did his yoga exercises. He went to bed at 9:30 PM.

ACT II

S AM SNEAD MADE IT A TOURNAMENT that golf fans had been anticipating for years. Snead versus Hogan for the U.S. Open. The
Tournament of the Century! Bob Feller on the mound, Dimaggio
in the box. Joe Louis and Billy Conn in a fifteen-rounder. On an
overcast, cool, and gray Friday the man who said earlier in the
week that the chill went right to his bones warmed the entire environment surrounding the 1955 U.S. Open when he improved his
first-round score by ten strokes. Ten! Sam Snead was back in it,
with a 69.

That Ben Hogan would be a party to the developing scenario
was confidently assumed. And indeed, although he had a com-
monplace round of 73, Hogan was definitely there. Actually, he
had a three-shot lead over Snead, but there were two rounds to
play on Saturday, and Slammin' Sam would surely have the physical advantage, at least. Look at the guy. A leopard, a cashmere-clad
Rolls-Royce. He had the stamina, the strength to do two rounds in
one day on the heavyweight Open golf course. Hogan looked like
he was going to collapse any minute. Poor guy. But look what he
did only eighteen months after the accident.

Hogan was widely admired, but his persona was so grim that only his astounding precision as a shot-maker could be enjoyed. Sam wore his straw hat at a jaunty angle, talked about his golf with a down-to-earth, mountain-boy turn of phrase, and of course handled the golf club with uncommonly beautiful rhythm. In fact, Snead could be very touchy and complaining when he played poorly, but his outward presence, and especially that marvelous swing, buried those character flaws. Many people would have liked to see Hogan win a fifth U.S. Open, but just as many, maybe more, wanted to see the Slammer finally break through, throw off the jinx or curse or whatever it was that had denied him this one championship, and complete, once and for all, his magnificent competitive record. How could such a talented golfer who had won everything else in the game not be able to take the Open? His age, the same as Hogan, was not an issue. Snead, clearly in excellent health, was a prime physical specimen. He didn't drink, didn't smoke, and, he liked to say, starting on Wednesday night, always went to bed early and alone.

There were subplots developing, of course, which could possibly become central to the final outcome. Every round of golf has the components of a play, and only two acts had been written. Tommy Bolt lost his magical touch on the greens and, of course, his temper as well. His second-round 77 culminated with a tee shot hooked into a bush on the 18th hole. With an unplayable lie, he double-bogeyed the hole and dropped into a tie for the lead with Harvie Ward, the smooth-swinging shot-maker and brilliant, fearless putter, who shot an even-par 70. While Bolt had been fairly magnanimous with the press the day before, after his second round he clattered off the premises without changing out of his golf shoes and would not talk to any of the newsmen except to complain that all they liked to write about him was his temperament.

American golf's mid-twentieth-century triumvirate, plus one, during a practice round over the Olympic Club's Lake Course. From left to right, Ben Hogan, Sam Snead, Cary Middlecoff (the plus one), and Byron Nelson. Notice the heavy amount of sand on the tee behind them. An over-sanded tee would finalize Hogan's fall to Fleck. AP/WideWorld

Moments after checking his scorecard following his completion of seventy-two holes, the usually undemonstrative Ben Hogan was talked into signaling that he had just won his record fifth U.S. Open. Two hours later he discovered that he hadn't . . . unless he won a playoff. Tournament Chairman Bob Roos is at his right side. Courtesy Olympic Golf Club

Jack Fleck hitting his second shot to the 18th green (72nd hole). His high follow-through indicates his successful effort to hit a very high shot that would stop quickly when it landed. It did, only eight feet to the right of the hole, from where he holed for a birdie 3 to tie Ben Hogan. *San Francisco Examiner*/Bancroft Library Archives

Jack Fleck is a picture of joyful relief at having just tied Ben Hogan for the 1955 U.S. Open. Ed Furgol, who was the defending champion, is at his side. Furgol helped Fleck make an endorsement deal following his playoff victory. BILL CROUCH, THE *Oakland Tribune* COLLECTION, THE OAKLAND MUSEUM OF CALIFORNIA. GIFT OF ANG NEWSPAPERS.

Ben Hogan plays from a bunker fifty yards short of the first green in the playoff. It finished seventeen feet from the hole—one of many good bunker shots he played in the tournament. But as in many of those instances, he only two-putted.

Golf Digest/CONDE NAST ARCHIVE © CONDE NAST

At the 11th hole in the playoff Fleck drove into the deep rough. With a three-shot lead he chose to simply play an iron out safely to the middle of the fairway and hope for a one-putt par. He bogeyed the hole. Hogan made a brilliant recovery from a greenside bunker, and this time converted a short putt for a par that reduced his deficit by a stroke. THE *Oakland Tribune* COLLECTION, THE OAKLAND MUSEUM OF CALIFORNIA. GIFT OF ANG NEWSPAPERS.

The seemingly impassive Fleck and Hogan march in lockstep down the 12th fairway in the playoff. The enthusiastic gallery had broken through the restraining ropes and play was halted for a minute or two to restore order and as a warning that such intrusions would not be tolerated.
COURTESY, OLYMPIC GOLF CLUB

A "fried egg," a very difficult lie from which to get close to the hole. Fleck mastered it on the 14th hole of the playoff, stopping the ball within three feet of the cup. He made the putt to save his par 4. BILL YOUNG, THE *Oakland Tribune*
COLLECTION, THE OAKLAND MUSEUM OF CALIFORNIA. GIFT OF ANG NEWSPAPERS.

Ben Hogan at the end of the road; his drive on the 18th hole of the playoff was pulled badly into extremely high rough when his right foot slipped on the sandy surface of the tee. It took him three swings to get clear of the heavy grass, by which time his chances were ended. AP/WIDEWORLD

Fleck and Hogan shake hands on the 18th green after Fleck two-putted to complete his monumental victory. *Golf Digest*/CONDE NAST ARCHIVE © CONDE NAST

Following the playoff, Ben Hogan waves his cap over Jack Fleck's putter, as if to cool it off. In fact, Fleck's good putting wasn't the only reason he won.

AP/WideWorld

Ben Hogan's warm and generous smile while congratulating Jack Fleck on his victory is one the golf world would have liked to have seen more. AP/WideWorld

The scores continued to be high, on average. Some of the favorites at the start of the championship fell even further back. Jack Burke, on the first hole, drove into heavy rough on the left and, as he more or less prophesied, didn't have enough wrist for it. He double-bogeyed the hole and finished with a 77. He wasn't out of it, though. Combined with his first-round 71, he was in a tie for third with Snead and Bobby Harris.

Middlecoff paired a 75 with his opening-round 76 and fell back into the bottom third of the field. Mike Souchak blew to a 79 but didn't feel he was out of contention. After all, Snead had one of those rounds, and look where he was. Gene Littler improved from 76 to 73 but didn't seem to be enjoying himself. He was not as close as expected but was there and thereabouts. Byron Nelson proved he still had some game with rounds of 77 and 74, a tie for sixth, but no one thought he would make a serious run at it.

Bob Rosburg had a steady 74 that put him into a tie for third, but he was not happy. Before the cut was determined he told a reporter, "Honest, I hope I don't qualify for the final thirty-six holes. They've ruined a good golf course."

Dick Mayer was going along well until the 8th hole, when his iron shot from the tee sent the ball up into the branches of a cypress tree hanging over the right edge of the green. The ball stuck in the branches, and Mayer had to take an unplayable-lie penalty that he capped off with three putts for a triple-bogey 6. He missed the cut. So did a few other notable potential contenders: Lew Worsham, Ted Kroll, Ed Oliver, and Walter Burkemo.

Hogan's second round of 73 didn't start out well, and not surprisingly it was his putter that was the culprit. He missed a two-foot putt for a birdie on the first hole. He rarely showed himself upset when he failed on the greens but after this miss shook his head slightly as if to say it was just another one of *those*. He had his tee-to-green game to bail him out. However, there appeared to be a slight crack developing in this part of his game. He missed a couple of fairways off the tee, which for Hogan was a lot.

The most flagrant example came at the 16th hole, the 603-yard par-5 that was playing at least thirty yards longer in the moist, salt sea air and on wet grass. Hogan's drive went straight right off the tee and into the trees. To everyone in the gallery—and to Hogan himself, really—such a shot was inconceivable. But he got lucky. The ball hit a tree and bounced straight left back into the fairway. It could have dropped straight down or caromed to the right in among more trees; it might even have gotten lost in the thicket of rough. As it happened, although he was only 150 yards off the tee, he could play from short grass and in the clear. He took full, even epic advantage of the break by first pounding a brassie just past the turn of the left-turning dogleg. He still had a full 2 iron left to the green but hit a terrific shot to within twenty feet of the hole. And lo, this time Hogan's putter worked. He holed the putt for the stoutest birdie of the tournament by anybody in the field up to that time. It was a splendid illustration of dogged determination and the unalloyed self-confidence that allows someone to hold his composure in the face of potentially self-inflicted pain.

Hogan's entire second round, in fact, was a clinic in resilience. He bogeyed four holes on the front nine but retrieved two of them with birdies that came from putts of some length—twelve feet and sixteen feet.

On the backside he had a bogey, that magnificent birdie at the 16th, and seven pars to finish with a 73. That put him in a tie for second place with three other players. One was Boros, the deceptively lackadaisical Hungarian-American who added to his gathering reputation as one of the best Open players of the era with a solid 69. Another was Walker Inman, who confounded tradition and stayed in the game by returning a gutty 75 to go with his opening 70. He was joined in second place by another golfer who came out of nowhere, in more ways than one. It was Jack Fleck, who fired a fine and, of course, surprising 69. The press corps immediately attended to Inman and Fleck, Will Grimsley putting it best in his write-up for the *Washington Post*. The two were "dark horses of the darkest hue."

It all began for Fleck on the fifth green. Something happened. It was inexplicable, or so it seemed. All of a sudden the putter became, in the supernatural sense, a wand with the magical power to turn dross into gold. It had nothing to do with a different grip, a change of position at address, or a new stroke path; it wasn't about mechanics. His stroke was the same short slap at the ball that many of the pros of the era used, including Hogan. It was a stroke necessitated by having to play most if not all their golf on (comparatively) thickly grassed, slow-running greens. One had to get the ball up on top of the grass and rolling as quickly as possible, and for many it was the slap that did it—and a putter with as much as five degrees of loft.

Even at the Olympic Club the greens were not as smooth as might have been expected for a well-to-do private club—and for a U.S. Open. They were overall in bent grass but, as with all greens in temperate climates, infiltrated with *Poa annua,* a weedlike grass strain that is uncontrollably distributed. It comes in on the wind and on players' shoes. *Poa annua* grows differently than the grass it invades. It grows faster, higher, and unevenly and, as the day wears on, puts bumps in the road to the hole. If an entire green is in *Poa annua,* it is fine. Oakmont's famously fast greens are all *Poa annua.* It just has to be cut more often, and lower.

On the long par-4 fifth hole, at 457 yards, Fleck drove into the fairway and just around the dogleg right. His approach was excellent, a 5-iron shot to twelve feet. He read the line from behind the ball and also took a look from directly opposite, on the other side of the hole. Standard reading technique. But this time, when he got over the ball, a new sensation went through him. He felt a weightlessness in his hands, his shoulders, and his body. The stroke itself was a kind of abstraction. The ball ran into the hole for a birdie as though it had no other place to go. It was as if the bumps caused by the *Poa annua* leveled out when they saw his ball coming. His stroke was so beautifully measured—a controlled, slower slap that sent the ball off at precisely the right speed and direction.

At the long, par-4 6th the enchantment continued. Fleck drove long but left. His ball ended up in the lip of the fairway bunker under a chunk of sod that had not yet meshed completely; it was one of the new fairway bunkers. He even had trouble finding the ball and was close to the five-minute limit on ball search when he spotted it. He had no alternative but to hack at it and hope it got back to the fairway. With one of his Ben Hogan wedges he did just that, sending up a huge chunk of turf and moving the ball into the fairway and about 170 yards from the hole.

He chose a 4 iron for his third shot and hit a grand one, striking the ball so purely he barely felt the contact. It arched high and with a slight draw landed just short of the hole and came within a foot of going in. He saved his par in spectacular fashion—more than spectacular. A paranormal aura was beginning to envelop him.

The genie left him briefly at the short par-4 7th, the only nominal birdie hole on the course. Fleck played it in a routine par. He drove in the fairway and then hit the green with a wedge approach shot and two-putted. But at the very next hole, the 139-yard par-3, *it* returned. Fleck used a 7 iron and, swinging with elegant tempo, flew the ball dead on line with the target. Ed Oliver, playing just ahead of Fleck, saw the shot and told Jack later that it actually went in the hole but jumped out. It finished only an inch from the cup—a leaner, in golf jargon.

He followed with a bogey at the long par-4 9th when he missed the fairway off the tee, but he finished the front nine with a one-under-par 34. Anyone shooting under par at the Lake course that week gained on the field, and Fleck did.

Fleck played very steady golf on the back nine. Nothing spectacular happened. He drove well, long and in the fairways. He hit all the greens but the 17th, where he made a good chip to save par. The putter continued to feel like the wand of the Good Witch. Just nothing fell. He had an even-par 35 for a total of 69. It was one of only three rounds under 70 on the day.

He was, of course, one of the two darkest of dark horses, but his friend Walker Inman got a little more coverage. He was a recently discharged serviceman, who only ten months prior was serving in Korea. Fleck was not dismissed entirely, although most reporters did not do their homework. One wrote that Fleck had been playing the tour for only a year. Another had him down as a driving-range pro.

In their phone conversation that evening Lynn Fleck heard something different in her husband's voice, in his articulation, in its tone. He told her of his day as though it had happened through a looking glass.

ACT III

WHEN THE U.S. OPEN went to a seventy-two-hole event in 1898, and until 1924, it was played in two days at 36 holes per day. Smaller fields allowed for that, but it was still a rough grind on the golfers. As the number of entrants increased the format expanded, and in 1925 it became a three-day affair with the last two rounds played on the third day. This made it a little easier on the body and soul. But either way, the tournament always ended on Saturday. Although it was not codified, the USGA's rationale for playing the last two rounds of the U.S. Open in one day was that it added a definitive physical-fitness constituent to the championship. It was a good point, especially in view of the general sporting public's misbegotten opinion—one that still holds in some quarters—that golf is not a very athletic game. But there was another reason that came before. The Saturday-conclusion format was rooted in the country's Puritan legacy, an observance of the religious foundation of America, which decreed that no pleasure be taken or business be transacted on the Christian Sabbath—Sunday.

By 1955 that dictate had ridden the steep slope to total abolition throughout most of the country. Baseball's Sunday dou-

ble-header had become a time-honored tradition. Families went
to Sunday afternoon movies and amusement parks. Merchants
counted on doing a good piece of business on this day when
almost everyone had a day off from work—everyone but caddies,
say, who toted the bags of private club members who teed it up
after they attended church services. Still, the USGA stayed rooted
in the old blue law—no fun on Sunday—even as golf adminis-
tered by other groups, and the nation's golfers at large, reflected
the evolved American popular and religious culture. The Sunday
morning round of golf with pals at the local public course was itself
a kind of sacrament. And all the other tournaments on the professional tournament circuit had become four-day events, eighteen
holes per day, concluding on Sunday. There was commercial value
in this, of course. Two separate days of competition covering the
entire weekend doubled the paid attendance.

In fact the USGA, in its characteristic fence-straddling if not
hypocritical way, did not strictly adhere to its Sabbath ritual. If
there was a tie at the end of seventy-two holes, the playoff was held
the next day, which of course was a Sunday. Ben Hogan wouldn't
have minded at all if the USGA had wholly joined with mid-twentieth-century American secularism. As it was, he would have to
play thirty-six holes on Saturday, June 18. It would be a long, difficult trudge on this physically exhausting Lake course.

As noted earlier, a few of the pros who had been around Hogan
over the years were not convinced he was in such poor condition
as he made it seem. Even if he wasn't playing in many tournaments
anymore, he was surely playing, and walking, rounds of golf. And
by all means he was hitting practice balls. He had to stand up to
do that. They knew his creepy silence on the golf course, seldom
saying anything at all to the other players in his pairing, had some

deception in it. His locked lips surely reflected his intense concentration on the work at hand. It was also a mark of his natural diffidence. *Effusive* was a word never associated with Ben Hogan. But not speaking to opponents was also an old gamesmanship ploy. When a player hits a very good shot and gets not a word or nod of recognition from others in the group it is like saying that player doesn't count, doesn't exist, that the shot didn't really happen . . . and if it did, who cares? Hogan himself didn't need the reassurance of a "nice shot" comment from others, but he was unusual in that. Most others get a bit of an ego sting from the silent treatment. Hogan knew that effect and used it. So why wouldn't he play the wounded-warrior card? Let them think he wasn't up to strength, and maybe they would feel they didn't have to push extra hard to beat him.

If there was any of that going on in Hogan's mind, it was on the far periphery. The hurt in his left shoulder was real and chronic. He had already had two operations on it. But his legs were the main issue. They didn't hurt as much as they were becoming less and less golf-strong. It was getting harder to stand still when beginning the full swing and even the shortest ones, especially near the end of rounds. Consistently good ball-striking can only be played off a solid foundation. Movement of the lower body to the right by just the slightest amount can put a full swing out of kilter and alter the swing path and timing. Any golfer endowed with hefty legs, those with significant diameter and density, has an immediate advantage over those with what is called "thin pins" in the lingo.

Hogan's legs weren't thin, but they didn't have the fundamental resource of size. What's more, the highway accident and the unique operation that saved his life involved reducing the flow of blood to his legs. As he recovered, this stopgap measure was relaxed but in the end rendered his legs extremely vulnerable to fatigue. It was probably why he was spraying the occasional drive to the left and right, most often in the last part of each round. The drive dead right on the 16th in the second round the day before was a good example.

The greater effect of the condition of his legs was the bearing it had on his short game, in particular his putting. Odd as it may seem, because the putting stroke does not require anything at all like the vigorous movement of the full or even half swing made with everything from the driver down to the short irons, the slightest body movement can have a negative effect on the result. Hogan was developing a classic case of the yips, the slang term for poor putting characterized by a nervous, jerky, poorly controlled stroke. It is generally recognized as a mental problem. But Hogan's poor putting was also a case of not being able to stand confidently stable or still over the ball.

Technically, Hogan had tremendous strength in his arms and hands that helped him direct the full swing with sufficient power and accuracy. And there is more margin for error with full-swing shots. If one can say putting is akin to heart surgery, hitting a drive is equivalent to splitting a block of wood. One can be a bit off center with the axe and still get a decent result. Not so with a scalpel. Hit a driver just a little out on the toe of the club and it may hook a few yards to the left. Still, it can very well end up in the fairway and leave a clear shot to the green. But hit a six-foot putt a hair out on the toe, and it will be enough to cause the ball to move an inch left of the hole or come up short of it. The count—the score—then goes up by one. A mis-hit iron shot can be atoned for with a fine recovery shot from a bunker, but only if the player can convert it with a good putt. One way or the other, a three-foot putt that is missed is missed forever. Holing out is what the game is all about. And that was becoming a real problem for Hogan.

Hogan wasn't totally hopeless with his short game, including the putting. A golfer has to make a few over the years to be so big a winner. Although in the third round he missed a ten-foot par putt on the 3rd hole after missing the green and playing a good pitch from heavy fringe, he holed an eight-foot putt for a birdie on the 10th. And he got another birdie at the par-3 15th after a fine 7 iron to within three feet. He played a solid fifteen holes and was one under par for the round. That was card par; he was three under by his accounting.

But then, on the last three holes the wheels (read: legs) virtually came off. He bogeyed every one of them with poor chipping and/or putting. At the par-5 16th, where he had made such a dramatic birdie the day before, he three-putted from twenty-five feet, the first putt ending up four feet past the hole. At the mighty 17th he came up short of the green with his 3-wood second shot and hit a chip to five feet and missed the putt. At the 18th he seemed even more disjointed. His short-iron approach finished just off the green to the left, about sixteen feet from the hole. The ball wasn't lying too badly in thick grass, but he was not sure how it would come out. He changed clubs twice before deciding on the sand wedge, then tried to be too precise with the shot. He decelerated the club as it moved toward the ball, and the slowed clubhead failed to bite through the heavy grass. He chunked the ball a mere eight feet, leaving him an eight-foot putt with a slight left-to-right break. When he finally got the putter moving, the ball came up short and right of the cup. A weak effort. At this he actually displayed a bit of irritation, something rare for Hogan. He swiped his putter a couple of times, actually simulating or repeating with even more quickness the stroke he made a moment earlier. He then tapped in for the bogey 5 to close the round with a 72.

With any sort of respectable putting he could well have been at least even par for the round. With all that, and for all his real physical issues, that he was doing as well as he was in this Open spelled out yet another tribute to his almost superhuman will to overcome his hurting body and mediocre short game and excel at the one thing on which his life was based.

The steep thirty-degree climb to the clubhouse and locker room was a bit more torturous in mind of what he had given back after so much excellent tee-to-green shot-making. Goddamn putting! Chipping, too. He slowly made his way up the stairs to get a bite to eat, a glass of ginger ale, and a good, long sit down. He would be teeing off again in forty minutes and starting the fourth round with a one-stroke lead, at 217.

In the third round Sam Snead continued to make his presence known. The gallery was becoming even more Snead-focused when he finished with a round of 70. As was his wont, he grumbled a bit and said that if he had made a few more putts he would have shot a 66. Or 64. He once had a round of 59 in an unofficial tournament and when interviewed said the same thing: "If ah'da been puttin' ah'da had 56." Right. And as he would put it, if the dog hadn't stopped to . . . defecate, it woulda caught the rabbit.

In his first-round 79 Snead drove ten times into the rough, hence the high score. In rounds two and three his driving accuracy was much improved, and he could play approaches from the short grass. This gave him a huge advantage, because of his length off the tee and his masterful iron game. All of which could make up for spotty putting. In round three he went out in 34 to pick up two strokes on Hogan, bogeyed twice on the back nine, but covered

those mistakes with a tremendous birdie on the exceptionally difficult par-4 17th. He hit the green with a 2 iron, where everyone
else was coming up short with 2, 3, and 4 woods. And he holed a
sizeable putt. It was one of only five 3s made on the 17th through
three rounds of play, two of which were the result of chip-ins. With
his even-par round Snead was in second place, one stroke behind
Hogan, and the mano a mano clash of the two giants of the game
seemed imminent. The gallery was buzzing about the thought of
being on the premises for a battle of the century, golf division.

However—and it is a big *however*—Snead was not at all exhilarated at the prospects before him. Bob Rosburg, who had earlier
demonstrated his pessimistic inclinations when he said he hoped
he didn't make the thirty-six-hole cut, found some sort of positive
energy and had a third-round 67. It vaulted him into contention
at only two shots off the lead. He was paired with Snead for the
third round and would be for the fourth as well. They had lunch
together after the third round, and at the table Rosburg confronted
a strangely depressed Snead, who was saying he didn't think he
could do it—win the tournament—because he was putting so
poorly. Rosburg encouraged Sam and told him he had a really
good opportunity to finally win the Open. But Snead showed little
enthusiasm. Sports psychologists would have quite a time contemplating this attitude. Was Snead afraid to win the Open? Was
he more comfortable, after all the disappointments, with not winning? Was he playing possum with his own psyche, tamping down
the prospect of winning in order to control his emotions?

Julius Boros, who broke up Hogan's two-in-a-row streak when
he won the '52 Open, shot a 73 to tie with Snead for second place.
He was a definite threat and, belying his casual manner, did indeed
give a damn whether he won or lost. He was good under pressure,

which he dealt with in an interesting way. The more important the shot he had to play, and especially if it was a short putt, the more quickly he went after it. When he won the 1952 Tam O'Shanter World Championship, he had a three-foot putt on the last green to take the huge $25,000 first prize. Without any hesitation, with what appeared to be only a glance at the line, he stepped up to the ball and tapped it in. He was avoiding tension by not letting it build up.

Jack Burke bounced back into contention with a third-round 72, and although Walker Inman had a round of 76, he was still something of a factor. Tommy Bolt's first-round 67 kept him in contention even after his 77 and his third-round 75. He was at 219, two strokes off the pace, and tied with Rosburg, who was more comfortable playing the Lake, "ruined" though it may be, than anyone else except Harvie Ward. Ward was at 220 and could not be counted out. He was tied with Jack Fleck, who had an ordinary round of 75.

Jack Fleck's frame of mind after his third round was just as it was after his first round. The score had no negative effect on him. He three-putted a green early in the round, missed a few greens with stray approach shots, and failed to get up and down. But he also made some clutch putts to save pars. It was not a good score in the round when, traditionally, the real contenders make their move into the center of the furnace, but he was relaxed and confident. After all, he had gotten the Word from up high, or wherever.

On Saturday morning while shaving, Fleck had heard a voice speak to him from the mirror. The voice said he was going to win the U.S. Open. Fleck couldn't characterize the voice—whether it was deep, a bass, or a Mario Lanza–like tenor. The accent seemed to be Midwestern, a kind of cornrow twang. It could have been him talking to himself without realizing it. But he was certain that wasn't the case. It was a voice from another world, he thought. He was stunned by the experience for a moment but then took it very much to heart, especially when it repeated the words: "Jack Fleck, you are going to win the U.S. Open."

ACT IV

J ACK FLECK HAD A QUICK TURNAROUND from round 3 to round
4. Only a half hour. He didn't mind, because he didn't plan on
eating lunch. He felt strong and didn't want to slow himself down
with food.

Dr. Paul Barton, a dentist in Davenport, was in town to see
Fleck play. Barton was a fine golfer who competed in prestigious
amateur championships around the country and had taken on
Fleck as a kind of sponsor when he was getting started as a professional. He paired with him in pro-am tournaments and otherwise
encouraged Fleck to work hard at his game. Barton had come west
with his wife to see their naval officer son, John, off to Japan from
San Diego. After the third round, Barton advised Fleck to eat some
sugar cubes during the upcoming round, explaining that no matter
how good a condition he was in, Fleck was bound to develop some
fatigue. He understood how much of a psychological drain playing
in competition was, especially for a national championship. The
sugar would give him energy bursts. Fleck was not comfortable
with the sugar intake—it went against his dietary program—but
he felt Barton had his best interests at heart. Barton said he would
hand him a few cubes periodically during the fourth round.

Fleck was off at 3:00 PM, two hours after Hogan and in the third-from-last group of the day. He was playing with Gene Littler, with whom he had been paired in round 3. Littler was just the kind of playing partner one would want. His swing rhythm could feed into Fleck's own game, his good form was also a plus to observe, and he was undemonstrative. Littler fit the mood Fleck had reached—the unusual composure, the easy poise that had been building up in him. The core of calm was enhanced by the fact that he and Littler, who was out of contention, had no gallery whatsoever. Fleck could play like an artist in his atelier.

The pairings and starting-times systems in the U.S. Open reflected a USGA attitude that said the association, like Ben Hogan, was not in the entertainment business. Nor did it seem to understand, or chose to ignore, the nature of competition and how pairings and their position on the course affected the outcome. For one thing, the leaders of the tournament after the second round of play were not among the last to start their third and fourth rounds. Nor were they paired, and if not they were not necessarily in a pairing just ahead or behind each other. If that happened, it was a matter of luck. When a tournament's competition develops and the leaders separate from the rest of the field, if the golfers at the top of the standings are playing together, the competition becomes more direct and therefore more intense and even personal. And if they go off at the end of the field, more interest is generated in the gallery. It can see what the leaders are doing, or can do, against a charge made by players ahead of them. Such a system always influences the players involved and how they respond under known pressure.

But Joe Dey, the executive secretary of the USGA, made the pairings and used an idiosyncratic method that no one understood. He never explained it either. The only sure thing, and no one ever realized it at the time, was that he would never pair Sam Snead with Ben Hogan. He knew how well Sam performed in a direct confrontation with the Hawk. Snead defeated Hogan four times in playoffs, one of the victories coming in the 1954 Masters. And if Snead was in contention Dey would always put him off before Hogan or anyone else who was ahead of him in the standings. In this, he had in mind Snead's history of throwing away chances to win the Open in the late going, starting with the 1939 fiasco in Philadelphia where, if he had known a mere par would have won it, he most surely would not have played the last hole so boldly. Thus he always put a contending Snead off before the leaders so he didn't know for sure what he would need in order to win.

Dey's animus toward Snead derived from their different class backgrounds. Dey was from the genteel Tidewater, Virginia, region of old money, large homes, and a kind of sophistication that was quite the opposite of Snead's upbringing in the mountains of Virginia. Snead could sometimes be quite crude socially, which not only went against the grain of Dey's personal sense of propriety—he had often mentioned that as a youth he considered becoming a clergyman—but also contravened the social order in which Dey grew up.

That personal eccentricity aside, it must be said that the double round to conclude the championship made it virtually impossible to pair the leaders in the fourth round who emerged after the third round. If it happened, it was a coincidence. This pairing system would be changed in 1961, with the coming of extensive television coverage. The change also included going to a four-day tournament. Now the leaders would be paired beginning with the third round of play. Although it was not the case in 1955, it is inter-

esting to speculate what might have happened if this had been the
system at the time.

For the last two rounds, Hogan was paired with Bobby Harris, a native Californian who was a club pro in Chicago. Harris
was an excellent player but was struggling that week and, with a
two-round total of 145, stood three shots behind Hogan after the
second round and nine behind after the third. On that basis, after
two rounds he had no business playing the third with the leader
or other close contenders. Hogan (145) should have been paired
with either Bolt (144), Ward (144), Boros (145), Inman (145), or
Fleck (145). Snead (148) should have been somewhere in that mix
of players.

In the fourth round, the pairings could have been or should
have been Hogan (217) and Snead (218) or Boros (218). Even
if Snead didn't get to go head-to-head with Hogan, he would be
playing only a group ahead. Just before the Hogan pair would be
Bolt (219) and Boros or Snead. Then Rosburg (219) and Ward
(220) or Fleck (220). Fleck would have some inkling of what he
needed to tie Hogan very early in his fourth round. And Hogan
would have known for sure what he needed on the 72nd hole to
win the championship. As it was, Snead and Boros were off a half-
hour before Hogan. And Fleck was off two hours after the leader.
Yet because the system was what it was at the time, the 1955 U.S.
Open, and indeed sports history, had one of the most dramatic of
finishes. Joe Dey was a lousy playwright, but he got lucky. Some
would say.

The cool San Francisco weather had a double effect on Hogan.
Had it been hot and humid, there would have been a further pro-
hibitive drain on his physical resources. Also the chill in the air

made it difficult to get his muscles loose—"oily," as Sam Snead liked to say. However, he had played eighteen holes already and was beginning to feel a rush of energy. Even a person of Hogan's austere emotional makeup, who prided himself on how he could control his disposition under stress, was having an adrenaline rush. The taste for the game was always in his mouth, but now it had become something more—he was salivating.

Hogan was not happy about his three-bogey finish of round 3, of course, but still, at 217 he had the lead with eighteen holes to play and was on the number he calculated would win. A round of 70, even par, would get a 287, and he'd have his fifth U.S. Open. Sam and Boros would be the ones to watch. Boros a bit more than Sam. Hogan had enormous respect for Snead's game but in truth felt he didn't have the head for this championship. Still, he would have to watch for him. There were no scoreboards around the course giving up-to-date information on who was doing what, but Hogan would find out.

Between rounds Hogan changed his shoes and socks, which had gotten soaked tramping over the moist grass of the Lake course. He wore the socks inside out so the raised ridge sewn at the toe end would not rub against his feet and cause irritation. It was a trick he had learned from Johnny Sain, the Boston Braves pitcher.

Hogan opened his fourth round with an excellent birdie 4. He drove into the left center of the fairway, played a 4 wood short of the bunkers, and hit a fine wedge third shot to within eighteen inches of the hole. Even Hogan could make a putt of that length, and he brushed it in. At the par-3 3rd hole, however, he hit the green with a 2 iron but three-putted from twenty-five feet. To show where his putting was—or, more to the point, his determination—at the 4th hole he holed a twenty-foot putt for another birdie.

At the 457-yard par-4 5th he drove into the trees on the right, a rare mistake in years past but one that was beginning to crop up in his game. With no clear shot to the green, and a poor lie, he had to play laterally back to the fairway. His third reached the green, and he two-putted for a bogey. He was not concerned. The 5, by his reckoning, was a half-bogey. The 5th was one of his two 4.5-par holes.

He played solid fairways and greens golf through the 9th hole and turned in an even par 35. A scoreboard at this point listed the scores of the leaders, and Hogan had a look at how Sam and Boros were doing. He saw that Boros was two over par early in the back nine and Sam was not doing any better. They were not making a rush. On the contrary, they must be struggling. Hogan didn't know the details of Boros and Snead's play and didn't want to know. When he saw their numbers on the board he knew that the two players who were the biggest threats were probably not going to be there at the end. The back nine had some very difficult holes. A slight smile came over his face. It was very slight, hardly noticeable to anyone other than close Hogan watchers. He was on his number and would play accordingly to finish the round.

Hogan had drawn a large percentage of the gallery from the very start of his final round, and it was increasing by a hundred or so every few minutes as people watched the scoreboard. The sophisticated San Francisco golf followers not only knew the game, they had a sense of history and wanted to watch with their own eyes every move Hogan made on his way to breaking the U.S. Open record. They saw it coming, as Snead was faltering and Hogan put up a front-nine score that by Lake course standards was very good.

The stoic Texan was relentlessly solid in his play and getting applause for every one of his shots. He didn't notice, and it made no difference to him, applause or no applause. There was no acknowledgement from him, no tip of the cap. He blocked everything extraneous to his job out of his mind, his vision, and his sensibility. He had learned how to totally ignore the surroundings if there was nothing in it that pertained to his golf. Many people saw this as discourteous, rude, and unappreciative. But they were at the same time enthralled by his single-minded intensity and his mechanized approach to the game.

Hogan was a very deliberate golfer in tournament play. He took more time than most golfers to prepare for each shot. Sometimes he would smoke at least half a cigarette when considering an approach shot. The players didn't complain about his pace of play, at least not to his face, if only because it was Hogan. Lloyd Mangrum might say a word. He didn't like Hogan and wasn't at all in his thrall. But Mangrum wasn't playing; he was out with an injury.

Officials were as daunted by Hogan's presence as most of the players and only once made a case in regard to his pace of play. In the 1954 U.S. Open, Joe Dey was refereeing a Hogan round and had his personal clock on him. Jackie Burke was the other player in the pairing, and at the 11th hole Dey asked Burke to suggest to Hogan that he speed up his play a bit, or he might have to penalize him. Burke at first said he wasn't about to tell Ben Hogan he was playing too slowly, but he finally did. When he told Hogan that Dey would like him to pick up his pace a little and was thinking of levying a penalty if he didn't, Hogan looked Burke in the eye with that awesome blue-eyed glare and said, "Tell him to put the strokes on me now and leave me alone." Nothing more was said about the matter. Hogan played in his own time the rest of the way, without penalty.

Once Hogan assessed the situation—how his ball was sitting, the direction and velocity of the wind, the distance he had to hit the ball—and determined what club he would use, he had a set routine for moving into position. It was not an uncommon procedure, but somehow his manner fortified the impression held widely that he was robotic, a machine cranking out one perfect piece of goods time after time. From behind the ball he faced his target directly, the club held vertically in front of him. He then moved around to the left side of the ball and stepped in with his right foot in the position it would be when his stance was completed. Now he moved his left foot into position, always a little farther from the target line than the right foot, which produced a slightly open stance. He set the club behind the ball, straightened his back, stuck his butt out behind him, and had a little flex in his knees, with his right knee angled to the left. His hands were even with the ball, with the driver slightly behind it. He waggled the club back and to the ball, the path of the waggle the same as it would be when he began his swing. The speed of the takeaway was relatively slow, or relaxed, but about midway back it would pick up speed, and in the downswing things got moving very quickly. The swing on the whole may have been quick compared to Sam Snead's metronomic rhythm, but it was Hogan's tempo, and he repeated it time after time.

At the 10th hole Hogan drove to the left corner of the dogleg-right fairway and hit the green with a splendid 4 iron to ten feet from the hole. It was an excellent chance for a birdie on a difficult hole. A 3 would almost surely pick up a stroke on the contenders. Paul Runyan, a champion player in the 1930s, made up for his lack of size—he stood only five feet five and weighed but 130 pounds—with a masterful short game. Not only did he have superb technique in chipping and putting, but, having grown up in Hot Springs, Arkansas, when it was a hot gambling town, he had mapped out the odds. Runyan believed 90 percent of putts from ten feet and in were makeable and that the odds of making any putts from eleven feet to fifty or sixty were the same—around 50 percent. In short, Hogan should make his ten-footer for birdie on the 10th. But he didn't even come near to it. After a long stand over the ball, he slapped it short and right of the cup. He tapped in for a par with the body language of someone who simply had no trust in what he was doing with the putter.

At the formidable 427-yard par-4 11th hole, the same scenario played out. Hogan drove well, a bit longer than he had been hitting it. As downcast as he was with his putting, he was still getting revved up over his chances of winning the championship. He played a 3 iron onto the green, the sound of the contact like a swiftly thrown hammer whose peen hits dead-center on a ten-penny nail. The mark of contact on Hogan's irons was remarkable—a small, round dot in the very middle of the clubface. A *mark*, not *marks*; he hit the ball on the same spot every time. The ball stopped only nine feet from the hole. Another very makeable birdie chance. He hit the putt too firmly, though, and ran it through the right-to-left break he was playing. Had he hit the ball a bit softer it would almost surely have curved into the cup. He two-putted for the par.

On the par-4 12th, at 387 yards—one of two par-4 birdie chances by length on the nine—Hogan drove well again. He had a 147-yard approach to the pin, an in-between distance—a little short for a full 7 iron, a little long for a full 8 iron. The pin was in the back part of the green, so Hogan opted for a firm 8 iron, not a hard-hit one. Better to come up a little short of the hole, where he could putt uphill. Long was not good here, with the heavy fringe grass behind and not much green to work with on a chip shot that would be hard to control. He struck the ball perfectly with the 8 iron, dead on line. It finished ten feet under the hole. Hogan handed the 8 iron to his caddie and strode slowly toward the green. He was not looking forward to the next shot.

Once again his putting failed when an excellent birdie opportunity presented itself. His ten-footer came up short, and he nudged the remainder of the putt in for the par 4. Three very legitimate birdie chances in a row, and not one of the putts touched the hole.

For once, it appeared, the failure to putt had an impact on his *golf.* On the 187-yard par-3 13th his 2 iron from the tee came up short, landing in the bunker just before the green. Although he had been playing well out of the bunkers all week, this time he did not. He actually bladed the ball, caught it thin, didn't take enough sand behind it, and lined it over the green into thick fringe grass. But he would not cave in; great players do not make double bogeys when they are in the thick of winning a major championship.

Hogan assayed his lie in the fringe. The ball was in deep, tangled grass, and he chose the same wedge he had just used out of the sand to play the shot. His concentration was so powerful one could almost smell it. He made a long backswing to make sure he generated enough clubhead speed to drive it through the grass, and the shot was beautifully executed. The ball landed some fifteen feet short of the cup, bounced softly, and began a smooth roll toward the hole. It was right on line and stopped at the very right edge of the cup. He saved a bogey. He did not fret. He was sure he had room for this mistake, and that would be it.

However, from the tee of the 410-yard par-4 14th Hogan drove to the right into the rough and among the trees. Luckily, he had a decent lie in grass that had been tamped down by the gallery. And he had a clear path to the green. Still, he was 210 yards from home. He rose to the occasion, hitting a magnificent 4-wood shot onto the green. He two-putted for a par and stood one over for the round.

The short par-3 15th, at 144 yards, had been good to Hogan. Or he had been good on it. The 7 iron he hit in the morning third round was as pure as he or anyone could do. With the pin in the middle-right portion of the green, his famous fade had been perfectly suited for the shot. He hit the shot with the machine-like efficiency that had become a trademark of his game. Indeed, his personality. The ball flew off at Hogan altitude—not as high as most but not low; Hogan played through his own personal air space. The ball tucked in a mere eighteen inches from the hole. A birdie that did not require a putting miracle. Hooray!

In the afternoon the hole on the 15th was cut in the front-left section of the green. The distance was some five yards shorter, but he hit the same 7 iron, slowing the clubhead speed a hair and aiming for the center of the green. With the championship in hand, he was not going pin-hunting, which was not his style anyway. The swing was what was by now the familiar, abbreviated one everyone noticed all week when he played short and middle irons— the clubhead getting just barely vertical. The strike was crisp, firm, solid, but not quite as accurate as he had planned. The ball finished some thirty feet from the hole, farther than usual by about fifteen feet.

He took a little more time to get the line of the putt and judge the slope of the green. Over the ball, he was even more deliberate than usual, a sign that his confidence in putting was waning even more. The stroke indicated that, too—short and very quick. But the ball was right on line. Thankfully, because it was going very fast. The ball hit at the very back-center of the cup and jumped straight up and straight down into the hole. Had it caught the lip of the cup, it would have spun away for a lengthy comeback putt. But not this time. A birdie! An accident, but a good one. The gallery surrounding the green erupted with a cheer and much applause. Hogan could barely contain his pleasure. But he did.

Hogan walked resolutely to the hole, picked the ball out of the cup with forefinger, middle finger, and thumb, and moved to the 16th tee. He was now even par for the day and one under par for the tournament, by his account, and his step had more bounce in it than it had all week. His weary legs had just been injected with a tonic, a shot of bubbly. He drove well on the par-5 16th, and as he made his way to his ball there was another miracle of miracles. He began to have a chat with Charlie Bartlett, the renowned golf writer from the *Chicago Tribune*, who, along with other newspapermen, was allowed to walk in the fairway a few steps behind the players. It was idle chatter, something about the weather, but that wasn't the point. Hogan the Silent spoke, on the course, in the heat of competition. It was as newsworthy as Garbo doing her first talkie and clearly indicated Hogan thought he had the tournament won. That putt on the 15th did it.

For his second shot on the 16th he played from the right side of the fairway, wide of the dogleg left, and struck a 3 wood with a finely controlled left-to-right trajectory that finished in the fairway 163 yards from the middle of the green. A firm 5 iron was his club of choice. He took a shallow divot, rectangular and exactly the width of the clubhead, and sent the ball precisely where he meant. It fell slightly to the right, like someone sliding sideways into a narrow entryway, and finished twenty feet right of the hole. He didn't make a real effort to hole the putt. He was not that sure of his touch, despite of or because of the way he hit the putt on the 15th. If he went for it and didn't hit the hole dead-center he was liable to blast it three feet past. The three-footers were the main problem. He tapped the ball up a foot short of the hole and eased that one in for a par 5. Now for the long 17th, on which he had made three 5s so far, pars in his book. A 4 would be nice, a bit of insurance against somebody sneaking up on him from behind.

The 17th fairway tilts at an eleven-degree angle from left to right, and one way to keep a drive on the short grass is to start the ball up the left side to allow for the cant in the terrain. The ball will trundle down to the right and hopefully stop before it reaches the right-hand rough. A left-to-right drive was in Hogan's wheel-house, it was his basic trajectory, and he could have hit the ball in such a way that there would be little roll after it landed. But instead, conscious of the fact that his driving was showing some uncertainty, he hit a soft draw. The ball landed into the slope and kicked right. Most of the rebound was taken out of the ball, which finished in the middle of the fairway.

He was well set up for a long second shot. He had a full 3 wood, and for the first time in the tournament he made a maximum effort to reach the green. He lengthened his swing a foot or so and hit a high and powerful left-to-right cut toward the left side of the green. He hit the ball extremely well, but it cut a little more to the right than Hogan had planned. He had a chip from just off the green of some thirty-five feet to the hole but did not have as thick a lie as he had on the 13th, where he had chipped well. And he chipped well again, with a firm chop down on the ball with his left hand bowed outward. The ball popped up out of the grass and, after a small bounce, rolled neatly to within a foot of the hole. He tapped the putt in for his first 4 of the week on the hole. He was at 283, with one hole to play. He had programmed 287 as the winning total, and a 4 on the last hole would accomplish just that.

The 18th had more to it in appearance than in how it really played from tee to green. The longest rough, nearly shin high, was far left of the fairway. A stand of tall, dark, thick trees bordered the right side all the way down. Yet, while the straightaway fairway itself seemed narrow, because of the length of the hole—only 337 yards—a driver was unnecessary. Many of the players had been using a 2 iron or 3 wood from the tee to be more assured of play-ing their second from the fairway. It would leave no more than a 7 iron, often less, using those clubs. The green was what protected the hole, at least when the hole was cut in the middle or toward the back, because the putting surface had a steep slope down from back to front. Only at the front quarter of the green was it fairly flat, and that's where the hole was cut for the fourth round. Front and right. Hogan had checked the position when he walked from the 8th green to the 9th tee. A par 4 was all he would need, and the deed would be done.

He played a 3 wood from the tee, started the ball at the middle of the fairway, and let it fall to the right. It finished on the right side of the fairway, which gave him a comfortable angle to play left of the pin and thus to the center of the green. He had no intention of cutting his short approach in toward the hole. Front middle was just fine.

He quickened his step a little more as he left the tee for what he and everyone else was sure was a victory march. There was some limp in his stride, but the shoulders were not as slumped as they had been for much of the week. After his tee shot there was some light applause from those who had followed his play on the course. In a few minutes, though, he would be in the middle of the stunningly impressive amphitheater that was the setting of the 18th hole. A high, wide, grassy hill rose up on the left side of the green, the top of it level with the first floor of the clubhouse. It was crammed with at least half of the day's attendants, many of the men in topcoats against the chilly air forming a massive blanket of humanity with all their eyes on the legendary Ben Hogan as he made his way to his ball 130 yards back in the fairway.

An ever-present cigarette in his mouth, Hogan assessed what distance he had left to the green. A 7 iron would do it. As he stepped into his address position an almost total silence fell on the scene. All one could hear were the birds in the trees surrounded by wisps of wind blowing through the leaves. Someone in the audience might have been whispering to a companion but not loudly enough to be heard. Everyone held their tongues and sat perfectly still to watch a man hit a golf shot. The silence was broken by the slight metallic click of Hogan's clubhead striking the ball, which on a medium-high parabola carried over the bunker fronting the green and landed softly on the putting surface. It was some fifteen feet to the left of the hole. The applause began as he put his 7 iron back in the bag, and it gradually grew as Hogan, now holding his right leg at the knee, came slowly up the slope that fronted the putting surface. He didn't look at the crowd. He felt the moment but would not concede to it. He knew what the occasion was, what it represented, but with steely resolve ignored it—or made out to ignore it. *Finish the work, finish the work.*

Bobby Harris was first to putt, and he ran his ball two feet past the hole. Then it was Hogan's turn. He did not get down in a crouch to assess the contour of the terrain between his ball and the hole. It meant getting up out of the crouch, and he could do without that. He did tilt his head from one side to the other while looking down the line to the hole, but since he wasn't going to try to make the putt, his main concern was with the speed at which he would send the ball. Done with that, he moved to the side of the ball and took his familiar stance—knees bent, back straight, the putter at a slight angle from his body to the ball. It was time, and for once he didn't hesitate, didn't stall. The stroke was not especially smooth; it was the usual slap, and the ball jumped off the clubface before beginning its roll. But it was a good putt by Hogan's standards, the speed judged just right. The ball stopped a few inches before the hole. It was too short a distance to mark it and then let Harris putt out before Hogan put a period on the last scene of the splendid play he had written. So Hogan tapped in, and a great applause rose from the huge throng surrounding the stage.

Hogan lifted the ball from the cup and raised his right hand straight up with his fingers splayed. Many interpreted his gesture as him saying he had just won his fifth U.S. Open. The gallery hummed its agreement and began to applaud once again. But Hogan was not a grandstander. What he meant with the raised hand was for the gallery to quiet down so Bobby Harris could putt out and finish his round. It was a gesture of politeness Hogan asked to be extended toward a fellow professional.

After Harris putted out Hogan did acknowledge the deeply resonant applause that came. He removed his cap for a moment, then walked over to Joe Dey, who was at the side of the green, and handed him his ball. He said that Dey might want it as a memento for the USGA to keep in its small but gathering collection of memorabilia, artifacts, and other assorted pieces of golf history. Here was the ball used to complete the record fifth U.S. Open victory by one man. Dey accepted it gratefully. Hogan again removed his cap to acknowledge the continuing applause, then walked off the green to the scoring tent to check his card, which Harris had kept, and sign off on it as correct. Harris shook Hogan's hand and congratulated the champion. Later Hogan broke with form and when asked to pose with his right hand splayed to show the five fingers, this time meaning he had won his fifth U.S. Open, he complied.

In 1955 the NBC network bought—for $12,000—the television rights to the U.S. Open for a total of five years. This was only the second time the championship was televised nationally. NBC sold its 1955 telecast to the Dodge Motor Company for $111,000. Quite a nice piece of business for NBC, which did not give the television audience much for its money. Broadcast time was only one hour on Saturday, the last day of the event. The network put a camera on the 17th fairway, another just behind the 18th green, and a third well above the 18th green on the first landing of the clubhouse. It was a short take, the "show" going off the air at 6:15 Pacific Coast Time. There was just enough time to show Hogan playing the 18th hole before signing off.

Lindsay Nelson, a professional sports announcer, did the play-by-play, although there wasn't that much in the scant hour that the program aired. Gene Sarazen did the color commentary. Sarazen did not play in this championship for the first time in thirty-three years. A cocksure man of small physical stature but the immense self-confidence of a storied champion (he won the U.S. Open twice, first as a twenty-year-old, the British Open, the Masters, and the PGA Championship, plus dozens of tour events, and was with Walter Hagen, the leading player in golf, into the early

1940s), Sarazen moved in quickly to interview Hogan once the play ended on the 18th green. The conversation between them was keyed around Sarazen's certainty that Hogan had won his fifth U.S. Open. Hogan was noncommittal but gave the impression that Sarazen was right. He knew that Snead and Bolt had finished with 292. He had them by five shots.

Snead's final-round 74 was the result of the poor putting he predicted for himself. Bolt's 73 was also the result of faulty putting. Julius Boros shot 77, a round that began to disintegrate early on when he very uncharacteristically played some poor bunker shots. His final total was 295, which tied him with Rosburg, who seemed to run out of steam and closed with a 76. Jackie Burke found the rough too often off the tee and shot a 77, his second score at that number over the four rounds, for a total of 297.

There were thirteen twosomes still on the course—twenty-six players—but Sarazen had only a few minutes of airtime remaining and completed his commentary saying loud and clear and with absolute certainty that Ben Hogan was the winner of the 1955 U.S. Open. Good night, and good luck.

Hogan slowly made his way up the steep incline to the clubhouse and locker room. This time his hand gripped his left leg just above the knee. Valerie, who had been sitting on the veranda overlooking the course, came over to her husband when he reached the top of the climb, smiled, and said, "Good playing, Ben." They did not touch. She went back to the veranda to wait for him. Hogan made it to his locker and sat down immediately on the long bench before it. His cap was off, his shoulders slumped forward, and his face was drained pale. He asked the locker-room attendant to bring him a Dewar's with a splash of soda. He planned on taking a shower, packing his golf shoes and a few sweaters in a small bag, and then dressing in a sport jacket and tie for the presentation ceremony at the 18th green. Then, he would get together with Valerie and meet his caddie in the parking lot, pay him, and pack up his clubs for the trip back to Fort Worth. But not right away. He needed to sit for a while. He had time for it; there were still some players on the course, and the ceremony wouldn't begin until all the players had finished.

Cary Middlecoff came by to shake his hand. "Nice going, Ben; that was a fine score to put up on this course." Hogan nodded, thanked Middlecoff, and took some questions from the sportswriters who were gathering around him.

"Did you think you had it won when you holed that putt on the 15th?"

"You don't win tournaments on one hole; there are seventy-two of them."

"How are you feeling? Your leg bothering you?"

"Only my knee. The more I walked, the more it hurt."

"You've been talking this week about giving up tournament golf altogether. Still feel that way?"

"Well, it's getting to be more and more of a strain. This one was particularly difficult."

And then a reporter came hurrying into the group and announced that there was a guy still out there who had a chance, a guy named Fleck.

Hogan's chin fell to his chest. He raised his head slowly and with a blank stare looked out past the people in front and around him. "Fleck?" he said. "Isn't he the one who's using my clubs?"

Jack Fleck's fourth round had gotten off to an ordinary start. He drove into the fairway, played his second shot short of the bunkers fifty yards in front of the green, and then pitched to within fifteen feet of the hole. He two-putted for a par-5. At the second hole, though, something unexpected happened, unexpected because for the first time since he had that wonderful feeling in his hands putting on the 5th green in round 2, he misjudged the speed of his thirty-footer and came up three feet short. And he missed the little one. A bogey.

In the past Fleck would have fallen into a black sulk over the three-putt green. He would have looked down at the ground as if to the treacherous devil who caused this inglorious error. But not this time. He did not seethe. Rather, he soothed his wound by ignoring it. He knew in his depths that it wouldn't hurt him in the long run, which was a good way down the road—two and half, perhaps three, hours down. Even when he missed the green at the long par-3 third and pitched his second shot from high grass to a distant thirty-five feet from the hole, he went about his task with remarkable self-possession. It led to a spectacular par. He holed the thirty-five-footer to avoid a bogey! His caddie, John Schroeder, had not said much to Fleck over the six days they had been together. It was largely because Fleck did not encourage conversation. And he didn't ask for advice on club selection or the line of putts. But Schroeder felt a good word was proper at this moment. "Fine putt, Mister Fleck, fine putt."

"Thank you, John."

He hit a long drive on the 433-yard par-4 fourth hole—he had been gaining length over the past week, a result of his excellent physical condition and a very sound swing, but it was his state of mind as well. A pioneer American golf professional, "Wild" Bill Mehlhorn, preached, "Muscles and joints should be at ease in their performance," and there was no better way to achieve that than to be free of psychological tension. Fleck's driver was going off like a cannon, because he was swinging the club with a kind of abandon—not reckless, by any means, but blissfully unaware. There were no swing keys and no second thoughts about strategy; he was in a free-flow of thought and physical movement.

For his second shot he used a 6 iron and easily reached the green. He two-putted without a problem. He played the even longer par-4 5th, one of the holes Hogan rated a par-4.5, with equal ease. A drive and 5 iron and two putts. All good, but he felt certain he needed a birdie or two to insure he finished in the coveted top ten. And then, the leprechaun landed on Fleck's shoulders. Everything he had for years worked on in his full swing and his putting came together and bonded with his mental state.

On the long par-4 6th hole he hit a very long drive that left him with only a 6 iron to the green. He hit the shot six feet from the hole. He made the putt, of course, and the birdie put him at even par for the round, six over par in all. If he were to par in, his score of 286 would almost certainly bring him a quite high finish, even a victory, according to his own pre-tournament assessment. But he wasn't thinking in those terms. It was too early. He was in the middle of an unusually abstract cerebral circumstance. He was very much aware of what he was doing in a practical way. He checked his yardages for club selection, read greens for their undulation, and observed the etiquette of the game—to be quiet and still while the other golfer prepared for and played his shot, not playing his shot out of turn, and so on. But all of that was suffused with a euphoric, in a way mindless, rhythm. Movement and thought were one.

At the very next hole, the short par-4 7th, he used a 3 wood from the tee to be sure he kept the ball in the fairway. With the length he was hitting the ball, a 3 wood was plenty to get past the rough and into the length-abbreviated fairway. From fifty-five yards he played a wedge second shot and struck the ball firmly and on line. It caromed slightly off the mound Bob Roos molded into the green and finished eight feet from the hole. Fleck took very little time over the putt, but it wasn't as if he were rushing. He was just not in a hurry. Not at all. He took a brief read of the putt, took no practice stroke, and eased the ball into the hole for a second-straight birdie.

He seemed to be floating as he walked to the next tee. The lightness of being. And he hit a soft 8 iron to the green of the 139-yard 8th hole. It concluded its travels fifteen feet from the cup. Once again he took very little time over the putt. He had played the hole so many times he knew the breaks almost as well as the lines on the palms of his hands. The feeling for the putter was as sensitive as it was when it first came to him on the 5th hole of the second round. The ball slid into the hole, and he had his third birdie in a row. Things were getting more interesting. At this point he began to think he could get in the top ten for sure. And maybe even . . . hmmm.

The rush slowed a bit at the 9th. Perhaps it was the noise and the crowd surrounding the nearby 18th green, where Ben Hogan was finishing his round. He saw Hogan limping noticeably onto the green but not without resolution even in the gimpy stride. Fleck nodded to himself, a nod that acknowledged the great champion's courage, tenacity, and exceptional ability. Distracted for the moment, Fleck hit one of his poorer drives, a hook into the rough to the left. He had a difficult lie, of course, and used a wedge to clear the ball from the deep stuff into the fairway. He had a lengthy pitch to the green, about sixty yards, and came up twenty-four feet short of the hole. Again he did not dally. He saw the line, felt the speed of the green, took his position over the ball, and let it roll. It was a good putt, but it stayed on the high right side and stopped a few inches from the cup. He holed for a bogey to finish at one under par for the nine—a 34.

He didn't know what Hogan's total score was, but from the gallery response he heard when he walked onto the green Fleck knew the master had probably done well and was probably the leader. *Good for him,* he thought. *He's a great player, one of the greatest ever.*

It was getting close to 5:30 in the evening, and the light was beginning to diffuse. The evening mist was making its late-afternoon entrance, shading the air in gray, and the late-afternoon wind was picking up a little, in places creating a soft whistle as it skittered around in the trees. A marshal named Tompkins, assigned to the last couple of holes on the front nine, was running out of players to help if necessary and had no gallery at all to oversee. He took an interest in Jack Fleck. He knew what Hogan had shot and recognized that Fleck was at a point where he could become a real factor in the outcome of the championship. He was also impressed by Fleck's stylish long swing and easy manner. Fleck seemed to him to be in some sort of trancelike state as he hit one fine shot after another. Tompkins had witnessed the Fleck birdies at the 6th, 7th, and 8th holes and began to follow him and Littler exclusively.

At the 417-yard par-4 10th hole Fleck hit another long and accurate drive. He was clearly not discouraged by the bogey on the 9th. He had only a 7-iron approach to the green and hit a high draw so accurate that it grazed the right edge of the cup and stopped but a few inches from falling in. It was a leaner and a resulting birdie that put him two under par for the round and eight over par for the championship. He was only one shot behind Hogan's seven-over final score, although he had no idea of that.

Tompkins thought this might be the time to mention the situation to Fleck. He wasn't sure if he should. He was leery that the information might put too much pressure on him and hurt his chances. Then again, if Fleck knew where he stood it just might encourage him to push a little harder and play even better. Tompkins straddled the line on the decision to tell or not to tell Fleck. As Fleck was walking down the 11th fairway after hitting another long, accurate drive, Tompkins slipped up to him and asked if he would be interested in other scores already posted. Fleck was so wrapped up in what he was doing he didn't hear Tompkins clearly. Tompkins repeated his offer. Fleck said he would be interested. Tompkins told Fleck that he was within range of the lead. Only that. Fleck nodded as if to say, "Well now." Tompkins fell back a few steps and stayed quiet. He also noticed, as did Fleck, that people were beginning to join the Fleck-Littler twosome as gallery. They were emerging like spirits out of the trees or an advanced company of soldiers scouting the upcoming field of battle. Word had gotten back that this fellow Fleck was making a move, that he was the last man standing in Hogan's way. Let's go see this fella, whoever he is. The gathering presence was hint enough to Fleck that he was getting very much involved in this affair at the Olympic Club. But he had known it all along, hadn't he? He parred the 11th.

Fleck drove well on the 12th, a medium-length par-4, and scored an easy par. At the par-3 13th, he hit an excellent 2 iron into the middle of the green and two-putted for another par. As he left the green, Marshal Tompkins approached him and asked if he wanted to know precisely where he stood. Fleck said he did, and Tompkins told him he needed one birdie to tie Hogan. Gene

Littler heard the conversation and interjected a realistic note: "He also needs to make pars. Four of them with the birdie."

That was true, and with the situation put to him, Fleck hit the longest drive of the day, in the fairway. He was closer to the hole than he had ever been and was in between clubs for his second shot. It was a hard 7 iron or a soft 6. Not wanting to overswing, he went for the 6 iron and eased up. But as was the case earlier, when he did that he pulled the ball. The length of the shot was enough. He was pin-high but in the greenside bunker. The ball was sitting slightly downhill, and Fleck dug his feet in sufficiently and played a good explosion shot. However, from the soft sand it was hard to put a lot of grip on the ball, and it rolled some eight feet past the cup. The putt was from right to left, and he hit the ball on the high right side but a bit too firmly. It ran through the break, and he ended up with a bogey.

He then needed two birdies and two pars to reach a tie with the leader in the clubhouse. He felt no pressure, and it showed. The gathering throng murmured about how cool he was, how happy-go-lucky he seemed to be in this competitive broiler he had gotten himself into. He looked like someone in a daydream. Was he unaware of what was going on? It couldn't be. He was making decisions of a very realistic nature—what club to use, where to aim the ball, how fast the green was running, and where the break would occur. Can someone cover that sort of ground in a coma, or even a semi-coma?

On the par-3 15th hole, at 144 yards, Fleck played a 6 iron with a smooth, effortless swing that sent the ball on a high arc just to the right of the hole, which was cut in the back portion of the green. It settled only five feet from the cup. He could get back that bogey on the 14th. He gave the putt a read, then stepped up to

the ball, placed the putter head just ahead of it, then behind it—
which was his routine—and tapped the ball smoothly. He read the
right-to-left break perfectly and holed for a birdie two. The gallery,
taking on size like a magnet in a batch of steel shavings, cheered
loudly and rushed to take advantageous viewing positions at the
16th tee and fairway. Hey, this tall guy has something going here.

The news had arrived in the locker room, where Ben Hogan
was sitting among the reporters with his Scotch and soda in his
hand, that Jack Fleck needed two pars and a birdie to tie for the
championship. Hogan took the news with a tight-lipped, dour
expression. He thought he had it won by five when he left the 18th
green, and now this fella had a chance to tie. *Hell, let him birdie out
and win it. I wish he would. Damn! Hell with it. Let the guy have it.
Let him do it so I can go home,* he thought.

When Valerie Hogan heard of the events transpiring she said
to a friend, "He's a nice young man, and Ben has won enough of
them."

The 16th was not the "birdie hole" the pros thought of most
par-5s. It was longer than usual at just over 600 yards and played
another twenty yards longer as the mist began to gather and make
the air even heavier. But Fleck was feeling feisty after having taken
a couple of sugar cubes from Dr. Barton, who was carrying the
sugar in the pocket of his topcoat. Fleck hit a huge drive. Although
he pulled it a few yards off line, he hit it so well it carried over the
rough at the corner of the dogleg and finished in the left side of the
fairway. He had a perfect lie, the ball sitting up as if on a tee. With
a 3 wood he drilled the ball down the middle, hitting it so strongly
he left himself with only a 9 iron to the green. In previous rounds
he had been playing a 7-iron third shot on this hole; other players
had been playing as much as a 5 iron. Fleck's adrenaline had been

spiked, and yet there was something else going on that the sugar stimulus had nothing to do with. He was in a very warm and cozy comfort zone.

However, unaccustomed to hitting a mere 9 iron to this green, he pulled his shot to about twenty-five feet left of the hole. It should have been closer with such a short club, but it wasn't. He exchanged the 9 iron for his putter with his caddie and with his high knee-bending stride loped easily onto the putting surface.

The lengthy putt was well judged in respect to distance, the most important component of putts longer than fifteen feet, and he had a simple tap-in for a par-5. He needed one birdie out of the next two holes (and of course a par), and the 17th was not a birdie hole. It was anything but. Few in the field all week had even hit the green in the regulation two strokes. Unlike Hogan, who turned his drive right-to-left into the sloping fairway and gave up some yardage to be safely on the short grass, Fleck, a very confident driver all week, played a slider just inside the left edge of the left-hand rough, the trajectory of the ball moving slightly left-to-right. He took advantage of the slope, and the ball ran forward a few more yards than it might have otherwise and stayed in the fairway.

Still, there was no contemplating what club to use for his second shot. It was all he had in the bag, the 3 wood. And he would have to hit it well. He did. He flushed it, hitting it as solidly as a sledgehammer on a flat rock but with flair. The ball slid left-to-right, landed just short of the green, and bounced up into the middle of the putting surface. Harry Von Zell, a popular radio announcer, was doing a radio broadcast of the tournament along with golf champion Lawson Little, who remarked that Fleck's 3 wood was the best shot under U.S. Open pressure he had ever seen.

The putt from twenty-five feet was almost as good. A downhill/sidehill right-to-left breaking putt, the ball looked like it was going in until the very last moment, when it slid a bit off to the left, caught the lip of the cup, and stayed out. What a birdie that would have been! Fleck now needed a birdie 3 on the last hole to tie Hogan. He was, of course, the last man standing.

Fleck had gathered a large gallery alongside, but in fact the entire attendance, some 12,000 people, were in place to see the finish by the unknown challenger to the great Ben Hogan. Many of those who caught up with Fleck on the last holes of the back nine, who weren't with him earlier to notice, were amazed at how collected he was as the pressure mounted. Everyone was deeply interested to see if, at this most crucial juncture of all—the last hole and absolutely needing a birdie—he would finally crack. After all, he had never been in such a situation before as far as anyone knew.

At least 90 percent of the crowd hoped he would not be up to it. *Hogan doesn't have many more left in him,* was the collective thought. *Look how he's limping, and look how frail he seems. How does he do it in the first place? Man has a steel backbone, huh? It would be good for him to set the record of five U.S. Open championships before he tosses in the towel. Then again, he's such a stiff-ass. No response to the gallery, all business, a machine. What did the Scots call him, the Wee Ice Mon? That's for sure.*

At the same time, a sporting-event audience can be so fickle that there was a desire for Fleck to hang in there and force a playoff. The flash, the stir, the excitement of the unexpected is an elixir, a shot of whiskey after a long day at the office. Either way, everyone on hand was witness to a stirring, unforeseen moment in sport.

Jack Fleck pulled the head cover off his 3 wood and teed his ball up to play the 18th hole. Was he conscious of the huge crowd he was playing in front of? Yes, but it had no great impact on him. It was too big, in his personal context. It was like an oversized sculpture in a small room; one doesn't really see it.

He released the clubhead just a touch too much at impact and turned the ball slightly to the left—a mild hook. It finished about six inches off the fairway, in the first cut of rough. But the ball was sitting up well. It would not be a problem getting all the clubhead on it. After Gene Littler hit his second shot onto the green, to light applause, a quiet seeped into the air. Or chatter seeped out of it. Indeed, as Fleck assessed his approach shot an eerie calm developed. The anticipation was palpable in the thundering silence.

Fleck chose a 7 iron for the shot. He would, of course, shoot dead at the pin, set in the front-right corner of the green. The ball would have to come in high so it would have little to no roll after landing. There was very little room to the right of the green, which was bordered by heavy fringe grass. It was a shot he had practiced often, having grown up playing on so many concrete-hard public-course greens. He had found a way to put additional loft on the ball without losing distance. He felt perfectly comfortable with the details of the task at hand and was fearless in contemplating it. In a way it was a no-brainer. He wasn't thinking of the consequences, of the past or of the future, or even of the technique involved. He had this shot to hit, and he went at it totally absorbed. And it was a beautiful shot to see. His follow-through indicated how he worked to get the ball well into the air, higher than usual even for a 7 iron. It was on target, carried onto the green, took one bounce, and settled eight feet to the right of the hole. It was an excellent shot, a fantastic shot under the circumstances, especially by someone who had had no such experience before.

Someone apprised Ben Hogan of the situation. He had avoided going anywhere in the clubhouse where he could see Fleck's play. He wished it wasn't happening. He was deeply disappointed in the possibility of a playoff. He was very tired physically and mentally. The brain drain from competing in a major golf competition is enormous. He would know whether Fleck made or missed by the gallery's response. He sat at his locker waiting, a refilled Scotch and soda in hand. Valerie was on the enclosed veranda above the locker room, dismayed that if Fleck made the putt she would have to stay on another day in San Francisco. She wanted to go home.

Gene Littler was away and putted first. He rolled his ball up to within a foot of the hole and then tapped it in to conclude his round. A 78. He was glad to be done with the tournament and the golf course. Tournament pros not in the mix at the end of a tournament generally have little interest in the outcome. But Littler realized something special was happening and was paying attention as Fleck prepared to putt.

Fleck took a look at the line of his putt and read a slight break from right to left—not much, an inch or two. He was not going to take a lot of time over the ball. He was not going to freeze on it. As he got into his address position the silence was deafening. There were at least 24,000 eyes on him. He aimed for inside the cup, inside right, and stroked the ball firmly so it would hold its line. And although he pulled the ball just a hair, the pace was enough that it held up and went down with absolute certainty. When it fell, the roar of the gallery was tremendous. High-pitched, low-pitched, thick, a Beethoven crescendo. Fleck stood up and, with his putter in his right hand, raised both arms to mid-height. His eyes closed for a moment, the look on his face a soft daze. It seemed to say, "What have I done?" What he had done was tie Ben Hogan for the

U.S. Open with one of only two rounds of 67 shot by the entire field.

Hogan knew what Fleck needed to tie, and when he heard the roar from outside, his head dropped to his chest and he muttered, "Son of a bitch." He didn't mean it for Fleck. He meant it for . . . who can say? Then he told the locker-room attendant to put his shoes back in the locker. He'd be playing golf again the following day.

ACT V

A s late as 1939, when there was a tie for the U.S. Open after the regulation four rounds, the golfers in the deadlock were required to play two more rounds to decide the winner. And if the combatants were still tied after those thirty-six holes, they had to play another thirty-six.

It happened once, and for the last time. This was in 1931, when Billy Burke and George Von Elm each shot 292 for seventy-two holes at the Inverness Club, in Toledo, Ohio. The next day Burke had rounds of 73 and 76 (149) and Von Elm had rounds of 75 and 74 (149), and off they went the next day to play two more rounds. Burke outlasted Von Elm this time, with rounds of 77 and 71 (148) to Von Elm's 76 and 73 (149). In all, they played seventy-two extra holes in two days, on top of seventy-two holes of regulation play over three days. As the last two rounds of regulation play were done in one day, Burke and Von Elm walked and hit shots over 108 holes in three days. In all, they played 144 holes to decide the winner. Burke, it might be said, won two U.S. Opens in one. Both golfers should also have been awarded endurance medals, with Burke's a little more embossed for having concluded the marathon with a final-round 71. Actually, Von Elm's 73 wasn't bad either.

It is not clear whether Burke and Von Elm would have had to play yet another thirty-six holes if they had tied after the second playoff. In any case, there was a modification of the playoff format in 1939, when Byron Nelson, Craig Wood, and Denny Shute tied after seventy-two holes at the Philadelphia Country Club's Spring Mill Course, in Conshohocken, Pennsylvania. In the first playoff round Nelson and Wood shot 68s the day after the championship proper ended. Shute shot a 76 and was eliminated. The next day, Nelson shot a 70 to Wood's 73 to take the title. So the thirty-six-hole playoff was done away with. Of course, Nelson and Wood would have had to go another eighteen holes if they tied after the second extra round, but they would do it the next day. Presumably. Nothing was writ.

However, although the eighteen-hole playoff format was retained and prevailed for Ben Hogan and Jack Fleck, in 1955 someone at the USGA must have felt a little more compassion for the players (or perhaps the limping Hogan), for in this case it was announced that if they were tied after eighteen holes it would go to sudden death. It was the first time this format was adopted. (The next time was in 2008, when Tiger Woods defeated Rocco Mediate on the first extra hole.)

Whatever the procedure, it was not a situation Ben Hogan was looking forward to. Having to play another full round on a golf course that took a terrific physical toll on him was not what he had planned. What's more, his performance in playoffs was not all that great for someone of his stature in the game. His overall record was eight wins and thirteen losses, and in major events he had lost twice (in the 1940 and 1953 Masters) and won once, for the 1950 U.S. Open.

It was suggested that Hogan's playoff record reflected that he was such a systematic player he programmed himself for exactly seventy-two holes, judged the score he would need to win, and geared himself for just those numbers. So intense was his concentration over the seventy-two holes that if he had to go into overtime he was mentally, if not physically, worn out. Or so disappointed that he had it figured out incorrectly he did not perform at his best. Or another force—like Jack Fleck coming out of nowhere—upset his calculations. Still, with his passion for the U.S. Open so deeply felt, and what apparently was an overwhelming desire to become the first to win five of them, it seemed unlikely he would let himself slack off against Jack Fleck. Then again, he was forty-two years old going on sixty. He had been playing professional competitive golf since he was seventeen, and because he gave every round of golf he played, including practice rounds, the full measure of his being (he once said, "I play golf with friends sometimes, but they are never friendly games"), he could very well be in the burnout stage of his golfing life both physically *and* mentally. His problem with putting alone could probably be attributed to that.

Whatever the case may have been, he would not take Jack Fleck lightly. Anyone who can shoot two rounds in the 60s on the Lake course had to have some talent. Then again, the fella might be intimidated by the occasion and his opponent. After all, Fleck had never been in such contention before, even in standard-issue tour events. But Hogan knew well that nothing could be taken for granted in the game of golf. He would get a good night's sleep and go about his regular routine: early up, bathe the legs and wrap the one, three eggs over easy for energy without weight, a glass of ginger ale, and make sure the driver goes slowly to the course. He would hit forty shag balls, maybe forty-five, stroke a few putts, and move on to the first tee.

After holing out for his birdie on the 72nd hole, Jack Fleck carefully checked his scorecard before signing it, then took questions from a press corps that was both upset with him and pleased. Upset because they had to rewrite the stories they had already prepared: Hogan Wins His Record Fifth National Open. Pleased because they had a different but fascinating story to write. They liked Fleck so far, because he wasn't the dour person he appeared to be on the golf course. Fleck teased the newsmen about having to work extra hours doing their rewrites. And, upon hearing that television coverage went off the air long before he had finished his fourth round and that Gene Sarazen had confidently announced that Ben Hogan was the 1955 U.S. Open champion, he said it reminded him of the *Chicago Tribune* front-page headline announcing that Thomas E. Dewey had won the 1948 presidential election. He then excused himself, saying he had to get some supper and rest, for he had a big day ahead. The newsmen went to their typewriters and *Roget's* to find as many synonyms as there were for *dark horse* and *upset*. They didn't think Fleck had a chance in the playoff, but, as Art Rosenbaum wrote, taking a line from Fats Waller, "One never knows, do one?"

A Pittsburgh sportswriter, Bob Drum, was in the scrum surrounding Fleck in the locker room. A young man who had a developing reputation as someone who liked to have a good time and usually found it at local bars, Drum called his wife at home to tell her he had to stay over another day in San Francisco. And why? Because a golfer named Fleck had tied Ben Hogan, and they were going to have a playoff the following day. His wife, who had heard many excuses from her husband for staying over an extra day or two, snickered and said that only he could come up with a name like Fleck to get an extra day on the road.

Walker Inman had been hanging around the edge of the gaggle of newsmen, and when Fleck broke away he congratulated his friend and asked if he wanted to go out for dinner. Fleck said no, he wanted to do his exercises and get his nine hours of sleep. He did make arrangements for Inman and Doug Ford to drive his car up to Portland, Oregon, where they would be playing in the Western Open the following week. Fleck said he'd drop the car off at Olympic in the morning and pick it up a couple of weeks later somewhere out on the tour. Win or lose, he would be flying home to Iowa when it was over.

Fleck was still feeling so calm it surprised him. He thought that, because it was over, more or less, he would come down to earth. He looked to see if his feet were on the ground and chuckled to himself for doing it, for thinking it. The voice in the mirror was on point. Almost. At least he had a chance to prove it right, to win the U.S. Open. But first, he had to call Lynn and Craig. And maybe his father, even if he didn't think much of the career. Maybe this would make him feel differently. He wished his mother could be there for it. She had come around, finally.

Doctor Barton invited him for dinner in San Francisco, but Fleck excused himself with thanks. He needed to be alone for a while. The doctor understood. He was a tournament golfer himself. He would see Fleck at the course the following day.

Fleck returned to the motel in Daly City and, after parking the car, looked at the sign for the next town, Colma, only fifty yards to the south. It was where all the gravestones in the Bay Area were made. When he took his room the previous Friday and learned that, he thought for a moment that it was a bad omen. But he let that notion pass. *Turn it around,* he thought. He would be burying all the other golfers in the field at the Olympic Club. Yes.

He went across the street for a light supper: a piece of broiled fish, an order of broccoli, a fruit salad, and a glass of water. In his room he performed his yoga exercises. Inversion, core strengthening, back bending, hip opening, side bending. And the peacock. He stood on one hand that held his body up and splayed his legs out. Then he stood on his head for a minute, with both hands on the floor to hold him steady. After the headstand he took a seated yoga position and let his mind drift until there was nothing on it. Then, to bed.

The playoff didn't begin until 2:00 PM, which meant a lot of time to kill before getting into the action. But he would get to bed at 9:30 PM anyway. Fleck remembered reading an anecdote about Walter Hagen, the great champion and bon vivant. On the evening before he was to play Leo Diegel for the 1926 PGA championship, Hagen was out having some fun and drinks at a local watering hole. Someone told him that Diegel had gone to bed at 8:00 PM. "Yeah," Hagen responded, "but he's not sleeping." Fleck would sleep and didn't need to set an alarm. He was on automatic.

Hogan dressed for the day: an undershirt, a white heavy cotton golf shirt, a dark V-neck cashmere sweater, light-colored gabardine slacks, and heavy socks. Valerie would come out a bit later and bring his sports jacket, a dress shirt and tie, and street shoes for the presentation ceremony. He put on his white cap and said to Valerie that he would see her after the round. She wished him luck. He nodded briefly and left the room.

He got into the car that would take him to the golf course, but the driver wasn't taking the usual route from the hotel. He was going the other way. Hogan asked why, and the driver said he was told to pick up two other people at a nearby hotel. Hogan was unhappy with this change of routine and that he would have to be with two people, strangers, for the twenty-minute drive to the

Olympic Club. He lit a cigarette and stared out the window. It was not the way he wanted his day to begin. He'd get over it.

Jack Fleck wore a pair of dark-colored gabardine slacks, a tan woolen V-neck sweater over a light-colored golf shirt, and a cap similar to the one Hogan wore, only fuller in the crown. Many people thought his wearing this cap was another way he identified himself with Ben Hogan. In fact, Fleck always wore a visor. He had brought this cap, which was made of wool, because it was warmer against the chill San Francisco air.

He brushed some sand off his trouser knees after having knelt on the beach and drove his car up Skyline Road and turned left into the Olympic Golf Club entrance. He showed his contestant's badge to the gateman, who wished him well. Fleck thanked him for his good wishes. He drove past the practice tee on the right, the pro shop and first tee a little farther up on the left, then down a small incline to the parking lot. Walker Inman was there with Doug Ford. He gave them the keys to his car.

"You've got the game, Jack; let him have it," said Inman.

"He's a tired old man, Jack," said Ford. "Keep it going, buddy."

"Thanks, fellas, I'll do my best. I think I can win."

"Damn right, you can," said Inman. "Give me a call when you're comin' back out on tour. I'll have the car for you. Oh, and Finsterwald is going to join us."

"Thanks, guys."

Fleck walked into the clubhouse, and there was Ben Hogan, who had also just arrived. They said good morning and went together down the stairs to the locker room. No words passed between them. After Fleck had changed into his golf shoes and was on his way out to the practice tee he passed Hogan, who was lacing up his shoes. Fleck stopped and said, "Ben, I was driving from El Paso when I saw and heard two motorcycle police and an ambulance coming toward El Paso. I did not know it was you until I read the newspaper the next morning. I understand that hundreds of well-wishers called and wired for your recovery and prayed for you. So no matter what the outcome is today, you will know what I mean. So, good luck and play well."

Hogan wished Fleck well too, then watched his opponent for the day leave. He couldn't for the life of him understand what Fleck meant by, "No matter what the outcome is today, you'll know what I mean," but he didn't dwell on it.

It was another chilly, overcast day on the coast of north-central California as the gallery filed into the Olympic Golf Club to witness this unusual matchup—the hitherto-unknown public-course pro, Fleck, against the magisterial Hogan. Many walked to the practice range to watch the two professionals hit their warm-up shots. Most gathered behind Hogan, who was deep into his work mode. He began by hitting some short pitches, then the 9 iron and through the rest of the set, hitting five or six balls with each club. For every shot he went about the process as though it were a shot he was playing on the course. He took his address position, set the club behind the ball, waggled the club, then made his swing. He followed the ball through its entire flight, saw it drop at the caddie's feet, then slowly pulled another ball into place and went about the process exactly as before.

The Hogan watchers chuckled enviously at how little the caddie had to move to retrieve each ball Hogan hit.

Jack Fleck set himself up to hit his practice shots at the far side of the tee. His aim was only to loosen his muscles and get his timing and coordination. He didn't hit the balls with the deliberation of Hogan, although he didn't rush the workout either. He was loose, relaxed. He swung each of the clubs, as he went up the ladder, with purpose but not urgency. He hit more than a few with his driver, which, of course, would be especially important against Hogan. He had been getting good length, in part due to his sweet tempo. But the length of his driver was also a factor. He did not use the Hogan driver, preferring a MacGregor Tommy Armour model with a hard plastic insert. And it was longer than standard in length—44.5 inches rather than the conventional 43 inches. Fleck was really more interested in getting in more extended putting practice, and after hitting thirty-five or so balls on the range, he headed to the putting clock, a few yards from the first tee.

Hogan hit a few drivers, then finished his warm-up with six soft wedge shots to get the feel back in his hands after the harder hitting. He then moved over to hit some practice putts. As tired as he had been, and more than a little depressed at how the tournament proper had ended, he was recovered and in a competitive frame of mind.

The time had come, the call to the first tee. And with it another set of nerve ends kicked in. Hogan knew the feeling well, of course. He had been in that situation so often. For Fleck it was different. A kind of numbness of mind hit him. When he reached the first tee he saw Dr. Barton at the gallery ropes and went over to ask him a question. "Doctor Paul, do we play this at match or stroke play?" Barton was taken aback. Jack didn't know the format? "It's stroke play, Jack. And remember, I'm going to give you some sugar cubes every few holes. It'll keep your energy up. I know it's not what you like to eat, but I think it'll help."

Fleck nodded, and then the Olympic Club's head professional, John Battini, poked his head out of the window of the pro shop, which was at the very back of the tee, and hailed Jack in a loud whisper: "Jack, Jack, phone call. Porky Oliver. He wants to talk to you. I told him you were about to tee off, but he said you had to take the call."

Battini held the receiver of the phone out the window, and Jack put it to his ear. "Jack," said Oliver, "you beat him today, or I'll kick your ass up to your shoulder. Hear me?"

"I hear you, Chops, I hear you." And Fleck handed the phone back to Battini. The phone call had brought him out of his brain freeze.

HOLE NUMBER I

Ben Hogan had the honor and received a nice applause when his name was announced. He did not acknowledge it. He propped his ball on a tee pushed down fairly low. He didn't tee it high, like so many of the others. They might hit it a few yards farther but not with the same control. He stepped into his address position, waggled twice, and hit a fine low-boring drive into the center of the fairway.

When Fleck was announced the applause for him was just as strong as it was for Hogan. The San Franciscans were not only polite, but they liked having this fascinating contest in their back-yard. Some history would be made, or could be.

Fleck felt a little unease in his stomach as he put his ball on the peg. He stepped back, took a couple of practice swings, then moved up to address his ball. His swing was a touch fast, and he caught the ball a little too high on the clubface. It was a kind of pop-up, but it went straight. It finished in the middle of the fairway fifteen yards behind Hogan's ball.

They walked off side by side but without a word to each other. The crowd rushed ahead to get in position for the second shots. They were bursting at the restraining ropes. It was a Sunday, and the attendance was as great in numbers as it had been for the previous day's two rounds.

Fleck was first to play his second shot. Being so far back from the green, and the bunkers fifty yards short of it, he felt comfortable hitting a 3 wood without fear of reaching the traps. He pulled the ball to the left into the first cut of rough about twenty yards short of them.

At this Hogan broke from his usual, conservative form. Feeling he had a chance at the very beginning of the contest to put pressure on Fleck, he decided to go for the green with his 3-wood second shot. He would start the ball at the edge of the left-hand rough and cut it to the right and onto the front of the green. He would need a big strike but was certain he could put a little extra on it and control the ball's flight. He couldn't. The ball was not hit quite as flush as he expected. It slipped off the clubface to the right, finishing in the rightmost of the two bunkers.

Fleck was surprised at Hogan's outcome. Something in him understood that Hogan had tried something different, didn't pull it off, and may not be as sharp as he could be. Fleck then played a 9-iron third shot and hit it well to twelve feet past the cup. He had a good birdie chance.

Hogan played an excellent long bunker shot, the most difficult shot in the game. He clipped the ball cleanly and on a low but controlled trajectory. It lit on the green, took one small bounce, and came to rest seventeen feet from the hole. He was first to play, and, after a long look down the line of putt, he got over the ball and held the clubface behind it for what seemed like a full minute.

Finally, he slapped at the ball, which ran a few inches past the hole. He tapped in for a par-5.

Fleck felt very comfortable with the putter in his hands. It was as if a genie had entered, or never left. He stroked his putt dead on line but just short by two inches. A little more hit, and it was in the house. Two pars.

Fleck (E)—Hogan (E)

HOLE NUMBER 2

Hogan hit another solid drive into the fairway. Fleck seemed prone to pulling the ball and here drove to the left into the second cut of rough, where the grass was as much as six inches high. Hogan hit a crisp 3 iron onto the green around twenty-five feet from the hole. A safe play, knowing Fleck was in deep grass to the left. Indeed, Fleck had so poor a lie he could not play for the green, which had a big bunker at its left corner. With a 7 iron he played out short of the green but in the fairway. From here Fleck hit a finely judged pitching wedge that took one bounce and stopped slightly more than three feet from the hole.

Hogan, as he had been doing most of the week, avoided the low crouch golfers take to get a look at the undulation of the ground. Getting down and up from a crouch was a strain on his legs. Standing, he bent halfway down from the waist to take a reading of what he had to deal with. After getting his read, Hogan stroked his putt on a line wide right of the hole. It didn't come to the left as much as he thought it would. But the speed was good, and he tapped in from one foot for his par.

Fleck had a tester, a short putt for a par that would keep him even. It was a putt that could define the rest of his day. A miss, and he would be one stroke down. It could have an effect on his confidence on subsequent holes. On the other hand, this early in the going there was plenty of time to recover if he did feel a strain. But he was feeling very sure with the putter, and, after a brief read of the putt—the target was inside the right edge, he didn't want to give the hole away—he stroked the ball with assurance and holed for his par. A very good and crucial save.

Fleck (E)—Hogan (E)

HOLE NUMBER 3

Hogan continued with the honors, which on a par-3 of this length (220 yards) could be an advantage for him, given his almost peerless iron game. A shot within birdie range would put some heat on the opposition. He pulled a 2 iron from the bag and, after his routine setting-up procedure, was just about to begin his swing when a rabbit came out of somewhere and took a stance some twenty feet in front of him. Hogan stepped away from his ball, and a marshal came out onto the tee and shooed the rabbit away. The incident drew a lot of laughs from the gallery. Hogan appeared neither amused nor upset over the diversion. Indeed, he simply put his 2 iron back into his bag and went through his setup routine once again, from scratch. He then hit a splendid shot that, with a slight right-to-left draw, bored into a mild left-to-right breeze off the Pacific Ocean. The ball stopped a mere five feet from the hole. The shot received considerable applause from the golf-savvy audience. It was a masterstroke made all the more remarkable for coming after the rabbit disrupted Hogan's routine. He was, to be sure, the "wee ice mon," the nickname the Scots put on him when he won the 1953 British Open. It referenced his remarkable imperturbability.

Fleck also chose a 2 iron for the shot. He was looking at Hogan's ball up close to the hole and knew he needed to make a good swing. He once again pulled the ball a bit to the left. But he got lucky. The ball had enough hit on it to just carry the bunker guarding the left-front part of the green. It landed on the rise just above the trap and skipped forward, finishing on the green only fourteen feet left of the hole.

Hogan went to mark his ball and discovered he didn't have a coin in his pocket. He asked Fleck if he had one he could borrow, and Fleck of course gave him a dime. It was the only conversation they had up to then, and it was very brief. Some galleryites up near the green witnessed the interchange and chuckled.

"They say rich people never carry any money." "Yeah, I've heard that. He's not that rich, is he?" "Think he'll give it back to him when the round is over?" "Depends on whether he wins or not." "Heh."

Fleck hit a good putt for his birdie try, but it came up a few inches short and right of the cup. He tapped in for his par. Hogan had an excellent chance to take the first lead in the contest. It was essentially a straight-in putt over pretty flat ground. Even if it had a bit of break to it, and there might have been an inch or two at most, from that short length one doesn't play the ball outside the hole. He wanted a firm hit to the center of the cup. He hit it firmly but was off line to the right. The ball caught the lip of the cup and stayed up. A visibly discouraged Hogan flicked the ball into the hole and walked dismally to the next tee.

Fleck had dodged a bullet.

Fleck (E)—Hogan (E)

HOLE NUMBER 4

Hogan hit another precision drive, this one with some length at 260 yards right down the middle. Fleck's drive was off line to the left, another pulled shot, but the ball caught a small mound in the rough and bounced to the right and into the fairway. He was a yard or so ahead of Hogan, who hit a 6-iron second shot that dropped slightly to the right (a classic Hogan fade) to within sixteen feet of the cup.

Fleck hit a 6 iron on the pin all the way, but it was a touch long. It finished twenty-four feet above the hole. Putting from the top of the green can be tricky in respect to speed, but Fleck showed good touch and eased his first putt only a foot past the hole. He tapped it in for a par-4.

Hogan, obviously not comfortable with the putter, took even more time than usual to play his first putt, which was from a makeable distance. He walked a complete circle around the hole from his ball and back, looking at the terrain to ascertain the undulations he had to deal with. At last he got over the ball, but where he was a bit too firm on the previous green, this time he overcompensated in the other direction and left the ball three feet short of the cup—a poor effort. He took a few minutes to gather himself for the short second putt, and when he finally did hit it, the ball just barely got in at the front of the cup. They were tied after four holes.

Fleck (E)—Hogan (E)

HOLE NUMBER 5

Hogan's uncertainty and mediocre-to-poor performance with the putter was something of a shock to many in the gallery, certainly to those who hadn't been following him at all during the week. Newspaper reports didn't make much of it. Certainly his legs were a factor, and here they got to his legendary driving accuracy. On this long, 447-yard par-4 he did not quite finish his swing—his hips did not make a full enough turn, and the clubface did not square up. The ball was pushed to the right into the trees and heavy rough.

Fleck teed his ball at the far right side of the tee box so he would automatically angle his body at address to be where he would be aiming at the left corner of the dogleg right fairway. He wanted no truck with the right side. If he missed his drive the way Hogan had, he would still catch the middle or right side of the fairway. As it was, he hit a very solid drive, so well and so long it ran through the dogleg into the rough on the left and fairly close to a line of trees.

With cypress trees in his line to the hole and the ball deep in the dense rough, Hogan had no choice but to play sideways back to the fairway. From there he would try to make a birdie for a par. That is, from where his drive should have been he would hit his third up close to the hole and make the putt. That was the plan.

Fleck saw an opening, of course, and was encouraged. He had to play a small or baby hook to clear some trees about five yards front-left of his ball in the rough, and he managed it well with a 5 iron, turning the ball from right to left. It landed in the front fringe of the green and ran up some thirty feet from the hole. He caught his caddie's eye, and they nodded to each other. Good job.

Hogan's 5-iron third shot finished on the green, twenty-eight feet from the hole. A good shot, but he needed a much better one. Fleck putted first and rolled his ball a half-foot from the cup. He tapped in for his 4. The feeling with the putter was somehow getting even more magical. He truly expected to make everything he looked at, and every putt he hit looked like it had a chance to go in. Not all would, of course, putting being what it is, but it was a good sign.

Hogan needed to hole to keep the match tied and this time made a decent stroke. However, the ball skimmed just past the right edge of the cup and stopped inches from the hole. He made a five, and Fleck now led by one stroke.

There was a murmur in the gallery. Could this be? Could this fellow Fleck have a chance against the great Hogan, head to head? Why not? He didn't look overexcited, not even excited.

Fleck (E)—Hogan (+1)

HOLE NUMBER 6

With the honor on the tee for the first time, Fleck boomed a big drive down the middle of the fairway; it traveled close to 270 yards, far above the average length the field in general had been getting during the week.

After the poor drive on the previous hole, Hogan took a little more time preparing to hit his tee shot on this long par-4. The bunker on the left was in his range if he hit the ball full flush, so he targeted the very right corner of it and cut the ball just enough to avoid the bunker. It was a very good drive, a fine comeback, although he was at least fifteen yards short of Fleck's ball.

Hogan was not flummoxed by the distance Fleck was getting off the tee. He never chased anyone with the driver and had always been able to put ten yards or more on a drive if he felt he needed to. He could even catch Snead at times. Here, he had a 4 iron left to the green. The ball was sitting down just a tad in the grass, so he'd have to go get it. He played the ball back a few inches in his stance to be sure he caught the ball first, then drilled it at the pin. The ball landed, took one hop, and settled into place around eleven feet from the hole.

He quick-glanced at Fleck to see what his reaction might be to the shot. He saw nothing, but his doing it in the first place was a sure sign he was concerned with how things were going.

Although he had not seen Hogan glance at him, Fleck recognized his opponent's shot as a statement that said he had plenty of game left. Fleck never doubted that. However, having driven so long, he had yet another between-clubs dilemma. He wasn't entirely sure of club selection for this shot to the green. A soft 6 iron? A hard 7 iron? He was opting for the longer club and swinging easy in these situations, but his swing tempo was somehow causing him to pull the shots just a hair. Still, he felt it was better to go easy. And again, he pulled the ball, which landed on the very left edge of the green and kicked left into the bunker adjacent to the putting surface.

As he was walking toward the green Dr. Barton called Fleck over to the ropes and handed him two sugar cubes. Fleck hesitated for a moment but followed the advice of his friend and mentor. He cracked the cubes between his teeth, then let them melt in his mouth.

The bunker from which Fleck had to play had a very low lip. It was just above the level of the green, and he had a good lie in the sand; the ball was sitting entirely on top. However, the hole was cut on the left side of the green, close to him. He was short-sided, and what's more, the green sloped directly away from him. He had no chance to get the ball close to the hole, no matter how well he hit the shot. And he did hit it well, clipping the sand just behind the ball to get as many of the grooves on it as possible to get holding spin. But the slope was too much, and the ball ran twenty-five feet past the hole, finishing in the fringe on the right side of the green.

It looked like the match might go even there. And Hogan being so close for a birdie, there could be a two-stroke swing with

Hogan going ahead. The chance of the latter happening was less likely, given Hogan's performance with the putter so far. Still, he had made a few during the week. Fleck could put all that speculation to rest with one fine stroke of the putter. But it wasn't going to be easy. He had to come up over a rise in the green. The ball would then move downhill a bit. But he had a good read of the putt, and his confidence was such that he didn't take much time with it. He made a firm stroke, and the ball ran up the rise, then down with beautiful pace. And in it went. A par.

"God*damn*, I've run into a putter," said Hogan to himself when Fleck's ball fell into the cup. "Sonofabitch. One of those guys. How the hell do they do it? Shit!"

It would not be correct to say Hogan was expressionless after Fleck's hole-out. There is no such thing, really. However, his primary facial conformation—tight-lipped, stern, even perhaps angry—intensified. You had to be an experienced Hogan-watcher to see the difference, but it was there. He despised golfers who made their game with the putter. They were bottom-feeders, in his estimation.

Hogan had an eleven-foot putt to gain a shot on Fleck's marvelous par save. He looked over the line of the putt, took a few practice strokes, which was unusual for him, then stood over the ball for a full fifteen seconds before he finally pulled the trigger. The ball was six inches off line to the right of the cup. Fleck retained his one-shot lead.

Fleck (E)—Hogan (+1)

HOLE NUMBER 7

It would appear on the surface that nothing anyone else did on the golf course bothered Ben Hogan. He was in his cocoon, his isolation booth. He learned to be that way with the same diligence he used to find his swing. Appearances, of course, are deceiving. Hogan had emotions like everyone else; he just tamped them well . . . most of the time. But he was upset by Fleck's par-saving putt. That didn't mean he was giving up, not by a long shot; it actually hardened his resolve, gave him a spurt of energy. But too much. After Fleck drove well, dead center, and very close to the bunkers guarding the front of the green on the 288-yard par-4, Hogan hooked his drive to the left into deep rough. On the only "birdie hole" on the course, he put himself in harm's way.

Hogan did have a clear shot to the green but heavy grass to play from. He took a good bit of time deciding how to play the shot, going through an entire cigarette, then finally powered a wedge out of the thicket and onto the green. He left himself with a thirty-five-foot putt for a birdie. Not what he needed.

Fleck had a simple little pitch shot from the fairway and hit a good one with his wedge. The ball came to a stop around nine feet from the hole. However, he would have to deal with Roos' Folly. The putt would run over a lower portion of the hump in the middle of the green.

Hogan hit one of the best putts he stroked all week and nearly holed out. The ball hung on the lip of the cup. The gallery *ooh*ed and *ahh*ed. It was a sympathy cheer. His putting issue had become clear to everyone, and the gallery was pleased for him to have made such a good effort.

Fleck, although he was putting for a birdie from only nine feet, had the mound to deal with. The ball was going to slide off it. Still, from that distance his odds were in the 65 percent range. Fleck made a good effort. He got the ball high enough, but it came off the mound more quickly than he had expected and slid by the hole.

He held his one-stroke advantage. Hogan dodged the bullet, this time.

Fleck (E)—Hogan (+1)

HOLE NUMBER 8

On this short par-3, only 139 yards, Hogan was in his wheelhouse. It was a distance from which his precision iron game was especially outstanding. It was only a 7-iron shot, but the pin was in the front-left corner, just behind a deep bunker. It was a situation in which he might take a more aggressive approach and shoot at the pin, but his conservative modus took over, and he played the safer shot to the fat part of the green and ended up around thirty-five feet from the hole.

Fleck was very confident of this shot. He decided to hit a soft 7 iron, despite having pulled a few of these "light" strikes. This time he hit it high, not unlike the 7 iron he hit on the 72nd hole that led him in his present situation. He smoothed a beauty, with a little bit of a draw. The ball finished seven feet under the hole. Perfect.

The applause for Fleck's effort was full and with more volume, as the green was very near the clubhouse. The gallery waiting on the hill to the left of the 18th green was watching the action, and everyone was sensing something special happening before them. The prospects were exciting and filled with wonder. Maybe this tall guy from corn country could pull it off. That would be something, wouldn't it?

Hogan was getting more concerned by the minute. Fleck's shot showed him that the fella might be more of a player than he had taken him for; maybe he was more than a putter. *Damn, that's not good.* And now he had a downhill putt on a green that was more beat up from the week's play than the others. With less grass on it, his putt was going to be pretty quick. Hogan lightened his grip on the putter and sent the ball off on a good track to the hole. Over thirty-five feet anything could happen, as he well knew, and this time one of those good accidents happened. The ball was going at a pretty good pace but was dead on line to the hole, and in it fell. A deuce, a birdie. *Take that, goddamn it.*

Fleck was unfazed. If Hogan was in his own world, so was Fleck. They were just different worlds. Hogan was married to hard reality, Fleck to the evanescent. And evanescence was in the ascendance. Fleck took very little time over his seven-foot putt. He saw the line clearly, as if there were in fact an inked path drawn for him. He stroked the ball firmly, followed through with the putter blade, and holed the putt. He went in on top of Hogan's thirty-five-footer with a birdie of his own. There is no better, more satisfying thing for the golfer who manages to do that. It increases or spurs on his enthusiasm, raises his spirits, gives him a huge boost of self-confidence. And for the one who has been topped the feeling is one of disappointment and, depending on the circumstances, frustration.

In any case, Fleck remained one stroke up. People in the gallery began looking at one another with astonishment. This guy wouldn't crack. Wow!

Fleck (−1)—Hogan (E)

HOLE NUMBER 9

Both players drove well in the fairway, with Fleck about ten yards ahead of Hogan. Hogan hit another fine 3 iron, the ball ending up pin-high to the right of the hole. Perfect distance. With a 4 iron, Fleck matched Hogan's accuracy and distance control.

The only difference? Fleck was pin-high left. Both had putts of twenty feet.

There was some question as to who was away and first to putt. In a match of this kind, the player who goes first has the advantage, especially if he holes out, although that didn't seem to bother Fleck on the last hole. The official, Joe Dey, came to the middle of the green to make a judgment. He didn't bother with a tape measure; he just looked both ways and after a moment declared that Fleck was farthest from the hole. He held his hands about six inches apart. It was that close. Fleck's putt broke about two inches from left to right, and he judged it perfectly. The ball slid into the cup for a birdie 3. The gallery cheered loudly. Fleck was beginning to pick up a lot of believers.

Hogan, with no visible reaction to Fleck's successful effort, walked along his line of putt to see if there was anything in his line—a bit of loose grass, anything that would deflect his ball if it made contact with it. He was taking more time to line up his putt than he had in all the preceding holes. Clearly, he knew the time had come . . . or time was running out. When he finally stroked his ball it was dead on line but without enough pace. It came up a foot short. He tapped in for a par-4 and was two strokes down with nine holes to play.

Fleck (−2)—Hogan (E)

HOLE NUMBER 10

Dr. Barton had given Fleck another two cubes of sugar when he concluded the 9th hole, but he didn't need an artificial lift. Although he took the cubes from his friend, he didn't partake; he handed them to his caddie when the doctor turned away to get a viewing position. Fleck's adrenaline was in full flow, which was indicated by his drive off the 10th tee. It was a smashing left-to-right slider that exactly fit the shape of the dogleg right fairway. He finished 263 yards out in the right center of the fairway.

Hogan also drove on the same line with the same trajectory but was at least fifteen yards short of Fleck's ball, which left him with a fairly long approach shot, at 177 yards. He would need a well-hit 3 iron to cover the distance, but that was not an issue. Valerie was said to have remarked some years prior, rather famously, when her husband complained that he wasn't making enough birdies, "Then hit the ball closer to the hole." Right.

Could he get it close to this 10th hole, from a good lie, when it was becoming clear he desperately needed it? Hogan hit the ball well, but it did not have enough holding spin and, after landing on the front of the green, it rolled near to the back fringe; he had a twenty-two-foot putt coming back. The hole was cut on the front-right portion of the putting surface.

Fleck had a much shorter approach shot and flighted the ball just right for the hole location. A high, slightly faded 5-iron shot settled nicely twelve feet left of the hole. His distance was exact, his accuracy nearly the same. He was playing with a graceful, elegant rhythm—his body language, the pace of his swing, everything happening as if in slow motion. That was how it felt to Fleck; there was no rush in anything he did.

Hogan seemed more determined than ever to make a good putt. Whether he liked it or not, he knew he would have to overcome his ragged putting. And he did, indeed, stroke the twenty-two-footer well. But putting being what it is, an unregulated science, as chancy as evolution, his ball got off to a good roll but appeared to make contact with a bit of risen grass, perhaps, and veered off line midway to the hole. It ambled just past the edge of the cup and stopped a foot from the Promised Land. He tapped in for his par-4.

Jack Fleck's putt broke about a foot from left to right, the most difficult of breaking putts for a right-handed golfer. The tendency is to not get the ball high enough or left of the hole. However, if one plays the ball a bit farther left in the stance—more off the toes than the heel of the left foot, thereby catching the ball a touch later in the stroke—the ball can more readily be put on the correct line. That's how Fleck addressed his ball. He then stroked it firmly so the ball would hold its line and not take too much of a left-to-right slide. Just right. The ball fell for a birdie 3.

The gallery roared once again and added a minute or so of applause. It then got unruly. Enthusiasm had grown as the contest progressed, and the spectators broke through or ignored the ropes holding them off the fairway. Many began racing along just behind the players. There was also a lot of chatter among the gallery; it was beginning to sound like a baseball game was going on. Joe Dey managed to get everyone's attention and announced that if the gallery did not observe golf etiquette and stay within the ropes and maintain proper decorum, he would suspend play. In fact, he called for a delay. It lasted for a couple of minutes. The crowd eased back behind the ropes, and the game went on.

In all the hubbub it was hard to discern if there was a particular favorite among the gallery, between Hogan and Fleck. After Fleck holed the twelve-foot slider on the 10th, though, there seemed to be a momentum shift toward him. Fleck had taken a three-shot lead, with eight holes to play. It was not insurmountable for Hogan, a famously strong finisher, but it didn't look like Fleck was going to come back to him. So far.

Fleck (–3)—Hogan (E)

HOLE NUMBER 11

At the straightaway 429-yard 11th hole Fleck opened the door a crack for Hogan when he drove into the right rough. Hogan followed with a pinpoint-perfect tee shot that split the fairway in half.

Fleck's ball was so deep in the thick grass that he had no chance to try for the green. With a three-stroke lead he could afford to play safe to the fairway, and he did just that with an iron he purposely kept short of the swale that begins forty yards from the green. He left himself with a flat lie for his third shot.

Everyone expected Hogan to respond forcefully to this opportunity. But they didn't realize that his legs were beginning to seriously tire. He didn't have the secure foundation needed to make his swing, which featured a hard turn of his hips to the left as he started the club down to the ball. Having to play so many long irons to the greens was taking its toll, and he again had a 3 iron to get home. He hooked his ball wide of the green. It landed in the far left side of the greenside bunker and plugged slightly in the upslope. He would have a very difficult shot because of the awkward stance and the ball sitting slightly below the surface of the sand.

Fleck pitched his wedge third shot onto the green. It didn't quite carry the rise in the middle of the green and came back down the hill, stopping about twenty feet under the hole. This portended a bogey, but his putting was so accurate that a 5 was not at all a sure thing.

However, Hogan wasn't in position to take advantage of Fleck's situation. He would do very well to scramble a 4, himself. Indeed, his odds for making a par were even longer given the type of shot he had to play from the sand. And then there was his ever-cranky putter. He carefully calculated the problem with which he was confronted. He was playing off a downhill lie out of sand that was thinner on the upslope of the bunker. His ball was not sitting up. And the hole was cut close to the left side of the green. He did not have a lot of room to work with in terms of footage between where the ball would land and the hole itself.

Wisely, showing the moxie of a longtime pro who had been in just about every conceivable situation, he did not use his sand wedge. It had a wide and angled sole, called bounce, and a somewhat rounded leading edge that in this situation might skid into the middle of the ball and send it on a line drive over the green. Instead, he used his pitching wedge. With its sharper leading edge and flat sole it could more readily cut through the sand with less chance of catching the ball first.

He dug his feet deeply into the sand and choked down on the club to balance out the inch or so his body was farther down in relation to the ball. Gripping down on the club would also shorten his swing, an important element in this play. It was a very delicate shot, and he hit it brilliantly. The ball had more loft than anyone would have expected, and it ran softly to a mere five feet past the hole. Those in the gallery who knew their golf well understood how good the shot was and applauded accordingly. One person shouted his approval: "Great shot, Ben, great shot!"

Hogan tapped the sand from his spikes, exchanged his wedge for his putter—which the caddie already had out for him—and moved resolutely, head down, onto the putting surface.

Fleck was very impressed with Hogan's bunker shot. He nodded his head and looked toward Hogan but didn't catch his eye. There was no chance he would say anything to the laconic Texan. Fleck went about his business, lining up a twenty-foot putt that had to come up a fairly steep incline. His main concern was to get the ball on top of the rise but with not too much speed after it got there and began its run to the hole. He would settle for two putts and a bogey. A double-bogey was out of the question. It was a touch-putt if there ever was one, and he had the touch. The ball rolled up the slope and then nicely along the flat. It stopped a foot from the cup. He tapped in for his first bogey of the round.

Hogan had a chance to close the gap by a shot, and he checked out his line carefully. He remembered putting to the approximate location of the hole during a practice round and recalled there was a small right-to-left break from where the ball was. He was right. The putt ran smoothly into the middle of the hole—center cut. A par-4. A great par-4! Fleck led by two strokes, with seven holes to play.

Fleck (−2)—Hogan (E)

HOLE NUMBER 12

On this medium-length, straightaway par-4 Hogan had the honor for the first time since the first hole. Again, going against form, he tried to power his drive to leave as short an approach shot as possible. But he hooked the ball into the trees on the left.

Fleck saw an opening but didn't force the issue. He wasn't forcing anything on this day. He hit another fine slider, as he liked to call his mini-fade, the ball landing in the fairway around 260 yards out.

Hogan's ball had hit a tree on the bounce and came back a few yards, leaving him some 170 yards from home. He drew a good lie, though, the ball sitting on some thinned-down grass where the gallery had trod during the week. Still, he had to keep his ball low to avoid the low-hanging branches of the cypress trees in front of him. He also needed to put a few feet of hook on it. With a 4 iron he hit a wonderful shot, low and hooking, that landed short of the green, skirted between the two front bunkers, and ran up onto the green about forty-five feet from the hole.

Fleck had only an 8 iron to the green, and he hit a fine, high shot that landed softly and stopped eight feet to the right of the hole. A very good birdie chance.

Hogan's long putting was actually pretty good, all things considered, perhaps because when putting from farther than twenty feet, one doesn't expect to make it. At least Hogan didn't, and with the pressure off, his stroke was better. This time was different, though. He hit a putt that was on line but didn't have the necessary pace. It came up three feet short of the hole, and, after marking it and stepping back, he looked back at what he had ahead of him. That sort of look after marking the ball hints at uncertainty.

Fleck, wasting little time while not rushing himself, made a good, solid stroke. But the ball just didn't take the borrow he played, and he missed a good birdie opportunity. Then it was Hogan's turn, and he did not look confident as he lined up the putt and got into position to play the ball. He had the onset of *yikkies*, a term Sam Snead made up for the nerves or yips golfers get with short putts they badly need to make. Actually, Hogan was already was in the throes. Indeed, he hit a touch behind the ball, which came up short of the hole by a couple of inches, a bogey. He went back to three strokes down, with only six holes to play.

There was a definite hum in the gallery, many of whom were rushing to take advantageous positions to watch the tee shots and approaches on the 13th.

Fleck (−2)—Hogan (+1)

HOLE NUMBER 13

They were at the far end of the golf course, with Lake Merced Boulevard on their left and the Pacific Ocean a half-mile away at their back. The gray sky had not changed, and the chill in the air was getting a bit more bite in it. Jack Fleck felt none of the weather, and although he was not oblivious to the reaction of the gallery to his play, the buzz of mass conversation came off as mere background noise, the inarticulate hum of a large crowd of people. He was totally immersed in his golf.

Fleck pulled a 3 iron from his bag for the sturdiest par-3 on the course. There was no long consideration of the elements and how they might affect his club selection. He was guided to the 3 iron and with it confidently hit a "slider" that fell to the right and stopped after one bounce around twelve feet from the hole. A very good shot.

Hogan, of course, took notice. How could he not? In stroke-play competition he was notorious for not paying attention to the other players in his pairing. Once, in the U.S. Open he won in Los Angeles, he was playing in the third round with George Fazio, a friend and substantial competitive rival. On the 3rd hole, a par-4, Fazio holed his second shot for an eagle. At the end of the round Fazio's scorecard, which Hogan was keeping, had no score on the 3rd hole, and Hogan didn't sign it when told that Fazio had made a 2. Hogan resisted for a time, saying he didn't remember the shot or hadn't seen it. He hadn't heard the huge roar from the gallery when the ball went in? He eventually gave in when Fazio threatened to drop out of the tournament if he didn't sign the card. Hogan was famous for his self-absorption, for his remarkable ability to concentrate only on what he had decided would be the winning score. But in this singular, one-on-one confrontation with Fleck, he couldn't help but be aware of what the other fellow was doing. He had to know in order to strategize his play, especially at this point in the game.

And so, with Fleck's 3 iron inside fifteen feet and three shots down with the holes running out, Hogan knew he needed to respond forcefully to Fleck's excellent shot. He did, poorly, but was gifted with an incredible piece of luck. Hogan once again did not complete his hip turn and sent his 3-iron shot well right of the target. It hit up in the branches of a cypress tree overhanging the bunker on the right side of the green. The ball did not drop immediately out of the tree, and there was concern it might stay up there. It happened often at Olympic, or on any course with cypress trees. It happened to Harvie Ward in the third round of this championship. On the par-3 6th his tee shot hit in a tree beside the green and did not come to earth. He had to take an unplayable-lie penalty and made a double-bogey.

Hogan's ball did fall, however, into the bunker. When it did the gallery let out a good-hearted cheer. What a break! Hogan was typically expressionless. It was for him, so he made it seem, the same thing as a carpenter dropping his hammer and simply picking it up and going on about his work. He walked to the bunker, drew his sand wedge from his bag, and went about playing his second shot. He was playing extremely well from the sand, especially the longer shots that required more art than the simple explosion from up close to the green. He nipped the sand just so, and his ball came to rest six feet from the hole. A fine shot.

Fleck made a good effort for a birdie that might well have put the match on ice, but it slid past the left edge of the cup. He could still gain a stroke if Hogan failed to save par with his six-footer. It was certainly not out of the question. Hogan, of course, appeared tentative as he prepared to play. He finally gave the ball a short, snappy tap, and it found the hole. A fine par after hitting such a poor tee shot. He took advantage of a very fortunate break. Fleck, though, was still three strokes up, and now with only five holes to play.

Fleck (−2)—Hogan (+1)

HOLE NUMBER 14

Jack Fleck had told his friends Walker Inman and Mike Krak early in the week that he thought he would do well in the championship because the course demanded accurate driving and that he was a straight shooter in that department. He had demonstrated that throughout the playoff so far and did so once again at the 14th, where he hit his Spalding Dot down the middle of the fairway at what had become his standard distance, around 260 yards. Hogan's decision at the outset of the tournament to give up some distance for accuracy off the tee had been effective—it had gotten him this far in the championship—but now, as the day wore on and he was playing his fiftieth hole in a two-day span, he was getting even shorter. He did have accuracy on the 14th but needed a 6-iron second shot where Fleck would have but an 8 iron to get home.

Hogan rose to the occasion, though, and hit a finely crafted fade to within eighteen feet of the hole. Remarkably Fleck, with a much shorter shot, put his ball into the bunker at the side of the green. What's more, he found himself with what is known as a "fried egg": his ball sat in the middle of the shallow crater it created when it landed. Fried eggs are very difficult shots. It is almost impossible to put any sort of holding spin on the ball, which almost invariably comes out with a lot of overspin and runs well past the target. But Fleck, in his wondrous mind-set, was up to the challenge.

To play a fried egg one must strike the sand at the back edge of the crater with a definite downward blow and with the blade squared. One can get the ball to come out more softly by relaxing the left arm, a bit of finesse not easily come by in a game that stresses a straight left arm, but that is precisely what Fleck did. The ball all but floated out of the sand, landed quietly, and stopped only three feet from the hole.

Richard Tufts, a USGA official who was on the scene and a member of the family that founded and ran the famed Pinehurst resort in North Carolina, was standing beside Joe Dey when Fleck played the shot from the sand. Afterward he remarked to Dey that it was a play that defined Fleck as a first-class player and that the shot might very well bring him the title.

No one in attendance—including Fleck—thought he would miss that putt to save par. He didn't, and it was a good thing, for Hogan actually made a putt of some length. He canned the eighteen-footer for a birdie. He gained a stroke, but if not for Fleck's excellent shot from the bunker and the sure putt for par, he could have gained two and been within a shot of a tie with four holes to play. As it was, two shots was not insurmountable. The fella might very well come out of his trance. There were a few good holes left to play.

Fleck (−2)—Hogan (E)

HOLE NUMBER 15

Both golfers played sound but unexceptional shots onto the green of this short par-3 and had putts of similar length—around sixteen to seventeen feet. Hogan was first to putt, and once again an odd distraction interrupted his concentration. It was hard to tell when he would finally draw the putter back, but it seemed that just about the time he was ready to begin his stroke, there was a loud crack and thump from somewhere near the green. It happened that a young boy had climbed up a tree to get a better view of the action and in the process broke off a heavy branch that came crashing down. Hogan stepped away from his ball and began his putting routine over again. He had to wonder if he was being singled out for this sort of thing by something or somebody.

In the third round he was about to play his second shot to the 10th green when a squirrel appeared in the middle of the fairway a few yards ahead of him. He stopped his procedure, put his club to his shoulder, and waited patiently until the little varmint scrammed off. Hogan then hit his 5 iron close to the hole and birdied. As with the other incident with the rabbit, once again Hogan didn't seem at all bothered by the incident and went on to hit a superb shot.

But at this late time in the day, with the contest coming near to a close, when he was playing the fifty-first hole in the last two days, his nerves were not quite as contained. If he had had a full shot to hit he no doubt would have overcome the interruption, but he had to putt, and he had enough troubles already in that department. To be sure, the putt he hit was not well stroked, and the ball slid past the edge of the hole. Hogan looked over toward where the branch had fallen. He gave no facial expression, but just his looking back did indicate he was peeved or upset by the disruption. Was he blaming the poor putt on it?

Fleck was unable to take advantage of the Hogan miss, however, hitting a solid putt but a few inches off line to the right of the hole. They tied with 3s, and Fleck carried his two-shot lead to the long par-5 16th.

Fleck (−2)—Hogan (E)

HOLE NUMBER 16

Both Fleck and Hogan drove into the fairway on this super-long par-5 hole and played 3-wood second shots. Both hit them well, to within 8-iron range of the green. As tired as Hogan might have been, he found the wherewithal to produce a powerful shot from the fairway. Fleck was merely doing what he had been doing all day.

The third shots could have developed some drama, but it was as though a brief lull in the action, a pause, a moment of respite from the intensity of the day was in order. Both hit ordinary shots to around twenty-five feet, not good from the distance, and while both made good efforts to hole for 4s, the end result was two mundane par-5s.

The next hole, the brutally strong par-4 17th, would likely be another story. It had the makeup to produce drama, if not tragedy.

Fleck (−2)—Hogan (E)

HOLE NUMBER 17

It was definitely moving time for Ben Hogan. Oddly, this was the hole where he felt he had his best chance to get a stroke back, maybe even two, and square the match. What made him think that is anybody's guess. For one thing, not only had Fleck shown himself to be an accurate driver, but he was outhitting Hogan by at least ten or more yards on every hole but the first. And sure enough, Fleck hit another fine drive up the left side of the fairway that, as expected, rolled to the right off the slope and ended up in the right side of the short grass.

Hogan had to give this one a ride and called on his many years of experience in dialling up that extra energy for an important drive. He wasn't chasing Fleck psychologically, just trying to get himself closer to the green off the tee. And he smoked one, his best drive of the day. He was only five or six yards behind Fleck's ball, in the fairway.

For all that, Hogan still had a full 3 wood to the green. He had a fine lie, the ball sitting up on the tight grass, and he converted an excellent drive with a championship fairway wood shot. With a refined piece of hand action at the moment of impact, he hit a low right-to-left burner that landed short of the green and ran onto the front of the putting surface. The pin was cut on the front-right side of the green, and he had only some fourteen feet of putt for a birdie 3.

Fleck was unmoved by Hogan's clutch play. He remembered well that in the fourth round his 3-wood second shot on the 17th had gone well past the hole, so he backed off this 3-wood shot and, in doing so, failed to fully square the clubface at impact. Furthermore, because he was hitting off a slightly sidehill lie, the ball beneath his feet, which prompts a ball going off to the right, his shot did just that. It came up about pin-high but to the right of the bunker at the right-front corner of the green. The ball settled in some heavy fringe grass.

Fleck took more time with this shot than he had been taking all round. He went well behind the ball and took a few practice swings to get a sense of how the club would come through this heavy grass. He would use his sand wedge, the heaviest club in the bag, to help get the clubhead through. Satisfied after that preliminary, he played a very good shot for the conditions and the situation. His ball came up five feet short but under the hole. He would have a straight-in uphill putt for the par-4.

The gallery, perhaps five thousand people, crowded in as close to the green as they could get to witness what they sensed would be two or three decisive shots.

Hogan was first to play, and his concentration on the work at hand was dogged. If one looked closely, with some sort of X-ray vision, one could see his brain spitting out direction and speed and ordering a short, tight stroke. His absorption in the task at hand and his determination to succeed with this effort were unmistakable. Indeed, for once he didn't stand over the ball very long, and he made an excellent stroke—smooth, with a lengthy follow-through. Alas, the grass or a dimple configuration or a bit of a breeze or a slight nervous tic kept the ball from holing. It crept past the left edge of the hole. With some reluctance, coupled with deep disappointment, he brushed the ball into the hole for a 4. *Well, OK, fella, let's see what you got.*

Fleck wasn't feeling any nerves, trepidation, or fear. He was as cool and collected as he had been all day—all week, for that matter. He just didn't put the short putt on the correct line. When his ball failed to fall there were some in the gallery who let out a brief cheer or at least a sound that said they were happy for Bantam Ben, playing on gimpy legs, clearly dog-tired. But now he was only a stroke behind, with one to play. It wasn't over till it was over.

Fleck (−1)—Hogan (E)

HOLE NUMBER 18

In late December 1954 the union representing San Francisco-area golf course maintenance supervisors sought an increase in the hourly wage of its members and threatened to strike if its demand was not met. The threat was directed primarily at the private clubs in the area, which of course included the Olympic Club. The greenkeepers were earning $1.80 per hour, and when their demand was not satisfied they went out on strike.

When the Olympic Club was given the 1955 U.S. Open and plans were made to lengthen some of the holes on the Lake course, the 18th was a special target. The final hole of a golf course is one everyone feels should be a demanding examination, because it is where the competition is so often decided. The 18th tee would be extended, adding another forty yards to the hole. The mounding for the new teeing area was in place by the end of 1954, but it had to be grassed. That meant planting grass seed, as placing slabs of already full-grown turf was not the way it was done at the time. However, because of the strike the seeding was not performed until early March 1955, when the club reached a settlement with the greenkeepers that brought them a raise to $1.83 per hour.

The seeding of the new tees on the Lake course got under way. However, in the Bay Area's cool late-winter and early spring weather, grass doesn't grow very much—or it grows very slowly, at best. As a result, the tees were not as fully filled out as they should have been by the time the 1955 Open came around. The club's greenkeeper, to make sure the spring rains did not make mudholes of the new tees—Northern California's basic subsoil is clay, which retards natural drainage—spread great amounts of sand on the new grass. The sand was also meant to keep the tees level, as new grass usually grows unevenly. Sam Snead was not the only golfer who complained during the practice rounds that it was difficult to get good footing on the new teeing grounds.

It could be said, given what occurred when Ben Hogan hit his drive on the 18th hole of the playoff, that the union movement in the United States got its licks in on an anti. Hogan made it staunchly clear that there would be no union workers in his Fort Worth factory, and if there were an effort to have one, he would shut down. So there.

Another aspect of Hogan's competitive approach came into play on that 18th tee, disastrously, along with a small but not insignificant quirk of fate. More often than not, when Hogan decided to go bold or aggressive with a shot, it usually did not come off well. That had been the case a couple of times in this playoff. And, finally, when Hogan had his golf shoes made, he had an extra spike put on the right shoe to give him increased stability. It didn't work in this instance.

Walking off the 17th green after gaining a stroke on Jack Fleck, and now only one shot behind, Ben Hogan would have the honor on the 18th hole. He decided he would take advantage of being the one who hit first and put some extra heat on his pesky and seemingly unshakable opponent. Having just missed a short putt, Fleck must be feeling some anxiety, Hogan thought. The 18th fairway is one of the narrowest on the course, and because the hole does not play especially long, a 3 wood had been the club of choice for Hogan and most of the field all week. However, Hogan felt that if he crushed a driver twenty yards closer to the green Fleck might get nervous, make the same club selection, and misplay his tee shot—drive it into the trees on the right or the heavy rough on either side. What was the risk? Hogan, after all, was one of the most accurate drivers the game had ever known.

Hogan put his tee in the ground a little higher than usual—he was after distance—and went into his familiar setup routine. The right foot was perpendicular to the target line—and the left foot flared out slightly; he had significant knee flex. The takeaway was nicely paced, but as he made his typically aggressive hip-turning downswing, a little more aggressive this time to get the additional yardage, his right foot slid backward, which severely altered the path of his club. His right elbow did not drop in toward his body, instead coming out and directing the club on same path it took at the start of the backswing. The ball was struck on the heel of the clubface and was pulled sharply left of the target. Oddly, it had a little bit of a slice on the trajectory but hardly enough to rescue its flight to some twelve yards dead left of the fairway. The pull-cut ball disappeared in the longest rough on the course.

The extra spike didn't hold his foot solid against the slippery sand and the extra force of the downswing. His tired, weak right leg added to the disaster. Some might add an irony—that the hooked drive under pressure that held back his career until he was in his early thirties had come back to bedevil him. But the drive on the 18th at the Olympic Club had nothing to do with faulty swing mechanics. It had to do with inappropriate course maintenance and, more to the point, an otherwise exceptionally astute competitor's misjudgment of the situation, the conditions of play, and his capacity to perform at his best at a decisive moment.

Jack Fleck had no intention of using a driver on the 18th hole, no matter what Hogan did, and upon seeing the result of Hogan's drive, he was even more confident not only of his club choice but of the swing he would make with his 3 wood. He hit a smooth, well-controlled shot down the center of the fairway.

Hogan's ball was on a sloped area where the gallery had not been allowed, so it was not tamped down at all. It took some minutes to find his ball, and when he located it, he saw that he would have quite a job just to get his clubhead on it. It was very deep in grass that came straight up nearly knee-high. Even if he could make some sort of decent contact with the ball, he couldn't hit it far enough to play it toward the green. There was too much rough to carry in that line. His only option was to play sideways to the fairway. If he could manage that with one swing there might be a chance to make a par-4. Ben Hogan was not delusional. He was quite the opposite. But he did see a possibility if he could clear the rough with one swing. However, looking down at his ball he knew he couldn't move it two feet. With a sand wedge he took a mighty hack and moved the ball a foot, at most. He took another hack and gained another foot. With his third hack, which brought up a great stash of grass resembling a healthy helping of spaghetti on the end of the club, the ball reached the fairway.

Hogan was still away, and with a 7 iron he hit a full shot that went to the very back edge of the green.

Fleck was loose and easy as he prepared to play his 8-iron approach to the green. He was, in gambler's terms, playing with house money. It was a simple shot in itself to a pin cut in the front-middle of the green, and all the more so for there being no pressure on it. He made a fine, smooth swing and sent the ball on a high arc. It landed on the green and settled to a stop eighteen feet below the hole. Perfect. An uphill, slightly right-to-left putt.

As Fleck and Hogan walked up toward the green they were greeted with a steady applause and some vocal cheering. Although it was hard to define who was getting the most applause, Hogan seemed to come in for a little more as he limped up the hill that led to the green if only because of his ashy complexion and haggard facial expression. He was the ancient warrior on his last legs coming home from a losing last battle that he had fought with all he had. Indeed, there were tears in the eyes of some among the ten thousand or so that encircled the 18th green. Hogan, of course, did not acknowledge any of this, if he sensed it at all. He was staying true to the public persona he had long ago established and behaved, in fact, the way all athletes of his era did on the field of play. It was deemed unseemly, not professional, a kind of bragging to display acknowledgment of or take pleasure in the audience showing its appreciation. When DiMaggio just barely tipped his cap to a roaring Yankee Stadium crowd, it was news. Hogan more or less exaggerated the subdued manner. Fleck was very much similar in his reaction to the cheers sent his way as he came to the 18th green, but he did drop his head a bit as his way of recognizing the appreciative ovation.

Hogan walked to the top of the green and gave his steeply downhill thirty-foot putt a brief look, stood beside the ball, and made a rather nice, smooth stroke. The ball was headed right for the cup. He thought to himself, *Don't you dare go in, you little bastard. I don't need you.* But it did go in. For a 6. A mighty roar accompanied the ball's entrance. Some of the cheering throng believed it was a birdie 3; they hadn't seen the troubles Hogan had back in the rough.

Herbert Warren Wind, the golf writer with the new *Sports Illustrated* magazine, wrote in praise of Hogan's professionalism in making the putt. To Hogan it was pure accident. He couldn't have cared less. He didn't bother to retrieve the ball. He sent his caddie for it. He stayed at the top of the green and—with his arms folded in front of him, his body language an ultimate expression of dejection—he watched Fleck complete the round with an easy two-putt par-4.

Fleck 69 (−1)—Hogan 72 (+2)

THE REVIEWS ARE IN

A FTER JACK FLECK HOLED the short second putt on the last hole
of the playoff to conclude one of the most unexpected results
in golf—if not sports—history, Ben Hogan came down from the
top of the green to shake his hand. He did it with a warm smile that
many thought he should have used more often in his public manner. A few minutes later Hogan and Fleck posed for a photograph
showing Hogan, again with a smile—although this one suggesting
something less genial, more in the way of condescending—as he
waved his cap over Fleck's putter as if to cool it off. Fleck grinned
at the gesture. Many officials standing behind them beamed widely.

Early in the week, in the days leading up to the start of the
tournament, Hogan had said, "This is a tournament in which the
putter will be relegated to a subordinate role." He was, of course,
dead wrong. In no U.S. Open, wherever it is played—indeed in
no tournament of any kind—does the putter play second fiddle.
Hogan's comment was but another example of the contempt he
had for the importance of this component of the game. What he
was also "saying" in the cap-cooling-the-putter photo was that if
not for that copper-toned John Reuter Bullseye Fleck wielded on
the greens, he wouldn't have emerged the winner.

Not quite. Statistically, Fleck played *golf,* as Hogan would describe it, just as well as the deservedly celebrated ball-striker himself. In the playoff Fleck hit more fairways than Hogan—eleven to ten—while outhitting him on average by fifteen yards. Both hit fourteen greens in regulation. Fleck outputted Hogan by only two strokes—thirty to thirty-two. The putting margin was skewed by Hogan holing the meaningless thirty-footer on the last hole. Had it not dived into the cup his ball would surely have run off the front of the green, and he almost just as surely would have ended up three-putting. But from the 1st through the 17th hole, when everything counted, Fleck had two less putts—twenty-nine to thirty-one. That's not a margin by which one could say Fleck won *only* on the strength of his putting. He did indeed hole some clutch putts, especially the twenty-five-footer at the 6th to save par. But on the whole Hogan didn't lose—Fleck won. He outplayed the Man.

The presentation ceremony was set up at the back edge of the 8th green, the principals facing the mass of people on the high slope beside the clubhouse. It was a terrific setting to see the golf played on the last hole (and the 8th, for that matter), and it also served as an outdoor auditorium for the speeches and trophy giving that followed. Hogan had on a tie and dark sport coat. Valerie was not at his side; she watched from the clubhouse. Fleck wore a light-colored sport coat over the shirt and sweater in which he had played. At one point, when all the participants in the ceremony were standing, Hogan sat, his face showing the same deep fatigue as his slumping body. No one felt he was impolite by sitting when the rest of the party was on foot. Everyone was well aware of the physical issues he was dealing with.

When he was called up to be presented as the runner-up in the championship and was handed a check for $4,000, Hogan drew very affectionate and lengthy applause. In his speech he offered congratulations to Fleck, sort of. "I want to congratulate Jack Fleck. His was a marvelous demonstration of superb golf. It was guts and fortitude. I never saw a fellow, *almost a beginner* [my italics], who performed so admirably. You saw how calm he was. I like that sort of fellow. He will wear the crown well."

Nice words. Boilerplate for the most part, except for the *beginner* designation. Then Hogan rained on Jack Fleck's parade. He went on to say how much he loved golf, that it was his life, but he was sorry to say he was through with competition. "Whether I won or lost [the playoff], I wanted to make a good show. I hope I've done that." An odd remark for someone who did not think for a minute he was in show business.

During the speech one could discern a slight catch in Hogan's throat. It was an unusual show of emotion for him, and the scenario drew tears from many in the audience. Real tears, as Bill Callan, a teenager at the time, remembers. He said, "I was crying myself."

Hogan's pronouncement took a good bit of the shine off the presentation of the winner's trophy to Jack Fleck. It reminded everyone who the *real* champion was. Or had been. Hogan may not have consciously tried to steal the show from Fleck with his throat-catching notice that he was departing from the golf scene. It was simply the act of a totally self-absorbed person. The term *solipsism* comes to mind. The polite thing to do would have been to make the announcement the next day, from his office in Fort Worth. And besides, he didn't really mean what he said.

The tenor of the scene around Hogan's locker immediately after the presentations, while he was packing his gear, was characterized as a wake. When asked how he would rate Fleck as a golfer, in this setting Hogan was a little less diplomatic. He said Fleck was a good golfer and added, "I never make predictions about golfers, but I'll say this. It's up to him. Anyone who wants to be good can do it, but he's got to work." A backhanded compliment, it would seem. Did he think Fleck just took up the game? Or only played on weekends? That he hadn't been playing the tour steadily for the past year and a half? Still, he was not nearly as blunt as the time when he was paired with Billy Casper in a Goodall Round-Robin tournament. Casper, a sometimes-erratic shot-maker but always a dazzling putter, had one of his best days on the greens. At the end of the round Hogan told Casper that if he couldn't putt he'd be selling hot dogs at one of those stands over there.

The interview session over, Hogan finished packing his small bag with a couple of shirts, a sweater, and a pair of shoes. He gave out a few new balls to lingering reporters and his white cap to the locker-room man. He then climbed the two flights of stairs to the main lobby of the Olympic Golf Club, where he met his caddie. He paid him $125 cash and gave him his shag bag and all the balls in it. Valerie was there to meet him. That evening they had dinner with a local club professional, George Mahoney. He and Hogan discussed selling the Ben Hogan brand of clubs in his shop. Valerie sat quietly by. The following morning they flew back to Texas.

For Jack Fleck the immediate aftermath of his victory over Ben Hogan was a whirlwind of events. A couple of them were high profile, one of them especially so. At 7:45 and 8:45 AM Monday morning Fleck was in the studio of KRON-TV, the NBC network's San Francisco affiliate station, to appear on the popular nationally televised program *The Today Show*. It was hosted by Dave Garroway (who, by the way, was a low-handicap golfer). Fleck received $1,000 for his appearance. His caddie also received some money for appearing.

The most notable event was a meeting with President Dwight D. Eisenhower, America's first golf buff, who was in San Francisco for the tenth anniversary of the founding of the United Nations. The meeting came about a few hours after the *Today Show* appearance. The president had come into the city on Sunday and was kept up-to-date on the playoff through aides and the radio broadcast. Eisenhower was not the only one with an interest. The local radio station, KFI, and all the city's newspapers were swamped with phone calls from golf fans asking how it stood as the match progressed.

Eisenhower wanted to meet Fleck and asked his Secret Service staff to round him up. They had some difficulty finding him. Fleck had checked out of the El Camino Real on Sunday morning, and when the golf was over he had no place to stay. Now that he was the National Open champion a little motel in Daly City would not do, but with the United Nations convention in town a hotel room was virtually impossible to find. Dr. Barton, the sugar man, came through. He put Fleck up in an extra bedroom in his suite at the Stewart Hotel but didn't register him as an occupant. The Stewart was directly across the street from the St. Francis Hotel, where the president was staying. When Eisenhower's men finally located Fleck, through Bob Roos, he was escorted to the president's quarters on the sixth floor, and they had a pleasant ten-minute chat.

The most memorable segment of the meeting was when Eisenhower, flashing his famous smile, held up the front page of the Monday edition of the *San Francisco Chronicle*, which had as its top headline, "FLECK BEATS HOGAN!" Just below it, in a smaller font, was "Eisenhower Arrives for U.N. Meeting." Golf and Jack Fleck topped the president at the box office. At least in San Francisco, and for a day.

That afternoon Fleck, Dr. Barton, and his wife, Clara, flew nonstop on a TWA Super-G Constellation to Chicago's Midway Airport. It was billed as a "Champagne Flight." Lynn and Craig Fleck had been flown to Chicago from Davenport in the private plane of a Davenport amateur golfer, Herb Elliott, so they could greet Jack as he got off the Constellation. The next morning Elliott flew the Flecks and Bartons back to Davenport for a civic welcome-home for the local hero. At the airport Fleck was greeted by city dignitaries—the mayors and heads of the Davenport and Betten-dorf chambers of commerce—and an estimated five hundred folks. He was cheered warmly. Two large signs were attached to a hangar and the terminal building that said, "Welcome Home Champ" and "Congratulations, We're Proud of You, Jack!" Beneath the latter was a twenty-foot reproduction of Fleck's putter. It would forever go down that Fleck won on the strength of his putter.

Fleck had tears in his eyes at the welcome, and in a thank-you speech he said it was much harder for him to make this one than the one he gave at the presentation ceremony at the Olympic Club. "I talked well there," he said to his fellow Iowans, "but I can't do it here." He thanked his "darling wife Lynn" and did manage to say that it was hard to realize he was the National Open champion and that he "realized, just as Ben Hogan said, that I am still a freshman in tournament golf. But I feel I have found something in the game. It came at once, with God's help. Golf is my life and always has been. I'm here to be with my family and my friends, but I'll con-tinue tournament golf. I can't go into hiding."

He was prone to odd remarks when being spontaneous. No one expected him to retire from the game. Go into hiding?

Jack, Lynn, and Craig were then escorted to a Cadillac con-vertible with the top down that was part of a multicar caravan that drove through downtown Bettendorf and downtown Davenport, where the streets were lined with an estimated two thousand cheering celebrants. Young Craig seemed not at all impressed with any of the proceedings. The boy said he was glad his dad won, but he didn't like that Ben Hogan lost, and during the arrival celebrations the boy appeared more interested in his Davy Crockett comic book than his father's moment in the sun. (Interestingly, in recalling this episode fifty-five years later, Craig Fleck said, "It took me a few years to realize that Mister Hogan was such a big deal.")

Louis Fleck, who had never seen his son play golf, was in attendance, although Jack didn't know it. Only when someone in the crowd shouted to Jack that his father was there and wanted to see him did they connect. Jack and his widowed sixty-seven-year-old father embraced, and both brushed tears from their eyes. Louis Fleck said he was afraid his son would forget him. Jack's brothers and sisters saw him pass in the parade down Bettendorf's Main Street.

There was a banquet dinner that night, and Fleck was given the keys to a new Cadillac car, a gift paid for by donations from citizens of Davenport and Bettendorf. John O'Donnell, the sports editor of the *Davenport Democrat*, was behind the gesture.

Three days later Fleck flew to New York to appear on the *Ed Sullivan Show* and meet with various people to discuss business opportunities.

It was commonly believed, or assumed, that in the year after winning the U.S. Open the champion reaped a small fortune from endorsements, golf equipment contracts, exhibitions, an instruction book, and other emoluments derived from his celebrity status. There was considerable speculation, even fascination, with how much the title was worth. In the San Francisco *Examiner* a week after the playoff a reporter revealed what he believed was Fleck's financial situation prior to his victory over Hogan. His column was headlined, "Fleck Had Only $3 in His Pocket—Then Hit Jackpot." He wrote:

> Cinderella Jack, prime candidate for one of Horatio Alger's success narratives, had only $3 in his pocket when he strode off the green a National Open champion. . . . This unhealthy state of affairs was revealed by the curly-haired Fleck yesterday during one of his public appearance speeches at Davenport, Iowa, the new golf king's home town. "Things were dark, indeed," Fleck related. "But all that is changed now." . . . Latest estimate has Fleck about to realize $75,000 from his National Open victory . . . but when Uncle Sam gets done his take home pay will be more like $38,000, the same as Ed Furgol pocketed in 1954 for his strike at Baltusrol.

Fleck did not have only three bucks in his pocket when he walked off the green after the playoff, and he didn't have curly hair either. But the three-dollar story made good copy.

Will Connolly, in the *San Francisco Chronicle*, wrote: "Winning the Open means a flat purse of $6,000 and between $50,000 and $75,000 in exhibition fees and endorsements. What will Fleck do with all that money?"

There was a Fleck family tale Lynn related after the playoff: "In past years whenever I wanted to buy something Jack always said, 'Wait till I win the U.S. Open.' Well, the time has come, but now I don't know what I want."

The first transaction Fleck made was with the Dunlop Company to play its golf ball. Dunlop didn't make clubs at the time. Ed

Furgol, who was contracted to the company, recommended Fleck and arranged for him to meet Vinnie Richards, the president of Dunlop's Sports Division. Richards signed Fleck to a two-year contract. Fleck liked Richards and asked him to arrange his exhibition schedule. Richards was well qualified for this particular business. He was one of the top American tennis players starting in the late 1900s, and a protégé of Bill Tilden. At the age of fifteen Richards partnered with the fabled Tilden to win the United States doubles championship. After playing on several U.S. Davis Cup teams and winning numerous amateur titles, Richards became the first male American tennis star to turn professional. He played an extensive professional exhibition series with Suzanne Lenglen, the great French women's tennis champion.

Fred Corcoran, a well-known man about golf who for a number of years was the manager of the PGA Tour, also advised Fleck in his business dealings for a short time in the early going. Corcoran helped found the Ladies Professional Golf Association and managed that circuit for a time. He had a long and glittery resume in golf and athletic agentry. He represented Sam Snead, Ted Williams, and Stan Musial, among a few other highly notable athletes. Corcoran connected Fleck with a New York firm called Endorsements, Inc., headed up by Jules Alberti, which developed some offers for him.

An anonymous writer for the *New Yorker* magazine had a "Talk of the Town" piece in a July 1955 issue of the periodical on a negotiating session Fleck had in Alberti's office.

Corcoran was also in the room. Fleck was described as wearing blue slacks, a gray tweed jacket, a blue-and-white tie, and as a "sort of golfing Gary Cooper, tall, slender, and soft-spoken, with an engaging diffidence of manner." Fleck sat with a ballpoint pen in hand examining an American Airlines contract that required him to have his photograph in an advertisement showing him checking in with his golf clubs at the airline's ticket counter. Fleck looked over to Corcoran for his opinion on the arrangement, and Corcoran nodded that it would be OK to sign on.

Then into the room came an executive with the McGregor Company, which produced Drizzler jackets. He sought to sign Fleck to endorse the garment. Along with posing for advertisements wearing the jacket, Fleck would consent to play ten exhibitions around the country for a total of $1,000, plus $300 and expenses for each of ten outings. In all, the deal was worth $4,000. Before signing the contract Fleck wanted to know if the jacket came in conservative colors—he had seen Furgol wearing a bright red Drizzler—as he preferred less conspicuous clothing. Assured that the firm had other, quieter shades and that he didn't have to wear a jacket every time he played golf, Fleck inked the contract. Oddly, in the ad Fleck is wearing a pair of bright red pants with his tan Drizzler.

The *New Yorker* writer also described a conversation he had with Fleck in between negotiations, noting that because Fleck did not drink whiskey or smoke he would not endorse such products. However, he might consider a beer endorsement because he did have the occasional glass of lager. Most significantly, Fleck at one point "groaned" that all of this endorsement bother "is sure a long way from playing golf."

Fleck found himself in a dilemma common to suddenly successful golfers. A lot of financial opportunities come streaming in very quickly, and they have no experience handling such heady stuff. What's more, almost all of the off-course deals take time and travel that detracts from their golf. They don't practice and play and compete as much and are mentally sidetracked. All the wheeling and dealing invariably hurts the quality of their golf. But when you've been living low on the hog, have been scrimping and just getting by for a long time, it's hard to turn down anything that comes your way involving money. Although Fleck was a quite frugal man, Lynn Fleck recalled, "It cost us eight dollars for every one dollar Jack won in prize money, especially the first winter he began playing the winter tour. We were still in the red as late as 1954."

Some agents other than Corcoran offered to handle Fleck's business, but they wanted 35 percent of the action they generated. Fleck choked on that number and decided to go it alone except for his arrangement with Vinnie Richards. It was not a wise decision. Corcoran would have been a good choice. He wouldn't ask for so high a commission, knew his way around the endorsement world, was honest, and was an inventive promoter. Once, between innings of a Chicago Cubs baseball game, he had Sam Snead hit a golf ball from home plate at Wrigley Field over the center-field scoreboard. Snead cleared the entire stadium with a 2-iron shot. If nothing else, Corcoran, or any other agent, would have taken a lot of the load off Fleck and given him more time to get back to his golf.

On his own, Fleck signed a contract with a start-up golf equipment manufacturer. It was not a fortuitous decision. Ben Hogan never offered him a contract, because he didn't have the budget to sign any pros. If Corcoran had been handling him Fleck would right off have signed on with any one of the big-three equipment companies—MacGregor, Wilson, Spalding—or Hillerich & Bradsby, the baseball bat maker that was also turning out first-rate golf clubs. Instead, Fleck went for an offer from the Chicago-based Nadco Golf Company, which had begun to produce a line of "diatomic" clubs. Fleck would receive a base salary, a duplication of the prize money he earned when he won a tournament, and he would get a bonus for a high finish in any of the major championships. He would also get a percentage of monies from Jack Fleck–model Nadco clubs sold in pro shops.

However, the big three and Hillerich & Bradsby did not like a new company entering a field that had a relatively small customer base and a narrow profit margin. They managed to get the True Temper Company, the game's premier golf shaft producer, to refuse to supply Nadco. Nadco was forced to obtain shafts from a smaller company that did not turn out quality goods. After testing the clubs at his Credit Island course ("He went to the back end of the range," recalled Bob Martin, who worked in the pro shop at the time and often shagged balls for Fleck, "because he didn't want to be seen using the clubs before he approved them."), Fleck told the Nadco man that he couldn't use their clubs because the shafts were not up to the best standards. He went back to using his Ben Hogan irons until he signed on with Spalding.

The upshot was that Nadco went out of business and sued Wilson, Spalding, MacGregor, H&B, and True Temper on grounds of restraint of trade. The lawsuits went on for two or three years, and all settled out of court. The last to do so was Spalding, and because Fleck was with Spalding he was a party to the Nadco issue. This caused a further disruption of his attention to his golf.

Ben Hogan had been saying during the week of the Open that he had worked very hard for this championship, harder than for any other, and that it was getting to be too much for him physically. He said he'd never train so hard again. When Fleck came in to tie him, Hogan said that if he himself won the playoff he would retire from competitive golf. And if he didn't, he would play from then on for fun, that from then on he was going to be a "pleasure golfer." No one remembered Ben Hogan ever playing golf for the fun of it.

To the point, in 1956 Hogan played in seven events, including the U.S. Open. That is three more than he played in 1955. In that string of competitions he tied for eighth in the Masters, tied for sixth in the Colonial National Invitational, played in the Dallas Centennial (T-13th) and Texas International (T-16th), traveled to England and won the Canada Cup individual title, and with Sam Snead as his partner took that event's team championship. In the U.S. Open, at Oak Hill Country Club in Rochester, New York, he tied for second with Julius Boros, one stroke behind Cary Middlecoff. Needless to say, leaving the other good playing aside, one does not finish second in the U.S. Open without training hard for it.

In 1957 Hogan had to drop out of the U.S. Open an hour before he was to tee off for the first round due to an attack of pleurisy. He did manage to play in five other tournaments that year, though. He missed the cut in the Masters, tied for eleventh at the Colonial, and tied for third in the Latham-Reed Pro-Am and the Palm Beach Round Robin. And he got fourth in the Greenbriar Invitational.

In all, from 1958 through 1967 Hogan played in forty-two tournaments. A couple of them were thirty-six-hole pro-ams, but most were full-scale tour events and major championships. He played in the Masters every year and finished in the top ten twice. In four U.S. Opens from 1958 through 1961 he was in the top ten three times and got fourteenth in the other. Hogan had stopped playing in the PGA Championship after his accident because the match-play format asked too much of his legs. But when the event went to stroke-play in 1958, he played in it twice. In 1960 he missed the cut by a shot, and in 1964 he tied for ninth. In 1959 he won the Colonial. It was his last victory.

In 1960 Hogan was in deep contention in the U.S. Open through seventy holes. When he tried to finesse a wedge third shot to a front pin on the par-5 17th hole it came up a foot or so short and spun back into a water hazard. He finished ninth. He did not play in the Open again until 1966, when he was awarded a special exemption from qualifying, the first ever given. Essentially, his competitive schedule after 1955, when he said he was retiring, was as busy as it had been between 1949 and 1955.

Hogan also made a special competitive appearance in which he reneged on his oft-spoken view that he was not an entertainer. As he once put it, "People pay to see golf, not a floor show." And yet, when he had a chance to make some nice money putting on a show, he went for it. In 1962 he was solicited to play Sam Snead in a match for the popular, groundbreaking television series *Shell's Wonderful World of Golf*. It was essentially an exhibition, a "show"; the matches had no real import. Hogan, however, demanded an appearance fee of $10,000, and such was the desire to have him on the program that the producer, Fred Raphael, and the Shell Oil Company agreed to it. Hogan was the only golfer in the nine-year run of the series to receive one. All the others, including Snead, played for the $2,000 winner's prize, $1,000 loser's share, and their travel expenses. Hogan gave good value for the money, though, creating an enduring piece of anecdotal American golf history.

The match was played in early summer 1963 and broadcast in the winter of 1964. It was held at the Houston (Texas) Country Club. In a remarkable display of tee-to-green ball-striking, Hogan hit all fourteen fairways and all eighteen greens in regulation. His putting was even more problematic than it had been. People in the gallery of some ten thousand, almost everyone a Hogan devotee, could be heard muttering, as Hogan stood for what seemed an eternity over every putt, "Get the damn blade started, Ben, for chrissakes!" Nonetheless, he defeated Snead 69 to 72. It was the only time Snead lost a head-to-head duel with his lifelong rival. The Shell Oil Company makes available videos of all matches in the series, and Hogan versus Snead is to this day the most requested of them all.

Perhaps inspired by that performance, Hogan played in seventeen tournaments from 1964 through 1970. His best results, not surprisingly, were in his hometown Colonial Invitational. He finished in the top ten all five times, including ties for third and fifth. To do his friend Fred Corcoran a favor, he played in the 1970 Westchester Classic, a longtime tour event played in a north suburb of New York City. Corcoran was promoting the tournament. Everyone knew it would be Hogan's last appearance in the East, but the tour officials on the site followed their standard pairing protocol and put him off at 8:30 PM on Thursday. Hardly anyone got to see him, and he withdrew after the first round, not because of the tee-time schedule but because his legs were not up to the terrain of the Westchester Country Club. He had forgotten how hilly it was.

Hogan's very last appearance as a tournament player was at the 1971 Houston Championship International, played at the Houston Champions Golf Club, which was founded and operated by his friends Jimmy Demaret and Jackie Burke Jr. He was doing them a favor, too, because he had been saying that his game was no longer fit for public display. Nonetheless, paired with Charles Coody and Dick Lotz in the first round, he played the first four holes in even par with excellent Hoganesque shots from tee to green. But at the par-3 5th, which has a deep ravine to carry, he hit his 3 iron fat and put the ball in the ravine. He dropped two more balls from the tee and put them in the ravine as well. Then, inexplicably, perhaps regressing back to his days as a poor kid, he went down into the ravine to either retrieve his balls or play one of them. On the descent his left knee buckled, and he almost fell headfirst into the creek. He finished the hole, making a 9, and continued the round.

He completed the front nine in forty-four strokes, but after double-bogeying the 11th his knee gave way when hitting his tee shot on the 12th. The ball finished in the fairway, and from a good distance he hit a fine second shot with a long iron that carried a pond and ended up on the green. With that, and forever true to his attitude about putting, he told his caddie to go pick up the ball. Then he said to Coody and Lotz, "I'm sorry, fellas, I'm through." He got in a cart and was driven in. It was not a grand exit by ordinary standards, but he ended his playing career on a high note by his own set of values, with a perfectly struck 3 iron.

From then on Hogan would spend all his energy on his equipment company, rarely traveling anywhere and becoming very reclusive. The Ben Hogan Golf Company made a dent in the market but never did become a major player in the industry. It wasn't because the top-of-the-line product—the clubs for the better golfers—weren't up to snuff. They were well made and attractive. He just wouldn't expand the line to include clubs for the average golfer. At the same time, he made influential innovations. He had a Hogan Apex shaft designed that did gain prominence. The idea was to fit the long irons with shafts a bit less flexible than the ones used in the short irons. It was a sound idea that was eventually picked up by other club manufacturers. Eventually, a few tour pros played Hogan clubs on contract. And for a couple of years in the 1960s he even put out a ball that met tour-pro standards. One would have expected that, given that the reason he left MacGregor was because he disapproved of their ball and wouldn't use it. But the Hogan ball didn't stay hot for very long.

In 1960, with his company unable to gain a firm toehold in the industry and operating money becoming harder to raise, he sold it to American Machine and Foundry. Hogan got in the neighborhood of $5 million and remained the head of the golf division in respect to the design and manufacture of clubs.

AMF sold the Hogan Company in 1984 to a private investor/businessman named Irwin Jacobs, who, four years later, sold Ben Hogan Golf to Cosmo World, a highly diversified Japanese firm. In 1992 Cosmo World was forced to sell Hogan Golf and did so to Bill Goodwin, who had no history in the golf business. Hogan was becoming more and more irritated with all the turnarounds in ownership and fell into a very deep funk when Goodwin moved Hogan's beloved plant to Virginia. It was like taking his child away from him. Hogan stayed in Fort Worth, but he did have input on the design of the better-player line. However, he would have nothing to do with the woods and irons that all the previous owners had been putting into the works—clubs with much larger clubfaces and other ungainly (to a pro's eye) features designed to help 90-shooters get the ball airborne no matter how poor their swings might be. It was sound business aimed at reaching the majority of golfers, but Hogan sneered when he did deign to look at them.

Finally, in 1997 the Ben Hogan brand was sold to Spalding Sporting Goods. It was the year Hogan died. Spalding eventually merged with Callaway Golf, and after a couple of years Callaway discontinued the Hogan brand.

At one point in the mid-1980s Hogan talked often about doing an autobiography. It came as a surprise to everyone in golf, for no one was more guarded about his private life than he was. I had an opportunity to help him write the book. In 1988 the PGA Tour initiated its triple-A minor-league tournament circuit, which it called the Hogan Tour. (It is now the Nationwide Tour.) To help promote his equipment and the new tournament circuit, Hogan agreed to sit for a long interview that was filmed so portions could be used in advertisements for both.

I was designated to ask the questions, which were directed exclusively toward Hogan's own experiences as a tour player. PGA Tour commissioner Deane Beman devised the circuit in such a way that the players would have to drive it in their cars, as was the case in the early days of the tour. When asked what advice he would give these young golfer/motorists, Hogan said, "Don't get hit by a bus." Indeed.

During the course of preparing the interview I got somewhat close to Hogan. We had crossed paths over the years—I was the writer on the *Shell's Wonderful World of Golf* show in Houston, and I had done a couple of magazine pieces on him. It wasn't chummy, by any means, but perhaps because I realized that by calling him Ben rather than the obsequious *Mister* that had become a kind of orthodoxy among golf people, he felt he did not intimidate me. Anyway, while having lunch after the interview I asked Hogan if he had made any progress on the autobiography he had been saying he wanted to do. He said not much, and when I asked why, he said he couldn't find a writer to do it. At that I hunched forward and said, "Oh?" and he said, "You might be the one." A few minutes later, when the others at the table had gone off, I asked him if he was serious about the autobiography. He said energetically that he was, that he wanted to tell the whole story, including Valerie's side of it. I said I would get on the phone and see if a publisher could be found. He said to go right ahead.

In a day's time there were three offers by publishers, all offering advances in the range of $50,000. I called Ben and told him. He said he thought the book had to be written first, then you get the money. I said, with a tone of incredulity, "Do you have any idea how many people want to know your story out of your own mouth?" There was a long pause, then he said, "I'll get back to you." I knew right then it would never happen.

I tried a few times in subsequent months to get him to do it, but to no avail. The Cosmo people wanted very much for it to be done, as it would further promote the brand. They told me that Hogan was put off by my telling him I'd have to spend a week or so with him periodically to get the material. He said he could do it in ten minutes. His life, in ten minutes! So it never came to pass. Ben Hogan was not going to reveal anything about himself. He was bound to take it all with him to his grave. But thanks to a couple of biographies of him, we got closer to the man. In *Hogan*, by Curt Sampson, the world at large learned of his father's suicide, which helped explain in some part, perhaps, Hogan's deep reserve. As might be expected, Hogan called Sampson a "broken-down old golf pro passing himself off as a writer." Sampson had been a golf pro for a while but turned out to be a much better writer. James Dodson's *Ben Hogan: An American Life* is the fuller, more detailed treatment of the man.

In 1966 the U.S. Open returned to the Olympic Club for the first time since 1955. Until then the USGA had given a five-year exemption to winners of the Open; for five years after their victory they did not have to qualify. In 1964 Hogan's exemption had run out, and he refused to go through the regular qualifying process, in part because it was a thirty-six-holes-in-one-day process. But for 1966 the USGA broke with historic precedent. It happened as casually as taking a sip of wine with dinner.

Under the big tree at the back of the Augusta National clubhouse, where a lot of golf business is made or at least started, Jay Hebert, a former PGA champion and an influential voice in the growth of the modern-day pro tour, mentioned to Joe Dey that the USGA ought to give Hogan an exemption into the Open being played at the Olympic Club. Dey thought it was a good idea, and he brought it up to the executive committee a few days later. It passed immediately, and Hogan was invited. He was surprised, said he was honored, and of course accepted. And at age fifty-four he hit the ball with the authority and precision always associated with him. The putting was no better, but he finished a very respectable twelfth. No thought had been given to offering Jack Fleck an exemption to that Open. He went through the qualifying process, made it into the field, but missed the cut.

In his first year after winning the U.S. Open, when everyone was watching to see if he really was of championship caliber, Jack Fleck did virtually nothing on the tournament trail. He missed the cut in the 1955 Milwaukee Open, his first outing after the victory in San Francisco. He did go to the third round of the 1955 PGA Championship, losing to Tommy Bolt 3 and 1, but otherwise he went unheard of for the rest of the year. The best he could manage the next year was to miss a playoff by one stroke in the 1956 Motor City Open. And in defense of his U.S. Open title he missed the cut.

Fleck's poor competitive performance in those two years was due in good part, if not entirely, to having played too many exhibitions and being busy with other off-course money-making activities. All he ever wanted to do was play competitive golf, but he couldn't pass up the chances to cash in on his celebrity. After all, he had a family to support and the long-suffering Lynn to make up to for all her sacrifices. In the end, over a two-year period, Fleck cleared around $40,000. It was probably more than he would have earned in prize money on the tour had he played reasonably well. The total purses were still in the $20,000 to $25,000 range, the number of money places was still below twenty-five, and the winner took 20 percent of the total purse. Of course, he was exempt from qualifying for the U.S. Open through 1960, which was four years better than his original goal when he got to San Francisco that Friday in 1955.

Still, he had lost his game. He didn't fulfill the performance clause in his Dunlop contract, which required he finish in the money with some regularity, contend often, and hopefully win a time or two so the company could herald its ball as an important component of his fine play. He didn't come close to any of that. But the failure to play well hurt not only in the pocketbook. He became a searcher in the wilderness for a taste of what he had back at the Olympic Club.

In 1958 Fleck moved the family to southern California, and a year later he was hired as the golf professional at the El Caballero Country Club, in Tarzana. It was a good arrangement financially, but after two years it went sour. The main reason, and the one that would spoil all other such positions he had, was he went off to play too many tournaments. He wasn't around the club and in the shop often enough. He had to keep trying to prove he was worthy of having won that U.S. Open title, and the quest kept him and his family always on the move and uncertain.

Bob Martin remembered a time when he was at a small, $5,000 pro-am at a course in rural Wisconsin, and to his surprise Fleck was there to play in it. "I asked him what he was doing at this little tournament," Martin recalled, "and he said he knew he should be back at his club—he was head professional at a club in Milwaukee at the time—because a big member-guest event was going on there. But he thought he'd come over to tee it up here. He left Lynn to do all the work back in the shop."

His travel out to play tournaments was an ongoing issue, but when he was on-site Fleck had a way of putting off the members of his clubs with his manner. Many perceived he was playing the part of a U.S. Open champ, was on a big ego trip. There may have been some of that, but he was basically a very shy man, an introvert who found it difficult to mingle, socialize, meet and greet. A head professional doesn't have to be an outstanding teacher, but he does have to do public relations with his membership, and Jack Fleck didn't have that capacity. To make it worse, his mien had an edge to it. He was often blunt, impatient, even rude. And he had a cheap streak. A story went around that he had sold a full set of clubs to a member and the total bill was one penny over the final dollar amount. Fleck insisted on collecting the penny. It might have been an apocryphal tale, but that it circulated was indication that Fleck was not well regarded.

The journalists covering golf projected the same attitude. After the short honeymoon in the glow of his marvelous victory over the greatest golfer of his generation, the newsmen just about forgot Jack Fleck. Of course, he didn't give them much to write about, but when the occasion did arise—when he missed the cut in

San Antonio, Miami, Paducah, Palookaville—they got on his case and referred to him inevitably as the dark horse who got darker by the minute and insisted that his victory in San Francisco was an anomaly, a glitch, a kind of mistake.

John O'Donnell, the sports editor of the *Davenport Democrat* to whom Fleck wrote the letter predicting that he had a chance to make a top-ten finish at the Olympic Club, tried to help Fleck deal with the press. O'Donnell had a lifetime of experience with athletes, and whenever the opportunity arose he would advise Fleck to let all the criticism, the barbs and gibes, and the innuendos roll off his back, to enjoy his moment in the sun, make the most of it, and let the chips fall where they may.

But Fleck was constitutionally unable to take heed. And in a day when the newspaper was still the main outlet for recognition, Fleck had fouled the reportorial air with his refractory behavior toward the ink-stained wretches, as reporters were still sometimes referred to. He didn't have the sloping, slippery, waterproof duck's back.

In his growing animosity toward the press, Fleck came to believe they reported not that he won the 1955 U.S. Open but that Ben Hogan lost it. He had some grounds for this feeling. One headline, in the *San Francisco Chronicle*, on Monday morning after the upset, had it, "HOGAN LOSES PLAYOFF—RETIRES." Another one bannered, "THE KING IS DEAD, LONG LIVE THE KING." Another read, "AMAZING FLECK STUNS MIGHTY HOGAN," which suggested that Fleck had pulled one out of the hat. Then there was the San Francisco *Examiner:* "FLECK (69) TOPPLES HOGAN (72)," which was OK in itself for Jack, but it was accompanied by a Hogan-dominated subhead: "One Stroke Back, Bantam Ben Is Foiled by Tall Grass on 18th;

Loses Final Bid for Fifth Crown." In the New York *Herald Tribune* it was, "Only Hogan Read Course Right, Made 1 Error." Which is to say Ben Hogan understood how to play the Lake course like no one else in the field, and he lost only because he hit a poor drive on the 18th hole. But wasn't Fleck one stroke up going to the 18th? Was it in the books that he would double-bogey the hole while Hogan parred it to win? And if Fleck didn't "understand" how to play the course, how come he was able to shoot three of the seven rounds shot in the 60s all week?

Fleck had a case for being underappreciated in respect to the headlines and coverage. But he didn't understand the nature of journalism and what makes news. Ben Hogan was a storied, hugely successful champion, and his name was going to share the headlines with whoever happened to beat him, be it Snead, Middlecoff, Boros, Bolt, or Fleck.

However, there were a couple of instances that would justify Fleck's distrust of the press. Fleck told of being on the plane from Chicago to New York three days after he defeated Hogan when a New York newspaperman introduced himself, congratulated him on his victory, and asked Fleck if he would tell him the story of his life and how he defeated the great Hogan. A naive or unsuspecting Fleck told him the story. When the interview was over the reporter asked him if he would sign his notes so his editor would not think he was making it all up. Fleck complied. The next day he learned that a deal arranged by Vinnie Richards to tell his story to the *Saturday Evening Post* for $5,000 was cancelled, because the reporter's newspaper had already run it. The story did run, soon after, in the Des Moines *Sunday Register* under his byline, but for how much is not known.

Another alleged occurrence has had a longer life and upset Fleck for many years. It revolves around an incident during the playoff itself. It is said that on the par-4 6th hole Fleck took a lot of time with a problem second shot, which he put into a greenside bunker, and consumed even more time to play out of the sand trap. When he finally got onto the green he allegedly remarked to Hogan that he was sorry to have taken so much time and that he would be out of Hogan's way in a minute. Hogan allegedly responded, "Take your time, Jack, we have nowhere to go." Or words to that effect.

It was said that when Hogan made his response to Fleck's apology, he gave up his intimidation factor, the stern, silent-killer aura he projected and that scared the hell out of his more callow opponents. With Fleck put at ease, he was able to go on and defeat Hogan. Hogan was said to have told the story himself, although he may have heard it told and nodded to agree that it happened.

It is highly unlikely any of it happened. First of all, Hogan was famous for saying nothing to anyone in his pairing during an entire round. As Sam Snead liked to say, "The only time Ben talks to me is to tell me I'm away." And Jack Fleck may have been even more close-mouthed during a round.

For another thing, Fleck didn't have much trouble playing his second shot on the 6th hole, because it was from the fairway. And the bunker he played from was very shallow; it had almost no lip at all, and he had a good lie. What's more, Fleck was playing very quickly throughout the round, far faster than Hogan, who was a very deliberate golfer. Finally, Hogan watched Fleck play from the bunker from the back of the green, a good distance from Fleck. It is unimaginable that Fleck and Hogan would have had any words between them from where they were at the time such a conversation would logically have taken place.

This story was put out by Dan Jenkins, at the time a young reporter for the *Fort Worth Press*. Jenkins wrote of the incident again in a brief historical piece on U.S. Opens that he did for the 1987 U.S. Open program. Fleck's take was that Jenkins, who went on to become one of the best-known sportswriters in America, made up the story to more or less protect Hogan or find an excuse for the incredible defeat of his hometown hero. Very improbable. When I asked Jenkins about that conversation between Hogan and Fleck on the 6th green, he said he did write about it but didn't see or hear it because he was somewhere else on the course. He got it from someone else. Fifty-five years later he couldn't remember who that was.

(A transparency note here. In 1988 I was told this story by Bruce Devlin, the Australian-born PGA Tour pro and golf course architect. He told me he heard it from Hogan himself, and he went on to say that Hogan surmised it led to his losing the playoff by giving up his psychological edge. I was fascinated by the story, mainly because it revealed that Hogan was aware of the impact of his personality and presence on other players, and he used it. At the time, I did not check the validity of the incident on the 6th green, trusting that Devlin had it right. I also learned, a few years later, that the late Shelly Mayfield, a former touring pro who had some friendship with Hogan, also told the story. When I wrote it up in *Golf Illustrated* magazine, for which I was editor-in-chief at the time [1986–1992], Jack Fleck called me to say the story was absolutely untrue and that whoever told it to me was a liar. And for that matter, so was I for furthering the myth. I began to doubt the story, but only when I took up this book did I really examine the matter. I have concluded that Fleck was right; the conversation between him and Hogan on the 6th green never took place. If anything, Fleck should know. He was there.)

Two years after all the off-course commerce ended for Jack Fleck and he got back to just playing golf, his game showed signs of revival. In 1959 he took second place in the Hesperia Open and the Orange County Open and was third in the Tijuana Open. These were smaller winter tour events but had good fields. Then early in 1960 he won his first regular tour event, the Phoenix Open. He showed the same kind of finishing talent he had displayed at the Olympic Club. He shot a fourth-round 66 to force a playoff with Bill Collins and defeated him at sudden death. Also in 1960 he lost a playoff to George Bayer for the St. Petersburg Open, finished third in the Houston Open, and, along with Bill Collins, lost in a playoff for the Insurance City Open to Arnold Palmer. He seemed destined to be a playoff man.

Then came the 1960 U.S. Open, at Cherry Hills Golf Club in Denver. Fleck came very close to becoming a decisive part of an Open that made an indelible mark on golf history. This was the Open in which Arnold Palmer made his famous last-round charge, shooting a 65 to overcome Mike Souchak's seven-shot fifty-four-hole lead to take the title. It was the Open in which Jack Nicklaus, still an amateur, finished second and prompted Ben Hogan to say (he was paired with Nicklaus in the last round) that if that young kid knew how to play he'd have won it. It was the Open in which Hogan, as mentioned earlier, needed a par-5 and a par-4 on the last two holes to record a 280 that would have been good for a tie with Palmer. When he watered his wedge third shot on the 71st hole and made a 6 he was so disappointed he made a triple-bogey on the last hole to finish ninth. This was also the Open in which

Jack Fleck made a serious run for the first prize, a fact few made mention of at the time, or since. Such was the scrim behind which he now resided in golf's consciousness.

On rounds of 70, 70, and 72, Fleck was in fourth place with eighteen holes to play. He was four shots behind the leader, Souchak, two shots behind Dow Finsterwald and Julius Boros, one behind Nicklaus and Hogan, and three ahead of Palmer. Palmer's smashing round began with birdies on six of the first seven holes. But Jack Fleck birdied five of his first six holes, and he had a two-shot lead on Palmer. However, Fleck missed a short birdie putt on the seventh hole, and his round deteriorated after that. He never got the putter going again and finished with a 71 to tie for third with Souchak, Finsterwald, and Ted Kroll.

Nonetheless, it was an excellent showing, and with that and his play on the regular tour in 1960 it signaled that while he might not be one of the game's very best players, he wasn't a hack. It could be considered, or reconsidered, that his win in 1955 at the Olympic Club wasn't exactly the sheer stroke of luck the golf world had come to believe.

Further evidence that Jack Fleck had some game arose when he won again, in 1961, at the Bakersfield Open. Again showing a flair for final-round drama and remarkable playoff verve, he shot a fourth-round 65 to tie Bob Rosburg and won the tournament on the first hole of sudden death.

But that was it. In 1962 he tied for second in the Denver Open, in 1963 he tied for third in the Texas Open, and otherwise Fleck had no imprint on the tour. He kept playing, but that was all.

In 1964 Fleck was hired as the head professional at the Green Acres Country Club in a north suburb of Chicago. It was a spring through fall position, and Craig Fleck remembers that the day after school was out in Laguna Niguel, California, he and his mother were on a plane to Chicago to spend the summer with Jack. When school began, they returned to California, and Jack went off to play winter tour events. While at Green Acres, in the PGA section with many fine players among the club professionals, Fleck won the Illinois Open and the Illinois PGA Section championship. At the end of 1965 he was terminated by the Green Acres membership. He was away too often playing tournaments. He moved around to different club jobs and kept playing the tour and not making expenses. Then, in 1975, came a shocking event.

In November of that year Fleck returned home to Laguna Niguel after playing a couple of tournaments. When he got in the house Lynn was not there. He had called to tell her he was on the way, and she was always there to greet him. Not this time. He went into the backyard to look for her and thought he heard the car running in the garage. He opened the garage door and recoiled from gas fumes that came pouring out. He saw his wife slumped forward in the driver's seat. He rushed to open the car door and pull her out, but it was too late. Lynn Fleck was dead. Asphyxiated.

He called his son, Craig, who was now out on his own, and told him the news. "He was hysterical," Craig recalled. "I got there just as they were closing the garage door."

Why? Lynn Fleck was an attractive, bright, intelligent woman with a degree in English Literature from Northwestern University. "Sometimes she would read twenty books in a week," Craig recalled. "Novels, histories, everything." She had wit. After her husband won the U.S. Open a reporter asked her what she thought of his achievement. She said, "He's the best-looking champion the Open ever had. He's got beautiful thick brown hair and green eyes and dimples. He looks just like Tyrone Power."

At the same time she was "a little odd, and tempestuous," recalled Bob Martin, who, as a young man, worked with Lynn Fleck in the Credit Island pro shop. Martin recalled the day Jack left for San Francisco in 1955. He was in the pro shop when Jack and Lynn were saying their good-byes. "Jack's car was packed, and they had a few words together. You know, 'Have a good trip, be careful, good luck.' They kissed, and out the door goes Jack. Then she looks at me and says the most curious thing: 'It would be nice if Sam Snead could win this time.' 'What about Jack?' I said, and she said, 'It would be nice if he could cash a check.'"

Why people commit suicide is a hugely complex question with no certain answers except that there is no one reason. On reflection, people who were close to the Flecks speculated that Lynn Fleck had over the years grown terribly frustrated with Jack bouncing around from one job to another and her having to run the pro shop while he was off playing tournaments. There was also all his travelling on the tour. She was alone a lot. She may have been going through menopause, when hormonal fluctuations can have tragically adverse effects on a woman's state of mind.

The reason for Lynn's sad demise that Jack Fleck proposes brings us back to his U.S. Open victory and his enmity toward the press. Fleck had never spoken of his wife's suicide until questioned about it for this book. He said that for a year or so after he won the Open she was getting phone calls from people she didn't know. She thought they were sportswriters from New York or Boston, and all of them made harshly disparaging remarks about her husband, that he hadn't done a thing after beating Hogan, that he was a bum, that he deprived a great golfer of his record fifth victory, and so on. "It was terrible, what they were saying," Jack Fleck recalled. "All I know is she couldn't take it because they were knocking me. I didn't know about it because it happened when I was away playing tournaments. Actually, I didn't know about it for a long time. Some years later, when he was grown up, Craig told me about the phone calls and all."

"Actually, I don't remember that conversation with Dad," said Craig Fleck in 2011. "I'm familiar with the story, but some other folks may have told him it, and he thought it was me."

Distance in time makes for uncertain recollections, but in any case, even if the phone calls were made, and they could only have been in the first year or two after 1955, it is highly improbable that it took twenty years for Lynn Fleck to react so tragically to them.

It took Fleck a couple of years to get past the calamity and begin playing again. The Senior PGA Tour was in the works, and as a prelude to it the PGA of America put on two of its long-standing Senior PGA championships in the same year, 1979. Jack Fleck won the February version, played at the Disney World course, in Orlando, Florida. Inevitably, he won in a playoff with Bob Erickson and Bill Johnston, holing a twenty-five-foot putt on the third hole of sudden death. The two players he defeated in extra holes were not front-liners, but the field as a whole had a strong list—Julius Boros and Roberto DeVicenzo, who tied for fourth, and Sam Snead and Charlie Sifford, who tied for eleventh. It was a good win for Fleck, another piece of evidence that he wasn't exactly an accidental victor. Of course, it is fascinating that all of his most significant victories came in playoffs. It must surely be coincidental but does have a kind of numinous charm to it.

Fleck remarried in the late 1970s to Mariann, a woman he met in California. He played on the Senior PGA Tour (now the Champions Tour) for ten years and earned some $400,000 in prize money without winning any tournaments. His exemption to this tour ran out after ten years, when his career winnings on the PGA Tour were no longer enough for one.

With nowhere to play competitively, and now sixty-eight years old, he and Mariann moved to Magazine, Arkansas, a rural community where his wife had family and some land. She was not well, and they felt she might be better in Arkansas. Fleck built a nine-hole golf course that he called Lil' Bit a Heaven, a name with an intriguing genealogy.

Davenport was the home of B. J. Palmer, whose father, Daniel David Palmer, founded the practice of chiropractic. B. J. is accepted as the first popularizer of the therapeutic system. His office in Davenport was decorated in an Eastern motif, all the furnishings, wall hangings, and other decorations coming from B. J.'s travels through Asia. He called the office A Litle Bit o' Heaven. Jack Fleck, like everyone in Davenport, visited B. J. Palmer's Little Bit o' Heaven if only to see the bizarre (for Iowa) ornamentation of the office. It was like a museum. The wonder here is, could this exposure as a youth somehow have drawn him to his later interest in hatha yoga?

The golf course in Magazine didn't follow an Asian decorative scheme and was anything but divine otherwise. It turned out to be another bit of bad luck for Fleck. When he proposed the project to the county government he was told a three-mile paved road would be put down from the main highway to the course. The promise was not kept, and golfers who wanted to play there had to traverse a dusty, bumpy dirt road. Even before that debacle, during construction of the course it was discovered that just beneath the surface soil was solid, impermeable hardpan. Construction costs escalated as a result, and, to meet them, Fleck sold at auction the medal he was awarded for winning the 1955 U.S. Open. It fetched

$32,500. Ironically, or sadly, the value of the medal, as writer Bill Fields pointed out in an article on Fleck, was because of its association with Ben Hogan.

In 2001 Fleck closed down Lil' Bit a Heaven and moved to nearby Fort Smith, Arkansas. Mariann had passed away before that, and Jack had married again, to Carmen Lewis. He has scraped by over the years and now lives largely on income from four "tournaments" on what is called the Super-Senior Tour. It is a formulation created by the PGA Tour for pros from the era before there was a pension program. Players including Gene Littler, Bob Goalby, Al Besselink, and Jack Fleck play four "events" per year—eighteen holes on a Monday of a regular Champions Tour tournament with local amateurs who support that tournament. Each of the pros gets $18,000 per outing, plus travel expenses. It's a living.

Sometime in 1995 Jack Fleck called Ben Hogan on the phone to have a chat. Jack brought up their playoff at the Olympic Club, reminded him that he used Hogan clubs, and so on. Hogan by this time was in the later stages of dementia, Alzheimer's disease, and couldn't remember anything about the time. "Was it a good course?" he asked Jack. Jack said it was.

Indeed, it was (and still is).

EPILOGUE

Upset

An upset in sports can only exist or be read in a historical context. When an athlete with a minimal record of achievement defeats one of great accomplishment it's an upset because the upsetter's past record doesn't warrant the victory. But any athlete who has worked at his craft and reaches a point where he can get into the same arena with the proven better player has a chance to come away the winner. The underdog who defeats the overdog just happens to be a better player that day than he had ever been before. It happens. Jack Fleck didn't figure, historically or statistically, to defeat Ben Hogan in the playoff for the 1955 U.S. Open. But he caught a wave, as they say, and his timing was impeccable.

The superior player is not pleased with having lost, of course, but odd though it may seem to say, he is accustomed to it. Jack Nicklaus, for example, entered well over five hundred professional tournaments and won seventy-two of them. It is the very rare athlete who goes through an entire career undefeated. The people who have a problem accepting that simple fact of competitive life are the fans. Great players are expected to win. When they don't, the loss disrupts the good order of things, and they are confronted with dread and uncertainty. There is enough of that going around, so the champions must win to relieve the anxieties of real life. It's *the fans who are upset,* not the players themselves.

Of course, every once in a while fickle fandom does like to see the little guy, the unknown, come through and knock off the big dog. Again taking a collective line, most of us are little guys when it comes to sports competition, and the upset winner stands in for us just as the champion does on the other end of the surrogate spectrum. However, the little guy has to be a person who projects himself in some way or ways that capture our interest. Just shooting the lowest score is not enough. In golf it could be the shape of his swing and the power he displays; it could be a rambunctious, take-a-chance style of play or physical makeup or body language. A good name helps. Jack Fleck just didn't quite make it under any of those categories. And to make it worse he defeated—upset—the wrong person.

Fleck? Change one sound and it's Fluke. Leave it as it is and one might think of inconsequential things—flecks of dust, say. He's a nice looking man but not distinctive. He is not overweight or underweight. He's tall but not excessively so. He doesn't smoke cigarettes; he is not known to have a drink or mess around with the ladies. He doesn't smile much at play or even grimace. His clothes are plain. He has an attractive golf swing, technically a quite good one, but somehow it has no special character.

None of this is Jack Fleck's fault, of course. He is what he is, and it all would have been acceptable except for one thing—he beat a deity. He was a kind of Judas. And not only that, he did the deed with such apparent ease. He didn't even break a sweat. That was *Ben Hogan* he did in with such seeming nonchalance. Who the hell does he think he is?

If it had been Sam Snead or Cary Middlecoff or Julius Boros who won over Hogan, it would have been just another U.S. Open. It would also have been just another one if Jack Fleck had beaten Middlecoff or Boros, Bolt or Littler. It wouldn't have been nearly as dramatic (or traumatic?); it would have been just an interesting incident. Even if Fleck had beaten Snead no one would have been terribly unhinged. There would have been the usual sympathy for Slammin' Sam, but by 1955 no one really expected him to win the title anyway.

That it was Hogan is what made Fleck's victory so enormous a disappointment to golfdom. Frank Hannigan, who worked for the USGA for more than thirty years and ended his career with the association as its executive secretary, remembered that Fleck was in some quarters widely despised, even hated, for what he did. If he had shown some winning form in the weeks or months after doing Hogan in, it would have helped his cause; he would have been held in some esteem. When he didn't at all, the sheen of that magical come-from-behind win over the fabled Hogan peeled away quickly and inexorably.

Herein, I have described the details of how Fleck did it, but there was something else going on that afternoon that was more than mere facts and figures, approach shots and putts. It was something that takes us to another level of understanding of how contests can be determined and that it is not only one man's physical dexterity or adroitness over the other.

Ben Hogan's approach to golf was that of a man of science or an engineer. He worked at his game as a physicist might, measuring forces in motion and seeking as much predictability as possible. Golf, by its nature, attracts an engineering mentality. The swing can be, and is by most who play it and teach it, broken down into parts the way one would see a multifaceted machine cranking out beer bottles. In Hogan's case let's say champagne glasses. His swing reflected that. And he thought of it in such terms. In the backswing the upper body turns seventy degrees, the lower body thirty degrees. In the downswing the lower body turns back seventy degrees while the upper body turns at thirty degrees. The wrists remain hinged until they get past the ball . . . and so on.

Jack Fleck was the antithesis of Hogan's methodical, disciplined mode of operation. To be sure, he stepped off yardages, made notes on the clubs he used from various locations on the course, took into account the direction and strength of the wind and its effect on the flight of the ball, and had the characteristics of his equipment thoughtfully specified. At one point in his career, early on, he thought about and worked out swing mechanics and technique. He did those nuts and bolts of golf, but by the time he reached San Francisco in June 1955 all the calculations had been sublimated, suffused in an amorphous state of mind. The information was in there but worked *instinctively*. Fleck's intuition won out over Hogan's science.

The origin of what brought Fleck to his state of mind during the 1955 U.S. Open was hit upon at some length earlier: his discovery of hatha yoga. It seems to have happened accidentally; he just noticed this book on the subject while taking a stroll one evening through the streets of Santa Monica. But it can also be said it was not so much an accident but predestined. The book in the window and Fleck happening by and eyeing it had been *arranged*, as some would say, from the beginning of time. Just as that iceberg and the *Titanic* were *meant* to collide.

Fleck was a man looking for a way to get control of his temperament and so was alert to anything that might be an answer. That book by Indra Devi was waiting for him, so to speak. The exercises, which attracted Fleck in the first place, became marginal to the meditative effects of the program. He was in good physical condition beforehand, and it was the calming of the mind that had the greatest impact.

Many observers that week, and especially during the playoff, used the word *trance* to portray the figure they saw doing a number on Ben Hogan. And that is what it was, in the yogic sense.

After the playoff Fleck spoke of winning with the help of another force. He wasn't exactly sure what it was. "I have to say it. There's no doubt about it. I had other help—power—to carry through to win." "Some Power Was Helping Me Because Some of My Shots Were Fabulous" was the headline for the story he told in the *Des Moines Sunday Register.* "'Lord Was With Me,' Fleck Says of Win," said another headline. But in the accompanying story Fleck is quoted, "The Lord was with me, *I think* [my italics]. Something was driving me all the way. I never played this well before in my life, and all of a sudden I just started to play."

It was the Lord; it was God; it was Something. Whatever it was, it conveyed or induced a level or degree of out-of-worldness that surpassed the particulars of grip and stance and so on and the pedestrian attention to the *meaning* of the moment or situation. There was no past or future history attached to Jack Fleck when he played for the *National* Open in 1955, for playing directly against *Ben Hogan*, for holing the putt on the 6th hole that began his surge to victory. There was only the doing of it, which was wrapped in some sort of mystical memory bag. We speak today of that state of mind, or mindlessness, if you will, as being in the "zone." Fleck was, perhaps without fully realizing it at the time, at least fifteen years ahead of the curve in American golf.

In 1972 Michael Murphy published a novel, *Golf in the Kingdom*, which for the first time articulated in a popular form the principles of Zen Buddhism as they relate to the game. Murphy, a passionate golfer and a pretty good player, cofounded the Esalen Institute, a kind of Eastern philosophy think tank situated on a promontory overlooking the Pacific Ocean just below Monterey, California. Murphy's book is a dramatic presentation of the mystical experience in golf. Sports psychologists picked up on it and gave it a more practical application. They began to advise golfers, especially professional tournament golfers, on, among other things, the value of detachment from the past and the future. You must play in the "present tense." You must play in a state of calm not unlike the state one reaches when smoking a bit of marijuana.

The hatha yoga Jack Fleck practiced is one form of yogic practice that shapes this state. If he had understood it fully in 1955 and expressed the concept to the newspapermen, the public, and his contemporary touring pros at the time, he would have been considered some sort of a mental case, a common term at the time for someone who was thinking well outside the norm. Saying it was God or the Lord was acceptable to the society in which he lived and performed.

It was not so much that "all of a sudden I just started to play," as Jack Fleck put it. The manifestation of over two years of exercises and meditation didn't happen overnight. The proof that it worked was that after he won the U.S. Open Fleck stopped practicing hatha yoga. When asked about it fifty-five years after his magical week in San Francisco, Fleck said it was one of the biggest mistakes he ever made in his life. "As soon as I won I went out and played all those exhibitions and made money. I was so busy I didn't have time for it. I knew it helped a lot, and I should have stayed with it. I think I might have won that 1960 U.S. Open if I did. When I got off to that start in the fourth round—five birdies in the first six holes—I was in there. But then the putter went bad, not because I choked. I wasn't a choker. It was because I got to trying too hard. That's what you learn from hatha yoga. To not try too hard."

There is a very fine line between wanting and not wanting what is important to you, and if you find a perch on it the issue is very likely to be decided in your favor. At least when it comes to winning a sports contest. On first reading, the statement seems to be an absurdity. How can you win the game if you don't absolutely, irrevocably *want* to? There can be is no "line" between the two; you care or you don't care. Caring is logical, even natural; it has to be the way to go. And yet, peculiar as it may sound, of the two attitudes, the not wanting or not caring, whether in fact or feigned, is often the better way to achieve the desired goal.

It is no secret that when there is a physical or athletic component intrinsic to winning, the mental input is going to have a significant effect on performance. The more your mind says, "I want," the more stress is sent to the ligaments, tendons, and muscles that produce the results. Tense muscles simply do not perform as well as those that are not. That's biology, with a side of the psychological. It usually also happens that decisions arrived at are not those one would make when not in a "want" mode. Jack Fleck slid around all that. Ben Hogan did not.

Without question, Hogan wanted to win every tournament he entered. Every athlete feels the same way. But Hogan had always buried that thought beneath intense concentration on the mechanics of his swing, on the immediate problems he confronted for every shot. Also, he deliberately, consciously ignored his immediate surroundings—the gallery, the other players, and the personal or general historical meaning or value of the victory. No one ever heard him openly express that he wanted to win any tournament. And he didn't say as much about the 1955 U.S. Open. But a few things he did during the championship indicated that *wanting* that event was definitely on his mind.

After holing out on the 72nd hole, he, unprompted, handed the ball to Joe Dey and told him he might want it as a USGA museum piece. And, when requested, he willingly held up a hand with all the fingers splayed to "say" he had just won number five. He was, in these acts, behaving like someone who had been mindful all along of the meaning of his performance. It must be thought of in this way because Ben Hogan was the antithesis of spontaneity.

And twice in the playoff itself Hogan went against his normally ironclad modus operandi and played more aggressively than usual. His try for the green with his second shot on the first hole, after Fleck's poor drive to start the playoff, was one example. The other was his choice of a driver on the 18th hole. In both cases he was trying to pressure Fleck into errors. Neither worked out that way, and the second of the two was a total disaster. In all, it has to be said Hogan departed from his normal conduct because he *wanted* to win so much, and that foiled his chances.

Jack Fleck was not unconscious all that week and especially during the playoff. He was simply on another plane of perception. He had found his way onto the thin blue line between wanting and not wanting. He was neither here nor there, in the best sense of the phrase. And because of that he had the greatest moment in his competitive career. He won the Big One, and even if it was a one-time-only achievement, it was more than almost anyone before or after him would ever realize. It was a wonderful coup d'état.

SELECTED BIBLIOGRAPHY AND SOURCES

BOOKS

Barkow, Al. *Golf's Golden Grind: The History of the Tour*. New York: Harcourt, Brace, Jovanovich, 1974.

———. *Gettin' to the Dance Floor: An Oral History of American Golf*. New York: Atheneum, 1986.

———. *The Golden Era of Golf*. New York: Thos. Dunne Books, St. Martin's Press, 2000.

Davis, Martin. *Ben Hogan: The Man Behind the Mystique*. New York: The American Golfer, 2002.

Dodson, Jim. *Ben Hogan: An American Life*. New York: Doubleday, 2004.

Fleck, Jack. *The Jack Fleck Story*. Ft. Smith, AK: JC Publishing Ltd., 2002.

Hogan, Ben. *Five Lessons: The Modern Fundamentals of Golf*. New York: Simon & Schuster, 1957.

Sampson, Curt. *Hogan*. Nashville: Rutledge Press, 1996.

Wind, Herbert Warren. *The Story of American Golf* (revised third edition). New York: Alfred Knopf, 1975.

OTHER SOURCES

The *Chicago Daily News*, the *Chicago Tribune*, the *Dallas Morning News*, the *Davenport Democrat*, the *Des Moines Register*, *Golf*, *Golf Digest*, *Golf World*, the *Guardian*, the *Houston Chronicle*, *Life*, the *Los Angeles Examiner*, the Los Angeles *Mirror-News*, the *Los Angeles Times*, *Newsweek*, the New York *Herald-Tribune*, the *New York Times*, *The New Yorker*, the *Oakland Tribune*, the *San Francisco Chronicle*, the *San Francisco News*, *Sports Illustrated*, *Time*, and the *USGA Journal*.

Conversations with Johnny Bulla, Jack Burke Jr., Bill Callan, Jim Dodson, Bill Fields, Dow Finsterwald, Craig Fleck, Jack Fleck, Bob Goalby, Frank Hannigan, Jim Hasley, Walker Inman Jr., Dan Jenkins, George Keyes, Gene Littler, Jack Luceti, Bob Martin, "Scrap" O'Donnell, Bob Rosburg, Vic Siegel, and Frank Tatum.

INDEX

For my daughter, Courtney, who shares my love of food, wine, and a mischievous sense of humor.

For my mother, Merle, who cooked for six children every night without complaining...too much.

And for my late father, Frank, whose immortal words, "Shut your mouth and eat," sent me on a fifty-year odyssey that continues to this day.

CONTENTS

CONTENTS

FOREWORD
BY NELSON DeMILLE

About fifteen years ago, I was in a restaurant (whose name escapes me at the moment), and one of the guys I was with asked me if I wanted to meet the chef. No, I didn't want to meet the chef, or the dishwasher, or even the head bookkeeper. The only people I'm interested in meeting in a restaurant is the bartender, maybe my waiter or waitress, and occasionally the hat check girl. But my friend persisted, "He's a celebrity chef."

What the hell is a celebrity chef? I'm an author. I'm a celebrity. Well, apparently there was a new phenomenon in America, to wit: the Cult of the Celebrity Chef. And I hadn't been paying attention to this interesting development in the culture.

And so that night I met Tom Schaudel, celebrity chef. He knew who I was (I'm a celebrity), and now I knew who he was. I was fairly certain I'd never spoken to a chef before—unless you count the short order cook at the Stop 20 diner in Elmont, or the various bartenders who knew how to microwave frozen pizzas—and I wasn't sure if we'd have much to say to each other. *So, Tom, how long do you cook your béarnaise sauce?*

I wasn't much of a foodie in those days, and to be honest, I'm still not, but I've refined my 1950s palate a bit, and I can now appreciate fine cuisine. But back then, my interest in restaurant food was limited to meat and potatoes, Italian and Chinese. Why would anyone choose to eat anything else? And why did I need to meet the chef?

Thankfully, Tom Schaudel and Nelson DeMille didn't talk about food on the occasion of this historic meeting; we talked about—

well—assholes, meaning some of the clientele. Tom is a *very* funny man, and I laughed so hard that the other patrons got very quiet. And that was the beginning of a beautiful friendship.

Tom sensed, I think, that I was not that interested in food preparation, and he's never invited me to inspect his kitchens nor has he ever explained to me what I was eating, and we've never swapped recipes. And for this, I am thankful. Similarly, he's never asked me about writing, where I get my ideas, what my next book is about, or who I think should star in the movie version of my novels. And for this, I am *very* thankful.

But then a few years ago, Tom crossed the line and started asking me questions about the publishing business. I asked him why he was asking, and my worst fears were confirmed when he said, "I'm writing a book."

I advised him, "Take two aspirins, lie down in a dark room, and wait for the feeling to pass."

But Tom persisted, bought me a bottle of wine, and sent me a partial manuscript. I sent him a note saying that if he didn't drop this idea, I was going to open a restaurant next door to one of his.

But then one day, for reasons that are still not clear to me, I began reading what he sent me. And now you can read it, too, because it follows this foreword. You won't get a free bottle of wine, but you'll laugh so hard that everyone around you will get quiet.

I'm not a good judge of food, but I am a good judge of writing, and I shouldn't have been surprised to discover that Tom Schaudel, who is funny, witty, and a sharp conversationalist, is also a hell of a writer.

Playing With Fire is a little like Anthony Bourdain's *Kitchen Confidential*, but actually better. Why? Because the kitchen is only half as interesting as the dining room. This may be the first culinary book that ever sliced, diced, and filleted the customers.

And you can't make this stuff up. I mean, I am absolutely positive that each and every story in *Playing With Fire* is not only true, but also toned down a bit to protect the identity of the guilty. I've heard Tom tell some of these stories over the last decade and a half, which have not only made me laugh, but also made me a better restaurant customer. No, I'm not a sensitive man, but I do now appreciate all the hard work, frustrations, and patience of the kitchen and wait staff in dealing with patrons who can be difficult, drunk, disorderly, or under-medicated.

If nothing else, this book will change your mind about opening a restaurant, and hopefully by reading these stories about Patrons from Hell, you will take note, as I did, and not behave in a manner that will get you a cameo in Volume Two of *Playing With Fire*. And if by chance a reader of this book *does* recognize himself or herself in one of these stories, then you've gotten your just desserts, and as a celebrity chef once said, "Revenge is a dish best served cold."

As an extra-added bonus, Tom Schaudel has included some nifty recipes in this book. They look simple enough, but you'll probably screw them up, so as another celebrity chef once said, "The best thing to make for dinner is reservations."

Enjoy reading these stories about those who made reservations at Tom's many great restaurants.

Nelson DeMille
Long Island, New York

Author's Note

One night while reading a magazine, I came across an article named "The Restaurant Customer's Bill of Rights." It went on to list ten "rights" that a customer was entitled to when dining out. It was mostly self-evident things like the right to a cheerful greeting, clean bathrooms, hostesses that respect reservation times, and waiters who serve food and wine at the proper temperature. As I was reading the article, it occurred to me, after all I had seen in dining rooms over the years, that maybe we restaurant workers could use a "Bill of Rights" of our own.

I decided right then and there that I would take it upon myself to write one. It included things like receiving a cheerful greeting back, actually showing up for a reservation when you make one, no snapping fingers or yelling across the dining room for your waiter, listening when someone is giving you directions, and an occasional please and thank you. It was written in a humorous, tongue-in-cheek style and published in *The Great Restaurants of Long Island* magazine.

Morris Sendor, the publisher of the magazine, called me to tell of the tremendous amount of attention the article received from both restaurant owners and customers alike. While we were talking he asked me if people really did some of the things described in the article. I told him that it was only the tip of the iceberg and proceeded to render him hysterical with some of the customer antics I'd witnessed over the years. He asked if I would be interested in writing a yearly article describing the things I'd seen people do. "Tom's Top Ten" was born, highlighting my ten worst or funniest customers of the year, and began running in the following issue.

This book combines some of the updated articles from the magazine as well as new unpublished material.

Several years ago I was talking to a food writer from *Newsday Long Island* newspaper, and we were discussing some of the articles I had written over the years.

"Are these stories really true?" she asked.

"Absolutely."

"Really, they're all true?"

"Yes."

"You haven't made any of these up?"

"Stephen King couldn't make this stuff up. It's wackier than fiction."

"I can't believe these things happen only to you."

"This happens in every restaurant, to some degree, every night," I said. "I'm the only idiot writing about it. And remember, I've been doing this for forty years, so I've collected a wealth of material. I talk to chef friends all the time, and most of what we talk about is how people, both customers and employees alike, behave, or rather misbehave."

"I would have bet some of it was made up."

"Nope, it's all true. Read it and weep."

The reason I brought up that conversation is because I want you to be reassured that every scene in this book actually happened. There are some conversations that after a long period of time are probably not exactly word for word, but they reflect the sentiments at the time and are as close as I can come with a middle-aged memory. I take both full responsibility and a little artistic license. Where I could use people's names, such as current employees, I have. They are my witnesses, and although you may find some of the things in this book hard to believe, they will absolutely vouch for me. Have fun. T.S.

Acknowledgments

There are so many people to thank for the last forty years that I'm sure I'll forget some. It's my memory and not their contributions that have been diminished. I apologize in advance.

This couldn't have happened without the exemplary work of Yvonne Kamerling and Janet Yudewitz of Legwork Team Publishing. Thank you for your patience and guidance.

Thanks also to my editors Andrea Deeken, Katrina Hill, and Russell Sacco for steering the ship in the right direction, and Christopher Donovan for illustrations that were right on the mark.

I'd like to give a heartfelt thanks to Nelson DeMille, a great writer, generous friend, and all around good guy. I appreciate it more than you know.

A debt of gratitude goes to Morris and Rosalie Sendor for publishing my unhinged ravings in their *Great Restaurants of Long Island* magazine, which planted the seed for this book.

A very special and affectionate thank you goes to Eddie Chernoff, who in spite of all the history, statistics, and common sense, continues to fund my hair-brained schemes. You are the only person I know who when asked, "Where can I find a gazillion dollars by Thursday?" answers, "Come by and I'll write you a check." You've taught me so much about philanthropy, friendship, and the meaning of a handshake, and I will take those lessons to my grave. I raise my glass to you...again.

This may be my only book, so bear with me for a few more thank yous.

To my daughter Courtney for who you are and for making me look good as a dad.

To Santon Curti, my mentor, for teaching me about food, a sunny disposition, ancient quotes from the Roman Senate floor, way too much abou the Civil War, the John "Boich" Society, and the writings of Gensel. Forty years has not been near enough time with you.

To my "brother" and first partner, Marty Smith, there's no one else who I would rather have my back, and no finer friend. You are the personification of integrity, honesty (sometimes to the point of pain) and character. I love you and miss you. Oh, and your golf swing's appalling.

To Dr. Michael and Cindy Buffa for pulling me out of the abyss and bringing me to Montauk.

To Bob and Deborah Ramsey: no one is more generous with their wine or waits longer to drink it.

To Mitch Rechler for *making* me take the *CoolFish* location.

To my sister, Ann May, who has the thankless job of trying to manage an out-of-control brother. I love you and owe you.

To Michael Dean Ross, my partner in crime, for his friendship, talent, heart, and chef-ness.

To Adam Lovett for taking such good care of the front.

To Michael Meehan for the great food, great times, guitar jams, and pushing me to improve.

To Steve Vai for your friendship, unattainable inspiration, and providing me with background music for my six words a minute typing marathons.

To Dave and Jim Winthrop for agreeing to sell the book and for the golf, the laughs, and the dinners: Dave, I think it's your turn to buy.

To Charles, Ursula, and Kareem Massoud for their winemaking skills and for allowing me to appear a lot smarter than I really am.

To Jeff Babey for "hermitizing," single-handedly keeping Pabst Blue Ribbon in the black, and a million laughs.

To Lisa Sari Schoen, my culinary soul mate.

To Diane Schaudel, Diane Flynn, and Mary Ellen Smith for typing with such unselfish good humor and putting up with me in the process.

To Marissa Candella for helping me through writer's block.

To my kitchen guys and girls, Lenny Campinelli, Rafacl Cardoza, Antonio Cardoza, Orlando Chavarria, sean Tehan, Devon Greene, Jill Deathwin, Jim Liszanckie, and Arnoldo Sandoval who keep everything running smoothly.

To Gail Gallagher for the photos.

To Mark Scordo, the most rock solid bartender on the planet.

To my dining room superstars, John Reeger, Alison Riconda, Mike Martello, Eileen O'Leary, Cindy McCarthy, Eileen Renshaw, Debbie Bowen, Evan Bucholtz, Kate Costello, Katie Muller, Ben Berliner, and Wendy Kammer-Strode: your patience, good humor and ability to remember how it went down made this possible.

To Dick Scholem, for your kind words, wit, and wisdom.

To Art Smulyan whose "guidance" helped get me into this business.

And finally, to the late Michael Todd, who did more to promote Long Island food and wine than anyone I know.

INTRODUCTION

'll start with a couple of questions: have you ever had an eighty-seven-year-old woman give you the finger, or had someone threaten to shove a potato up your ass? Or have you, on occasion, misplaced your dentures between your appetizer and your main course? Don't for one second try to tell me that you have never accused a waitress of stealing your lobster's claws, been stuck on a toilet seat for an hour and a half, walked out of a ladies' room with a birdcage on your head, or asked for a discounted dinner check because your waiter had the audacity to have a heart attack near your table.

This is my reality, the part of the restaurant business that no one tells you about before you jump in. I'm assuming it would be a pointless exercise to warn newcomers, as they probably wouldn't believe the worst about people, and you really need to experience these scenes first hand in order to understand the boundaries (or lack thereof) of human behavior.

My journey began at a very early age. I was blessed to have a great grandmother who, as a young woman, worked as a cook in hotels in Switzerland. In the early 1900s, women were not permitted to rise above the level of what would be considered today's pantry position. As a result, my great grandmother became very good at cooking vegetables, making salads and dressings, and baking. She, in turn, taught my grandmother how to cook, which is pretty much where I had my earliest experiences in the kitchen.

Visiting my grandmother's house when I was growing up was always something to look forward to. She would make a huge Sunday supper with a special dessert for my brothers, my sisters, and me. My personal favorite was what she called "Homemade

Cake." It was a simple white cake with a sugar frosting baked in a deep cake pan with a hole in the center. To this day, I've never had a cake that was as light, moist, or as purely satisfying as that one. One of the few regrets in my life is not asking her for the recipe before she passed away.

Whenever I could I would *help* her in the kitchen while she was making dinner. I'm sure I was in the way most of the time, but she always gave me a job to do and made me feel important. The aromas of that kitchen stay with me to this very day, and I'm sure they have played a part in the path I have chosen.

As I got to my teenaged years, my life took a turn toward music. After seeing the Beatles on the *Ed Sullivan Show*, I was convinced that being a rock star was my destiny. I practiced hard and played in bands and at school dances, but being a marginal guitar talent at fifteen, I started to think that I needed a "Plan B" for employment. I was starting to like girls more than guitars, and knowing that at some point I would have to buy them *something*—a bracelet, a movie ticket, or an egg cream—I decided to look for a job.

It was 1968 and in 1968 if you were under sixteen years of age and wanted to work, you needed what were called working papers. I'm not sure what they said or who they protected because I ultimately never got them, but they were required. I found that lying about my age was way easier than dealing with the government, so that year during my summer vacation, I lied my way into a dishwasher job in a newly opened steakhouse at the age of fifteen. Largely because I was one of the few employees who actually kept showing up for work (I desperately needed the money), I was promoted to line cook, eventually taking over the kitchen from a "chef" whose daily consumption of two bottles of cleaning products was kind of getting in the way of his kitchen performance.

I discovered a whole new world and was very much drawn

into the insanity of the restaurant business so I continued to work through high school, concentrating way more on cooking than learning. Because of my rather casual attitude toward school, and the fact that I couldn't seem to get there quite as often as they would have liked me to, I was sent to see a guidance counselor for some—well—guidance. Art Smulyan, my guidance counselor, asked me what I planned to do with my life upon graduation.

"Have you thought about college?" he asked.

"I have but I'm not sure I know what I want to do."

"Let's talk about it. Why don't you consider Mortuary Science?"

"Why would I do that?"

"Well, you wear black a lot."

"That's the best you can come up with? Maybe I should study to be a guidance counselor; it doesn't seem like it could be all that hard."

He laughed and said, "Oh Thomas, Thomas, Thomas."

Due to the fact that I was a bit of a problem for most of the administrative staff and just about every teacher in the school, Art and I spent a lot of quality time together, if you know what I mean, and we grew to be very friendly. Whenever I would get under someone's skin, which was practically a daily occurrence, they would send me to see Mr. Smulyan for yet another guidance session, and we would spend the hour talking about everything and anything. He was, in my opinion, the brightest light in the school. We talked for a while longer, and after confiding in him that I loved to cook, a fact that was hard to let out in the crowd I hung out with, he suggested that I try to enroll in a cooking school. He helped me with the application, and the following fall I was at the Culinary Institute of America. We're friends to this day, but I still hold him somewhat responsible for getting me into this business, and we laugh about it whenever we see each other.

I bounced around for ten years after graduating from the C.I.A., learning the craft of cooking, and then in 1983, along with a couple of friends who were as naïve as I was, opened my first restaurant. Twenty-five years and fifteen restaurants later, I'm a little wiser, a little more experienced, a little battered, and still pretty much having the time of my life. I always tell people that I have turned two bad habits into a career: eating and drinking. Who's having more fun than me?

Playing with food is like never leaving kindergarten. You get to paint, mold, draw, write, play with others, snack, rest, wear a smock, and clean up. That's some valuable stuff right there. I can't think of anything else that I would rather do. This journey has been a dream realized through generous partners, hard work, more luck than I have deserved, and the great people of Long Island who have supported me at every stage of my career. You have stuck by me through both good times and bad and have allowed me to do what I love to do, on my own terms, for more than twenty-five years, which is an eternity in this business. You are the best and most loyal customers a chef could have, and I would like to thank each and every one of you for allowing me to feed you all these years and to have had the pleasure of your friendship (except of course for the eighty-five customers that you will meet in the following chapters of this book).

On second thought, I would like to give a heartfelt thanks to some of my "all star" customers because they really have taught me so much over the years. Here are some brief examples of their life lessons: I have learned that lamb isn't really lamb, and that when you are trying to find your way to a restaurant, traveling north or south is an irrelevant point when deciding whether to make a right or left turn. I have learned that the word "allergic" can be synonymous with "neurotic," that pigeons swim, ducks workout, and that saline is preferable to silicone. I have learned that although fish is sometime "fishy," meat is rarely "meaty," and chicken is never "chickeny," Botox, on that rare occasion, can be "Botox-y." I have learned that I'm not only an asshole; I'm a "friggin' asshole," a "fucking asshole," a "stupid asshole," and an "arrogant asshole." It's hard to hold up against that kind of reinforcement.

Most importantly, I have learned how to smile while being screamed at, to laugh in the face of threats, and that patience is not only a virtue, but an acquired skill. I've always believed that I have learned more from my failures than my successes. Success is easy; ask any failure. Failure, on the other hand, requires introspection and hard work to rectify. The same is true for the difficult customer.

By my math I have fed over two million Long Islanders in the last forty years. One million, nine hundred ninety-nine thousand, nine hundred and fifteen have been wonderful; eighty-five have made this book. It is a miniscule percentage of my customer base and although their numbers are small, they are the most memorable cast of characters you will ever come to know. Having to deal with them has made me a better chef, a better restaurateur, and a better person. They have taught me the meaning of the phrase, "When given lemons, make lemonade," and have given me the gift of being able to see the humor that resides in the unimaginable circumstance.

I invite you to come meet them all: the neurotics, the psychotics, the allergic, the afflicted, the affected, the manic and the depressed, the Atkins disciples, the South Beach diet crowd, the anemic, the bulimic, the bingers and the purgers, the gastrointestinal groupies, the dreamers, the schemers, the "Is it made with cream?"-ers, and all the people who torture restaurant workers on a daily basis, seemingly just for sport. You guys rock. You are an inspiring lot, and I thank each and every one of you for providing me with such wonderful material and enriching my life in ways I would have never thought possible.

FRESH HERBS,
Tom

WARNING!

This book contains adult language and references, and as a result would probably garner an R rating if it were to be made into a movie. So, because of the inevitable language and content necessary to be true to the events of this book, I feel an overwhelming social responsibility to warn certain segments of the population.

If you are currently under the age of seventeen, over the age of one hundred seventeen, a vegetarian, a card-carrying member of PETA, a Democrat, a Republican, carrying a business card listing your forty-seven favorite allergies, in anger management therapy, salt-free, a recovering alcoholic, a raving alcoholic, enjoying the miracle known as Botox, sexually attracted to lemons, sporting a cheap toupee, a male under 5'3", use adjectives such as "tensile" to describe your favorite new Cabernet, in the clutches of menopause, or take more than three prescribed medications that end in "zak" or "zine," you may not wish to subject yourself to any further abuse, unless you find, as I do, humor in the absurd.

My First Day
On the Job

This actually took place on the opening night of a brand new restaurant called Kipling's in Farmingdale, which happened to be my very first job as a head chef. I should have known right then and there what I was getting myself into and changed careers, but the fates had a different plan for me and the rest is, as they say, history.

Kipling's was built from scratch by a very talented man who knew very little about the restaurant business. He had partnered up with a Cornell graduate who had been managing restaurants on Long Island and the Caribbean for several years. I was hired as the head chef, largely due to my ability to not let the fact that I had never had a chef's position get in the way of the delusion that I could somehow pull it off. Favoring hubris over humility, and in the possession of more balls than brains, I talked the owners into giving me the job. (Oh, and I was also willing to work for much less than the average chef salary to get a shot at my own kitchen. Just thought I'd mention that.)

Having your first head chef's position is rough enough, but I was not only biting that off, no pun intended, it was also a brand new restaurant. This meant there was no history, experienced employees, systems or procedures, or anything else to guide me through the initial days. Everything I learned there was learned the hard way, in the heat of battle, one battle at a time.

Being a brand new restaurant, we had a brand new crew. I was one of the last hires so most of the staff was already in place when I arrived. It was a few days before we were to open and everyone, both in the front and back of the house, was working feverishly, cleaning, stocking, cooking, and trying to get to know one another. I had just turned twenty-four years old and in concert with overstating my ability at the interview, I was totally overwhelmed with the enormity of opening a restaurant from scratch. Like I said before, I didn't hire any of the kitchen staff; they were already there. But I couldn't have found a wackier, more hysterical, hard-working bunch of functional abusers if I had handpicked them myself.

I had a sous-chef, a couple of cooks, a prep guy, and a dishwasher, and since none of us had ever worked together, it turned into a very interesting couple of days. The crew was looking to me for direction, which, looking back, was pretty amusing since I had no idea what I was doing either. Don't get me wrong, I was a very experienced cook, but I'd never run my own kitchen and the word delegation had not yet found its way into my vocabulary. We somehow got through a friends-and-family practice night and three nights of grand-opening parties—with an open bar that seemed to go on forever—before we were ready to debut for the public.

Here was my kitchen staff: I was a twenty-four-year-old head chef who was a reasonably good cook, but had no experience in managing a kitchen, making a schedule, or ordering food. Chuck, my sous-chef, had an associate's degree from some cooking school I'd never heard of, six month's work experience, an incredibly infectious laugh, and a penchant for drinking nine beers before breakfast. Debbie, the grill cook, was just out of cooking school and not exactly sure what a grill looked like, but she had an insane sense of humor and could outwork any of us. John, the line cook, got all his experience in the army, and you could pretty much taste it in his food. His two distinct qualities were an ability to make foie gras taste like "C" rations and an extremely limited vocabulary of mostly four letter words. He was so ridiculously vulgar and profane that you couldn't even be offended, if that makes any sense; more on that in a minute. Juan, the prep guy, was a fairly normal, well-adjusted Salvadorian man—at least until we got hold of him. And last but not least, Ernst, as we called him, (his real name was Ernie) was the last true American dishwasher. He smoked a ton of pot every day, looked like Greg Allman, and in that language that only pot smokers use, would walk around saying, "This is sooo coool, man, I love working with foood, man. Foood and tuuunes, man, foood and tuuunes. Hey, turn the radio on, man." I never had the heart to tell him that scraping it off the plate into a garbage can is not necessarily working with foood.

For better or worse, we were a team, and for four or five days, we were running around the kitchen like the Keystone Cops trying to get ready to open. This was the seventies and every night was a party, so even though we were working twelve hour days, Chuck, Debbie, and I would be out every night until 5:00 am, then get up, have breakfast (or in Chuck's case a few beers), and do it all over again. These were two of the funniest people I have ever met, so if you combine these two maniacs, a couple hundred Amstels, my silly ass, Ernst, a half ounce of weed, a Tom Waits cassette playing at ninety decibels, and John's ability to turn "Waltzing Matilda" into something disgusting, you begin to imagine what that kitchen was like. I still see Chuck from time to time and neither one of us can look at the other without breaking up, and we're talking about stuff that happened thirty years ago. It's still funny.

So there we were on opening night, each of us with a hangover the size of a small Balkan country, and on only about three hours sleep, chopping, slicing, grilling, sautéing, frying, cursing, smoking, and singing our way through the prep work for the eighty or so guests that were breathlessly awaiting the opening of yet another new restaurant. If they only knew. We had two drop-dead gorgeous sisters, Debbie and Valerie, who worked there as servers and kept coming into the kitchen to advise us of how much time we had before the first guests were to arrive. Four hours to go, three hours to go, and so on...this turned into a problem. They would distract the kitchen so much when they came in that I would lose a half hour of prep time. Chuck would turn into Rico Suave, John would say something profane, Juan would try out a broken English pick-up line, Ernst would eat a brownie, and Debbie would spend twenty minutes telling the boys that the sisters were not all that hot. Being the consummate professional, I eventually convinced the sisters to stay out of the kitchen so we could make some progress.

The first reservations were at six. To my absolute shock, by five thirty we were very close to being ready. I told Chuck and Debbie to check the stations while I had a word with the wait staff.

As I was talking to the servers, Chuck came out of the kitchen and said, "I think there's something wrong with the stoves."

"Stoves, like with an *s?*" I said.

"Yeah, stoves with an *s*."

"What's wrong?"

"I'm not sure, they don't look right."

I was thinking that this guy drinks beer for breakfast and had about eight hours of sleep all week; what could possibly look right? I followed him back to the kitchen and at first I didn't see it. As I'm staring at the ranges it dawned on me that all the flames were yellow, not blue, and just as I was about to say that to him, the fires went out one by one. The six burners, the ovens, broiler, grill, and steam table; they all just went out. I had forty people about to sit down, with forty more behind them, and I had no flame. I was paralyzed. I looked at Chuck, he looked at me, and neither one of us knew what to do.

Just when you could have cut the tension with a knife, John said, "I'll bet some woman crashed into a fucking telephone pole rushing home to get laid and fucked up the gas lines."

I must confess I never knew that gas came from telephone poles. The tension, stress, and lack of sleep combined with the most creative use of profanity I'd ever heard—not to mention the genius behind the telephone pole-gas connection—gave me maybe the hardest laugh of my life. It was a full ten minutes before any of us could speak, let alone call the gas company. As funny as this was, and it was, we still had a *huge* problem. I called the owner into the kitchen.

"We have a problem," I said.

"What's up?"

"We have no gas."

"What?"

"We have no gas."

"Did you order propane?"

"What's propane?"

"You didn't order propane?"

"I didn't know we needed propane. I've always worked with gas. Someone should have mentioned the fact that we were using propane and put it on some kind of automatic delivery. This is a first for me."

The owner said, "I'll call right now."

While we were standing in the kitchen wondering what we were going to do, my crack staff weighed in on the problem.

Chuck said, "I could use a beer."

Debbie said, "I can't wait to try out the grill."

John said, "Fucking American tech-fucking-nology."

Juan said, "Heffe, dees no so guud."

Ernst said, "Anyone for some tuuunes?"

The boss came back in and told us he had called the propane company and because it was a Saturday, they wouldn't be able to send a delivery for a couple of hours. This should have been the moment I decided to go to law school. Instead I walked out into the parking lot behind the restaurant, and as I was cursing the fates, I looked up and saw the answer to our problem right in front of my eyes: a diner. There was a diner located caddy corner to our parking lot on an adjacent street. They had a brisk breakfast and lunch business but since we were in sort of an industrial area, dinner was quiet.

I called Chuck out of the kitchen and asked, "Do you think the owner would let us use his kitchen?"

Debbie and John joined us in the parking lot. I told them that I was going to ask the owner if I could rent his kitchen for a couple of hours.

Debbie said, "Chef, you're a genius."

Chuck said, "I think you're out of your mind."

John said, "Fucking Greeks."

I ran to the diner, asked for the owner, and explained our situation about the propane, the fact that I had eighty reservations and it was opening night. I asked if could I rent out his kitchen for a couple of hours.

Surprisingly enough, he said, "Yeah, no problem. You can use it, my friend. Just clean up after yourself."

He took me into his kitchen, introduced me to his staff, and told them to help me any way they could.

I don't think I've ever received a more generous gesture in my life. I ran back to the restaurant and when I told the owner what we were planning to do, he looked at me as if I had lost my mind.

"You can't cook our menu, get the food right, then run it over here," He said.

"You have any other ideas?"

"Actually, I don't."

"Then that's what we're going to do, and be prepared to buy some cocktails. Service is going to be slow."

He just looked at me, shook his head, and went back to the dining room. Ten minutes later the servers started taking orders. They gave the orders to Chuck and Debbie who would then assemble the ingredients in a bus box. John, cursing, would then run the bus box across the parking lot, over the guardrail, and into the back door of the diner. We would then unpack the order, and together with three cooks named Nick, I would cook the order, tray it up, hand it to a waitress who would run it back over the guardrail, across the parking lot, into the kitchen, through the service station and into the dining room to be served. It really was insane, but after two successful tables, we were getting the hang of it and starting to believe that we really could pull it off. I was just getting into the zone, and I think even the Nicks were having fun, when the unthinkable happened: it started to rain.

John came into the diner with the next bus box, and he was soaked to the skin.

"It's a fucking downpour out there. Fuck this shit, this is fucking stupid. I'm soaked to my nuts."

"I don't believe this. What's next, Bell's palsy?" I said.

As one of the beautiful sisters was waiting for her tray, she took one look at John and said, "I'm not going out in that rain. No way. Uh uh. Not me."

I told her, "Look, this is no time for a mutiny. We can do this."

"I'm not serving food with wet hair and makeup running down my face."

Just as I was about to lose it, one of the Nicks, in his very thick Greek accent said, "My friend, use bag."

"What?"

"Use bag for garbage."

"What are you talking about?"

"Put bag for garbage over wait girl."

"Holy shit, that's brilliant."

We took a couple of fifty-five gallon garbage liners, cut eye holes out, put them over the servers and their trays to keep them dry, and sent them back out over the guardrail, across the parking lot, and into the restaurant. This went on for about three hours and honestly I can't remember ever having so much fun on a Saturday night.

Even the diner owner was rooting us on. Chuck was high-fiving the waitresses as they were coming through the kitchen, and Juan was marveling at some real American ingenuity. Debbie was asking if there was a grill in the diner. John was cursing the restaurant business, me, and since he completely soaked, the onset of diaper rash, and Ernst was smoking a doob and shaking his head outside by the dumpster. When it was all said and done, we had served sixty-six guests. We had ten no-shows and a party of four declined to eat with us because as they were parking their car, they saw waitresses running food across the parking lot from the diner and announced to anyone who would listen that we were serving diner food at gourmet prices.

Miraculously we only had two complaints. The first was from a man who thought his dinner could have been a little hotter, which was a perfectly legitimate complaint considering the circumstances. The second came at the very end of the night. After it was all over and we had cleaned up, I decided to go to the bar and have a drink, largely because heroin wasn't available. As I was coming down from the most adrenaline-drenched night of my young life, a woman approached me and asked if I was the chef.

"Yes," I said.

"I enjoyed my meal very much, but I do have one small complaint that I think you should know about."

"What is it?"

"The new potatoes that came with my fish were a little soggy."

"Soggy?"

"Yes, soggy."

"Well, you know, it's pouring outside."

Sourpuss

Do you believe I have a friend who would do this to me? *Steve* eats about three or four meals a week in one of my restaurants. He *is* a Mench and this is nothing that I haven't told him to his face so I'll lay it out for you right here: He's a major pain in the ass. You can hear the collective groan from the wait staff when he arrives. From the time he comes in and until he leaves, he requires the undivided attention of no less than twenty people, usually tipping for five. From the water glass to the coffee spoon, he has some kind of problem that has to be addressed, at that very moment, by a team of highly trained professionals. He thinks nothing of walking into the kitchen to explain to the pantry how he would like his salad washed, and he'll stand there yapping in the middle of service until I throw him out. He thinks he's funny, and I admit that I do get a chuckle out of it sometimes, but when you are busy you tend to lose your sense of humor.

I once told him not to come in on Monday nights anymore because it's usually the slowest night of the week, and I don't have enough servers to treat him like the king of Dubai and still take care of the normal people. He was stunned.

"Am I a pain in the ass?" he asked.

My turn to be stunned.

"Are you a pain in the ass? Are you kidding? If they had a Pain in the Ass Hall of Fame, your jersey would be hanging on the wall."

"You're hurting my feelings, dude."

"And you're killing my servers. Why are you so crazy anyway? How in the hell could you have developed that many neuroses in only forty-five years?"

"It's what makes me _me_. I've always been kind of fussy."

"A thick black hair sticking out of the end of your nose would make you _you_, but you'd likely have it removed, no? And another thing, you aren't fussy, you're a pain in the ass. There's a difference."

But he's my friend, so there you go; he's _him_, and I'm stuck with him. A mutual friend introduced us about ten years ago. Lucky me. Of all the special needs he has, there's one that's particularly irritating: he uses a boatload of lemons. He needs three pieces of lemon with his water. Then he usually has vodka on the rocks with lemon, and after that a salad with lemon on the side. Dinner is chicken, fish, or pasta, all with lemon, and an iced tea with—you guessed it—lemon. If we have a dessert made with lemon, he'll have it; if not, he'll make one by squeezing three or four lemons dry on anything served to him. He'll end the meal with decaf espresso with a lemon twist, and a warm wet napkin, with lemon, to wash his hands. I've got to be the only restaurant owner in history who, when he sees a certain customer, checks to make sure that we have at least half a case of lemons in the walk-in box. Quite a distinction, don't you think?

After saying all this, you'll be surprised to learn that it's not the amount of lemons he uses that I find so irritating. It's the fact that he has to have them cut across and not end-to-end. Most restaurants cut lemons end-to-end because you cut through the core and that keeps more of the juice in. If any of his lemons are cut end-to-end, he sends them back. I kid you not.

Once I said to him, "What's with you and the lemons? You've ruined cases of fruit on me over the years. What difference does it make whether they're cut this way or that way?"

"The juice flows out better when you cut across the fruit. And it's easier to squeeze."

"Easier to squeeze? You're not wringing out a towel. It's a lemon for God's sake. You're out of your mind."

"I am what I am."

"Yeah. Popeye with lemon issues."

The last straw came on a busy Saturday night. I came out of the kitchen, and when I looked into the dining room to see where he was sitting, I couldn't believe my eyes. The area around his table looked like a Ben-Hur movie. There must have been twenty people crowded around watching what was going on. My entire wait staff, four or five customers, a hostess, and three busboys were all watching him demonstrate how to properly cut a lemon.

"What are you doing?" I asked.

"I'm just showing them how to cut lemons."

"I'm just showing them how to cut lemons. That's great. Perfect. You've cramped up my entire restaurant on a Saturday night giving lemon cutting lessons?"

He looked at me and said, "Am I being a pain in the ass?"

THIEF IN THE NIGHT

T ease was a small restaurant that seated about fifty people, and the bar and the dining room were adjacent to one another in the same space. I thought it would be fun to frame and hang some menus of special dinners I had eaten while traveling around the world. The problem was where to hang them. We didn't want people standing in the restaurant reading them because *Tease* was a small restaurant, but we wanted to share them and thought they'd make for great decor. The brainstorm was to hang them in the bathroom so while you're sitting there, or standing as the case may be, you could pleasantly pass the time.

I had hung a menu from *Charlie Trotter's* in Chicago over the urinal. No reflection on Charlie; it just happened to fit there. I hope he's not pissed. Anyway, it was a twelve-course-tasting menu that Charlie had prepared for my girlfriend and I, and it had a lot of sentimental value. Food, when it's great, has the ability to freeze a moment in time very much like a photograph. When I looked at that menu, I was transported right back to that night in Chicago. I could remember all the different dishes, the flavors, wines, and about one third of what I had said or heard. We tend to drink a lot of fluids in the course of the night in the kitchen, so I was transported to Chicago rather frequently. I would always catch a little smile while standing there reading that menu.

One night, I decided to take a little bathroom break, and I headed for the men's room. As I walked up to the urinal, I saw that the menu wasn't hanging there. I was thinking how strange it was because it was Velcro-ed to the wall and couldn't just fall off.

I came out and asked the staff, "Who took the Charlie Menu

41

out of the men's room?" Nobody knew anything about it.

One of my waiters made the following observation, "Maybe you took it down and forgot to put it back up."

I've always believed if you're thinking something stupid, you just say it. It removes any doubt the rest of us may have had and gives a clear look at a thought process that probably shouldn't be ignored.

"That's your contribution? Maybe I forgot to put it back up?"

"I'm not trying to insult you or anything, I just thought maybe, that, you know, that maybe you forgot or something. Don't get mad at me. I was just trying to help."

I said, to him, "Could you do me a favor? If you ever see me choking, please, do not try to help. I'd hate to compound the terror of not breathing with the thought that you may be my only hope."

I went back to the kitchen, questioning my choice of careers. We had an open kitchen at *Tease* so I told all the cooks to keep an eye on the dining room in case they saw anyone with my menu. I was trying to see under the tables and had all the servers on red alert. I told them he must have put it down the back of his pants considering that anything that could be seriously injured is in the front, so if they saw anyone with an unusually flat ass walking out, to call me immediately. I'd considered a full pat down, but customers frown on that kind of thing.

No one saw anything: the damn thing vanished. I just can't imagine some guy walking out of the men's room with an 8 1/2" x 11" framed menu stuffed down his pants. Whoever took it was very smooth but the big question is, who would want it, and what possible value could it have had for anyone other than my girlfriend or me? Oh well, I still have the memory of the dinner, but it would still be nice to have the menu. I guess it's the best excuse I can think of for a return visit. The waiter left shortly thereafter. I believe he went into politics.

BUSTED

I believe that there is as much cosmetic surgery on Long Island as there is in Hollywood. If I only had it to do all over again, I may have gone to medical school. What a business that is. Having an office filled with scantily clad women sure beats checking in two hundred pounds of recently deceased fish.

I don't know if it's a media thing or what, but in the good old U.S.A., we seem to have an inflated interest in boobs. You can't go anywhere without seeing the glorification of boobs. In fact, we celebrate them. They're everywhere. They're on television, in print media, advertising, radio (Howard Stern), music videos, department store windows, sporting events, beer commercials, magazines, the Internet, and as I recently discovered, the bar at *CoolFish*. I know guys, and girls for that matter, who routinely spend ridiculous amounts of time and money in bars that feature boobs. I personally don't get it. I think if you've seen three hundred, you've seen them all, but apparently I'm part of the minority.

I was standing at the bar one night at *CoolFish*, having a glass of wine. A very nice looking party of three couples was close by, and it was hard not to eavesdrop (it's also great fun). The guys were talking about the New York Jets, and not being much of a sports fan, I tried to focus on the ladies. It was like being in an episode of *Sex in the City*. They were comparing plastic surgeons and discussing the procedures that each of them had recently undergone. It started to get a little competitive between two of the women as to whose doctor did the best work. Back and forth it went

"My guy's the best on Long Island."

"Your guy's on Long Island because he's not good enough to

work in the City."

"My guy doesn't need the City because everyone out here goes to him."

"I've seen the work he's done. He should be ashamed of himself."

"Your guy made yours too big."

"Yours are on an angle."

"Mine aren't on an angle. Yours are lopsided."

"Your guy knows nothing about Botox."

"You look like Joan Rivers. You look Botox-y."

On and on it went and then just like that, the idea came.

"Let's ask the guys."

"Okay, let's see."

Before I knew what was happening, each woman had a breast out showing it to the men in their group. This is in the middle of a packed bar on a Saturday night. Their husbands at first were taken aback but quickly recovered. One of the men in the party seemed to be giving half of one of the new augmentations an impromptu exam. I guess you have to judge on both looks and feel. Everyone got a quick look and a quick feel.

The last thing I wanted to do was to go tit for tat with a partially defrocked party of six, but someone had to do something. I did. I marched right into the office and explained to the manager that two sets of twins needed reuniting in the bar, that she needed to take care of it right away, and to keep me abreast of the situation. Rank has its privileges.

THE AUCTIONEER

We have a policy in our restaurants about gift certificates. If the amount of your gift certificate is greater than the amount of your bill, we do not give the change in cash. What we do is subtract the bill amount from the face value of the gift certificate and issue a new gift certificate for the remaining amount. It's not about giving up the cash; it's a bookkeeping nightmare.

One night a couple came in for dinner at *CoolFish*. It was a fairly busy weeknight. Diane was their waitress, and she led them through the menu and the specials for the evening. It was as normal as normal could be. They had a couple of drinks, appetizers, entrées, and they split a dessert. They lingered over coffee for a long time, talking quietly and holding hands. Diane had the impression they were on a second or third date because you can usually tell that sort of thing by the body language.

Finally, he called Diane over and said, "Can I get a check?"

Diane added up the bill and returned to present the check. As she placed it down he asked her, "Is it okay to pay this with a gift certificate?"

Diane said, "Of course."

He placed the gift certificate in the folder and Diane took it to the computer to process it. She saw that the gift certificate's amount was greater than the bill, so she had to go to the office to have a new gift certificate issued for the remaining amount.

She returned to the table and handed him the check folder with the new gift certificate inside.

He said, "I thought you got lost."

"Sorry, I had to process a new gift certificate for your change."

45

"What do you mean?"

"There was a difference in the amount of your gift certificate and the amount of your bill, so I had a new gift certificate made for that amount."

"I don't want another gift certificate. I'll just take it in cash."

Diane explained that it's not our policy to do that, and he'll have to take the gift certificate. He wasn't happy, but he also wasn't angry; he was somewhere between extremely disappointed and very sad.

He said to Diane, "That really sucks."

"Sorry. It's house policy."

"Alright. What can you do?"

We thought that would be the end of it. I should have known better. They stayed at the table for another twenty minutes or so, leaning toward each other and talking in hushed tones. He was very animated, and she was shaking her head back and forth.

Finally he looked to his left and said to the couple sitting next to them, "Excuse me. Are you going to pay your bill in cash?"

The man at the table was trying to comprehend the question. He said, "Excuse me?"

The first guy said, "I'm sorry to bother you but I paid with a gift certificate, and they gave me my change with another gift certificate, and I was hoping that if you were going to pay your bill in cash, that you would buy this gift certificate from me and use it towards your bill."

"You're kidding me, right?"

The guy said sheepishly, "No, hey, sorry, I just thought we could maybe, you know, work something out. It's not enough for a whole dinner, and I don't know when we'll be back here."

The man at the table said, "Sorry. I'm paying with a credit card."

"Okay. Thanks anyway. Sorry to bother you."

He started talking to his date again, who now had her forehead in her hand and her elbow propped on the table, staring at him in disbelief. She was still shaking her head back and forth, but now much more slowly, as the realization of what he was about to do set in.

He turned to the table on the other side and went through the same song and dance. The couple was looking at him like he was some sort of circus freak. They told him they were paying with a credit card. He started talking to his girlfriend again, but now she was staring at the floor. He then got up and started going from table to table, asking if anyone was paying with cash while explaining his problem. As insane as this was becoming, people were getting a kick out of it. The sheer shamelessness and the tenacity were something to behold. There was a buzz in the room.

On the other side of the dining room, one of the customers said with a big smile, "Hey buddy, I can help you out."

The guy said, "Really? Oh, that's great." He walked over to the man's table.

The man said, "What's that baby worth?"

"Five dollars and thirty-seven cents."

The man took some bills from his pocket, peeled off a five and handed it to our hero. He placed the billfold back in his pocket and started feeling around for change.

Our hero said to the man, "Don't worry about it. Just give me a quarter."

The Allergist's Wife

One summer Saturday afternoon at *Downtown Grille* in Montauk, I was tasting wines with one of my salesmen, looking for some new Gruner Veltliners. A couple came in and asked to see a dinner menu. After looking it over, the wife said that she would like to make a reservation. Her husband chimed in and said that he could not eat there because he was allergic to everything on the menu. I must tell you that the word "allergic," when used in a restaurant, more times than not is a synonym for "I don't like it," or "It's too expensive." (Example: Veal Chop for $42.00...Achooo!)

I told him that was fine, that not every restaurant was good for everyone, and that I understood. The woman was undeterred and after a *private* meeting in the foyer, including several four-letter words and some clenched teeth, they decided to make a reservation. Saturday night is a very busy restaurant night, as you know, and reservations usually have to be made weeks in advance.

The husband said to me, "Look, chief, I really don't want to eat here, but my wife insists so put us down for six people at eight o'clock."

Don't you just love the *chief* thing? I explained to him that I had no reservations available at eight and that all I could do for him was reserve a table at five-thirty.

He said, "That's totally ridiculous, who eats at *five-thirty*!?"

"Unless we're talking about half the population of Florida, most of the time it's people who don't already have an eight o'clock reservation," I responded.

"I don't want to come here anyway. That's unacceptable! Let's go."

The wife turned to me and said, "We'll take it."

The husband's face was so red, I suspect that if you hooked his heart up to LIPA, he could have lit up Long Island for an hour.

He turned to me and said, "Okay, you win. (*I win?*) We're coming at five-thirty and for these prices, the dinner had better be perfect!"

I told you. You can always see where these situations are headed. They returned at five-thirty, a party of six, and he was on a mission. He insisted the sodas had to be filled to the very tops of the glasses with ice on the side. He was furious that our sixteen-ounce wine glasses weren't filled to the rim. Two servers were on their hands and knees adjusting the "wobbly" table with matchbooks. Salads and appetizers were, of course, rearranged to being unrecognizable, and all the entrées came back to the kitchen at least once, some twice. And as a fitting conclusion, he announced that the desserts sucked.

He said to the server, "I made this reservation with the chef this afternoon. Is he still here?"

"Yes, sir. He's in the kitchen right now."

"Get him out here."

The server came into the kitchen and said, "Chef, the man on table twenty-three wants to see you."

I said, "What's he want; do you know?"

"No, but he's been a problem since he arrived."

"Is that the five-thirty *six top*?"

"Yup, the one and the same."

"This ought to be rich."

I went out to the table fully prepared for a fight.

He said, "This is the worst meal I have ever had in my life!"

I said, "Me too."

"Your food was disgusting!"

I got slightly offended. You may like or dislike my food; you may think it's inspired or dull, but I assure you that it's not disgusting.

I said, "Really?"

He said, "What are *we* going to do about this?"

"Do about what?"

"Do about this being one of the worst meals I've ever endured! Not one thing that came out was edible."

I said, "You know what? I've been cooking for over thirty years, and I can't remember ever going zero for six on a table. Actually zero for eighteen if you include appetizers and desserts, which you did manage to suffer through. So I think what we should do is that I'm going to go back into the kitchen, and I'm going to practice my ass off so that the next time you eat here, hopefully it will have improved."

He looked at me and said, "You're not taking anything off of this check?"

I said, "I would rather stick a fork in my eye."

I've got to tell you, at this point the service staff started doing the wave in the service station, listening to all this going on at the table. Then he decided to bring out the heavy artillery.

He said, "I just want you to know, if you don't adjust this check, that I will never, ever come back here again and…I'm telling everyone I know how horrible it was!"

This was a threat? I said, "Okay. Hold on one moment."

I went to the bar, got a napkin and a pen and wrote, "I will never come here again and neither will my friends," and brought it to the table.

I handed it to him and said, "Could you just sign this to assure me that you are serious?"

"You think I'm kidding around here? We are never coming back here unless you pick up this check!"

"Oh, I heard you. Everyone heard you, and in fact I've never seen my staff quite so giddy. I'll just need a signature so that if you change your mind I'll have some legal recourse."

He said, "You're a fucking asshole."

Want to open a restaurant yet?

Veg Head

This one made the book because in my experience, it is unique. One night a woman and her husband sat down for dinner. I swear I can spot a vegetarian from forty-feet away. Many of them don't look healthy. How ironic is that? They spend way more time worrying about sickness, sunlight, and humane animal husbandry than they should. All that hand-wringing seems to result in low weight, pale skin, and in most cases, glasses. It's hard to put on weight eating alfalfa sprouts and B-12 capsules, impossible to get color avoiding the outdoors, and reading all that PETA literature can certainly cause diminished eyesight.

I know that I'm generalizing, and I must confess that it doesn't apply to *every* vegetarian. I know two who are the picture of health. But the chances are high that if you look around a dining room, the person who weighs less than a European supermodel, has the pallor of Morticia Addams, and has a pair of pharmacy-bought 2.25 specials perched on the end of their nose, there's a strong possibility that person is a vegetarian.

Back to the story. The woman said to the server, "I'm a vegetarian. Do you have anything I can eat?"

The server asked her, "Do you eat fish?"

"No. I just told you I'm a vegetarian."

He said, "I know but some vegetarians eat fish."

"I don't, so is there anything for me to eat?"

"Yes, we have a grilled and roasted vegetable plate. How's that? It's actually very good."

"What's on it?"

"Faro, potatoes, roasted peppers, spinach, beets, mushrooms, asparagus, fennel, and hummus."

"I don't like hummus, could I have something else instead?"

He asked, "What would you like?"

"What do you have?"

"How about we give you some dried cherry chutney?"

"Great. I'm also not crazy about beets. What else can I have?

"I could ask the chef to substitute carrots maybe."

She said, "Carrots would be fine. Oh, and would you mind asking him if he would give me broccoli rabe instead of the asparagus? I saw that you were serving that with something else. Asparagus makes my urine smell."

He said, "Well, we can't have that now can we? I don't see that being a problem, the broccoli rabe that is, not the smelly urine."

"That would be great. I don't mean to be a pest, but I wasn't feeling well some months ago, and I went to a healer, you know, someone who deals in alternative medicine, and he put me on a vegetarian diet, gave me some herbal extracts, and I've never felt better."

The server then said, "That's great. One veggie platter with no hummus, chutney instead, carrots replacing the beets, and broccoli rabe instead of the asparagus for reasons I can't believe we were discussing, coming up."

Vegetarianism is a religion of sorts, just as dogmatic, and like religion, the recent converts are usually the most zealous. They always seem to need to tell total strangers something about the event that sent them to the asparagus altar, occasionally mentioning the unconscionable treatment of veal, and certain bodily processes no one wants to discuss. Go forth and spread the word.

The server sent the order into the kitchen and followed it in. He said, "Hey Chef-o, I've got a fussy vegetarian out there with that veg plate, so could you make sure it's served just how I ordered it?"

Believing the term non-fussy vegetarian to be an oxymoron, I pronounced his question rhetorical, and said we would do our best.

He added, "I'm just giving you a heads-up. I've got a feeling about this one."

We paid careful attention to the veg plate and made all the changes that she asked for. It was a challenge of sorts so we were having fun with it, and when it was ready to be served it was, in a word, gorgeous. I called the server into the kitchen to pick up the order. We were sending out, as far as I was concerned, the finest veg plate ever made, for those who keep records of such things.

I said, "That ought to do it, no?"

He said, "I can only hope so."

Guess what. Five minutes later, he returns to the kitchen with the veg plate. He throws it on the serving line and says, "She doesn't want it. I told you I had a feeling about this one."

I asked him, "What was wrong with it? We made it just like she asked us to."

He said, "Chef, you are not going to believe this one!"

"Dude, I've heard them all."

"With all due respect, I don't think you're quite ready for this."

"Believe me, I've heard 'em all man. Hit me with it."

He looked at me and, pronouncing every word very slowly, said, "The woman doesn't want it because there are too many vegetables on it. Now she tells me she'll have the gnocchi but with the broccoli rabe instead of the asparagus. Asparagus, it seems, makes her urine smell. Did I mention that before?"

I said, "That's it, I surrender."

Say No To Crack

Some people, whether it's because of karma, ignorance, or the fact that they may have been raised by wolves, just can't get the whole social-grace-in-public thing together. What you do in the privacy of your own home—or *den* as the case may be—is certainly your business, but what you do in public should be governed by rules of decorum. Your right to be an asshole has to be weighed against my right to not care to be affected by you *being* an asshole. It's really just the "yelling fire in a crowded theater argument" applied to eating out. The rest of us shouldn't have to endure the boorish behavior of others just because they are unaware or unwilling to act in a civilized manor. I don't believe it would be tolerated in any other environment without the mandatory two-week sensitivity training imposed by those claiming to be, ironically, the most tolerant among us. (Wink.)

We need some sort of required class in high school to teach basic etiquette. I'm not talking complicated stuff here like finger bowls, fish knives, or how to eat fugu without dying, but it seems to me that if we can take the time to teach sixteen-year-old students how to have sex, which I'm sure most of them have figured out by now, why can't we teach them not to talk and chew at the same time? Just teach simple manners; it's way more useful than knowing how to diagram a sentence. The fact that I don't know what year Washington crossed the Delaware has had no meaningful effect on my life to date, but knowing that blowing your nose at the dinner table is likely to upset some folks has no doubt spared me the horrified countenance of more than one dinner date.

Get my drift? The man you're about to meet never attended

the previously discussed classes, but he did manage to stretch my tolerance to the limit while making me laugh out loud. For the two people on the planet who don't know what plumber's crack is, let me describe it for you. Plumber's crack is simply that bare patch between the top of a pair of low-riding pants and the bottom of a high-riding shirt. Oh, it's a beautiful sight. The funny thing is, you never see it on anyone like Gisele Bundchen, which would make it model's crack, and therefore highly addictive. No, it's always a guy who is too short for his weight with the body hair of a silverback gorilla, and most times he's kneeling behind someone else's toilet.

Tease was a small restaurant that seated about fifty people, and the bar and the dining room were adjacent to one another in the same space as I said before. This guy came to meet some friends for dinner. He was a little early so he said to the hostess, "I'm meeting some friends and they're not here yet, so I'll just wait at the bar and have a drink."

The hostess turned and said, "The bar is right this way," and when he passed her, it was the first time any of us noticed it.

We have a very clothes-conscious clientele, so to see a man showing that much skin was unusual. She started to giggle and headed to the window of the open kitchen to report in.

She said to me, "Check out the back of that guy's pants. He's got plumber's crack."

I looked over to the bar where he was standing, and it seemed like the back of his pants were down around his knees.

I said to the hostess, "That can't possibly be comfortable," and the two of us broke up in conspiratorial hysterics.

The dining room was filling up, so I said to the hostess, "You better get back *behind* the podium; I'll keep an eye on that *asshole*." Cheese ball humor, absolutely, but it achieved the desired effect.

Neither of us could look at one another for the next hour.

The guy then says to the bartender, "I'll have a Dewar's on the rocks with a twist," and plopped his half naked rear end on one of the stools. Leaning his elbows on the bar, this motion raised the back of his shirt, and he proceeded to moon the entire dining room and half of western Europe. It was what I would call a room with a view. It looked like a cross between a side of beef that was hit with an axe, and a convenient place to park your bicycle.

As I marveled at the sight, I knew I had to do something.

I called the hostess and said, "Can you discreetly take a picture of that with your cell phone?"

She said, "Are you out of your mind? I can't do that. Why would you want to memorialize that, anyway?"

"If we could get a picture of that ass, and blow it up to poster size with the words, "Say No to Crack," we'd be retired in sixty days. This is the money making opportunity of the century staring us right in the puss, and I'm sure they could airbrush out the lint."

She was useless for the rest of the night. From where I was standing in the open kitchen, I could see that I wasn't the only one who was amused. Some people were laughing, some were staring, but everyone noticed.

These situations are delicate. You don't want to embarrass anyone, but by the same token, you don't want anyone to have to see someone's rather large and hairy ass while eating dinner, lint or no lint. I was about to go out and tell him to—well—the truth is, I really didn't have any idea what I was going to tell him, but it became a moot point when his friends arrived. He paid his check at the bar and the party was seated in the dining room. He was still showing a lot of skin, but it was now facing the bar at chair level so it wasn't as noticeable.

I've been a keen observer of human behavior for a very long period of time. My experience has been that quirky people are very rarely limited to one or two quirks; they usually have a shitload. If I see someone acting or dressing unusually, I remain a bit wary because I know there's probably more to come.

As the guy was looking over the menu, he removed his shoes from his sock-less feet. He then began what turned out to be a self-administered, ten-minute foot massage. I can only imagine the stress on one's feet while trying to decide whether to have the fluke or the pork loin.

He finished the massage and ordered his dinner; I believe it was the fluke. He then took his cocktail napkin and, for some quirky reason, wiped only his left big toe, crumpled the napkin into a ball, and tossed it over his right shoulder toward the bar. Are you kidding me?

The bartender was standing there in a complete state of disbelief, I was in the kitchen with my mouth open, and the hostess was later hospitalized for observation. We couldn't believe what we were seeing. Who could?

The bartender came into the kitchen and said to me, "Okay, you've got to go say something to that guy."

"What do you want me to say? I've never before told anyone to pull up your pants, stop wiping your toe, put your shoes back on, and pick up your napkin. That doesn't sound quite right to me. It doesn't really flow, if you know what I mean."

"Tom, he wiped his toe with a napkin that he threw at me," and then he broke up laughing.

"See, you can't even say it to me with a straight face. How do you expect me to survive that at the table?"

"Coward."

I said, "Just go put on some rubber gloves and pick up the napkin, and if he does it again, call me and I'll go out there and kick his ass. I certainly won't have any trouble finding it."

The guy behaved himself for the duration of the meal, so I never had to go out and say anything to him. Frankly, I'm surprised no one at his table said anything either, but like I've said before, with some behavior, there's not much you *can* say. Besides, I don't think that I could have said anything without cracking up anyway, *ha ha*, so that would pretty much take the sting out of the discipline routine.

He wound up finishing his dinner and leaving without anyone getting hurt.

Everyone was saying, "Did you see that? Do you believe that guy?"

I said, "Yeah, for a minute there I thought we were going to have the only restaurant on Long Island with a naked dining section."

I'm sure if I turned up the heat a little and hung a sign that said, "No Pointing or Laughing," half of Field 6 (the naked beach at Jones Beach) would show up.

Mistaken Identity

Anyone familiar with the Yiddish word *chutzpah* will get a kick out of this. A woman walked into *CoolFish* on a very busy Friday night without a reservation. My sister Ann, who at the time was manager at one of my other restaurants, happened to be filling in for a hostess who had called in sick. Sometimes things just work out that way.

There was a huge crowd of people around the hostess desk asking about their reservations, confirming that their parties had arrived, and threatening the occasional lawsuit for being seated two seconds after their scheduled time.

A woman sliced her way through the assembled lynch mob, approached the hostess desk with a confident stride, and announced, "Table for four."

Ann looked up asked, "Do you have a reservation?"

"No. Do you think I need one?"

"Yeah, we're very busy tonight. I don't have a table right now, but if you would like to wait at the bar, I may be able to get you seated in about a half an hour."

Check this out. The woman hesitated for a moment then looked Ann dead in the eye and said, "How about the little fact that I'm Tom's sister. Does that change your mind about my table there, honey?"

Ann was flabbergasted. I do have two other sisters, but unfortunately for the woman, Ann knows what they look like.

"You are who?"

"I'm Tom's sister and I would like a table immediately."

"You're Tom's sister."

"Yes."

Ann said, "You're talking about Tom Schaudel, the guy who owns the place, right? The chef?"

"Yes, the one and the same. Tom, he's my brother."

Ann broke into a broad grin. "You know, I'm Tom's sister, too, and come to think of it, I haven't seen you at any family gatherings lately. How have you been? Even better, where have you been?"

Not even batting an eye, the woman looked Ann and said "Well you can't blame me for trying. I guess we'll just have to wait at the bar." What are the chances?

Urine a New Job

A new waitress was working her first Saturday night at *CoolFish*. She had come to us recommended by a chef friend with whom she had worked. He told us that she was a great worker and great with people (the latter part being of utmost importance, since five to twelve percent of the people we deal with on a daily basis are certifiably insane, depending on which server you ask).

The restaurant she came from had great food and a loyal following but it was very small. *CoolFish* is not. *CoolFish* is rather big and very busy on Saturday nights. It's like the difference between an argument and World War II. The transition can be difficult for some servers. I think the expression, "A deer in the headlights," pretty much summed up her demeanor. She was very nervous because it was her first night, and I'm sure she wanted to make a great first impression.

She was waiting on a party of six. She brought out the drinks without any problems. She then took and brought out the appetizer orders without a hitch. Finally, she took the main course orders and I think at that point she was beginning to relax. There were a few special requests, but nothing she or the kitchen couldn't handle.

Fifteen minutes later, the busboys cleared the appetizer plates. Five minutes after that, the food runners brought out their main courses, and the waitress stepped up to the table, uttering the nine words she would forever remember.

"Is there anything else I can do for you?"

A woman at the table looked up and said, and I kid you not, "Yes. Go to the ladies' room, reserve me a booth, and hold it until I get there because I'm not waiting in line to pee."

Who thinks like this?

The waitress said, "You've got to be kidding me, right?"

"Do I look like I'm kidding?"

"No. Come to think of it, you don't."

The woman then said, and this is word for word, "Listen you, I'm dead serious. Now get away from this table and get me that booth. Get going. Now!"

She's going all right: going straight to heaven.

QUIT YER WHINING

The popularity of wine has exploded, and everyone is into wine. That's great for me for a couple of reasons. First of all, I love wine; sometimes too much. I also love to share wine and some of the knowledge I've managed to retain over the years. Wine can also change the perception of a bad habit. It has—unlike beer, whiskey, or drugs—a birth year, a pedigree, a grape varietal, and it is the world's only living beverage. Wine is actually alive in the bottle. This makes for interesting conversation. Adjectives are thrown around wildly, and there are discussions, to the point of pain, about legs, noses, and finishes. Wine elevates drinking alcohol to noble endeavor. If you and I drink two bottles of tequila, we're two morons, but if we drink two bottles of *Pinot Noir*, we're two aristocrats. Same buzz, different perception.

Secondly, I get to sell it to a willing clientele, and that means occasionally I make a profit. Here's a quick lesson: Winemakers are moving away from using corks to seal their wines. There are a couple of reasons for this. The first is there is a serious cork shortage; they are literally running out of cork. Secondly, and more importantly, about ten percent of corks fail, allowing air to penetrate and spoil, or oxidize, the wine. They have tried, to some degree of success, plastic and rubber corks, but it is common knowledge that the only foolproof method of preserving wine in the bottle is with the dreaded screw cap. It's not a real sexy solution, but it's one hundred percent effective and practical as hell.

When a wine has been spoiled by oxygen due to cork failure, the term to describe the spoiled wine is "corked." Once a wine is corked, the wine is assumed to be undrinkable and for restaurant purposes, un-sellable. Many fine winemakers have gone to screw caps already, and many more will soon follow. I predict in twenty years, all wine will be screw-cap sealed. It removes the ceremony of a waiter "romancing" a cork from the bottle at the table, and screw caps have always been associated with cheap wine, but I think eventually it will come to be universally accepted. More importantly, it will save us from all that spoiled wine.

For background information, we have thirty wines by the glass at *CoolFish*. Our policy is that we will let you taste any of them before buying one to make sure that you are happy with the selection. Armed with that information, we proceed. A woman ordered a bottle of Kim Crawford Un-oaked Chardonnay from New Zealand. It has a screw-cap. The waiter brought the bottle to the table and presented the wine.

The woman said, "That's great."

He unscrewed the cap, to the horror of the guest, and poured a taste. She said that it was fine, but the look on her face suggested otherwise. About five minutes later, it became apparent that she had a problem. She was suspicious of the screw-cap and didn't want the wine, but she needed a reason to send it back.

We'll always take a wine back, no questions asked, if a customer doesn't want it because we want them to leave happy, but some people still feel compelled to create the illusion that they are savvy, and have a perfectly good reason for returning a perfectly good wine. People who are truly wine savvy never send wine back unless it's corked or badly faded. The rule is: You buy it, you drink it. If you want to window shop, go to Macy's.

She called me over and said, "There's a problem with this wine, I can't drink it."

"What's wrong with it?"

"It's corked."

(Heh, heh, heh.) Me, trying to look serious, "I don't think it could be corked."

She said, "I know wine and this wine is corked."

"That's amazing because there's never been a cork in that bottle. It has a screw-cap, so while I'm perfectly willing to consider that your wine may be 'screwed,' it's certainly not 'corked.' But if you don't like it, we'll take it back, and I'll bring you a wine-by-the-glass list so you can taste them before you buy them to be sure you like what you get."

She said, "Fine."

She looked over the list and said, "I'd like to try the Sauvignon Blanc."

We brought a taste.

She said, "Nah, maybe the Chardonnay."

We brought the Chardonnay.

She tasted it and said, "No. How about the Gruner Veltliner."

We brought the Gruner.

"It's too spicy. I'll try the Pinot Grigio."

We brought out the Pinot Grigio.

"Too dry. Maybe the Riesling."

We brought the Riesling

"Sorry."

To make a long story short, she tried eighteen tastes out of thirty possible wines.

The waiter finally went to the table and said, "So have you landed on one you like yet?" She said, "No, but I can't drink any more because I have to drive home."

WIGGED OUT

Here's a date story. Apparently we have very romantic restaurants. I've written extensively about some of the hijinks that go on, but this one is a little different.

One of our bar regulars, who is in every day, is an intelligent, fun, sweet, and recently divorced man. He's also quite a character and that you'll just have to trust me on. I love the guy. So does Mark, the bartender. We argue politics all the time, breaking every drinking rule there is, but it never gets to the point of anger and it's always great fun. And of course I'm always right.

One day he was sitting at the bar and this woman, who was very attractive in a Billy Idol kind-of-way, walked in. They started a conversation and were talking and laughing—and drinking. Some people subscribe to the fact that absence makes the heart grow fonder; I believe *martinis* make the heart grow fonder.

A couple of martinis later, the couple became a couple and hung out all night. This was one of those "hook-ups" where everyone—except the happy couple—knew it didn't have a prayer of working out. He's a very mild-mannered, gentle, middle-aged, upper-middle-class professional. She's younger, edgy, confident, and looks—well—she looks like Billy Idol.

They went out a couple of times. I guess it was going okay; then something went wrong, end of story; the end of the relationship.

One night Mark said to him, "Hey, you still seeing that woman?"

Joe said, "No."

Mark said, "She must have gone into the witness protection program or something. We haven't seen her in a while."

I said, "Maybe she's touring Asia with the band."

Joe said, "That's not funny."

I said, "Sorry, sometimes I have these 'Idol' thoughts."

Mark and I cracked up; he didn't. The three of us were sitting there at the bar talking and who walked in but "Billy Idol." Mark saw her and gave me a subtle nod, careful not to let on. She saw the customer, stopped dead in her tracks, spun around, and left. Mark said nothing, I said nothing, and the customer never saw her.

Five minutes later, the front door opened. In walks Billy Idol with a wig on that makes her look like Ginger from *Gilligan's Island*. I swear I'm not kidding. She sat down three stools away from Joe and ordered a drink; a Martini, I believe.

Two martinis later, the regular looked at her and nodded a polite hello. He didn't recognize her. Mark was wetting his pants.

She had a drink at the bar. A guy came in to meet her and had another drink at the bar with her. They paid their check and went to the dining room for dinner.

An hour passed, and Mark couldn't contain himself any longer. He said to Joe, "Did you see that woman that was just here?"

He said, "Yeah, she was nice looking."

Mark said, "That was the woman you were just seeing."

He almost fell off his chair, which actually isn't all that uncommon for him.

He said, "Get the hell out of here."

He refused to believe it at first, but as time passed, curiosity got the best of him. The problem was, how do you nonchalantly walk past a table of two, staring at the woman, and not get knocked out? We finally convinced him it was her. I don't know if he was more upset about her being on a date or not recognizing her. But two nights later, he made a remarkable recovery with a woman who loves martinis and who looks nothing like any rock star I know.

More Whining

I have a customer whose sole purpose in life is to ensure I don't make a profit, and he's very good at it. He's a very successful guy and very nice, but it absolutely kills him that I make a living selling him food and wine. He comes in quite frequently, and he'll always whine about the price of wine by the glass. We have thirty selections, priced between six and twenty-five dollars. They're all too high. If I had a glass of wine for $1.35, he would feel ripped off. The man throws nickels around like they're manhole covers.

The funny thing is, he's in a tough spot. He lives alone, can't cook, and his estimated net worth is about $220 million. I laugh like hell because it drives him crazy to pay restaurant prices for wine and food, but he has little choice. Since he's resigned to the fact that he has to eat out, he has designed some ingenious ways to save money and to make sure, at the end of the day, that I don't make one dime more than I'm entitled to. Which, I'm already on the record as stating, isn't much.

Check out the moves. He'll order a glass of wine and finish almost all of it. When the bartender sees very little left and asks if he would like another, he'll say, "Just give me a splash." To him a splash is the metric equivalent of six ounces. You see, no one can be expected to pay for a splash, so he'll have six or seven splashes in the course of a night. Shamu doesn't splash as often.

Here's another: order a dinner, eat three quarters, and send it back.

"Would you like something else?"

He'll say, "No, I lost my appetite. Just take it off the check."

And yet another: When there's nothing he can think of to

complain about, he will eat, along with his dinner, twelve seven-grain rolls and four pounds of marinated olives just to make sure I lose money. He will often bring in his own wines because we don't charge a corkage fee for regular customers. He never checks his coat and never tips a dime over double the tax. He expects a free dinner on his birthday, which comes about seven times a year, and if he brings in a large group of people, he expects his dinner to be on the house.

It's always been a comic wonder to me how someone could amass a $220 million fortune while spending so much time and energy personally making sure that I don't. The really funny part is that he's convinced he's one of my best customers. It's hilarious. He always tells me, "I'm here all the time. What would you do without me?"

I've always thought, "Gee, I don't know, make a living?" All in all, he's not a bad guy, just nuts, but funny nuts.

Anyway, one night he came in with a date. He can't let her see the cheap side, right off the bat, if he wants to make a decent impression. He called me ahead of time, telling me he had a date for the first time in a long time, and asked if we'll make a big VIP deal when he arrives. Then he asked me to choose a really fine wine for them. Something in the thirty to thirty-five dollar range, and could I extend the *Prix-Fixe* ($26.95) dinner to seven p.m., because he couldn't possibly pick her up and get there by six-thirty. The *Prix-Fixe* menu is in effect from five p.m. to six-thirty p.m. to try to stimulate early business. It's a three-course dinner for $26.95 and targets seniors and early diners, not multimillionaires.

"No problem," I told him.

He arrived, we made a huge deal for him, and sat him at table eight, the romantic/power table. I chose a Liberty School Cabernet Sauvignon for them, which sells for thirty-five dollars. It's the second label of Caymus Vineyards, and I believe a great wine for the money.

They ordered their appetizers and as the waiter was bringing the wine to the table, another customer, who apparently knew my buddy, stopped him and said, "I'm a friend of Mr. Smith's, and I would like to buy him and his date a drink."

The waiter said, "He's just ordered this bottle of wine."

The man said, "Okay, then put that wine on my tab. I'd like to buy it for him."

The waiter said, "Okay, no problem."

The waiter proceeded to the table, and as he presented the bottle to my buddy, said, "That gentleman over there would like to buy your wine." As the waiter presented the wine, and without as much as a second's hesitation, he looked at the Liberty School Cabernet Sauvignon ($35.00) and said, "That's not what I ordered. I ordered the Phillip Togni Cabernet ($225.00). He scammed his friend, who was trying to be nice and buy him a bottle of wine, and upgraded himself to a wine he would have never dreamed of paying for himself. I mean the guy never flinched, although I suspect his friend did when he saw the check.

After dinner he pulled me aside to tell me what he did and said, "See, what other customer would do for you what I do?"

I said, "Probably no one."

He said, "You made an extra one-hundred-dollar profit on the deal.

I said, "Wow, that's great. How can I ever thank you?"

He said, "You can buy me a drink."

BARRED FROM DRINKING

A woman wanted to book a shower at *CoolFish*. The problem was that she essentially wanted it for free. She carried on, "How much is this, how much is that. That's too expensive. Can't you do any better?" Where are we, Juárez?

After an hour of intense negotiating, I was exhausted. She wore me out. She ultimately settled on a basic party package, but decided there would be no alcohol served because you have to pay for it. We were all looking forward to a nice dry shower.

About a week before the party, the phone calls started. With only seven days left until the party, she put on a full-court press to lower the price.

She asked, "How about cutting your staff a little, would that lower the price? What if we don't use waitresses and we serve ourselves, would that lower the price? What if we don't turn on the air conditioner, would that lower the price?"

I said, "Why don't you have it in the parking lot? That would certainly shave it down a tad." (I know what you all are thinking, but I couldn't possibly make this up.) I think we said three or four "Nos." I really don't remember.

The big day came. The party was to start at one o'clock. At 12:55, the woman arrived. She walked in the front door, stopped dead in her tracks, pointed at the bar and screamed three or four times, "What's that! What's that! What's that!"

Stunned, we said, "What's *what?*"

She said, "What is that!"

I was looking around, half-expecting to see an ax murderer. I had no idea what she was pointing at.

73

Finally, I said again, "What's *what?*"

"That!"

"You mean the bar?"

"Yes, the bar. You have to get it out of here. If my guests see it, they'll order a drink."

"Get it out of here? Where would you have me put it?"

"I don't know, but it's got to go."

Okay, let's say we can find a spot for those 427 bottles of liquor in the next three minutes; don't you think the big mirrors, a forty-foot shelf, and those fourteen stools are a dead giveaway?"

She said, "Can't you cover them with tablecloths or something!"

"You're kidding."

"Do I look like I'm kidding?"

We said, as the realization began to sink in, "She ain't kidding."

So there we were, covering the entire bar with tablecloths, when one of the waiters asked the obvious question. "What are you doing?"

We gave him the obvious answer, "Covering the bar."

"Why?"

We told him, "The woman doesn't want her guests seeing the bar. She's afraid they'll order drinks. And I couldn't get a Hollywood set builder to fly out here on an hour's notice to make it look like Dry Gulch."

"You mean the woman who's throwing the party?"

"Yeah."

He said, "Hey Chef, you're not going to believe this. She just asked me for a glass of ginger ale."

I said, "So give it to her. What's the big deal?"

The waiter was now hysterical. He said, "No, listen to me. You don't get it. She wants it as a mixer."

"What are you talking about?"

"Chef, she has a flask of booze in her pocketbook, and she's sneaking drinks when no one's looking." I'm still in therapy and healing very slowly.

SHORTAGE OF
CUSTOMERS

I never thought I would be writing about someone in my own profession, but I guess bad behavior knows no job description. Here's the deal. There's an ironclad, steadfast rule in this business: you never, ever, under any circumstances, at any time, for any reason, poach someone else's employee. It's just not done. Not once, never. If someone applies for a job from another restaurant, I want a phone call from that owner saying everything's cool. Period. I've just learned not everyone thinks that way.

In a restaurant I've opened recently (hint, hint), the owner of a restaurant down the block stopped in. I was thinking, what a nice guy, he came to wish us luck, which is what a classy person would do. He came over and said hello, talked for a couple of minutes, and then did a curious thing: he went to the bar and ordered a half-glass of wine.

I've got to say something here and some of you may think I'm being bitchy: the man is short. Really short. Still, if you're over 5'2", you should be able to drink one glass of wine. He finished his wine and left.

The next night, it was the same routine. He had a half-glass of wine, and he was whispering to the bartender nursing his drink and looking around the dining room. Two nights later, I took a manager and a hostess over to his place and ordered a bunch of *apps*, four bottles of wine (they were out of the first two we chose), then overtipped and left. That's just restaurant etiquette. That's how most owners behave in someone else's restaurant.

The next day, he changed his tactics. He walked by the window, counting our customers. He seemed to be obsessing over how many customers we had each night. It was getting funny. He followed that pattern for several days, walking past the window and counting. We actually started a one-dollar pool to guess what time he would pass by.

Then, just when we thought we had him figured out, he changed the routine again. He came in the next day, ordered his half-glass of wine, walked through the dining room talking on a cell phone, and pretended to go to the men's room-six times. I don't care how short you are; you can't pee six times on a half-glass of wine. He followed this new routine for several more days.

The next day we were getting ready for service, and I went out to the bar. My staff was talking about him saying, "Do you believe that guy?"

I said, "What's up?"

They told me that whenever he would come in, he would say to them, "Why are you wasting your time here when you could work for me? Why don't you bag this job and come down the block."

I'm always the last to know. He even asked my girlfriend to work for him when she was briefly helping me out. I guess nothing is sacred.

The funny thing was that all of my employees were laughing at the guy. And I wasn't really upset; I was more bewildered.

I was thinking, "You're a big (little) restaurant owner. Shoot the lock off your safety deposit box and run a twenty-five dollar ad on Craigslist. Come on, dude. I've had it up to here with you." (Try to picture my hand cutting across my navel.)

Oh, and you should at least tip twenty percent on a half-glass of wine.

Cheers.

ONE FOR MY BABY
AND ONE MORE FOR THE ROAD

I've always been a fan of quality over quantity. It's not for everyone, but for me that's the deal. I know people who judge restaurants by how many sandwiches they can make from the doggie bag. Not for me, but for some of my customers, it's all that counts.

A woman came into *CoolFish*, sat at the bar, and ordered a glass of wine. We serve five to six ounces (an industry standard pour) in a sixteen-ounce glass to allow the wine to breathe.

Mark served it to her, and she looked at him like he just insulted her mother.

She said, "What's that?"

Mark said, "Pinot Noir."

She said, "Where's the rest of it?"

"The rest of it?"

"Yeah, the rest of it. Fill it to the top."

Mark said, "That's a half bottle of wine. We serve it in a large glass so it can breathe."

"I don't need it to breathe; I need it full."

Mark, who has heard it before said, "Okay, bombs away."

He filled it to the top and walked away. Three or four minutes later, he saw her trying to get his attention.

Mark looked at her and said, "Yes?"

She said, "How am I going to drink this? It's too full."

"You asked me to fill it."

"Well, now I'm asking you to un-fill it and put it in two glasses."

She now had two glasses of wine, both about the size of a single serving, but it was good material for me so we went with it.

Here's the rub: I don't mind losing the glass of wine, but now she's had one glass of wine that was sixteen ounces. That's a good amount if you're planning to drive. She may be a pain in the butt, but she doesn't deserve an accident or a DWI. You could probably blow .08 NYS blood alcohol content after sixteen ounces of wine, depending on your body weight, and she was petite. That's something I always thought was patently unfair. Someone who is in great shape at, say, 150 pounds could blow .08 or higher after two glasses of wine, where someone who is out of shape at, say, 300 pounds may only blow .05 after two glasses of wine. It's just not right, and it makes a strong case for not exercising.

Here's a better idea. Why don't we develop a handicap system for drinkers like they have for golfers? In golf your handicap is the average, minus a small percentage, of your most recent scores. The higher your scores, the higher your handicap; the lower your scores, the lower your handicap. They use these as adjustments to make the betting or a tournament more fair. People who drink on a regular basis would naturally have lower handicaps because, presumably, practice makes perfect, so they would be better at handling it. On the other hand, if you drink infrequently or tend to make an ass of yourself when you do—driving off bridges or singing *"Danny Boy"* on karaoke night—your handicap would be higher, and that number would alert the rest of us as to what to expect after your third cocktail. It would also make it easier for the police to gauge what kind of shape you're in when they pull you over.

"Good evening sir. Can I see your license, registration, insurance, and handicap cards? Oh, you're a 27 handicap? Could you please step out of the car."

I'm a professional, so I would be considered a scratch drinker; a zero handicap. I've practiced long and hard to get good at it, and I should not be held to the same standards as a 17 or 22 handicap should be. I know zero handicap drinkers that could complete the Indy 500 at .08 without a problem. A zero handicap drinker blowing .08, and a 22 handicap drinker blowing .08 are two completely different .08s. Trust me: I see it on a daily basis. The high handicap drinkers don't practice as much and therefore are not as accomplished as we professionals. You'll never see a zero handicap drinker running through a party naked with a lampshade on their head. That's a high handicap move. Give it some thought. I believe the idea has some merit. It works for golf, why not drinking?

Anyway, the woman drank both glasses of wine and ordered another; another *two* that is. She then got up, and while bringing back the lost art of staggering, headed for the ladies' room, wobbling all the way in her Jimmy Choos. I don't understand how women walk in those things to begin with, do you? She wasn't really drunk, she just could have used a pair of sneakers.

After ten minutes, she came out, returned to the bar, and had one more sip of her glass of wine. Make that *two* glasses of wine. Or was it one glass? I'm confused; whatever. She took a sip.

Mark asked, "Are you okay?"

"I'm fine."

And she was. She paid her check and walked into the lobby. Then she did a curious thing. She then took her shoes off, placed them on the floor, rubbed her aching feet, and left.

One hour later, another customer left the bar to go home. He went into the lobby, turned around to the bar, and said, "Someone left a pair of high heels in the lobby."

Mark said, "Really?"

The customer said, "Yeah, they're right here."

"Give them to me. I'm sure she'll be right back to get them."

That was the last we saw of her. She never came back. It's hard to imagine someone doing the *walk of shame* through the parking lot with no shoes. Or better yet, forgetting you didn't have them on in the first place, but then again, I'm a scratch drinker.

ONE HOUR
MARTINI-IZING

I have a soft spot for seniors. I was lucky enough to have two sets of the best grandparents that anyone could possibly ask for. They were loving, kind, nurturing, selfless, and a blast to hang out with as a child. They spoiled me rotten. The only things I couldn't do when I was with them were things that were bad for me or could otherwise have caused me harm. Those memories are evoked when I see seniors today, and I feel a natural affection and a sense of protectiveness toward them. Not that they need it, of course, but it's something I just can't help.

So, just like when a loving grandparent would not let a child do anything to harm himself, I've recently thought about instituting a policy in all my restaurants that will not allow anyone with an AARP card to order a Martini. Call it tough love.

Here's a quick word on martinis: A Martini is an attitude, not a cocktail. Four to five shots of liquor in a glass is not a drink, it's a roadside bomb. Martinis are the express train to stupidity. The only reason they gave the damn thing a name is because you couldn't have some socialite (strange job description, don't you think?), dripping in diamonds and wearing a designer gown, asking a bartender for a glass of gin. How crass. So instead, they ask for a "Martini." It's a more civilized way to order, and very *chic*, but also very strong. A Martini is what you order when you need to get the job done and time is an issue.

Another reason for seniors to avoid martinis is flexibility. They don't possess as much as when they were younger and one's body may be required to move in several conflicting directions at the same time. There's nothing sadder than watching an eighty-year-old walking to the restroom like he's on one of the crab boats from the show *The Deadliest Catch*.

Here's what made me consider the ban. A party of five arrived for dinner one Sunday night. It was Mom, Dad, the two kids, and Grandma. They looked like the perfect family.

The server asked, "Anyone care for a drink?"

Grandma said, "I think I'll have a Martini."

The server returned with the drinks and prepared to take their dinner order. Grandma slammed down the first Martini and ordered another. The server returned with the second Martini, finished getting the dinner order, took the menus, and left.

Grandma drank the second Martini before the appetizers arrived. I was told that as she was finishing her second, she got this really dreamy look on her face, and as she tipped the glass up to drain the last couple of drops, she leaned back and went ass-over-head onto the floor, out cold. All hell broke loose at the table. The parents were trying to deal with Grandma, the kids (a son about twelve-years-old and a daughter of about eight-years-old) were flipping out, the wait staff cramped up, and I was informed there was a problem at table twenty-three.

As I arrived, Grandma was on her back, out cold, and her son-in-law was trying to revive her. Her daughter said, "I think there's something wrong with Mother."

I said, "I'd say that's accurate."

The woman asked, "Can you do something?"

I said, "We've already called the EMTs. Is she on medication?"

"No."

"Has she had anything to drink?"

"Two martinis."

"When did she have them?"

"In the last, oh, ten minutes or so."

"Was there a contest that I'm unaware of?"

"Can't you please do something?"

"What would you like me to do?"

"Give her mouth-to-mouth resuscitation."

"Huh?"

I will do almost anything to help someone in trouble, but you have to admit that giving mouth-to-mouth to a very old woman is a pretty large order. I figured that that responsibility resided with the son-in-law. He could have used it as a bonding moment, cementing their relationship, while buying himself a get-out-of-jail-free card for the rest of his marriage.

Just as I was about to pronounce her dead, unofficially of course, the EMTs arrived. They revived her with some oxygen and got her back to her chair and awake.

The daughter launched in and said, "Mother, you shouldn't drink like that. That's dangerous. You could have hurt yourself. What about the children? What kind of an example are you? I don't believe it."

I think the best part of growing old is that you just don't care what anyone thinks anymore, the best evidence being the clothes.

So after everybody, including the EMTs, was finished doing their best Dr. Phil on this woman, she issued the line of the night.

"I don't know why everyone is getting so crazy already. I'm just a little tired. How's my hair?"

The server came up to me later and said, "Can you believe that old lady?"

I said, "You mean the Kettle One suicide?"

"I've never seen anything like that before."

"What did you see?"

The server said, "Here we go. Why, what did you see?"

"I saw a new world record in the senior division."

The server laughed. "What are you talking about?"

I said, "That was the first time in my entire career I saw a person get totally hammered, pass out, get revived, adjust her clothing, coif her hair, and ace an intervention all in less than twenty-three minutes. I don't believe it's ever happened before."

You're a Corker

know I say this often, but just when I've thought I've heard it all, someone steps up to the plate and hits one out of the park. I won't lie to you: dinner at *Jedediah Hawkins Inn* can be expensive. We decided to do a three course *Prix-Fixe* for the off-season, and it was a huge success. It gave people who ordinarily wouldn't be able to spend that much for dinner a chance to come, as well as rewarded our regular patrons for their continued off-season support. It literally kept us full all winter. That being said—and combined with my belief that six percent of the public is certifiably insane— shit was bound to happen as they say, and it did.

A man called to make a reservation for four people for the *Prix-Fixe* dinner. He made sure to emphasize that he wanted to have the *Prix-Fixe* menu, *seven times*. We told him the *Prix-Fixe* menu was in effect all night and there were no restrictions. He said that he'd heard that one before and was not going to be a bait and switch victim. He wanted to make sure he got the *Prix-Fixe* menu. That made eight times he'd mentioned it. We said we would make sure he got it. He seemed reassured. (A side note: Why would we think of doing a *Prix-Fixe* dinner, make the menu, advertise it, prep the food, instruct the staff, and then when someone comes in for it, tell them, "We don't have one. Ha, ha, fooled you!"? It's just a question.)

Anyway, we were about to hang up the phone when the man said, "Wait. I have a question."

I said, "What is it?"

"Do you allow people to bring in their own wine?"

"We do, but there are some restrictions."

"Like what?"

I said, "It really shouldn't be on our wine list, you shouldn't bring in more than two bottles per table, and there is a corkage fee of twenty dollars."

"Twenty dollars?"

I repeated, "Twenty dollars."

"For each bottle?"

"For each bottle. One bottle is twenty, two bottles, forty."

The man then said, "Okay, thank you. Oh wait, the wine I have is an older Bordeaux. Do you have a decanter and will someone decant the wine for us? Oh, and we'll need good wine glasses. You have those, don't you?"

I reassured him, "We will and we do."

The man said, "Okay. See you Thursday night."

Sensing a certain potential for trouble I said, "Can't wait."

I have a sixth sense about these things. You get a kind of tingling sensation somewhere private that lets you know that something wacky is coming.

I'd like to say a word or two about bringing in your own wine before we go on. I'm a card carrying "wine-know," and I get the fact that sometimes you want to share a bottle of special wine with friends. That's totally cool. There are two things to consider. First, please make the arrangements in advance with the restaurant. It spares both you and us the pain of an embarrassing moment because some restaurants won't allow it, which is their prerogative. Try to imagine the reaction of your local Jiffy Lube team if you brought in your own oil and filter and said, "Here, use these."

Second and just as important, try to make an attempt to bring a special wine. There's nothing worse than asking a waiter to decant your favorite White Zinfandel when he's in the weeds on a busy night. Also, it's a nice gesture to offer the owner a taste for allowing you to bring it in. See, we can have fun and learn at the same time.

I'll get back to the story. The man arrived and was seated with his wine. He told the waiter he had pulled the cork an hour before to aerate the wine, but would still like it decanted, and to make sure he got the *Prix-Fixe* menu (the ninth time he had mentioned it). We gave him and his party the menus—*Prix-Fixe* menus in case you were wondering—and they ordered dinner.

He then tells the waiter, "I'll be tasting the wine."

The waiter comes into the kitchen and asks me for a decanter. He said, "Chef, that guy that brought the Bordeaux in, just told me he'll be tasting the wine for the table."

I said, "What's he going to do if he doesn't like it, send it back? He brought it. Just pour the damn thing." The two of us were howling imagining the possible scenarios: *"Where'd you get this rotgut from? I've been all over the world and I've never had wine this bad. Get me the sommelier this instant."*

The waiter decanted the wine and poured some in his glass. He tasted the wine, pronounced it exquisite, and everyone had a glass. That was pretty much that. All three courses—*Prix-Fixe*, by the way—went off without a hitch. They all had a great time. No one ordered coffee. (It is extra you know.) The waiter presented the check with the twenty dollars added for the corkage fee. The man looked at the check and called the waiter over.

He said, "There's a twenty-dollar corkage fee on this check."

The waiter said, "I assumed it was discussed before you came, because it was written in the reservation book that you were bringing in a bottle of wine."

"It was discussed, but I'm not paying it."

"Why not?"

My friends, I hope you're sitting down for this. The man, with a straight face, said, "Because I took the cork out before I got here in order to air it out."

The waiter, now speechless said, "I'll get a manager."

He came into the kitchen and told me what was going on. It was hilarious. This is great, great stuff. Who thinks like this? I had to go see for myself.

I approached the table. I said, "I hear there's a problem."

The man said, "Yes. I was charged a corkage fee on a bottle of wine that had no cork in it, and I won't pay it."

I said, "Really? Okay, I'm willing to take off the twenty-dollar corkage fee, but I'll have to put on the thirty-dollar decanting and glass-washing fee. You can pay twenty for corkage or thirty for decanting and glass-washing; it's up to you. I'm assuming you used the glasses because there's lipstick on two of them. Just let the waiter know what you decide, and he'll make any corrections needed. Thanks for coming."

As he was paying the check—with the original corkage fee included—the waiter told me he heard the term "highway robbery" bandied about. How about a big high-five for imagination though? He certainly deserves it.

FRANC-N-STEIN

There's something about the subject of wine that tends to put some people in touch with their inner asshole. I think it's because, for so many years, wine was associated with the upper classes, and it was assumed to be an elitist undertaking—a snobby hobby if you will. Anything that requires seventeen adjectives to describe the nose, legs, and body should be the envy of even the most self-absorbed supermodel.

I once witnessed a fist-fight at a dinner party started by an argument over the finish of a late harvest Gewürztraminer. One of the combatants thought the finish went on forever and said so, twelve times. The other thought the finish to be considerably shorter, with a harsh alcohol edge. They argued about it back and forth until they couldn't control themselves any longer and turned a relatively civilized dinner party into the UFC. I later told the two women I thought they both had it wrong, but only after they were too tired to throw another punch.

Wine fires up the same kind of passion as religion and politics and, come to think of it, has probably left its mark on both, judging by the headlines. The standing rule in my bar is no arguing about religion, politics, or who makes a better Cabernet, France or California. It's a good rule.

We have a customer whose lack of wine knowledge is only exceeded by his need to display it. Wine is a very big subject that takes years to get a grip on, and knowing that Cabernet is red, Pinot Grigio is white, and liberally throwing the word "dry" around will not get you a master sommelier certificate. These facts have eluded my man, and he jumps on any chance to enlighten the rest of the world with his kindergarten wine smarts. Combine that with an unnatural affection for the sound of his own voice, and you can hear the fingernails scraping the blackboard.

I can't tell you how many times I was forced to ignore a running diatribe of, "It's pretty dry; it wasn't really dry; I didn't think it was dry enough; now that's dry; it has great legs; no legs; one leg; a peg leg."

Funny enough, though, his lack of wine knowledge has paradoxically increased mine because every time he starts talking, I start drinking. One night, he came in straight from an adult education wine course, all fired up.

He asked the bartender, "Is Tom around?"

The bartender, who's no longer with us by the way, said, "Yeah, he's in the back. You want me to tell him you're here?"

"Yeah, I'd like to say hello."

The bartender came into the kitchen to tell me that my man wanted to say hello.

I said, "You didn't tell him I was here, did you?"

"Yeah, why, you don't want to talk to him?"

"Oh man, I'm not in the mood for a wine lesson."

"Sorry, I'll tell him that you left."

"No, forget it. I'll go say hello. Just remind me to thank you properly at some point in the future."

I went out to the bar, and my man greeted me warmly and said, "I just came from a wine class."

"I thought you knew everything about wine already," I said somewhat sarcastically, with a smile.

He stared at me for a second, got the joke, and laughed. "The class is on California wines. I'm a Francophile, as you know, so I took this course just to find out what it is that some people see in California wines."

"How's it going?" I asked.

"It's going well," he answered and then said, "It's confirming everything I always knew. They make shitty wine in California. I don't know why they bother. Frankly I don't know why they make wine anywhere *but* France. No one else seems to know how to do it. I've tried some Italian and Australian wines, and I've got to tell you, they pretty much suck."

"So let me ask you," I said. "You never drink any wine other than French?"

"No, except of course, for this wine class."

"No Italian, Austrian, or German?"

"No. They're terrible."

"Terrible?"

"Terrible and I'll tell you something else. The German wines are way too sweet."

"The reds or the whites," I asked, rolling my eyes.

"The whites; they're too sweet. Nobody makes wine like the French. I've never had a French wine I didn't like."

I'm assuming he thought it was a serious question.

I said, "Apparently you don't drink enough. How do you feel about Long Island? Tried 'em?"

"Are you kidding me? The worse wine I've ever tasted. What a waste of real estate."

"I have some friends out there who would probably disagree with you. What about the time Lenz took out the Pétrus in the blind-tasting of Merlot?"

"It was fixed. It had to be."

"Fixed? Some of the judges were French, and I believe the French come from France."

"I'm telling you it was fixed. They were trying to market Long Island wines. Big money talks bro! It was fixed, trust me."

I said, "You're probably right. I'll bet it was those bastards at Halliburton."

He said, "You'll eventually come around to see that I'm right. You need to drink more French wines and stop wasting your time with swill."

There comes a point when talking to someone who is clueless, that you realize you look as foolish as they do for just being involved in the conversation, and giving them a platform for their stupidity. It was starting to get to me. I realized the mature thing to do was just shrug my shoulders and let it go. So, of course, I continued.

"I would never limit myself to one region; it would seem like eating chicken every day. Why not *expand* your palate?"

"At least I've limited myself to the best. You're just wasting your time. But you'll see, you'll come around," he answered.

Exhausted, I asked, "Are you having dinner tonight?"

"Yeah, I guess we better sit down. Got any French wine? Ha ha."

I said, "Yep, plenty. See you after dinner."

I returned to the kitchen and finished dinner service. After cleaning up and putting in some orders, I went back out to the bar to have a glass of wine. My man was at a table in the bar area and called out, "Hey Tom, thanks for dinner. It was great. I'm curious, what are you drinking?"

"Steininger Gruner Veltliner, Kabinett; it's from Austria. I was at the vineyard last year and loved the wine. You should try it, I'll buy," I told him.

"I wouldn't waste the calories, my friend. Why don't you try a real wine? We have some St. Véran left, I'll pour you some," he said.

"I'm not big on Chardonnay these days. Thanks anyway," I answered.

He then issued a shining example of a *quit while you're ahead* statement: "It's not Chardonnay, it's St. Véran."

St. Véran *is* Chardonnay, for those who may not know. I was sitting at the bar with my fingers in my eyes, desperately trying to control myself. It would have been very easy to embarrass him, but ultimately what's the point? I decided, for the fourth time in my life, to act my age.

"No thanks, I'll stick with this," I said.

He just couldn't stop. "Once you start on French wine, I swear you'll never drink anything else. I'm telling you, man."

"Thanks for the tip."

"I'll even buy you a glass. Pick out whatever you want."

"No thanks. I'm fine."

"Pick out something comparable to your Austrian wine and drink them side-by-side. You'll see. There's nothing that compares to the French. Besides, it would be my pleasure to contribute in some small way to your wine education. Go ahead, order something."

That was it. I simply couldn't listen to another word.

I said, "You know what? Let *me* buy *you* something. You're the customer after all. Besides, I really don't want another glass of wine." (The first time that's ever happened, I believe.) "Let me buy you an after-dinner drink."

He said, "Okay. That's nice of you."

"Well, you're a good guy, and we can certainly agree to disagree like two mature adults."

He said, "I agree to disagree, that is. But I suspect deep down you know I'm right."

I said, "I was going to have Cognac before I go. Care to join me?"

"Oh yeah, I'd love to, that would be great."

I poured us each a glass of German-Robin Brandy. Sorry, I had to do it. His wife wanted Grand Marnier, I'm assuming because it's French. I brought the three snifters over to the table, sat down, and proposed a toast.

I said, "Here's to our ever expanding knowledge of the grape, French or otherwise," and we all clinked glasses.

He finished a sip, held the glass before his eyes, and said, "Oh man, that's good. Man, that's good. It's everything you want in a Cognac. I taste a little caramel. Do you get that?"

"You like it?"

"It's fabulous."

"What Cognac do you usually drink?"

"I like Hennessy XO and Cordon Bleu."

"How's it compare?"

"I think this blows them away."

"Me too."

"Whose Cognac is it?"

"German-Robin. It's a little boutique producer I was turned on to. I love the stuff."

He took another sip, looked at his glass and in a serious tone said, "Tom, this is why I drink French. Seriously, taste this: It's unbelievable. No one...no one can do what the French do. The proof is in the glass. You ever taste grappa? It's like lighter fluid, but this—it's—it's *France* man."

I said, "Yeah, those French. Listen, I've got to go. Let me bring the bottle over for you so you can see the label, in case you're in a store and want to pick it up sometime."

"Yeah, please. I would definitely buy some for the house, thanks."

I got the bottle, returned to the table, placed it down, shook hands with him and his wife, and said, "Goodbye."

He laughed, lifted the glass, and said, "Viva la France."

I walked out of the bar area and glanced over my shoulder to see him staring intently at a label that read, German-Robin *Alambic* Brandy, *Mendocino, California*, in the good old US of A. I have an inner asshole too, apparently.

FREE AT LAST

There are only two ways to get something for free: someone can give it to you, or you can take it. One is a act of generosity and one is larceny, an act referred to in some circles as stealing. There is—in a minute percentage of the population, thank God—something about the concept of *free* that causes some people to experience symptoms such as sweaty palms, an elevated heart rate, and a dull ache just above the kidneys. Along with these physical manifestations, there also resides a will to deceive, rationalize, and justify actions whose sole purpose is to avoid parting with a piece of paper sporting a mug shot of a dead president.

There must be some kind of orgasmic fulfillment in getting something for free that I've never experienced, because I have seen people take great personal risks for the smallest of rewards. But hey, free is free, which is a reward in itself, right? And what's most amazing to me is that when these people are caught, instead of being embarrassed, as I imagine any normal person would be, they become defiant, angry, or my personal favorite, indignant. We're not talking grand theft here; this is restaurant stuff, petty at best. It's just that some people possess a character flaw that will not allow them to keep their cotton-picking fingers off of other people's things. And although it may be a disease, it's one amusing sickness. The symptoms to watch for are involuntary eye-shifting, a general feeling of thrift, and a strong odor of entitlement. I hope it's not contagious.

We were recently catering a party on a Saturday afternoon. One of the gentlemen attending the party brought his own wines. He had three bottles, one Magnum and two 750s.

He called over one of the waiters during the cocktail hour and without even bothering to ask if it was okay, said, "Could you chill down these two whites and open the Magnum to let it breathe? We'll drink these with our dinner, and don't worry, I plan to take good care of you. Just make sure you keep our glasses filled and only pour these wines at our table. This is very good wine, you know. I go to Napa quite frequently, and I brought this back with me. They're very expensive and very hard to get."

I saw the wines, and they were decent, but not at all hard to get. As far as expensive goes, they weren't what you would call low-priced or bargain wines, but I've paid more for a glass of wine than the bottles were worth collectively, including the Magnum. Wine is a lot like sex and politics in that the more someone talks about it, usually the less they know, and although some people may indulge you by listening to your adventures and opinions, no one really gives a shit about what you've done or what you think. Josh Wesson, a noted wine expert, said it best while addressing the wine snob phenomena, "Put your pinky down, shut up, and drink." That pretty much says it all.

Apparently our hero never read the quote. As the party was being led into the dining room for dinner, he flagged down the waiter, saying, "Hey, don't forget me. I'll take the first white now. Bring it over, and we'll take the second one right after that, and then the Magnum for the entrée. Don't worry, buddy. I'll make it worth your while."

The waiter brought the first white and poured it for the table. Our hero said, "Yeah, I bought this when I was out in Napa. I go there a lot. I've got a lot of frequent-flyer miles so it doesn't cost me anything to fly. What's even better is that I have a friend in the wine business, and he hooks me up with free accommodations when I go. I pretend to own a store, and I get the tours, drink the wines, and it doesn't cost me a cent."

The waiter's eyes glazed over. "That's nice," he said.

Our hero, looking around the dining room, said, "You have a lot of bottles displayed on the shelves. Is there wine in them?"

The waiter said, "Only in the *CoolFish* Riesling bottles. The rest are dummies."

"There are a lot of Riesling bottles."

"Yeah, it's the chef's private label. I guess you could call it a shameless plug."

"Oh." Then he said to the waiter, "Could you do me a favor? Could you get me a piece of tuna for dinner instead of the sea bass? I don't like sea bass."

"It's not on this menu so there would be an up-charge. I would have to have the manager ask the hostess if it's okay with her."

Our hero then said, "No, you don't have to ask anybody. Just do it. I told you I'm going to take care of you. You see the wines I'm drinking; just do it for me. Work it out with the kitchen. Sea bass won't go with the red, and I don't want meat. Go ahead and work it out."

"Alright, I'll see what I can do."

"You can do it. Just do it. Work it out."

The waiter okayed the tuna with the kitchen and served it with the red and the Magnum for the main course.

Our hero said, "See this *Cab*? It's the best Cabernet in Napa. I know. I go to Napa all the time. There's not much of this around."

Not only was this wine not allocated, there was plenty to be had, and it wasn't even the best *Cab* on the block, never mind Napa. Excuse me for being bitchy.

Dinner proceeded uneventfully with him enjoying his tuna, drinking his wine, and pontificating about the pleasures of traveling at the expense of others.

The woman who was hosting this party for her son was first class all the way, and as a result, threw a wonderful party. As dessert was being served, she gave out swag bags to the boy's friends; they were between the ages of eleven and fifteen. In each bag was a basketball jersey from her son's favorite team, with each corresponding friend's name printed on the back—a very nice touch. The kids were thrilled and some of the boys put their jerseys on over their shirts.

Our hero spotted the jerseys and said to the waiter, "Where did they get those jerseys?"

"In the gift bags."

"Can I get one?"

"I think they're just for the kids."

"Are there any left?"

"I don't know."

"Could you check? I told you I'm going to take care of you, right?"

The waiter checked and realized some of the kids had left before the bags were given out, so there were a few still unclaimed.

He went back to the table and said, "There are a couple of bags left, but I don't know if anyone is coming back for them. Maybe she will take them with her and her son can give them to the friends that left early."

"Oh come on. They don't care. Just bring me one."

"All right, but you're taking full responsibility if there's a problem. I'm going to say you took it."

"Yeah, yeah, okay. Just get me one."

You would have thought it was Christmas morning when he got the bag. He pulled out the jersey—with someone else's name on it by the way—and put it on over his suit, resembling an NBA straitjacket with the bottom of the jersey three inches above his navel. He would have looked less ridiculous naked.

The waiter said, "Nice jersey."

"Ain't it great?"

"That's not your name on the back of it, is it?"

"So what, it's on the back. I can't see it anyway."

Shaking his head, the waiter left the table and started cleaning up. Everyone was starting to leave. Our hero took his swag bag and what was left of his Magnum, the best Cabernet in the universe, and walked to the bar.

As he passed his waiter, he says, "Here, I told you I'd take good care of you," and slips him a five-dollar bill.

He continued on into the bar and walked past John, the head waiter. John noticed that he was the only adult carrying a swag bag, so it caught his attention. He looked at the bag and saw what he thought was a wine bottle. He followed our hero to the bar to get a better look. Inside the bag was a bottle of *CoolFish* Riesling. Since I'm the only person who makes it and the only person who sells it, there's only one place he could have gotten it: off one of the shelves in the dining room.

John asked him, "What's in the bag?"

"What's in what bag?"

"The bag there in your hand. Is that one of our wines?"

"Yeah, I'm taking it home. I don't have any wine at home."

"Did you pay for it?"

"No. It's complimentary."

"What would make you think it's complimentary?"

"It was on the shelf in the dining room so I assumed it was complimentary."

I can't wait to try that one out next time I'm in Barnes and Noble looking to fatten my cookbook collection. *I'm sorry officer; they were on the shelves so I assumed they were complimentary.*

John continued, "Sir, these wines are displayed; they're not free. If you want to take it with you, you'll have to pay for it."

"How much is it?"

"Fifty dollars."

"Fifty dollars, are you kidding me?"

"Actually I'm not. It's fifty dollars."

"My wines were worth twice that. No way."

John said, "Well, then I'll have to take it back." And he did.

About five minutes later, John saw me and told me the story. He was fuming about the guy. I was in awe. After getting caught stealing red-handed—or white-handed, it was Riesling after all—he was still sitting in the bar, chatting like nothing had happened. No embarrassment, no shame, no contrition, nothing; he was unembarrassable.

I told Mark, the bartender, and the managers, Ann and Eileen, what had happened, and we were all just standing there laughing at the guy. I guess he finally decided there was nothing left to steal so he started heading for the front door.

As he passed me he stopped and asked, "You're the owner right?"

I said, "Guilty."

"Great party and what a nice place. You guys did a great job. Service was good, too. I took extra care of the waiter."

"Yeah, I heard."

"You know, I have a party coming up, but I already put down the deposit on another place. I wish I'd come here first."

"Yeah, well too bad. I'm sure it'll be fine."

"Okay. Thanks again."

"You're welcome."

I think everyone was shocked that I made no reference whatsoever to the wine bottle, but sometimes there just *are* no words other than, "You're under arrest."

APPETIZERS

Repeat Performance

It doesn't happen very often, but every once in a while a customer will get called out for their behavior. One Sunday night, an elderly woman ordered soup as an appetizer. On Sundays, it's always the soup.

For some reason, our Sunday customers tend to be a little older. I hope I don't get in trouble for saying this, but I've never had a customer over the age of sixty-five whose soup was the proper temperature. Before you go getting your politically correct panties all in a bunch, ask any person who has ever worked in a dining room, and I'm sure they will back me up. There has to be some mathematical equation between your age and the temperature of your soup. I think it's that the temperature of your soup has to roughly equal the square root of your age, plus half of your IQ, times five hundred. I don't know why, I just know it is.

I have actually witnessed an elderly uncle eating white-hot soup like it was gazpacho. Not to mention the noises emanating from his side of the dinner table. To give an idea of what it sounded like, try pronouncing the letter "P" loudly and rapidly, while inhaling hot soup through your mouth. Nice, huh? There had to be blistering, but according to him, the soup could have been a little hotter.

So it came as no surprise when a bowl of soup came back to the kitchen one Sunday night because it was "ice cold." We reheated it and sent it back out. It came back. It wasn't hot enough. She wanted it heated again. I heated the soup a third time, but I went one better. I heated the bowl until it was very hot. I sent it out. The soup came back. Why you ask? You guessed it. It wasn't hot enough.

There's a rumor going around in some kitchens that says liquid starts to evaporate at 212 degrees, so I was beginning to get nervous. The last thing I wanted to hear is, "Where's the rest of my soup?"

I heated the soup a fourth time, reheated the bowl, and in what I considered the move of the day, I gently heated the spoon. Didn't matter, the soup came back.

"It's not hot enough," she said.

As you can imagine, this was starting to get past the point of fun. While all of this was going on, a table of four that was sitting next to this woman had reached the end of the line.

One of the men at the table stood up and said, "I can't sit here and listen to this shit anymore. I was at Boccaccio's last week, and I saw you do the exact same thing over there. You're a nutcase! Shut the hell up, eat your friggin' soup, and stop torturing these people!"

She sat there with her mouth wide open—and steam pouring out.

Who *was* that masked man?

SALAD IMPLANTS

It is going to be very hard for me to get this right, but believe me, this can't get as close to being as ridiculous as the original event. It was all about salads. To give you some idea of what it was like on that day, the food runner, Dino, made by our count *twenty-six* trips to that table. That's four-point-something trips per salad. I believe it's still a record.

That day changed him forever. He started out professional, concerned, and polite. By the end of lunch, his hair was a mess, the knot of his tie was on the side of his neck, there were Xs where his pupils once had resided, and he was in full-blown Spanish Tourette's.

The first seven or eight trips were all the usual stuff.

"The room is cold."

"The room is hot."

"Turn the air conditioner up."

"Turn the air conditioner down."

"It's too light in here."

"It's too dark in here."

"I don't like my fork."

"I need another knife."

This, believe it or not, is pretty tame stuff. Six customized salads were served to six customized women after forty minutes of menu reorganization, a discussion of the Atkins diet, and a ten-minute dissertation on allergies.

All of a sudden, one of the women uttered the six words that sent Dino into his mental decline, "Her salad is bigger than mine."

That's about when all hell broke loose. Dino took the smaller salad back, and we made it larger. Dino took it out. Now the table was in a frenzy. No one was going to be out-fussied.

"I need more endive."

"Hers has too much dressing."

"I can't eat radicchio."

"Onions make me fart."

"My lettuce is wilted."

"I want the dressing on the side."

Dino brought them all back, we fixed them, and Dino took them back out.

Now the woman whose salad was originally too small had a bigger salad than the woman next to her. Dino took it back. We fixed it. Dino took it out.

While he was out there—breathing heavily, I might add—they decided they needed fresh water glasses. Dino removed the glasses. Dino brought new glasses. Dino filled the glasses.

Here's where it gets a little tricky. The woman who just had *her* salad enlargement now has a bigger salad than the other three, but the other three had been nibbling through all of this activity. So, in reality, they're salads are not smaller, just somewhat eaten.

This matters not.

The woman said, "Excuse me waiter."

Dino went to the table.

She then said, "Now *our* salads are too small."

Dino brought them back. We fixed them. Dino brought them out.

All six women were staring at their salads, and in their eyes you could see sort of a mental micrometer carefully measuring, taking a vegetable inventory, and counting the salad leaves.

Just as all six seemed finally satisfied, the leader emerged. The alpha female, in one final display of pure salad envy, announced,

"I'm short a tomato."

Dino brought it in. We added a tomato. Dino brought it out. Finally, they ate.

We were rolling on the floor in the kitchen. We were all laughing so hard it was impossible to work, except for Dino, who was weeping quietly by the bread warmer.

They all split a *Chocolate Bag* for dessert. Thank God they didn't order two, or we may have lost Dino completely.

"Waiter, our spoons have spots."

Dino took them away. Dino brought new ones back.

"We'll just have coffee and a check please."

Dino brought the coffee. Dino brought the check.

"By the way, this is decaf, isn't it, because otherwise I'll be up all night." This one always gets me. This is at twelve-thirty in the afternoon.

Dino said, "Yes ma'am."

And when he returned to the kitchen, Dino was finally smiling.

CLUELESS

I won't garnish this story because it requires none. There's really not much to say, as you will soon see.

It can be pretty scary out there. I have perhaps the greatest restaurant employees on Long Island. I know everyone thinks that they do, but they don't. I do. Some of my employees have recently gotten involved with the Pediatric Cancer Care Unit at Winthrop Hospital. They have been visiting the children and helping with the fundraising.

One day last year, they came to me to ask if I would do a luncheon and a chocolate demonstration for twenty-five of the children. We had the luncheon the following month and had a ball. We used one of the dining rooms and set up all the round tables. All the kids had lunch, and afterward we taught them how to make our *Chocolate Bag* dessert.

To see these children having so much fun in spite of everything they were going through was a life-altering experience. There really wasn't a dry eye in the house. The kids were all covered with chocolate, whipped cream, and ice cream and had turned the dining room into one magnificent mess.

For the sake of clarity, I must tell you that it was impossible not to know that these children were ill. Some had lost their hair due to chemotherapy and were wearing bandanas to cover their heads. I even got a bandana-tying lesson from one of the girls. It was obvious to anyone with an ounce of humanity that these kids were special.

At about one o'clock, five women walked in for lunch. The hostess seated them in the other dining room. Here's the quote.

"Are these kids going to be here much longer because they're very loud. Oh, and we would prefer a round table."

The hostess explained that all the round tables were being used for the chocolate demo for the kids.

The woman said, "That's ridiculous. How can you inconvenience your regular customers for bunch a of children?"

I'd love to tell you I had a clever response, but what can you possibly say?

THRIFTY FIFTY

Being in the restaurant business exposes you to a wide range of people and professions. In my experience, there is one particular profession where almost all the people I have met who work in that profession are inherently thrifty. I can't tell you why, but I *can* tell you it is true. The profession involved shall remain nameless for the sake of civility. I certainly don't want to mention it and have someone try to *teach me a lesson.* But I assure you that if you ask anyone, *anyone*, in my profession which profession has the greatest number of the cheapest people, they will get it on the first try.

We were having a retirement party for a person of this profession. I think it was for about fifty people. The negotiations with the person in charge were great.

I said, "Would you like to do a lunch or dinner party?"

She said, "Is lunch cheaper?"

"Yes."

"We'll do lunch."

"Do you have any menu items in mind?"

"The least expensive items that you offer."

I said, "Okay. How would you like to handle the bar? You can run a tab on what's consumed or you can have a per person charge by the hour."

"Which is cheaper?"

"I don't know the people involved so I can't really tell you."

She said, "How about we do this. At the end of the party, add them up both ways and charge me for the least expensive of the two."

I said, "What a great idea!"

"How much is the tax?"

"Eight and a half percent."

"That's a lot of money."

"I just collect it; I don't get to keep it."

"Okay, how much for the gratuity?"

"Twenty percent."

She asked, "Isn't that a little high?"

I said, "Not according to my wait staff."

"Isn't there anything we can do about that?"

I told her, "Maybe we can dress them up in candy-stripe shirts and call them volunteers."

"You're so funny."

"Yes, I'm hysterical."

She finally said, "Okay, let's book it. We're all excited about this. This should be quite an affair."

I agreed, "Oh yeah. It's going to be a barn-burner."

The day of the party arrived and in all honesty, it was very nice, in a chicken and pasta kind-of-way.

About ten minutes into the party, the woman who booked it went to the bar for a drink. She had decided not to include liquor because adding that to the price made the party prohibitively expensive and she was concerned no one would show. So everyone had to buy their own drinks.

She said to the bartender, "How much is a Martini?"

Mark, the bartender, says, "Ten dollars."

"That's very expensive. Can't you do any better?"

"Sure how about fourteen?"

"I only have eight dollars with me."

Mark, the big softy, said, "Okay, I'll make you one for eight."

"Thank you so much."

The woman now has to walk about fifty feet with a Martini back to the dining room. If you don't think wait people are talented, try carrying four martinis fifty feet with no spillage. Knowing this, Mark left a little room for error in her glass.

She said, "Where's the rest of my drink?"

Mark said, "I didn't want you to spill it. I didn't fill it to the very top because I thought it would be easier for you to carry. And besides, it's a ten-ounce glass."

"I paid for this drink and I want the rest."

Do you believe this? She paid eight dollars for a ten-dollar drink and she has volume issues. Mark filled the glass to the top. She carefully picked it up and proceeded to spill about a quarter of her drink on the bar.

She said, "This isn't going to work."

Mark said, "I'm shocked."

"Put it into two glasses so I can carry it, and don't forget to replace what I spilled. That wasn't my fault."

Mark, totally amused, said, "No problem."

While Mark was splitting the Martini, the woman made a move that would be the envy of any three-card monte dealer in New York. She palmed a two-dollar tip left previously by another patron.

After negotiating the price, making him add more—twice actually—splitting the Martini in two, and wiping up the mess, she said, "Thanks, this is for you," and handed Mark the two dollars that the previous customer had left on the bar.

Mark caught the whole move out of the corner of his eye, smiled, and said, "Thank you." He then turned to me at the end of the bar and said, "Chef, I have another one for the book."

Sports Hero

Over the past forty something years in this business, I have met many famous people. A remarkable number of them have been athletes. Athletes are different from other famous people in that they are not only physically impressive, but also the best in the world at what they do. They are very different from you and me and their size and grace are hard to miss.

I have fed the likes of Gerry Cooney, Clark Gilles, Bob Nystrom, the Sutter brothers, Don McCauley, Boomer Esiason, Tom Kite, Marvin Jones, Siupeli Malamala, Curtis Martin, and a Salvadorian housekeeper named Anna whose sweeping skills would be the envy of any Irish curling team. Who would have thought that on a Saturday night, on Long Island, at eight o'clock sharp, that I, Tom Schaudel, would be privileged enough to discover "The Phenom?"

We're talking about a breakout talent whose skill eclipsed anything I'd previously seen in his chosen sport. If I could convince him to let me manage his career, I could give up all the bright lights and glitter of the restaurant business, and maybe even finally relax. All I have to do is convince the International Olympic Committee officials to consider adding napkin-throwing to the current lineup of events. We must have the Michael Jordan of napkin-throwing right here on Long Island. The man can do with the napkin what Tiger can do with a golf ball. He can draw it, cut it, pull it back, or turn it over, and his short name has no equal.

Here's how it went down. *PassionFish* was brand new and sometimes in the beginning, things can be less than smooth. This man thought that his dinner was taking entirely too long to come out, which I'm sure could have been the case. We're far from perfect.

He announced to the rest of the table that he was going to take care of the "problem."

He took his napkin off his lap, walked through the dining room, down the center hall to the hostess desk, and said, "Why is our dinner taking so long? This is UNACCEPTABLE!"

And then, like any other well-adjusted soul, he proceeded to throw his balled up napkin into the face of the twenty-year-old hostess' assistant. I can't imagine the amount of therapy it takes to "let go" of being hit in the face with a used napkin, but she survived.

This is a brilliant resolution skill, don't you think? Imagine this: you go to the dentist, and if you wait too long for your appointment, you just smack him in the face with one of those *Better Homes and Gardens* magazines he has hanging around the waiting room. No one reads them anyway. Homes maybe; gardens? I don't think so.

Or how about this? You go to a mechanic to fix your car, and you wait too long, so you beat him repeatedly in the kisser with one of the floor mats.

Hey, here's one more. You're in that line in the supermarket that's for ten items or less. A woman in front of you is taking all night trying to find exact change in one of those little change purses that women always have twelve-dollars-worth of nickels in. Just whack her upside the head with a box of frozen peas.

I've got to admit it, it does sound tempting.

HOSTAGE NEGOTIATOR

There are only two things I know about plumbing. Number one: your pants have to be at half-mast so your ass looks like the crack of dawn. Number two: shit does not run upstream. That's it. That is the entire content of my knowledge of plumbing. I don't even know why they spell it with a "b" in the middle. It serves absolutely no purpose. Beats me.

Commercial plumbing needs constant attention, as you may imagine, and the result of that attention is that you rarely have a problem, but every once in a while...shit happens. So when my crack staff informed me that we had a slow drain in the ladies' room, I sprang into action. I called a plumber. An hour later, this guy showed up dressed like Ricardo Montalban.

I said to Diane, the manager, "Who's that?"

She said, "That's the plumber."

"Where's Tattoo? That's the best dressed plumber I've ever seen."

She rolled her eyes.

I walked into the bathroom and said, "Hey, what's up?"

The plumber said, "You've got a slow drain. I'm here to clear it."

"Oh, you're the plumber?"

"Yeah."

"You're the snappiest dressing plumber I've ever seen. Shouldn't you have some plumbing stuff all over you or something? Maybe pull your pants down a little?"

He laughed and said, "I'm the boss. I usually don't go out on jobs, but we're short a couple of guys today, so you're stuck with

116

me."

I said, "Okay, carry on. I'm just glad you're here."

Twenty minutes later, he gave me the "all clear," and he walked out of the bathroom without a spot on him. I was skeptical. He was way too clean.

Here's the result. Three elderly women came to *CoolFish* for lunch. Twenty minutes after their arrival, Mark the bartender, hears muffled cries for help.

They were soft at first ("HELP, HELP, HELP."), then grew louder and louder ("HELP. HELP! HELP!")

He determined that it was coming from the ladies' room so he asked Diane, the manager, to see what was going on. She opened the door to the ladies' room, and the muffled cries turned into a roar. The floor drain was backing up, sending water and various other plumbing liquids all over the place.

This elderly woman was sitting on the bowl with her pants down and her legs straight out, screaming "Help, help! I have open-toe shoes! Help, I have open-toe shoes!"

And, for the kicker, "I want a free lunch!"

You had to see it.

I said, "You have to come out of there."

She answered, "I'm not coming out until someone cleans this up. I have open-toe shoes and I want a free lunch."

I've got to tell you, sitting on a toilet bowl with your legs up in the air, a half an acre of bloomers around your ankles, screaming for free food, is not the strongest negotiating position I've ever seen.

I told her, talking through the doorway, "Just pull your pants up and come out."

She said, "Not until someone mops this up!"

I have a wonderful nineteen-year-old Salvadorian porter. It would be unthinkable to reward all his hard work by asking him to do this.

I said, "Just come out; it's not that deep."

She repeated, "I'm not coming out until someone mops this up, and I want a free lunch!"

Again with the free lunch. So now I have to break the news to Moises, my porter. He's willing to do anything I ask, but I just don't think he knew what he was in for. I mean, really, a half-naked elderly woman on a toilet bowl, screaming for a freebie?

I explained to him that he had to mop the ladies' room. He told me it was no problem; I vehemently disagreed. I tried to tell him what it would be like, but unless you've been there, you can't really know. I told him he had to keep his eyes closed, but we decided that mopping in Braille was too difficult, so we settled on one eye half-shut and the other closed. I was really concerned that if this were his first experience with nudity, he would be scarred for life.

I said, "Whatever happens in there, don't look."

As he was standing in front of the ladies' room, weighing one hundred twenty pounds (including his mop and his bucket), I imagined what all generals over the years must have thought when they sent their young soldiers into battle: *"Dudes, you are seriously screwed."*

Moises bravely entered the bathroom. I couldn't look. He emerged fifteen minutes later, alive but somewhat shaken, followed by the woman.

Diane came back into the kitchen and said, "The woman wants to talk to you."

I said, "Does she have her pants on?"

Diane, laughing, said, "Get out there." I go out.

The woman said, "So do I get a free lunch?"

"Absolutely. For this kind of material, I would have given you a free wedding."

"Well, thank you. But, I have no plans to marry. Lunch will be fine."

All night I had this picture in my head of people jumping off the stern of the *Titanic* screaming, "I want a refuunndd," and Moises swabbing the deck.

DRUGS:
Ya Gotta Love 'em

My ex-wife is one of my best friends and works for me part-time helping out with the front desk duties. She's patient and friendly and has a great sense of humor. (She needed one to be married to me.) These qualities, especially her sense of humor, are what make her such a good hostess and allow her to smile through any situation that may arise. But everyone, including my beloved ex-wife, has a limit (a fact I should have been more aware of considering that we're not married any longer).

A party of four, waiting for a table, was informed there would be a thirty-five minute wait. We didn't take reservations at *Starfish*, and there was a crowd at the podium posturing for Diane's attention.

One of the men in the party was very antsy and kept coming over to Diane and asking, "Is it ready, is it ready, is it ready? Is our table ready yet?" He was like an eight-year-old on a road trip.

Diane patiently told him, "As soon as it's ready, I'll let you know."

Five minutes later, the table directly behind the hostess desk became available. Diane informed the party that their table was ready and brought them over to seat them. I will readily admit that it was not the best table in the restaurant, but if you have no reservation on a Saturday night and you're really hungry and you are in a casual, very busy restaurant, you should consider taking whatever table is available.

The antsy guy turned to Diane and said, "This is unacceptable. I will not sit here!"

Diane, taken back, said, "Okay. It's just that I thought you were in a hurry, and I was trying to get you a table as soon as possible."

The antsy guy said, "Sorry, unacceptable!"

Diane, getting slightly annoyed at the guy's tone, said, "Fine *sirrr*, I'll let you know when another table is ready."

He said, "Fine *ma'ammm*! I can hardly wait."

Fifteen minutes later, the table behind the first one became available. Diane brought the party over, and they sat down and seemed somewhat happy.

The antsy guy said to Diane, "I'm sorry I yelled at you. It's just that I'm taking medication, I'm very hungry, and if I don't eat, I'll be sick."

It never ceases to amaze me that sick people always tell you that if things don't go their way, they will become sick. If they weren't sick to begin with, would we even be having the discussion? Sorry, I digress.

Diane said, "That's okay, enjoy your dinner. I'll be back to check on you later."

The party had finished their meal without further incident, which I believe to be a miracle considering who was at the table.

Then Diane returned to the table after they were finished and asked, "Is everything okay here?"

I'm still unclear what it was about the question that caused the guy to lose his mind.

He grabbed Diane by the arm and, squeezing a whole lot harder than he should, said, "You get away from me! You call yourself a hostess? Get away from this table! Get away right now or I'm not responsible for what I'm about to do!"

Diane—momentarily in state of shock—recovered before losing it herself, saying, "Get your hands off of me! What the hell is your problem anyway? You've been a pain in the ass since you walked in."

She stormed back to the front desk, muttering under her breath.

I hadn't seen her that mad since we were married. The manager went to the table to try to calm the guy down.

He told the manager, "Keep her away from this table. I'm not responsible for what I'm about to do. She's no hostess. I DON'T NEED THIS SHIT, I'M ON MEDICATION!"

That was the one thing I was absolutely sure of; it just didn't seem like it was the right prescription. On the way out, he stopped at the front desk and said something else to Diane. I believe she then said something off-color about his mother, and they had to be separated again. It was nuts, like Ali and Frazier after the bell. Diane had to be physically restrained.

After we finally pulled them apart and he left, she said, "Do you believe that lunatic?"

I said, laughing, "Hey, don't talk about my customers like that. Besides, I thought I detected a little spark between the two of you." Then we all just lost it.

CURRYING A FAVOR

Sometimes all it takes is the four words, "I'll have the mussels," to set off a psychodrama of unimaginable proportions. A woman came to *Starfish* one night to have, what we thought, was a quiet dinner with her husband. It was a slow Sunday night, and she said she was glad that it wasn't busy so she could relax and have her dinner in peace. We took her at her word. She ordered the mussels as an appetizer. The menu reads, "PEI Mussels/Red Thai Curry/Coconut/Basil/Lime." It's one of our signature appetizers.

The dish came out and she was not happy. She called the waitress over and said, "There's something wrong with my mussels."

The waitress asked, "What's the problem?"

"This isn't the same broth that I had the last time I was here. Did the chef change the recipe?"

"I don't believe so but hold on, I'll check."

The waitress asked Dan, the chef, if the recipe had changed.

He said, "No. It's always been the same."

The waitress then said, "The lady says it's not the same as last time she was here."

Dan said, "It's the same broth. I've been making this broth so long that I have dishwashers who can't read English who know the recipe by heart."

The waitress returned to the table and said, "I checked with the chef, and he said that it's the same broth that we always make."

The woman said, "No, I'm sorry but it's not."

Ann, the manager, heard what was going on, went to the table, and said to the woman, "It's the same broth we always use, but if you're not happy and would like something else, we would be glad

123

to make it for you."

The woman said, "No thank you. What I would like is the mussels with the same broth that I had the last time I was here. You people are lying to me. You must think I'm stupid. I know what probably happened. It's Sunday and you probably ran out of broth on Saturday night and the chef was too lazy to make it, so he probably bought some in the supermarket on his way to work, and now you're trying to pawn it off on your Sunday customers because you think, since we're in our golden years, we're too old to notice."

How's that for a conspiracy theory? Ann went back to the kitchen and asked, "Dan, are you sure it's the same broth?"

Dan, annoyed, said, "I've made five-thousand gallons of the stuff. It's the same broth."

Ann returned to the table and said, "Maybe you were mistaken about what you had. Could it have been one of the nightly specials or something like that?"

The woman looked at Ann in disbelief and exclaimed, "What do you think? Do you think I'm crazy?"

At that point I was very proud of my staff because that was the first time the word *crazy* came up in the conversation, and none of us had mentioned it.

Pointing at another guest two tables away, the woman says, "That woman over there had the mussels too. Let me taste hers." I swear I'm not kidding.

Ann said, "Although I'm sure she wouldn't mind at all, I'd prefer to keep this between us."

The woman, sensing a weakness, said, "Oh sure, you don't want anyone else to know that you're a bunch of liars and you serve supermarket food."

She then got up, went to the kitchen window, and asked for Dan.

Dan said, "Hi, I'm Dan. What can I do for you?"

She said, "You're a liar and you're serving supermarket red curry broth."

Dan was dumbfounded.

She then proceeded to tell Dan, Ann, and anyone else who would listen that she was a food critic (for the *Lunatic's Home Journal*, I'm sure), and she was going to write a column telling everyone that, again, we're liars who serve supermarket food, and she'd expose us for the frauds we are. These people are out there, my friends, just walking around.

Ann was at the end of her rope so she called me, explained what had been going on, and asked what to do.

Since I have more experience with crazies than Hannibal Lecter's attending psychiatrist, I knew exactly what this woman wanted.

I told Ann, "Tell her that you called me and that I said to fire Danny, effective immediately."

"You want me to tell her I'm firing Danny?"

I laughed and said, "Yeah, tell her I said that even though Danny is a decent family man, an exemplary employee, and a fine chef, I will not tolerate anyone lying to one of our valued customers. And if it wasn't for her laser beam palate, I would have never known that he ran out of Thai red curry and was too lazy to make another batch. Tell her I'm grateful."

Ann tells her word for word what I said and she was thrilled. She told Ann, "At least Tom had the courage to admit that I was right. Now I'll give you another chance."

Ann said, "So can I have the kitchen get you something else?"

The woman said, "No. Have the chef make me another order of mussels, just don't put it on our check. Heh, heh, heh."

Montauk Mussels/Thai Red Curry/Coconut Basil Recipe

This dish was on the opening menu at *Lemongrass*, a restaurant I had opened in Roslyn in 1997. These mussels have all the flavors that make Thai cuisine so interesting. I love Montauk mussels. A local fisherman friend of mine, Larry Keller, (who I affectionately call Captain Grumpy) used to bring me tons of local mussels at the *Downtown Grille* in Montauk. They were always very clean (no sand), plump, and had an incomparable flavor. If you can get them, do so. For a small fee, I'll give you Larry's number. Make sure you serve this with lots of bread and soup spoons. I guarantee there will be very little of the broth left.

Ingredients:

2 tablespoons sesame oil

1 teaspoon garlic, minced

1 teaspoon ginger, minced

1 teaspoon lemongrass, minced

½ cup onion, finely diced

4 ounces unsweetened coconut milk

2 ounces Coco Lopez

1 cup fish stock

2 teaspoons Thai Red Curry paste (available at Asian markets)

3 tablespoons soy sauce, to taste

2 pounds mussels, scrubbed, rinsed, and debearded

2 tablespoons basil chiffonade

2 tablespoons cilantro leaves, roughly chopped

In a thick-bottomed pot or casserole, heat the sesame oil, being careful not to let it burn. Add the garlic, ginger, *lemongrass*, and onion and sauté until the onions are softened but not browned (5-8 minutes). Add the unsweetened coconut milk, Coco Lopez, fish stock, Thai red curry paste, and soy sauce. Bring the mixture to a boil and simmer for 5 minutes. Adjust the seasoning with soy sauce. Add the mussels and cook, covered, 6-8 minutes longer until all of the mussels have opened. Remove from heat and discard any mussels that haven't opened. Stir in the basil and cilantro. Divide the mussels into four soup bowls and pour the broth evenly over each serving.

Chef's tip: *The broth can be made a day ahead and refrigerated. You can use this broth to steam fish such as skate or red snapper. If you reduce the broth by half, you can use it as a sauce.*

Wine pairing: Bedell Gewürztraminer

Is This On The Level?

We have two levels in the dining room at *CoolFish*. The left side is at street level, the right side is one step up. I can't tell you how many times people have tripped up or down on that step. If I could remove it, I would, but it's impossible. Not that there haven't been some incredibly creative attempts at self-destruction, but in spite of the best efforts of some very talented customers, no one has managed to kill themselves—yet. There are times when the dining room looks like an audition for Chevy Chase doing Gerald Ford. I hate to laugh, but watching my clientele sailing across the dining room floor like the Flying Wallendas while keeping a straight face is close to impossible.

We have, by law, a light on the step. We also have had, at various times, reflector tape, a handrail, white paint, a sign, and a waitperson saying, "Watch your step." It simply doesn't matter. No matter what we say or do, there are usually at least one or two suicide attempts per week. So now, I just wait patiently for someone to succeed in killing themselves, so I can turn the restaurant over to the surviving family members and retire.

Here we go. A middle-aged couple was being led to their table in the right-side dining room.

The hostess said, "Watch your step."

The man was leading the way. He negotiated the step with the grace of Gene Kelly.

The woman was right behind him. The hostess repeated, "Watch your step."

Bang. Ignoring the warning, her instep hit the riser. She was catapulted forward two-and-a-half-to-three feet in the air, at a speed of approximately four-miles per hour. She wore a look on her face that indicated that she knew she had royally screwed up.

I'm no gymnastics expert, so I can't really tell you if it was a front somersault with a double lutz or a figure eight with a half gainer, but I will tell you that it was the most incredible digger I've ever seen. Her shoes were about two feet above her head when she landed. Try it. It ain't easy. If she had the presence of mind to point her toes, she would have easily scored a perfect ten. Luckily, she broke the fall with her nose. Her arms were flailing uselessly at her sides, and the rest of her was bouncing and screaming past table seventy-one. She skidded to a stop under the exit sign by the emergency door. Thank God, because if she had gone through the door into the parking lot, I don't think I would have been able to recover. As it was, it took over an hour before I was able to look at her.

Four of us were standing there when she went down: me, the hostess, a server, and the lady's husband. Three of us ran to help the woman. Her husband ran the other way. At first, I thought he was going for help or just panicking, but it gets better. I watched him step down off the dining room level, bend over, and check to see if the step light was on. His wife was lying in a heap, wondering if she'll have to spend the rest of her life in a wheelchair, and he was thinking he had just hit the lottery.

I walked up behind him and when he noticed I was there, he looked up. I said, "Looks to me like it's on. Too bad, huh?"

He said, "Well, I was just checking to see if it was working."

I said, "Maybe you should see if your wife's still working."

With that he went over to the wife who was just beginning to realize what country she was in. We got her up and into a chair, and after icing her down and giving her a glass of water, she seemed okay. They stayed and had dinner, and I never received the requisite lawyer's letter, but on the way out she said to the hostess, who basically *tried* to save her life with the "watch your step" warning, "You really should do something about that step. Someone could get hurt." That's quite a line when it's issued by someone with carpet burned knees, a black eye, and three-inch lump on their forehead, no?

I Came to Bury Caesar

A woman came to the bar at *CoolFish* and ordered a Martini. She had a few sips and started to relax. She was by herself. The bar was filling up with regulars, and everyone was talking and yucking it up. She really didn't know anyone, but she was friendly and wanted to mix in.

She said to one of the regulars, "Have you ever eaten here?"

He said, "Yeah, all the time."

She said, "Have you ever had the Caesar salad?"

"Yeah."

"Me too. I think it's horrible."

He said, "I don't think it's horrible, I kind-of like it."

She said, "I've eaten here many times, and I like everything I've had, but the Caesar salad sucks. The chef has no idea how to make a Caesar salad. He doesn't know the anchovy to cheese ratio, he uses too much lemon, and not enough garlic. It really sucks."

The man said, "Well, you can order other salads."

"Yeah, but I really like Caesar salads and his is terrible. There's too much mustard."

The guy wanted out of the conversation, so he introduced her to a couple standing on the other side of him.

She asked them, "Are you having dinner here?"

The couple said, "Yes."

She said, "Don't order the Caesar salad, it sucks. I've eaten Caesar salads all over the world, and this chef just can't make it. It's horrible."

The couple said, "Thanks for the tip," and they went into the dining room.

She turned to the bartender, Mark, and said, "Do you sell a lot of Caesar salads here?"

He said, "Yes."

"I can't believe it. His is the worst Caesar salad I've ever eaten."

Mark said, "It's kind of popular here."

"It sucks."

She ordered another Martini. A party of five was at the bar, waiting for a table. They all struck up a conversation, and finally she said, "Are you guys eating here tonight?"

The group said, "Yeah, we eat here once a week."

"Ever had the Caesar salad?"

"Yeah."

"Sucks, right? Too much mustard."

"Nah, we kind-of like it."

She said, "I think it's awful."

She went on like this for an hour. She must have told twenty people how bad the Caesar salad was. Finally, her friend came. They paid her check and sat down for dinner. They had another cocktail at the table and looked over the menu. Diane came over to take their order.

The woman said, "I'll have a crab cake appetizer, and can I get a Caesar salad for an entrée?"

She finished the entire Caesar salad, croutons and all. Diane went over to the table and said, "How was everything?"

The woman said, "The crab cake was delicious, but the Caesar salad sucked."

Hey, at least we're consistent.

Caesar's Salad Recipe

No matter how many new salads are created, new ingredients discovered, or new techniques invented, this simple salad remains as popular as ever (except, of course, for the woman you just met). This salad has stood the test of time since 1924, and it looks like it has a pretty bright future. So, here it is.

Ingredients:

½ cup croutons
1 egg yolk
2 teaspoons garlic, finely chopped
2 anchovy filets, mashed
2 tablespoons lemon juice, freshly squeezed
6 tablespoons extra virgin olive oil
2 drops Worcestershire sauce
4 tablespoons Parmesan cheese, divided
1 head romaine lettuce
Ground black pepper to taste

For the croutons: Preheat oven to 375°F. Trim crusts from day-old French bread and cut into ¾ inch cubes. Sprinkle lightly with salt and spread out onto a baking sheet. Bake 10-15 minutes until light golden brown and cool.

For the dressing: Place egg yolk, garlic, and anchovy in a blender and blend for 30 seconds. Add lemon juice and Worcestershire sauce and blend 5 more seconds. With the motor running, slowly drizzle in the olive oil until thickened and well-combined. At this point, you can add a little lemon juice if the dressing is too thick, or olive oil if it's too thin, to get the right consistency. Add the parmesan cheese and blend.

For the salad: Separate, wash, and dry the romaine leaves. Tear into bite-sized pieces and place in a wooden bowl with the croutons. Toss with the dressing until well coated. Divide among four salad plates, sprinkle with the remaining Parmesan cheese and season with the ground black pepper.

Chef's tip: Cut baby red and green romaine heads in half, lean them against one another, and drizzle on the dressing for a more dramatic presentation.

Wine pairing: Croteaux Rose

Chewing Gum

Perhaps you've noticed as I have that as you get older, life gets a little harder, you move a little slower, and forget pretty much everything. It's just harder to keep your shit together. I have recently developed a soft spot for middle age, largely because I've finally arrived. And let me tell you, we can be a pretty funny group.

One night, a middle-aged woman came into *CoolFish* with her husband. They had drinks and appetizers, and they were on their entrées when we noticed a commotion in the dining room. She was panicking, waving her arms, standing up, sitting down, and kneeling on the floor looking all around the table. Then it hit her.

She started yelling, "THEY TOOK MY BREAD PLATE! THEY TOOK MY BREAD PLATE! THEY TOOK MY BREAD PLATE!" She kept repeating it over and over again. It was like *Rain Man* without the math skills. We ran into the dining room.

"What's the problem?"

She said, looking down at the table, "They took my bread plate!"

"We got that part. What's the problem?"

I've always heard that the gunshot victim never hears the gun. The bullet is too fast; it hits you before you hear the sound. This was kind-of like that. She looked up at us, and we realized what was wrong before we heard the sound of her voice.

She said, with her lips curled over her upper gums, "My teeth were on it."

We were incredulous, "Holy shit."

I would have thought she would have needed those.

She said, "Go find my teeth."

I've been at this a long time, and I have to tell you that was absolutely the first time I ever saw someone take out their teeth in a restaurant. That's the course I want to teach at the Culinary Institute of America when I retire. The one they never tell you about. "Welcome, ladies and gentlemen, to Denture Recovery Class."

We set about to find the missing choppers. Three people in latex gloves up to their armpits in garbage, laughing uncontrollably, with an APB out on a set of uppers are quite a sight. We were looking and laughing, laughing and looking, and then I spotted something. Halfway down the garbage can, past the steak bones, chewed fish, and assorted bar refuse, sat a two-pound lobster carcass with a smile like Martha Raye. Bingo.

We took the teeth out, sprayed them down, and ran them through the dishwasher. Here's the second problem: How do you bring them back out? What plate do you use? What garnish? We ultimately chose a plain white plate so the teeth would blend in better. We figured there was much less of a chance of traumatizing one of the other guests. It's just not what you want to see right before tearing into your dinner. Just for the record, we decided not to use parsley as a garnish; it always seems to end up getting stuck in a tooth. We went with mint.

Dead Man Sitting

Every once in a while, I win one. Not often admittedly, but every once in a while.

We had a customer for about a year or so who was maybe the worst we had ever had. Like I've said before, I believe it's okay to fire a bad customer, much the same as a bad employee, and that needed to happen. This guy was not only unhinged, but loud, mean, and nasty. It took an average of a half an hour to get his seat right.

"No, not there. Not there either. Nope not that one. What about that table?" he said.

"Sorry sir, four people are already sitting there," the hostess answered.

"Ask them to move."

"Sure, not a problem. I'm sure they'd be happy to move for you." She said and thought to herself, *"After all, you are you."*

You get the picture. You could finish half your dinner while this ass was still shopping for a table. After his highness finally got his rather rotund rear end in a chair, through dinner he got worse.

"Everything sucked, the wine was warm, my waitress was rude, the busboys are stupid and inept, and you never change your desserts."

Why I subjected myself to this for a year, I'll never know. Oh, I remember: it's my staff who get the abuse. I hide. Trust me on this, he is worse than it sounds. I was in front one night when he came in.

He said to me, "Where's the hostess?"

I said, "What's the difference? You're not going to sit where she takes you anyway."

137

He said, "That's pretty funny, you're getting to know me. I must be coming in too often."

I said, "Yeah, I had the same thought. Why don't you do your Magellan routine around the dining room, and let us know when you *discover* your table. Then I'll send her over with menus."

"Okay."

What amazes me is that it never occured to him that he's a buffoon, my sarcasm notwithstanding.

Twenty minutes later he found a seat, his third choice. (The first two were already taken.) I sent the hostess with menus.

The waitress working that station saw him sit down, came to the hostess desk, and said, "I'm not waiting on him. He was so ridiculous last time he was here. He did this and that and this..."

I said, "Yeah, okay, I hear you. I'll get Lee to do it. Lee, pick up table seventeen."

Lee looked at me and said, "Oh no. That's not my station and I can't stand that guy."

I said, "All right, forget it. Diane, pick up seventeen."

Diane said, "No way. You can fire me if you want, but I'm not waiting on him."

And so it went. Every time I asked someone to wait on him, they said no. It got funnier and funnier. By the time I got back to his table, I couldn't control my giggling.

I said, "Well you finally did it."

He said, "Did what?"

"You've abused every server to the point that no one will wait on you."

"What the hell are you talking about!"

"You heard me. I can't get a server to your table."

He said, "That's ridiculous. Get someone over here!"

I said, "Can't help you."

Getting redder, he said, "You should fire all those people."

I asked, "All eight of them? I'll let you in on a little secret: good servers are way harder to find than bad customers."

He said (get this), "If you don't get a waiter over here right now, I'm never setting foot in here again."

I said, "Come on, don't *tease* me like that. It's cruel."

"That's it, I'm outta here!"

Have you ever seen eight waiters, three busboys, one hostess, one bartender, and one owner running through the dining room to hold the door open for a departing guest? I have.

LOST AND FOUND

You ever notice that there has never been, in our two-hundred-and-something year history, one great explorer from Long Island? We've got musicians and authors, actors and actresses, business titans and sports figures, but not one great explorer. Not one. You know why? It's because we, on Long Island, couldn't find our asses with a set of directions, two maps, and a LoJack.

You think I'm overreacting? Ask any hostess if you don't believe me. We just can't get *there* from *here*. It's true. When you give directions over the phone, no one listens the first three times you go through it. Then, on or about the fourth or fifth attempt you sometimes get a pertinent question. On attempt number eight or nine, there may be some feigned interest, and maybe some writing. When it finally dawns on them around attempt number ten or eleven that they have no idea where they are going because they've been yelling at the children, giving instructions to the housekeeper, or listening to Dr. Phil the whole time, you have to start from the beginning.

And you must go very slowly so they can repeat every line.

"You take 495..."

"I take 495..."

"Get off on seaford-Oyster Bay Expressway..."

"I get off seaford-Oyster Bay Expressway..."

That's about how it goes. Simple direction calls usually last about forty minutes to an hour, so that's why I employ twenty hostesses. Thank God for them because I don't have the patience. Not often, but every once in a while, I'll still pick up the phone. It's God's way of telling me that I have too much free time.

Ring. Ring

I picked it up and said, "*CoolFish*, Tom speaking."

She said, "I need directions."

I said, scared, "Where are you coming from?"

"Hauppauge."

"Okay, take the LIE to exit 44 north."

"*Brandon stop hitting your sister!* Excuse me. What was that?"

"Take the LIE to exit 44 north."

"Exit 44. Is that north or south?"

"North. Take that to Jericho Turnpike West."

"*No, don't put them in the dryer with the colors. Yeah, chicken is good. They love the fingers.* I'm sorry. What did you say?"

"To Jericho Turnpike West."

She asked, "West?"

I said, "West."

I should tell you here that the woman had a very distinctive voice. It was kind-of like-Minnie Mouse on steroids. So as excruciating as this was becoming, every time she said something to me—or one of the other thirty-seven people she was conversing with—I had to stifle a laugh.

She said, "Okay, I go west on Jericho."

I said, "Yes."

"Then what?"

"Then you go about ..."

She said, interrupting, "How far—*John did you call the Miller's?*—I'm sorry, what did you say?"

"I didn't say anything. I didn't get the chance."

She said, "Oh, sorry. There's a lot going on here."

"Here too, believe it or not."

She asked, "What do I do when I get to Jericho Turnpike?"

I said, "Turn red.."

"You're pretty funny."

"Just wanted to make sure you were listening. Take Jericho about two and…"

She asked, "Can I put you on hold a minute?"

I said, "Sure, take your time. I've got all day."

The funny thing about call-waiting is the second caller gets all the respect. You call first, then you get kicked to the back of the line when the next person calls. I'm always tempted to hang up and call back so I can get to the front position. Mature, right?

She said, "Sorry that was my babysitter. Okay, where were we?"

I said, "Take it two and a half miles…"

She screamed, "*Give her a piece! What's the matter with you! God!* Sorry."

I said, "Two and a half miles. Go under the overpass…"

"Where's the overpass?"

I said, welling up, "Two and a half miles…"

"Oh, you said that."

"Go under the overpass, and our sign is three-tenths of a mile on the left."

She asked, "Three miles on the left? *John, could you please do something with these two!* Three miles on the left?"

I said, sobbing, "Three-tenths of a mile on the left, *tenths* of a mile."

"On the left or the right?"

"On the left."

Every direction call, just when you think you're done, has the recap. I love the recap.

"Okay, so I take the LIE to exit 44 north. Then I take Jericho Turnpike West two-and-a-half miles. I go under the overpass and you are three miles."

I interrupted, "Three-tenths of a mile."

"Oh, that's right you said that. Was that on the right or the left?"

"Left."

She said, "That was easy."

I said, "Yeah, a piece of cake."

Notice the witty food reference? I thought about having the proverbial after-sex cigarette for the first time in twenty-five years when I finally hung up because I was so exhausted. Little did I know that later that night, I'd have to do it all over again.

A frantic call came to the hostess station about seven o'clock.

The hostess buzzed me in the kitchen and said, "There's an extremely agitated woman on the phone with a funny voice asking to speak to you."

"Did she tell you what city she was calling from?"

The hostess said, "What are you talking about? Pick up the phone, okay?"

I answered, "Tom here."

The lady—in one of the longest run on sentences in recent history—said, "I called you for directions and now we're lost and I have a seven o'clock reservation and my friends are already there and we're going to be late and I don't know where we are and my husband won't ask for directions and it's your fault and I want a free drink when I get there."

"Calm down. I'll guide you in on the phone."

"I can't believe we're lost. It's your fault and your directions sucked."

I said, "Try to find a street sign and give me the name, or find out what state you're in and we'll figure it out."

"This is your fault. Some directions. I hope you cook better than you direct. This sucks...wait; I think we're coming up to a light."

I said, "Okay, look for the sign."

She, "Yeah there it is. I can't read it yet. Hold on...hold on. Wait. It's Jericho Turnpike!"

"That's good."

She asked, "Do I make a left or a right?"

"Are you heading north or south?"

I swear to you this next exchange is verbatim. She said, exasperated, "What does it matter?!! Left or right?!!"

I said, "Okay, make a left."

I hung up. Five minutes later, I got another call from Minnie.

She said, "We still can't find you."

"Where are you?"

Once again, I feel compelled to tell you that the next exchange is absolutely verbatim.

She said, "We are in your parking lot. We can't find the entrance."

"I'll send out a search party."

By this time, my staff knew what was going on, so about six of them go out the front door and start waving.

When she finally walked in, she said sheepishly, "From where we were parked, the bush blocks your sign."

I said, "I would have thought the three-foot blue neon fish on the twenty-foot awning would be a dead giveaway."

"I'm so embarrassed. Did you have to send six employees out?" (Even she was laughing at this point.)

"I was afraid you wouldn't see the first five."

She said, "You're pretty funny."

"Yeah, I'm a scream."

"Are you going to buy us a drink for our trouble?"

I said, "You're pretty funny yourself."

BED SPINS

I've always thought it would be cool to own a boutique hotel. I think every chef harbors thoughts of those little inns in Europe where you cook out of the garden in your backyard, drink the local wines with your guests, and sit in front of a roaring fire discussing subjects as interesting as, what effect does the driving of SUVs have on the mating habits of the ostrich, and does every person who protests the building of a nuclear power plant own a tie-dyed shirt? Who wouldn't want to do that?

Be careful what you wish for. I got lucky.

I'm a partner in a beautiful boutique hotel. I do get to cook out of my own garden, and I do get to drink local wines with the guests, although my discussions rarely hit the lofty levels of the aforementioned Europeans. As you may have learned by now, from my unhinged ravings in the previous pages, some of my restaurant customers can be, well, a little *picky*. I'm now beginning to understand the same is true of some of my hotel guests. I've also become aware that the people who are picky in restaurants are also picky about their hotel rooms. Isn't that a remarkable coincidence?

A couple checked into *Jedediah's* for the weekend. I knew them from up-island and thought him to be a rather peculiar fellow. He's not a bad guy, just peculiar with a capital "P."

Debbie, the innkeeper, was busy checking them in, showing them around, and giving them the "things to do on the North Fork" speech. Being a rather peculiar fellow, he would interrupt her as she was talking to ask peculiar questions about the subject at hand.

Debbie said, "Here we have a guest refrigerator with water, orange juice and..."

Mr. Peculiar interrupted, "Is the orange juice fresh-squeezed?"

"Yes sir, it is. We also have snacks like yogurt, granola bars..."

Mr. Peculiar interrupted again, "Are the pits strained out?"

Debbie patiently said, "Yes sir, they are."

Mr. Peculiar, on cue, "At what temperature do you keep the refrigerator?"

"I'm not sure. I'll have to check with the chef. He has a thermometer."

"If fresh-squeezed orange juice is too cold, you really can't taste it."

Debbie said, "I didn't know that."

Mr. Peculiar asked her, "Can I ask you to put some prunes in there? I don't like yogurt."

"I'll see what I can do."

Get the drift? These aren't bad people, but they're emotional vampires, sucking the energy out of you with unending questions and needs. This orientation, for a normal couple, takes five minutes. Forty-five minutes later, Debbie and Mr. Peculiar were still discussing the brand of coffee used at breakfast, and did we have another artificial sweetener other than Sweet'N Low, because apparently Sweet'N Low will shave years off your life.

Questions like his will shave years off your life, not Sweet'N Low. I could snort Sweet'N Low three times a week and live to be eighty, but I wouldn't last two weeks living with Mr. Peculiar.

They finally got their bags and headed upstairs.

His wife walked in the room and said, "Oh, it's gorgeous."

And it is. The rooms at *Jedediah's* are crown-molded, plush-carpeted, Frette-appointed, exquisitely furnished oases of luxury, complete with your very own fireplace and a heated bathroom floor.

He walked into the room, went over to the bed, laid down, and

immediately announced, "I can't sleep on this mattress."
Debbie asked, "What's the problem?"

He said, "This mattress is uncomfortable. I'll never be able to sleep on it. You'll have to get us another room."

"We don't have another room."

"Then get me another bed."

Isn't that great? Yeah, no problem sir, we'll get you another bed. We just happen to have thirty or so set up in the cellar so you can give them a test ride. Try 'em all out and when you find the one you like, dial 1-800-MATTRES, and leave off the last "S"; that's the "S" for psychosis!

We are talking about a five-thousand dollar pillow top, hotel-rated, lumbar-approved, sex-tested mattress, with two-hundred-million-thread-count Frette sheets, custom pillows, and a comforter with enough goose feathers in it to tickle half of Canada, and this guy can't sleep on it.

Debbie came downstairs and told Adam, the manager, what was going on.

Adam went to see if he could help and asked the man, "What's up?"

The man told him, "I can't sleep on this mattress. It's uncomfortable."

Adam said, "It's the only one we have right now and all the rooms are full, so I don't know what I can do about it."

"Okay, then turn the mattress over."

Adam said, "Huh?"

"Turn the mattress over. Maybe the other side will be better."

Adam said, "Sir, this is a pillow-top mattress. There *is* no other side. It's one-sided."

The man then said, "Okay, why don't we try turning it around instead of over, so the head is at the foot side and vice versa."

"You want me to turn the mattress around so the head is where the feet are, and the feet are where the head is?"

He said, "Yes."

Adam asked, "And just what exactly is it that you think that's going to do?"

"I don't know, but it can't be any worse than this side."

"Okay. Are you going out this afternoon?"

The man said, "Yes. We planned on visiting some wineries."

"Okay, when you go out, we'll turn it around so it'll be ready when you get back."

He looked at Adam suspiciously for a second and said, "How will I know that you really turned it around if you plan to do it when I'm gone?"

Adam said, "Look, I promise I'll turn it around, but we're busy right now so it may take me a little while to get to it. Besides, if it's that uncomfortable I'm sure you'll notice the difference."

"Okay, thank you."

Adam, laughing, said, "Don't mention it. Anything else you need? Do you want the sheets on backwards or the pillows turned inside out?"

The man started to laugh also and said, "No, just the bed." At least he could laugh at himself.

The hardest part about turning the bed around was explaining why to the kitchen guys who I recruited to help Adam. Try explaining to three guys who come from a country whose gross national product barely exceeds the price of two Posturepedic pillows that some guy can't sleep on his mattress until it faces the other way.

We went up to the room, undid the comforter, pillow, and sheets, picked the mattress up by the four corners, and with three of us moving one way and one moving the other, we tippy-toed that mother around from north-south to south-north. Debbie came up to remake the bed and then punched out and went home.

Two hours later, as dinner service was beginning, the girl who worked the night desk came into the kitchen and said, "One of the guests wants to speak with you."

I said, "Who?"

She said, "Mr. Peculiar. There seems to be a problem with his bed."

"Now what?"

"I don't know, he insisted on talking to you."

I walked out, saw him, and asked, "How were the wineries?"

He asked me, "Why didn't you turn the bed?"

I said, "We did turn the bed."

He said, "Do you think I'm stupid?"

I was thinking, "*Nah, I'd have to go with nuts,*" but I said, "No, I don't think you're stupid, maybe just mistaken."

He then said, "I can't sleep on that mattress until you turn it around."

Staring at him for a second and trying to figure out what to do, I finally said, "Okay, you want it turned around? We'll turn it around."

Sometimes it's just easier to give 'em what they want.

If you think explaining to my kitchen guys why we were turning the mattress around was hard the first time, you should have been there for number two. We went back up to the room. He was waiting there with his wife. We undid the bed, grabbed four corners, and this time thankfully, all going the same direction, moved the mattress back to the original position that it was in when he first pronounced it uncomfortable. Adam made up the bed as my crew and I went back downstairs muttering under our breath, one in English, two in Spanish.

The rest of the night was relatively quiet. I ran into him the next morning when he was checking out.

I asked, "Hey Mr. Peculiar (I used his real name), how'd you sleep?"

He said, "Pretty good. I've got to tell you something though. I was a little annoyed at you and your staff yesterday. I think Adam was trying to take me for an idiot, telling me he turned the bed around. I could tell right away when I lay down last night. It was actually pretty comfortable once you turned it."

I thought it was time to have some fun.

I said, "You noticed that much of a difference when we turned it last night?"

He said, "Yeah, absolutely."

"A big difference or just a subtle difference?"

"It was like night and day. I can't believe you people thought I wouldn't notice."

I said, "I feel terrible about that. I guess they got busy and forgot and then told me they'd turned it, thinking you wouldn't notice. Sorry. You know, I always tell them, 'You've got to get up pretty early in the morning to be pulling those mattress tricks.'"

He chuckled and said, "Well, no harm done, but I probably did you a big favor by having you turn it. If I were you, I'd leave it just the way it is. It's so much better."

I said, "You know what? That's a good idea. I think I will."

Unreserved Nerve

Montauk Point is located at the very tip of the South Fork of Long Island. The town itself is three or four miles west of the Point, just east of the world-renowned Hamptons. It doesn't have the same cache as the Hamptons, but I prefer it because of its small town, resort-by-the-sea-charm, and as the bumper stickers attest, "Montauk is a quaint little drinking village with a slight fishing problem." Need I say more? The seven or eight years I spent in Montauk were probably my favorite years in the business. Montauk is a magical place, and I have a spiritual connection there that has to be related to some past life. There's no other explanation for going out there and thinking you can do fifty-two weeks' worth of business in eight. But the combination of the natural beauty, a very interesting cast of local characters, and my seemingly endless capacity for self-delusion was way too strong a brew for me to resist.

Don't get me wrong, we had a pretty good run out there, but winter is winter, and Montauk is Montauk, so the reality of that limits how much business you can actually do, no matter how good your product might be. It becomes a lifestyle choice in essence, and you make whatever concessions you have to make in order to wake up there every day.

It also takes a tremendous amount of financial and personal discipline to be in a seasonal business. All your revenue comes fast and furious in a couple of months and then shuts off like a faucet for the rest of the year. You need a plan to conserve the funds in the summer to dole out in the leaner times. On a personal level, there is a lot of downtime, and as my friend's grandmother used to say, "Idle

151

hands are the devil's workshop."

Most people, when they think of the restaurant business, talk about the hours and how brutal they are. For me, it was one of the hooks. I learned a long time ago that having the right-brain artist's imagination and being a child of the sixties conspired to allow me a certain level of "creativity" in my use of time off, if you get my drift. I am frankly, capable of some really stupid stuff when given the opportunity and the time to pursue it, so I found out early on that increased work hours were, oddly enough, a health benefit. If you combined my off-hours antics with the fact that I've never had a plan in my life, and my tendency to spend money like a drunken Democrat, I probably wasn't the best candidate for a seasonal business. But there I was in Montauk, trying to make it work.

Maximizing your intake in season is critical to your success. Once the summer finally gets under way out there, every night is like a Saturday, and being busy every night puts a lot of pressure on the restaurant as a whole, but on the dining room staff, it's especially difficult. You only have so many tables and so much square footage, and you have to feed as many people as you can—while making them comfortable and not feeling rushed, with dessert and five cups of coffee—in as little time as possible, so you can do it again, and then hopefully again.

When we book a table on a busy night, I consider it a real estate transaction: it just happens to come with a meal. We're selling square footage. I don't mean to sound chilly, and we certainly want you to enjoy yourself, but in reality, we need to sell the tables to survive. Last I heard, Berkshire Hathaway was not awash in restaurant stocks.

The other problem in Montauk is that since it's a beach, golf, and fishing town, no one goes out to dinner before seven. This decreases the time you have to feed the guests and increases the pressure on the dining room staff.

One August night at about 6:40 p.m., a couple walked up to the hostess stand and asked, "Do you have a table for two?"

The hostess asked them, "Do you have a reservation?"

The woman said, "No, but we were hoping that since it's early, we would be able to get a table."

This is where a good hostess is worth a fortune. Shifting tables and times, dealing with no-shows, early arrivals, late arrivals, and over-bookings is a very delicate and difficult job. That night we had one of my superstars on the door.

The hostess said, "I'm sure we can do something here; just give me a minute."

She looked at the reservation sheet and after two or three minutes of adjusting said, "Okay, if you'll follow me please," and led them to a table for two.

As they arrived at the table, the man said, "I don't want to sit here."

The hostess looked around the dining room, pointed to another table for two, and said, "How about that table over there?"

He said, "No, I want a bigger table. I'm a big guy. I won't be comfortable at a small table."

The hostess patiently explained to him, "Sir, I can't give you a table of four for two people. We would lose two seats."

Looking at the empty dining room, he said, "Well, you really don't look all that busy to me."

She said, "It's not busy yet, but in twenty minutes I'll need all the seats I can get. I can't give you the bigger table."

You would think that someone who didn't have the foresight to make a reservation, in Montauk, in season, would be just a little bit grateful that she was willing to take a chance to seat him in the first place. When a hostess takes a chance like that, somewhere in the course of the night, she is going to pay for it.

As all of this was going on, I decided to walk out to the hostess desk to look at the reservations to see what I was up against that night. The hostess and the couple were back at the desk, and she was studying the reservation sheet for any possibilities, while trying in vain to get him to sit at a table for two. As I approached the desk, I got wind there was some kind of problem.

I asked the hostess, "What's up?"

She said, "The gentleman doesn't want to sit at a deuce. He wants a table for four. He thinks he'll be more comfortable."

This really comes down to a Hobson's choice. Do I make one difficult customer, without a reservation, happy at the expense of four people who already have a reservation, or do I make four people with a reservation happy at the expense of one difficult customer without a reservation? Even I can figure that one out.

I said, "Sir, if I could give you the bigger table I would, but I can't. I realize that you probably think I'm nuts because no one is here now, but if you look at this reservation sheet, I'm about fifteen minutes away from being fully committed here, and frankly, we're risking a bit of a log jam seating you at the deuce. Maybe we can give you a reservation for another night or you can come back when it's not so busy, *say in November*. I don't want you to be uncomfortable, but I can't give up the two seats."

Here it comes. The man looked at me and said, "Fine, but let me tell you two something. I know Tom Schaudel, and when I tell him what's going on out here, heads are going to roll!"

I didn't know quite what to say. The man just said he knew me, was going to call me, tell on me, then have me fire—me. That's a lot to digest right there.

The hostess and I looked at each other, not knowing what to do. She figured it out first. She pinched her nose shut with her thumb and forefinger, covered her mouth with the rest of her hand, and ran into the kitchen howling.

Still standing there stunned, I asked, "You know Tom?"

He said, "Damn right I know him, and I'll let him know how I was treated here!"

What could I do?

I said, "Look man, I'm sorry. Sit wherever you want. The last thing we need is him coming out here all pissed off and throwing a tantrum. I apologize."

The man and his wife sat at a table for four, had dinner, and I'm assuming that they enjoyed themselves, since he never called me to tell me to fire me. The reservations for that table were backed up all night, for which the hostess endured endless abuse.

I had to buy a round of appetizers and a bottle of wine for the first four customers scheduled for that table that was seated forty minutes late, and had to pick up the total bill for the second party scheduled at that table because their wait was even worse.

Later on that night, I was having a glass of wine at the bar and relaying the story to one of my regulars.

He said, "No way."

I brought the hostess over to confirm the story.

We were all laughing about it when the hostess said, "I can't believe you didn't say anything. Why didn't you tell him?"

I said, "I thought about it for a second, but quickly realized it would take all the fun out of it."

"Fun? You call three hours of pissed-off customer abuse fun? Do you have any idea what I went through with that table's reservations after you decided to just give it away? And, by the way, how much did it cost you in comps?"

I said, "You're young, you'll recover, and anyway, it's not about the money. How many times in your life do you get to see a perfect ten?"

"What are you talking about," she asked.

I said, "A ten, a perfect ten. I'm forty-five years old, and I've only seen two before: Bo Derek in the movie *10* and Mary Lou Retton at the Olympics. This guy was a ten, the perfect knucklehead. If I had said something, he would have immediately fallen to a seven-point-five or an eight. It would be like watching someone do the perfect gymnastic routine and then seeing them break their ankle on the dismount. I couldn't do it. Besides, at some point he'll probably figure it out. Every once in a while, even a knucklehead can have an enlightening moment and far be it from me to screw with enlightenment."

THE NAME GAME

I guess it's just part of being thorough, but I'm always suspicious of people who have two minutes of conversation about a reservation or a party, and they need to know your name. Some people, when they ask for my name, have that *tone*. You know, the one that says, "If anything, *anything* goes wrong, there will be hell to pay."

I've had people ask for my name and then threaten my job. I love that one: "I'll have your job." My thought is, *You're welcome to it*. Be careful what you wish for. Oh and by the way, what's *your* name? Besides, who's going to fire me? I'm the boss.

Anyway, a woman came into *CoolFish* to see about booking a party. She was going to have a bridal shower for her daughter She talked to Diane, giving her a list of about 367 special requests, saying that her daughter was freaking out about the shower and everything had to be perfect.

Showers usually include a champagne punch, salads, lots of gifts, a wishing well, and a silly hat, which is all pretty much standard stuff. But the woman had so many other needs that the party was complicated to the point of ridiculous. Diane decided she couldn't deal with it. She told the woman that she had to talk to the manager.

The woman said, "Fine. What's your name?"

Diane said, "Diane."

The woman called Ann, the manager, on the phone to talk about the party. After an hour's speech about all her special needs, Ann said, "You're going to have to talk to the owner."

The woman said, "Fine. What's your name?"

Ann said, "Ann."

The woman called me and said, "I'd like to have a bridal shower for thirty-five women. The punch has to be blue, the salads have to be organic, the wait staff needs to carry out the gifts, the wishing well has to be a certain size, we need a silly hat, twelve gift tables, cocktails for the men, coffee picked fresh in Jamaica, chemically-free raised fish, etcetera, etcetera. Got it?" I was thinking, "*Yada, yada, yada.*"

I said cleverly, "We really can't do a party that small (or that neurotic), but maybe you could call our other restaurant, *Thom-Thom*, and they could help you." (Heh, heh.)

She said, "Fine. What's your name?"

I said, "Tom."

She called *Thom Thom* and spoke to Jason, the manager, who booked the party, warts and all, and just when he thought it was done, she said, "How do I know the food will be good? I've never eaten here."

Jason said, "Why don't you come in on Saturday night, and we'll buy you dinner. That way you can be sure it's good, how's that?"

She said, "That's great. What's your name?"

Jason said, "Jason."

Friday came and she walked into *Thom Thom* at 6:45 p.m. She wasn't supposed to be there for another twenty-four hours.

She told the hostess, "We couldn't make it on Saturday so we came tonight instead." She continued, "My husband is parking the car; he'll be right in."

Here's the problem and as you can see, it happens often.. The dining room was relatively empty, but fifteen minutes later, all the reservations were due to show up and we wouldn't have any seats available. It's a tricky explanation. Lana, the hostess, tries her best.

"We don't have any seats available right now, but if you can wait about twenty minutes I'll sort out the reservations and see if we can get you seated."

The woman said, "You are kidding, right? There's no one here."

Lana said, "I know, but all the first-turn reservations are due in fifteen minutes, and since you don't have one, I have to make sure I have a table for you. The only other thing I can do is seat you at the bar."

The woman lost it. "I am not sitting at the bar!"

Lana, exasperated said, "That's all I can do right now," and went back to the reservation book.

The woman yelled, "You look at me when I'm talking to you! What's your name!"

Lana said, "Lana."

"Get me the manager!"

Jackie, the manager on duty that night, is one of my nicest employees. She's very patient, tolerant, and kind, and usually has no trouble making a guest happy.

Jackie came over and said, "What's wrong?"

The woman said, "I want to be seated."

"What time is your reservation?"

"I don't have one."

Jackie said, "Okay, if you could just be a little patient, we'll get you seated."

The woman screamed, "I'm not waiting! Don't you get it? I booked a party here! You don't know how to run a restaurant! I've been in the restaurant business, my husband's been in the restaurant business, and my family is in the restaurant business! I want a seat!"

Why didn't her family book her party? It's just a question.

Jackie, trying to calm the situation, said, "Ma'am, please don't speak to me that way. We're trying to help you here."

The woman screamed, "Fuck you!"

Isn't that nice?

Jackie said, "That's it. I'm done. We don't have a table for you."

The restaurant was starting to get busy. Jackie walked away from the woman, and the woman screamed, "Don't you walk away from me!"

Jackie continued walking.

The lady, now much louder, "What's your *naammee!*"

Jackie turned around and screamed back, "Michelle!"

The woman yells back, "Oh yeah Michelle, I'll have your job" and turned and walked out the door past her bewildered husband who was just walking in. She grabbed him by the elbow and dragged him, backwards, out the door.

I can spot 'em comin' a mile away.

Happy 60ᵀᴴ...No, 50ᵀᴴ... No, 60ᵀᴴ Birthday

Remember Leslie Gore? She had a bunch of hits in the early 60s and every one of her songs had the word "cry" in them. Her biggest hit was, "It's My Party (And I'll Cry If I Want To)," and with that in mind, we begin.

A man booked a table for eighteen people on a Saturday night to celebrate his sixtieth birthday. He sat with Ann and did the menu, pricing, and the cake; no special seating arrangements were discussed. This part is the key to grasping what happened.

Eighteen people on Saturday night at seven o'clock is tricky business, so we handle the seating arrangements. You want to shop for a table, come on a Monday. We could use the entertainment. If you let the professionals run the dining room—God forbid—things will go so much smoother.

A couple of days later, one of our regulars booked a party of twenty for his fiftieth birthday on the same day. The man literally lives at *CoolFish*, so when he requested to sit in the Fishbowl, we said, "Sure."

The Fishbowl is the glassed-in seating area in the bar. It just so happens to seat about twenty people so it was perfect for his party.

The fateful night arrived and balloons and flowers were delivered for the regular customer's fiftieth birthday party. They said, "Happy 50ᵗʰ Birthday." Go figure. We placed them on the table, not knowing that at that very moment a storm was forming in the parking lot.

The man who was having the sixtieth birthday party arrived first. He had only three of his party of eighteen people with him. He walked in, told the hostess his name, looked at the Fishbowl with the balloons and flowers and said, "Great, our table is ready."

161

Ann, the manager, said, "Sir, that's not your table. Your table is in the dining room."

Ann is 4'11" tall. The man was 5'2". It's always the short ones isn't it?

It took this guy fifty-nine years to find someone short enough to yell at, and he absolutely unloaded on Ann. "I'm not sitting in the dining room! I am sitting at that table!"

Ann calmly said, "I'm sorry sir, but that table is booked for another party."

"Then move the other party! I'm sitting there!"

He then proceeded to go and sit at the table, by himself, with the balloons that said "Happy 50th Birthday." His three guests, not knowing what to do stood mute at the hostess desk. He was my first squatter. We asked him to get up but he refused. We wanted to drag him back to the hostess desk but were afraid he would take the tablecloth with him.

Ann finally convinced him to follow her into the dining room to see his table, which was a huge mistake. This is a public place and so the public was there. Upon seeing his table, the man lost his mind.

Screaming, he announced, "I will not sit at this table! This table sucks!"

Ann said, "How about a table along the banquet with a privacy screen?"

The man said louder, "What the fuck is wrong with you people! I'm not sitting here! I'm going back to the other table!"

As they walked back to the hostess desk, Ann was getting annoyed.

She said, "Sir, you are not getting that table."

"I want the owner!"

"He's not here."

The man screamed, "Then get him on the phone!"

Ann asked, "I think he's out of the country, and besides, he's not too stable either. You may not want to do that."

As the man demanded the table yet again, he was screaming, clapping his hands together, and literally jumping up and down. I kid you not. He actually left his feet; about as high as Phil Mickelson did when he won the Masters. Maybe two inches, three at best.

Just when you think you've arrived at the outer limits of bizarre, he uttered the absolute showstopper.

He screamed out, "I'm calling my lawyer!"

Ann said, "Huh?"

The man, now on a very loud roll, said, "I'm calling my lawyer right fucking now!"

And what exactly would he say to his lawyer? Can you possibly envision that conversation?

The man calls and says, "Hello, Perry?"

The lawyer answers, "Yes."

The man says, "I have a huge problem."

The lawyer asks, "What happened?"

"I'm at CoolFish for a birthday dinner, and they are trying to seat me in the dining room!"

The lawyer says, "Those dirty bastards! Can you imagine the nerve of those people? I'll sue the asses off them...no, better yet, I'll close them...no, you know what, let's go for the death penalty."

Thankfully, his family talked him out of calling. They decided to leave. He was very pissed-off and was leaning towards killing someone, and the other three people were just plain mortified, so it was a timely idea. And we couldn't have been more thrilled by the way.

But there were two problems: The rest of his party still hadn't arrived, and where the hell were they going to take eighteen people at seven-thirty on a Saturday night on Long Island without a reservation? (Heh, heh.) Try to picture eighteen people sitting in Burger King with a sixty-year-old man wearing a paper crown, chomping on a Whopper.

As he announced he was leaving—like this was some kind of threat—he said he would tell everyone he knew not to come here anymore. Do you have any idea how many times I've heard that speech? Yawn. Besides, no one actually listens to lunatics, you just kind-of stare at them.

As he walks out the door he yelled, "I'm calling my lawyer! I'm fucking suing!"

Again with the lawyer. You know, I've been sued for some pretty weird shit in my day: kitchen accidents, assorted burns and self-inflicted stab wounds, three or four suicide attempts stepping in and out of the front door, nonperformance of a catering party due to a hurricane, and by someone who cut a testicle on the bathroom toilet door latch. Don't ask. But never, ever in my forty years in the restaurant business have I been sued for trying to seat someone in the dining room. But I'm sure that there is a struggling lawyer out there, with way too much time on his hands, willing to spring the argument of "Fishbowlus Limitus" on an unprepared court. Pray for me, my friends.

A Lamb by Any
Other Name is Still a Snapper

Have you ever had someone say something to you that made you get that look on your face that a dog gets when it stares at its owner, trying to comprehend what's he's saying? It's the look where his head is slightly cocked to one side, the eyebrows are scrunched down, and he's straining to understand English.

Try this one. One night a woman ordered a rack of lamb as her entrée. She seemed to be a little *eccentric*. How did we know that, you might ask? Good question. She had on a hat.

I've always subscribed to the theory that if you wear a hat, have a fashion sense that includes bow ties, or smoke a pipe, you are a full-blown nut. It's been proven true time and time again. If you give it enough thought and pay careful attention to those around you, you will eventually come around to see that I'm right. The bigger the hat, the bigger the problem, the more colorful the bow tie, the more *colorful* the character, and God help you if someone is smoking a pipe that curls in the shape of the letter "S" below their chin.

I'm not completely sure why bow tie wearers and pipe smokers are crazy—and they are—but I have developed a theory about chronic hat wearers. I call it "cranial warming." I believe that the constant wearing of hats causes a slight warming of the brain over a long period of time. Think about it for a minute. If one degree of global warming over a period of one hundred years can cause the environmentalists to go apoplectic about the destruction of something the size of planet Earth, then how can an organ the size of your fist have a prayer of surviving the long-term effects of wearing a hat? We've always been told that heat escapes from your head, right? Well, hats trap the heat and the heat cooks the brain,

166

so it's not as farfetched as you may think. Where's Al Gore when I need him?

Let me try to describe this hat for you so you can have some sense of what we were dealing with. It was the first time I ever saw someone wearing a hat in a restaurant that was bigger than the table they were sitting at. It resembled a flying saucer with fake fruit on it. The front was slightly turned up—the only reason she could see where she was going—and the sides and back cast a six-foot shadow in three directions. There was a ribbon wrapped around the bowl of the hat, which spilled off the back, down her to her waist. The fact that someone could see a hat like that in a store and think, "Yup, that's one good looking hat," remains to be one of the great mysteries of our time. I'm guessing that she was in her seventies; that's about the age where it appears that most people stop giving a shit about what other people think about how they appear. But again, it's only a guess. Her husband was dressed relatively normal. No Don Ho rum punch shirt, and nothing that said, I love Myrtle Beach.

The server brought their entrées to the table. Two minutes later she called the server over, pointed to her rack of lamb, and said, "Take this back. I don't want it."

The server asked, "What's wrong with it?"

The woman said, "It's not lamb."

"It's not lamb?"

"No. It's not lamb."

The server, who fully realized seconds after seeing the hat that she was in for an interesting evening, picked up the plate and said, "Okay, I'll let the kitchen know. Is there anything else I can get you instead?"

The woman said, "Yes. You can bring me a rack of lamb, real lamb."

Her husband, I assume from years of experience, remained silent. These types of displays are rarely an isolated incident for hat-wearers, and as I mentioned before, her hat was only slightly smaller than Rhode Island; which just for the record, is not an island..

The server brought the lamb back to the kitchen and said, "Table fourteen doesn't want her lamb rack. She wants a lamb rack instead," and started laughing, anticipating my reaction.

At first I couldn't formulate a response, and I'm sure the look on my face was the same as the dog trying to comprehend what its owner is saying.

I finally said the only thing you could say to a statement like that. I asked, "What the hell are you talking about?"

By that point, between the hat and my reaction to the lamb crisis, the server lost it in a laughing fit. Trying to speak—and not too successfully—I might add, she said, "That nut with the hat, *ha ha ha*, you know, the one I told you about, *ha ha ha*, she says that's not lamb, *ha ha ha ha*, *ha ha ha ha*, and she wants another one *ha ha ha ha!*"

Trying to get a grip on this and now laughing myself from watching her lose it, I asked her, "It's not lamb? Not lamb, huh? Did she tell what she thought it was?"

Trying to regain her composure, she said, "No," and lost it all over again. I'm sure it was the look on my face.

I decided to go to the table. As I walked out onto the patio, I spotted the hat right away. Frankly, you couldn't miss it, since it occupied about forty square feet and shrunk my seating capacity by about ten percent.

I walked up to the table, introduced myself, and said, "What a lovely hat. I understand that there's a problem with the lamb."

She said, "Absolutely there is!"

I said, "What's wrong?"

She said. "That lamb rack you gave me was not lamb."

I said quizzically, "Really?"

"That's right. I've eaten lamb all over the world and whatever that was, it wasn't lamb."

I said, "I'm curious. What do you think it *was?*"

"I don't know, but it wasn't lamb."

Trying not to stare at the hat, I said, "Well, the only other animal that has a rack that size is a Labrador retriever."

She exclaimed, "Great. Now every time I order a rack of lamb I'm going to think of eating a dog. Thanks for the reference!"

I wanted to say, "And every time I see someone with a hat, I'll think of you, my dear," but instead I said, "I was just trying to assure you that it couldn't be anything but lamb. I don't know what else to say. If I make you another lamb, it's going to bear a remarkable resemblance to the one you just had, so maybe you should order something else."

Her husband—who had been eating the whole time this had been going on—looked up from his halibut and said, "Make her a piece of fish."

That was easy. I was speechless. Recovering, I asked him, "What if she doesn't believe the snapper is a snapper?"

Not even looking up from his plate he said, "Then I guess I'll have to eat it."

She said, "OK then bring me the fish."

Is it me?

Blackened Snapper Recipe

Back in the early eighties in New Orleans, Chef Paul Prudhomme brought redfish and the blackening cooking process to the attention of the rest of the country. As with any other cooking fad, chefs everywhere were blackening everything from oysters to ice cream, and what was a brilliantly simple cooking method became a clichéd afterthought in our culinary lexicon. I think that's a shame because when applied properly, blackening is a great way to spice up milder tasting fish. The heat of the pepper reminds me of the weather, the women, and the music of New Orleans and those flavors always bring a smile to my face. Here I use our local blackfish, also known as tautog, instead of Paul's redfish.

Ingredients:

2 tablespoons sweet paprika
2 teaspoons salt
1 teaspoon onion powder
1 teaspoon garlic powder
1 teaspoon chili powder
¾ teaspoon cayenne pepper
¾ teaspoon ground white pepper
¾ teaspoon black pepper
1 teaspoon dried thyme
3 ounces soy or canola oil
Six 8-ounce snapper filets, about ½ inch thick

Mix the dry ingredients in a medium sized bowl. Heat the oil in a cast iron skillet over high heat until very hot. Thoroughly coat the fillets with the seasoning mix by either dredging them in a bowl, or sprinkling the seasoning on the filet and patting it with your hand. Place filets in the skillet, being careful not to splatter the hot oil. Cook uncovered until blackened, about 2 minutes. Carefully turn the filets over and cook an additional 2 minutes. (The cooking time will vary with the thickness of the filet. The fish is done when it appears white throughout the filet.)

Chef's tip: Any fish can be substituted for the blackfish, as long as it's at least ½ thick and not more than ¾ inch thick; any thinner or thicker will throw off your cooking time and result in dry or partially-raw fish. The exception is tuna because it's better served rare. Be very careful placing and turning the fish in the pan. Hot oil can cause a nasty burn.

Wine pairing: Blue Point Summer Ale

Tasteless

I don't know why I continue to hand out menus. Giving some people a menu is an exercise in futility. They can't eat anything on it until they complete a redrafting, and then they will grudgingly order a dish, provided they either don't like the dish, or every element of the dish has been thoroughly changed to maximize the confusion in the kitchen. It's a Long Island thing.

A party of four arrived for a Thursday night dinner. One of the women was interested in the tuna with foie gras, portabello mushroom, and red wine glaze. The problem, however, was that she didn't like tuna, foie gras is fattening, and the red wine glaze has alcohol and veal stock in it. Anyone with a shred of sanity would pick another dish, but crazy people usually don't know they are crazy, right? For her, I'm sure this was just another routine Thursday night dinner with the homies.

The waitress came to the table to take their dinner order. She told the waitress—for the whole table, I might add—that they will have four tunas. She would like two prepared as they are on the menu for their husbands. There's a novel concept. She said that her friend would like her tuna well-done (not recommended) with black and white sesame seeds, the foie gras well-done (again not recommended), shiitake mushrooms instead of the portabellos, and a Dijon mustard sauce (which I haven't made since the seventies) instead of a red wine glaze. That was, as I later discovered, the easy one.

Ready? She said, "I want salmon instead of the tuna, prepared like *her* tuna but with only white sesame seeds. (Did I mention that sesame seeds, white or black, were not on the menu?) I would like the salmon grilled, not seared."

The waitress interrupted her and said, "That's not going to be good for the sesame seeds."

She didn't care. She continued, "Take the foie gras that was going to be on my tuna because I can't have it, sear it with some kind of fruit, and give it to my husband as an appetizer. The portabellos are okay, but they will need to be steamed and sliced, and I want a sauce made with only lemon, and I can't have any butter. It can't even touch the plate. I'll get deathly sick if there's any butter. No butter!"

The waitress came into the kitchen and said, "I've got a live one on table twenty-one."

I asked, "What does she want?"

She asked, "How do you know it's a *she*?"

Truth be told, I average seven out of ten for the women in the "I need to drive someone crazy" department, so I was betting the percentages.

I said, "Uh, lucky guess? It is a woman though, isn't it?"

I got the look. The waitress repeated the order to the best of her ability. I've had some all star orders in my time, but this was up there in the top three.

I said, "That can't possibly be right."

Annoyed, she said, "That's exactly what she told me."

I said, "Let me go talk to her and get it straight. I may have to fly in a team of specialists for this one."

I literally went to the table twice just to try to understand the order. Truthfully, I can't even say if she told me the same preparation both times—it was a rather detailed list of requirements—but it was also a slow night and in a twisted way, I was kind of having fun watching her go though her act. It was like the proverbial car wreck; you don't want to look, but you can't turn away.

After learning the second version of "the meal," she told me all about her twenty-seven food allergies, the requisite gall bladder operation, and the possible early onset of Alzheimer's caused by cooking in aluminum pots.

I said, "Maybe instead of the having the salmon you should be hospitalized. They could give you an IV, perhaps with white sesame seeds or something." Three of the four of them found that funny.

Knowing all along I didn't have a prayer of getting it right, I headed back to the kitchen. I explained the order to the cooks. You can only imagine the looks I got, but they marched through it like the good soldiers that they are.

I yelled, "Hey guys, pick up twenty-one," and out went what I considered to be a valiant attempt at the impossible.

Five minutes later, both of the special orders were returned to the kitchen. What a surprise. The first one only needed more fire on the already well-done tuna; no problem. The salmon was another story, actually a novel. The salmon needed more fire also, so I returned it to the aluminum pan for a few minutes, hoping that Alzheimer's would help her forget how to get to the restaurant. Although she requested the portabello steamed, it was too *mushy*, and although she requested no butter, the sauce was nine times too thin.

We fixed the order and sent it back to the table, but it looked like our second attempt to correct the uncorrectable had also crashed and burned.

I was summoned to the table for an audience with the queen.

She said, "I'm very disappointed with the food."

I said, "What's wrong?"

She said, "Everything. Nothing was cooked as I asked you to."

"Which time?"

"Look at her tuna; it's too well-done."

I said, "I hope you realize that it was well-done the first time you sent it back. Then you said you wanted it cooked more, after it was already well-done, just as you ordered it."

"She didn't want it *that* well-done! And my salmon is tasteless."
No shit?

I said, "When you decided to play Rachael Ray with your dinner order, you removed any possibility of flavor."

She then said, "Whatever, take both of these back! We don't want them."

I said, "Okay. Can I get you anything else?" I was hoping she would say, "The check," but it seems that whenever my ship comes in, I'm standing in the train station.

She said, "We're not that hungry anyway, so will you split a vegetable plate for us?"

I said, "Sure, no problem, but I'm not changing anything on it. Okay?"

She asked, "Are there enough vegetables on it for the two of us?"

I said, "You know, the last I heard there were."

The Rare Threat

Here's the pecking order for the firing of a customer. If we just need to end a relationship with a difficult customer, any one of my managers will handle it. If someone is drunk or belligerent, it's usually handled by Mark, the bartender. He's very diplomatic and patient, but he's also the size of Texas. I trust them all to make the right decisions, but if the situation gets out of hand or potentially dangerous, then I feel responsible to step in. With that background information, we'll proceed.

Bullies like to prey on the weak or those whom they perceive to be. I was working a Saturday night on the kitchen line with a million tickets hanging in front of me, when a manager and a very upset waitress walked into my station.

The manager said, "You may have to go out there and deal with this one yourself."

I was crazy busy and I didn't need any more problems than I already had just trying to get through service.

I said, "Deal with what?"

The manager said, "I have a huge problem on table forty-one and I don't even want to tell you what happened. You may have to go out there."

I said, "Out with it. What happened?"

A little more background information is necessary here. We only cook tuna rare or well-done in my restaurants. The problem with medium rare and medium well, especially with tuna, is that everyone has a different idea of what that is. I'm just not talented enough to cook sixty orders of tuna fifty different ways, and get them all correct for sixty people who don't know what those particular temperatures mean to begin with. See my dilemma?

Knowing that it tastes better rare and considering my lack of talent, we choose to take the easy route. It's also listed on the menu as "Rare Yellowfin Tuna," and the servers are told to let the customer know it's only cooked rare, or completely well-done for the Bumble Bee fans.

Some people just don't play well with others. This man ordered tuna and told the waitress he would like it medium. The waitress explained that the chef will only serve it rare or well, and if he wanted his fish cooked medium, he should order something else.

Get ready, here's the quote, "Tell the chef to shove his pride up his ass and cook it the way I want it."

I still don't believe it. Who would say this to a twenty-five-year-old woman? What do you even say to someone like that?

The manager recounted the whole scene to me, and I completely lost it. Now I just wanted to know who I was dealing with—a crazed biker, Mafioso, the KKK, or a Black Panther—and did I need a gun, a meat cleaver, or three dishwashers and a leg of lamb.

So I said to her, "Who is this guy?"

She said, "I don't know."

"What does he look like?"

"He's about 5'3", weighs about, I'd say, 120 pounds and he's probably about seventy-five years old."

I said, "You can't be serious, now what?"

The manager said, "Can I handle this?"

I said, "Please. I've got enough going on in here."

I have to tell you I wanted him thrown out.

The manager said to him, "Here's the deal. You have absolutely no shot at a medium tuna. Your choices are: have it rare, well-done, order something else, or leave."

He said, "I can't believe the chef won't cook my tuna medium."

She said, "I can't believe that you said what you said to my server. You should be ashamed of yourself, at your age. I also can't believe the rest of your party would even eat with you. Choose something else or leave, and, by the way, no one will miss you if you go."

He said, "All right, all right. I'll have the sea bass. God-damned chefs are such prima donnas."

I'll bet a thousand dollars right now that there's a sign on his license plate that says, "World's Greatest Grandpa."

Grilled Yellowfin Tuna/Seaweed Soba Noodle Salad Recipe

*O*f all the preparations of tuna that I have cooked or eaten, I prefer it paired best with Asian ingredients. I spent a considerable amount of time studying martial arts and, consequently, eating in Chinatown. This preparation is probably the result of those experiences. The sweet, salty, and spicy flavors of the dish and the richness of the tuna is a marriage made in culinary heaven. I don't recommend this to anyone who needs their tuna cooked to the "Bumble-Bee" state. This is meant to be and best served rare; the rarer the better.

Ingredients for the marinade:

1 cup soy sauce

½ cup soy oil

6 tablespoons rice wine vinegar

6 tablespoons plum wine or Aji Mirin

1 teaspoon sesame oil

1 tablespoon cilantro, minced

2 tablespoons garlic, minced

2 tablespoons ginger, minced

1 tablespoon black sesame seeds

1 tablespoon white sesame seeds

1 pinch red pepper flakes to taste

Four 6-ounce tuna steaks

6 ounces soba noodles, cooked al dente

3 ounces wakame seaweed

Whisk marinade ingredients together in a medium sized bowl. Place the tuna in a shallow bowl and using half the marinade, marinate the steaks, turning every 15 minutes for 1 hour. In a separate bowl, combine the cooked soba noodles and the wakame, mixing until the wakame is evenly distributed throughout the noodles. Add the remaining marinade to the noodles, toss, and set aside. Preheat outdoor barbeque to very hot. Remove the tuna steaks and drain the excess marinade. Grill the steaks 1 ½ to 2 minutes on each side. The outside should be nicely charred with a warm, rare center. Remove from the grill. Divide the seaweed-soba noodle salad among four plates. Slice the tuna across the grain into 1/8 inch slices, arrange beside the salad. Serve.

Chef's tip: Salmon works very well with this preparation as well. The tuna can also be seared in a cast iron skillet on the stove if the barbeque is inconvenient.

Wine pairing: Paumanok Chenin Blanc

THE BILL

In what other business could you even think about trying this? A man booked a holiday party at one of my restaurants. He wanted us to set up a buffet for about two to two and a half hours and have an open bar for the entire length of the party. We settled on a price for the food but he didn't want to be charged per person by the hour for the bar, which is standard for a party like his. He wanted to run a tab and pay for it at the end because he was not sure everyone was going to drink. We were pretty sure they would. Who goes to a holiday party and doesn't drink when it's on the company? I must tell you, the gentleman who booked the party was not the owner of the company.

The party went off without a hitch, and it was one hell of a party. As the party was nearing the end, about twenty of the guests were still going at it hard at the bar. The manager asked the host if he wanted to continue with the tab or switch to a cash bar. He said that everyone was having a good time, and to continue the tab and let them have fun. And fun they had. What's better than free cocktails on the boss? They ordered cigars, single malt scotches, Sauternes, the works. At the end they all left in taxicabs and limos. The host paid the bill, thanked us for the party and said, "Good night."

The next day, he called and asked to speak to the manager. He told her he needed to meet with her that afternoon.

She asked, "About what?"

He said, "The bill."

He stopped by that afternoon and told her that he couldn't hand the bill in to his boss because he spent too much money and the boss would be livid, so he wanted her to lower the bill. Is that beautiful or what? *I spent too much and I'm going to get in trouble, so I want you guys to bail me out.* How did this become my problem?

The manager, I guess in the interest of future business—and completely without my knowledge, by the way—felt his pain, and to my subsequent disbelief, decided to discount his bar bill.

She told me what happened, and in shock I said, "You *what?*" She assured me it was good public relations because they have an office in the building, and they are always in the restaurant.

It took a while for me to get by that one, but a few days later I let it go. Hey, it was the holidays, goodwill towards man and all that. Just as I was recovering, I received a call a week later from the host of the party. Between you and me, I was expecting a "Thank you."

What I got was, "We have to talk."

I said, "About what?"

He said, "The bill."

I said, "What about the bill? Wasn't it already discounted?"

He said, "Yeah, but it's not low enough and I'm still worried about submitting it. You see, I asked everyone in the office how much they drank, and no one said they had more than two cocktails."

I said, "Let me understand this. You told everyone there was a problem with the bill, then asked them how much they had to drink and they all said two, correct?"

He said, "Yeah. That's correct."

I asked, "Did the subject of cigars come up?"

"No."

"Did anyone mention shooters of Johnnie Walker Blue at $28.00 per shot?"

"No."

"How about Chateau d'Yquem at $25.00 per ounce?"

"No."

I asked, "If no one had more than two drinks, then why did my parking lot look like the entrance to Penn Station with all the limos and cabs out there? And how could a four-hour party get extended two hours with no one drinking?"

He asked, "Why would my people lie to me?"

I asked him, "If you asked the prisoners in Attica State, how many do you think would tell you that they were guilty?"

No answer.

He then says, "So you aren't going to take anything off my bill?"

"We did take something off your bill. We're just not going to take anything *else* off your bill."

I don't know what happened ultimately with him and his boss. I suspect nothing did, and I sure hope that's the case. But I mean, really, you can't be serious.

FISH ORNAMENTS

We try to decorate the restaurants as best as we can for the holidays. It's fun but stressful, because God forbid you inadvertently leave out one of the more obscure religions. I guarantee you that the one practicing parishioner of that religion lives in my neighborhood.

Every year we add a new religion to the decorations. We have, as you would imagine, a Christmas tree and a menorah. We have also now have an Islamic crescent moon and star, as well as Kwanzaa decorations to go with the dreidels, reindeer, poinsettias, Santa Claus, Christmas balls, lights, and garland that help make the season so festive. As crazy as this may sound, it's the Christmas tree and the menorah that cause me the most grief.

First, I'll deal with the menorah: I can never remember which side to light first. The last thing I want to do is offend anyone, but every time I ask, I get a different answer. I finally consulted a customer who was a rabbi and got it straightened out. The second problem is that my Spanish workers think the menorah is a Christmas decoration, so whenever they see that some of the lights are unlit, they screw the bulbs back in. This drives me crazy, as you can imagine, because I have to constantly monitor the menorah.

The tree is my other dilemma. It has to be decorated, and although the staff usually gets into it, it's a pain in the ass trying to find the decorations year after year and replacing what has been broken or lost. We usually place the tree as close to a door as possible because we have to move it in and out of the restaurant occasionally, and it can be awkward. We do a lot of catered parties and the last thing anyone wants to see is a Christmas tree at a Bar

Mitzvah, or a fully lit menorah in the Communion photos, so we move the decorations accordingly.

My staff knows that I don't like gaudy Christmas tree decorations. One of my employees came in one day with a fish-shaped Christmas tree ornament for me to look at. It was brilliant. A glass fish ornament for a restaurant called *CoolFish* was perfect. The only problem was that they were very expensive.

The whole staff was cranked up about these ornaments. They promised to carefully store them so they wouldn't break. They told me they were an investment; we'd have them every year, and that they would look great on the tree. I was totally down for the ornaments, but I was worried they were going to disappear.

Diane asked, "Can't we just get them, they'll look great on the tree."

I said, "No they'll just disappear, and they're way too expensive."

"You are such a pessimist."

"No my dear, I'm a well informed optimist."

Forgive me, I'm jaded. The fish ornament lobby was so powerful that I relented. I think we bought twenty-five ornaments, and I'd be embarrassed to tell you how much they cost, but they were so cool.

I think we lost eight on the first day. I flipped out. It wasn't about the money, although it should have been; it was that I just really liked them.

On day two, three more disappeared. Now I was pissed off. I decided that instead of hanging them, I would get fishing line—no pun intended—to secure the ornaments to the tree. I used the old Fly Fishing knot, or whatever it's called, on the fourteen remaining fish, secure in the fact that they would be around to see another season.

All was quiet for about three days. The fourth night I had

gotten off work and was hanging at the bar. I noticed a large party leaving the restaurant. As the last woman in the party walked by, I saw the Christmas tree slowly bending toward the front door as she passed. The closer she got to the door, the more the tree bent over. She had one of the ornaments in her hand but the knot was hanging on. The tree was another story.

The Inspector Clouseau in me kicked in, and I realized this woman was trying to take one of the fish. I decided to confront her.

I said, "What are you doing?"

She said, "What do you mean?"

Exasperated, I said, "I can't believe you would try to take an ornament from the tree. I mean, it's Christmas! You're stealing, for God's sake."

She looked me right in the eye, one eyebrow down, and said in her best low voice, "Well if you're going to be an asshole about this, I'm not coming back."

I said, "Let me get this straight. You are dragging a ten-foot Christmas tree out the front door by a small glass fish, and I'm an asshole?"

She said, "You heard me."

I said, "Hopefully Santa will bring you a mirror on the big day."

She looked at me and said, "You're a friggin' asshole," and walked out.

Can you believe that?

TABLE EIGHTEEN

 One Saturday night at *Tease*, a party of six walked in and was seated at table eighteen. *Tease* serves multiple courses of small plates, and this party each ordered three courses. Everything was wonderful, according to the table, until the third course. That was when one of the men decided there was a problem. The entire table was happy to get their third course, but he decided that his came too fast.

He said to the waiter, "Hey chief, take this lamb back. It came out too fast, and I don't want you to bring it back for at least a half-hour."

Meanwhile the rest of the table continued to eat. About twenty-five minutes later, Chef Ron fired up another lamb rack. He plated it and sent it out. The waiter brought it to the table.

The man said to the waiter, "Hey pal, is this the same lamb you served me before?"

The waiter assured him it was not.

He then said to the waiter, "Then let me tell you something, big guy. Someone stole one of the chops."

Ron is a lot of things. He's a talented chef, a nice guy, hardworking, and honest, not a lamb thief.

So now he wanted the pork instead. We brought him the pork and everything seemed fine until the check came. He paid with a credit card, signed it, and on the line where it says tip, he wrote in very bold print, $00.01. He and his party then left the restaurant and proceeded across the street to another restaurant to have an after-dinner drink. I'm assuming the rest of his party was unaware of his generosity because there was no additional money left on the table.

The manager at *Tease* saw the tip and decided to confront him and ask him if something was wrong.

He went across the street, found the man in the bar, and said, "Excuse me sir, we noticed that your tip was rather small, was there a problem with the service?"

The man said, "Well, there was a problem with the lamb, but it was fixed."

The manager said, "Was the food okay?"

"Great."

"Service, drinks, atmosphere were all okay?"

The man said, "Yes, very good."

"Then why the lousy tip?"

"Tipping is a prerogative, not a requirement."

The manager told me later that he was at a complete loss for words.

The epilogue to this story is that a few nights later, a man came in and was talking to the manager while waiting in the bar for a table. After he was introduced, he said, "I heard my brother-in-law was in here the other night. Did he leave a penny for a tip?"

The manager said, "Oh, you heard about that?"

The man said, "Nah, I was just curious. He does it everywhere he goes. He finds some little inane thing to whine about, and then leaves a penny. He just can't stand to part with the money. That's why we're here tonight. We refuse to be seen in a restaurant with him."

Body and Sole

Body language is a subject I have got to study in some formal way in my next life. It's incredible how much you can tell about someone by watching them move. A hand on the hip with the eye rolling bit, and the head pitched forward with an exaggerated exhale can spell *mucho trouble*. Especially when it's aimed at someone who just said, "I'll be right with you." .

After their interminably long two-and-a-half minute wait, the hostess seated a couple for dinner. The woman looked over the menu and decided she didn't like anything on it. She told the waitress that she just wanted salad with piece of fish on it. Diane, her waitress, suggested the Grilled Salmon Salad. Basically it's salad with a piece of fish on it. We keep it on the menu to satisfy the occasional customer who needs to have—well—a salad with a piece of fish on it.

The woman said, "No, no, no. I don't want that!" *That would be way too easy*

Her husband ignored her and ordered his dinner. The woman was still perusing the menu and contemplating the necessary changes. She finally looked up and said, "I'll have the salmon salad, but could I get Chilean sea bass instead of salmon? Oh, and no dressing, no smoked tomato relish, no tomato, hold the onion, and if I see one chive I'm sending it back."

Diane said, "Hold on, I'll see if I can do that."

Diane asked the chefs if they would make the changes and they said yes, but they wouldn't take responsibility for what it tasted like.

Diane returned to the table and said, "That's fine, but we

189

take no responsibility for what it tastes like. Once we make it, it's yours."

The woman said, "Fine."

The dish went out; the dish came back.

The woman said to Diane, "Take this back to the kitchen. I don't like it; it has no flavor." Imagine my surprise.

Just as Diane was about to remind her about the no-responsibility contract, the woman dove through the loophole and said, "And half of this dish is cold."

Did I mention that she ordered a salad?

The manager decided to take charge. She walked over to the table and said, "Ma'am, we went over this with you before we cooked it. We made it exactly like you asked us to."

The woman said, "I don't care. I don't like it and half of it is cold."

The manager said, "We'll be happy to heat the salad for you and bring it back out."

The woman said, "No, and you know what? The sea bass was a little *fishy* so I think I'd rather have the sole. Can they do that?"

The manager said, exasperated, "Okay, we will make you a sole, but you will have it exactly like it is prepared on the menu. Your salad greens and your dressing will be warmed and the dressing will be served *on* your salad and, like it or not, you will be charged for it. And it's going to take about ten minutes, just so you are aware."

The woman said, "I don't want to wait that long. My husband is almost done eating."

The husband was rolling *his* eyes by this point, but said nothing. I think that people who marry crazy people should be required by law to warn the rest of us. Crazy is communicable and we should be prepared..

The manager was starting to lose it. "We don't have cooked sole lying around waiting for someone to change their order three times, tell us their salad was cold, and then expect to get it immediately. It has to be cooked, ma'am!"

The woman said, "*Fine.* I guess I'll just have to wait, won't I!"

Out came the sole; back went the sole.

The woman said, "I don't want this. It's terrible. Besides, I've lost my appetite trying to teach you people how to make a simple salad with a piece of fish on top."

Check, pleeease.

NERVES OF STEAL

Stealing is a problem. I'll tell you something funny. We have a fifteen-dollar pepper mill charge on our computer that we add to the bill if someone steals a pepper mill off the table. It's the only charge, in twenty-five years of being in my own business, which has yet to be disputed. Go figure. I guess that "honor among thieves" thing is true. Or at least I thought so.

I'll give you a little background. We have metal menu holders at *CoolFish*. They are brushed metal clipboards with the *CoolFish* logo cut out at the top. My cost is thirty-five dollars per clipboard. What possible value these have for anyone else is a complete mystery but, believe it or not, it's the winter season's hottest item. There's a delicious irony to someone sticking a thirty-five dollar menu holder under a ten-thousand-dollar fur coat and running out the door.

A table of eight mature sixty-or-seventy something's sat down for dinner. Their waiter took their drink orders and brought them from the bar. He then took their dinner orders and as he collected the menus, he realized that he only got five of the eight back. He made a mental note to get the other menu holders but he got busy and forgot.

At dinner's end, the eight people were leaving and one gentleman in the party turned in his menu holder. Another one of the party had one under his coat and was on the way out the door. The third grabbed the menu from the table and was walking out, trying to stuff the menu holder down the back of his pants when the waiter said, "Excuse me, sir, I'll take that menu for you."

The man said, "That's my menu. I'm taking it."

The waiter said, "It may have been your *menu*, but it's not *your* menu. I can't let you take it, but you can buy one if you'd like for thirty-five dollars."

The man said, "That's ridiculous."

I ask you, is it any more ridiculous than a seventy-year-old man trying to shove a metal clipboard with a fish on it down his pants?

The man gave the waiter the menu and proceeded to the front door. Then, in a carefully choreographed ruse, complete with subtle head nods, eye contact and a distraction, he swiped one off the hostess stand while the rest of the party occupied the hostess, and shoved it under his coat. As he turned to walk out, it fell out of his coat, clanging on the floor. Busted and dejected, they finally left.

The waiter had a sneaking suspicion about them, so he followed them outside and to his amazement, he saw the entire party high-fiving each other over the two menus that they had managed to liberate. While all the commotion was going on, apparently one of the ladies managed to slip one under her fur coat. If you've never seen eight members of the "greatest generation" jumping up and down, high-fiving each other over stolen menu holders, you owe it to yourself. Although, to tell you the truth, I don't know exactly how you would set that one up.

The waiter came back in and told me what was going on outside and that I should confront them. I went outside to do just that, but after witnessing eight retirees humping each other in a pile like they had just won the World Series, all I could do was laugh.

I called an impromptu management summit, and we decided that some guerilla warfare would be more fun. We waited an hour (eleven-thirty p.m.) and then called up the person whose name was on the reservation. We left a message saying that we would be charging his Visa with an extra $105.00 for three stolen menus. They really stole two, but I was looking for a reaction.

I wish I had access to one of those spy satellites so I could have listened in on the ensuing phone calls. The lines must have been glowing. The calls I got—and there were more than a few— were filled with denials and accusations, not to mention cursing, swearing, threatening, and whining. It was a hoot. I don't think any of the eight people are talking to each other to this day. They had 105 reasons to be mad at each other. Oh, by the way, the charge was never disputed.

Hands Down

The manager of *CoolFish* was summoned to table sixty at eight-thirty on a Saturday night. It seemed there was a woman who was unhappy with her fish. I know by now you must find that hard to believe.

There must be some kind of contest for bad restaurant behavior. I'm sure there are points awarded on a yearly basis for performance, style, and degree of difficulty, with prizes for whoever has accumulated the most at the end of the year. I imagine the rule book would look something like this:

Changing your table two or three times:
Five Points.
Sending food back for no apparent reason:
Seven and a Half Points.
Completely destroying the ladies' room:
Eight Points.
Making a waitress cry:
Ten Points.
Then add 'em up at the end of the year to see who won!

First Place: A trip to Maui, meals included, of course.
Second Place: A shopping spree at DKNY.
Third Place: Dinner at one of Tom's restaurants,
no menus necessary.

The problem that night for that particular customer was the manager was not the crying type. She approached the table to see what was wrong.

The lady, after three Cosmos and in a display of articulation, told the manager, "The salmon is dry and tastes like shit. I have eaten all over the world, and this salmon tastes like shit."

Funny, I've eaten all over the world also, but I can't ever remember trying shit.

You know the one thing that all chronic complainers do? Whenever a chronic complainer is about to file yet another complaint, they always start with, "I've eaten all over the world," before airing the rest of the complaint, and then follow up with a sentence that is a complete fabrication in order to buttress their bitching.

It's hysterical. I've never met a chronic complainer who hasn't eaten all over the world. If you've never been out of the U.S., you can't be a chronic complainer. It's just not allowed.

"I've eaten snapper all over the world, and this isn't snapper."

"I've eaten foie gras all over the world, and it's never pink in the center."

"I've eaten local corn all over the world, and this isn't local."

Take it from me, this is one well-traveled group. Can you picture all of them showing up for the same Love Boat cruise? Abandon ship!!

We don't require a food resume every time there's a small problem: We get it. You're a well-traveled and sophisticated foodie who just happens to not know the difference between a snapper and a Whopper. I won't even get into the well-done foie gras or the single vineyard corn thing. We'll always make you another dish because we want you to leave happy—*leave* being the operative word.

Anyway, now that the woman had established her credentials as part of the "I've eaten all over the world club," she made it to the fabrication part of the program, and it's a classic.

She said to the manager (get this), "I can make better salmon than this at home."

What do you think the Las Vegas odds would be that the cardboard is still in her oven? I can just picture her coming home from a hard day at the spa and saying, "Honey, could you take the cardboard out of the oven and hook up the gas? I thought I'd surprise you tonight with my famous non-shit-like salmon."

The manager explained that we would be happy to take it back and redo it, gesturing animatedly and talking with her hands. As she was talking, her hands were out in front of her, palms up.

The woman picked up the salmon with her fork, placed it in the manager's hand, and said, "Get it out of here."

The manager now has an eight ounce piece of half-chewed salmon in her hand. She started to shake. Her veins were popping out, her muscles tensing, and then she calmly said, "Take the salmon out of my hand. Now!"

She then placed the salmon back in the woman's hand, grabbed her napkin off the woman's lap, wiped her hand, threw the napkin (it's an epidemic) onto the woman's plate, and said four very distinct words, "Now you get nothing!"

The woman started, "But..."

The manager interrupted, "Nothing!"

They finished their dinner and left. The woman got nothing and like I said before, sometimes you just have to fire a customer, especially when they get a little "out of hand."

Grilled Salmon / Spring Veggie Sauté / Sweet Pea Purée / White Truffle Cloud Recipe

What's better for shedding that winter funk than the first warm day of spring? The world turns green, flowers bloom, the birds return, and a couple of very interesting vegetables make their debut. Ramps (wild leeks) and fiddlehead ferns make a brief appearance at this time of year. Morel mushrooms, asparagus, sweet peas, and fava beans, though around for a longer period of time, also show up in the spring. I wanted to showcase these wonderful vegetables together in a celebration of the season. I used salmon with this preparation, mainly for the color. It plays very well with the bright green of the Sweet Pea Purée. The White Truffle Cloud is just, well, a white truffle cloud. Fire up those grills.

Ingredients:

3 tablespoons olive oil

Four 6-ounce salmon filets

2 cups spring veggies (asparagus, favas, morels, ramps, fiddlehead ferns)

2 cups fresh peas

Warm water (enough for thinning the pureed peas to a sauce-like consistency)

½ teaspoons sugar (as needed)

¼ cup heavy cream

2 teaspoons white truffle oil

Salt and pepper to taste

Preheat charcoal or propane grill. Brush the salmon filets with 1 tablespoon of olive oil and season with salt and pepper. Place on grill and cook approximately 5 minutes on each side (medium rare) or until cooked to your liking. At the same time you put the salmon on the grill, heat the remaining 2 tablespoons of olive oil in a sauté pan. When the oil is hot, add the spring veggies to the pan and sauté until the vegetables are cooked through, but still firm to the bite (5 minutes approximately). While the salmon and the spring veggies are cooking, place the fresh peas in a blender and blend on high speed, thinning with warm water until the purée has a sauce-like consistency. season with sugar, salt, and pepper, and reserve. To plate, place a pool of the purée in the center of the plate and arrange the veggies in the center of the purée. Place the salmon on top of the veggies and a dollop of the cream on the salmon.

Chef's tip: The peas, morels, fiddleheads, and favas have their distinctive shapes so leave them whole. Cut the asparagus to mimic, as closely as you can, the size of the other veggies. The sweet pea purée and the white truffle cloud can be made in advance if there are time constraints, but no more than a half hour. You can substitute frozen peas if you must, but the flavor will not be the same.

Wine pairing: Jamesport Pinot Noir

High Steaks

On opening night at *Thom Thom* restaurant, a man came in by himself and sat down for dinner. The waitress took his drink order and informed us that there was something a little strange about the guy.

She told us vaguely, "I can't put my finger on it, but he's a little off."

This is always great news.

The appetizer course passed without incident. He'd ordered a filet mignon, cooked medium, as his main course. The waitress brought out the filet, placed it on the table, and asked if there was anything else she could get for him. He muttered something unintelligible under his breath and waved her away. He then picked up his knife and fork and proceeded to cut one-sixteenth of an inch off the end before putting his knife and fork down. He looked up and called the waitress back to the table.

He said, "This steak is not medium. I don't want it.

She said, "Sir, how would you know? You haven't cut into it yet.

He said, "I did cut into it and it's too well-done. Take it back."

She brought it back to the kitchen and said, "This is too well-done. I need another filet for table six."

I looked at the steak and said, "He never even cut into it. How would he know?"

I cut the steak in half and it was a perfect, and I mean a *perfect*, medium. I sent the same steak back out to show him that it was medium.

He told the waitress upon its return, "Nope, I don't want that one. I want another steak."

The waitress brought the filet back into the kitchen and said, "He said he doesn't want that one. He wants a new filet."

I asked her, "Is this guy nuts or something?"

She said, "I told you he was a little off."

It's not worth the fight to me, so I told the grill guy to put up another filet and to cook it medium rare instead of medium. It went out. Three minutes later, the waitress returned the new filet, with one-sixteenth of an inch sliced off the end, to the kitchen.

"It's too well-done."

"You can't be serious."

"I'm just telling you what he said."

I decided that I had to see this guy for myself. I went out to table six and introduced myself. I said, "Hi, I'm the chef and I understand that you're not happy with your filet."

He said, "You people can't seem to make it medium."

I said, "Sir, it's a culinary impossibility to have your steak medium all the way out to the end. That's the part that sits on the grill. The medium part is on the inside."

He said, "Sorry, I don't accept that so I don't want it. I'm not going to only eat the inside of my steak and besides, it's tough; I tried a piece. Just bring me my check."

I said, "I could read through the piece you tried. How could it be tough? It's filet mignon; tasteless maybe, but not tough."

He said, "Sorry, it's tough."

Baffled, I returned to the kitchen. The waitress said, "What do you want me to do?"

I said, "Unless you're a licensed therapist, just take it off the bill."

She did and brought the check out, placing it on the table.

He looked at the bill and said to the waitress, "I didn't mean for you to take it off the check."

You've got to love that line. I've heard it a thousand times. Let me try to understand this. You ruin two perfectly good pieces of steak at a combined cost of seventy dollars, just so you could pay for them, leave hungry, and tell your friends at the asylum what a great time you had at dinner. Have I got this right?

Just when I thought it couldn't possibly get any more ridiculous, the waitress came to me and said, "Check this out."

There, in the leather check holder where you place your credit card or cash for your bill, was a gift certificate for one hundred dollars from the restaurant that was previously at that location and had gone under; and he asked for his change in cash. Still think I could make this stuff up?

OUTED

C heck this out. A couple came to *CoolFish*, sat down at the bar, and ordered cocktails. The bartender asked if they would be having dinner. They said that they would be, but they were going to wait a while and enjoy their drinks.

After about an hour and a couple of drinks later, they were ready to eat. The hostess seated them in the dining area we refer to as the Fishbowl. It's really still part of the bar, but it's enclosed on three sides by glass, so it can be seen from both the bar and the dining room. They ordered another round of drinks, but they were still not quite ready to order their food.

After about ten minutes, the man disappeared. Vanished. Gone. He was gone about twenty minutes when we realized something was wrong. We looked in the bathroom, he wasn't outside smoking, he wasn't at the bar. He was gone. We assumed they had a fight and he had left. Hey, it happens.

She was sitting there alone and we were wondering what to do. We didn't want to make her feel uncomfortable by asking her what had happened, and she didn't appear all that upset, so we decided to give her privacy and wait until she called us over for something.

Then about forty minutes later, her boyfriend returned with a large brown shopping bag. He placed it on the table, removed his coat, sat down, and proceeded to unpack an entire Italian take-out dinner, complete from semolina rolls to tiramisu. They each picked up a fork and the two of them dove into the food like they were going to the electric chair. I swear, I'm not kidding. (I find myself saying that a lot.)

The two of them were eating an Italian take-out meal in my

restaurant, with my silverware, on my table, using my napkins, and soiling my tablecloth when the man flagged a waiter down and said, "Can we please get some water here?"

The wait staff was speechless. You're watching it all go down, and your eyes see it, but your mind can't grasp it. At that point there's really nothing you can say short of, "Get out!" that would remotely apply to this situation.

It was a truly surreal moment. I decided to have fun with it. We were all laughing uncontrollably anyway saying things like, "Can you believe these two? What's fifteen percent of take-out? How's the eggplant?" The only one who wasn't laughing was the waiter. He'd lost a table and presumably a tip, so he wasn't very happy.

The waiter asked, "Can I throw them out?"

I said, "Nah, this is too rich to miss."

We let them finish.

The man, completely missing the fact that he's a freak and with a straight face, asked the waiter, "Could you bring me a check?"

How's that for bliss? The waiter brought the check for the two drinks ordered at the table. It was nineteen dollars, plus tax. Oh, by the way, fifteen percent of nineteen dollars plus tax is two dollars and eighty-seven cents. Thanks for coming in.

SNAPPER RETRIBUTION

Someone out there has to write me to please tell me if this happens in any other business but mine. I'll set the scene for you. A party arrived for the *Prix-Fixe* menu on a Friday evening at about five-thirty. The *Prix-Fixe* menu at *CoolFish* is from five to six-thirty, Sunday through Friday, and costs, for three courses, $26.95. I think this is a pretty good deal. Some of my customers think I should do a little better. On the deal, that is.

We don't skimp on the *Prix-Fixe*. We give the same portions as dinner, and some of the same items. Admittedly, we use some of the cheaper items, but that's okay. It's supposed to be a good deal, and it is, but at the same time I'm not obligated to go broke in the process. There are usually three fish, three meats, one vegetarian, and a pasta choice on the menu, along with five or six appetizers, and three or four desserts.

The table of five looked over the menus for about five minutes and decided they were ready to order. Four out of five ordered Chilean sea bass as their entrées. To this point, things were going remarkably well. But there's always one, right?

The last gentleman couldn't find anything he liked and wanted to know if he could substitute the truffle-crusted snapper instead.

The waitress said, "That's not on the *Prix-Fixe*, sir, and it's a more expensive dish. I'm sure the kitchen will make it for you, but there will probably be a surcharge.

The man said, "If I wanted to pay a surcharge, I wouldn't have come for the *Prix-Fixe*."

I have got to try this technique out sometime. Picture this. A florist has a sale on gladiolas. No thanks, I'll have the roses—at the gladiola price. Winter clothing sale: two sweaters for the price of one. Uh uh, give me two Roberto Cavalli shirts instead, and you know what, throw in a pair of sunglasses—for the same price. Hey, here's one: Ford Smart Lease on a Taurus, $199.00—36 months, no money down. Love the price, love the terms, love the Expedition—for the same price. Why does it sound so much more ridiculous when this thought process is applied to any other business but ours?

Anyway, at some point you have to take a stand.

The waitress said, "The kitchen won't make it without a surcharge."

We're only talking three dollars here, but it's the principle.

The man said, "I've eaten *Prix-Fixe* dinners all over the world (here we go again), and they always let me order what I want." Yeah, those French are so accommodating, aren't they?

The man then said, "You know what? Forget it. I'll have the Chilean sea bass."

I know—through years of pain and suffering—that when someone who really wants a menu rewrite and gives up that easily, it's not over. And it wasn't.

All was well with the appetizers. Then the entrées came out, five orders of Chilean sea bass. Four of them were fine. Guess who? Yup, he's got a problem.

He called the waitress over and said the one thing I've never heard a man admit out loud, "Mine is smaller than everyone else's."

Pardon me sir, but that's how rumors start.

He continued, "You purposely gave me the small one because I wanted the snapper."

The waitress said, "Sir, I didn't bring them out; the runner did."

He said, "You told him to give me the small one."

The waitress said, "Let me get you another piece."

The man said, "No, forget it, I'm not hungry now. I'm too upset."

"Come on, sir, let's fix this. What can I do to make you happy?"

He looked up at her with a gleam in his eye and said, "You can have the kitchen make me the snapper, at the same price."

Visitors 596, Tom zero.

BERRY SHADY

Once again I find myself saying, "It didn't take long."
We were only open three days at the *Jedediah Hawkins Inn*
when we got our first "all-star." The woman sat down to dinner with
her husband and told us she was in for the second time. We thanked
her for her support and took her drink order. The server returned
with the drinks, explained the specials, and told her she'd be back
momentarily to take her order.

She took a sip of her drink, perused the menu and decided to
have the duck. Here's the menu description, word for word: "Roasted
Jurgielwicz Farms Duck/Blueberries/Farro/Asparagus." I think
that's pretty straightforward, no?

We served her the appetizer, I really don't remember what it
was, and things were going swimmingly. As you know by now I can
usually spot 'em, but I have to admit this kind, gentle, seemingly
charming, little old lady had us fooled. We cleared the table; out
went the entrées, led by the duck.

The waitress asked, "How's everything?"

The woman answered, "Fine."

The waitress asked, "Can I get you anything else?"

The woman answered, "No thanks."

The waitress said, "I'll be back to check on you."

Ten minutes later, she returned to the table. "How are we doing
here?"

The woman looked up and says, "Terrible."

"What's wrong?"

The woman said, "The menu says half of a duck. I only got a
breast and a leg. Where's the other half?"

The stunned waitress said, "A breast and a leg is half of a duck."

The woman said, "No it isn't, and I want the other half." Then she continued to say, "And the chef didn't disguise the blueberries." (Huh?)

The waitress said, "I don't understand."

"The blueberries weren't disguised at all. They just sat on the duck."

The waitress, now grinning said, "I'll tell the chef."

I gotta tell you right here, I've heard some menu critiques, but this is up there. The waitress told my partner, Michael, and me, and as we are looking at each other in disbelief, we simultaneously burst out laughing. Then it started.

"What would she like them disguised as, strawberries?"

"Perhaps a Ferrari."

"Hey how about a serial, or *cereal*, killer? Then you wouldn't have to serve a knife with the duck."

You've got to hand it to me: I'm always looking to improve the service. We took the half or one-quarter or one-eighth or one-sixteenth of duck off the check and she was happy. I've checked every costume store on Long Island since, and can't find one single disguise that would fit a blueberry. The best business advice I've ever had was, "Find a need and fill it." I now have the need. Hey, what about small Groucho Marx noses and glasses? Nah, then they'd probably start robbing banks or something.

A word of caution: The next time you order duck with raspberries, blackberries, gooseberries, or boysenberries, look very carefully at those berries. You just never know.

LA CAGE AUX FOLLIES

Dating is a funny thing. So much time and effort go into it. Look at any steak house on Thursday night, and you'll see what a popular sport it has become. There are Web sites for dating, advice for dating, agencies for dating, dating for money, speed dating, dating for food, dating, dating, dating. And now a new twist: married dating.

A married (we were to find out later) woman came into one of the restaurants on a date, not with her husband. They looked like the typical forty-something first date couple, listening to each other, laughing, winking, eating, and—drinking.

As the alcohol goes down, the temperature goes up. They were hand-holding, kissing, and hugging when all of a sudden the woman looked up as if she'd seen a ghost. But it was worse. The woman saw her husband sitting on the other side of the dining room, also on a date. She panicked. She got up and walked, head down, to the ladies' room, unseen by her future ex-husband, and there she stayed for an hour. She came clean and explained her dilemma to Diane, who by virtue of the fact that she had to pee, was now a co-conspirator. Together they tried to devise a plan to get her out of the restaurant without being seen. Her date was sitting there wondering what happened, so Diane went out to the table and told him she was sick.

Unless you're Bob Vila, there's not much in the bathroom that can help you make a stealthy exit. Walking out of the restaurant with a garbage can on your head or a toilet seat around your neck is likely to get looks from the most jaded of diners.

I had an idea that Diane and I discussed during one of our

several strategy meetings during the ordeal. I said, "Break into the tampon machine, hang them from her ears, nose, and fingers and sneak her out as a Christmas tree."

Diane said, "If you're not going to be helpful, just shut up." I guess she didn't like the idea.

Anyway, we have a birdcage in the bathroom. They planned to have the woman carry the birdcage on her left shoulder and walk out, hiding her face. These are the same two women that thought the tampon idea was ridiculous. Why not just put your head in the cage, paint your face yellow, and walk out as Tweety Bird?

They were dead set on plan "A." The bathroom door opened. Diane came out, followed by an inconspicuous woman with a birdcage on her shoulder. You believe this? I was in awe. They walked right through the bar and out the door. It worked. Diane brought the cage back in and put it back in the ladies' room like nothing ever happened.

I have one question for that woman. How focused on the other woman was her husband that he didn't notice someone, who should at least look *vaguely* familiar, with a three-foot birdcage on her shoulder? Hmm? Maybe it wasn't her husband after all; maybe he was a blueberry in disguise.

Hot Potato

Ever had someone threaten to shove a potato up your ass? I have. Let me start from the beginning.

A guy and his date sat for dinner. The guy was a little bit macho, and his date was kind of pretty and furiously cracking her gum. They ordered a bottle of "Pully Fusey" (his pronunciation of Pouilly Fuisse, not mine) and looked over the menu. He was trying to match his dinner to a wine he couldn't pronounce, and she was looking for something that would go with her gum.

They both ordered *apps* and entrées, and we started the dinner process. He was telling her that "Pully Fusey" was one of the best wines in the world, but he had a real treat for her for dessert. She showed her appreciation with her full attention—thirty seconds of gum silence.

Appetizers went out. He was impressing her with his storied and colorful life, and she was falling in love—presumably with Wrigley's Peppermint. The entrées went out. She had fish; it's perfect with gum. He had a hanger steak with asparagus and fingerling potatoes.

One man's al dente is another man's hard. I thought the potatoes were al dente. He did not. After chasing his potato around the plate with his knife and fork for two minutes (maybe they were extra al dente), he gave up in frustration and called the busboy over. This is where the lack of judgment occurred, no doubt fueled by testosterone.

He said to my busboy, "These potatoes are hard. Tell the chef to give me some others or I'll shove these up his ass."

Isn't that precious?

"I'll shove these up his ass."

I had to write it twice because I still find it hard to believe he said it. The busboy didn't speak much English, but you don't have to be William F. Buckley to get that message. He should have just asked me for some more potatoes, but I guess in the interest of feedback, and with the good intentions of full disclosure, he gave me the *whole* package.

The busboy ran into the kitchen and said, "Heffe, the mang at table twenty-four, he say he going to chub the papas upa you hass."

I said, "Huh?"

The busboy said, "He say he wan to chub the papas upa you hass."

The waitress, knowing I'm unbalanced, came running in to the kitchen saying, "Just give me a side of fingerlings. Just give me a side of fingerlings."

Too late. The potato was out of the bag. I'm a pretty Zen guy and have little interest in the tough guy thing, but I do have a limit. And I'm not exactly built like Woody Allen. This was the rudest thing I'd ever heard, not to mention what it would feel like. I decided to take the high road—and cripple him.

I went into the dining room with a napkin over my wrist and a plate of fingerlings in my hand. I walked up to the table and said, "Hi, I'm the chef. Start shoving." He started copping more pleas than the Colombo family. I wasn't done.

He was saying, "Come on, I was kidding."

I said, "You weren't kidding when you thought I was some old French guy. Start shoving."

"No, really. It was all in fun."

Fun? Here's an idea for your next house party. Invite five or six couples, clean out the vegetable aisle at your favorite supermarket, and supply everyone with olive oil. What fun. What a jerk. Now he wanted to make everything okay.

He said, "Hey come on, don't be mad. I'll buy you a drink after dinner."

I believe in always giving someone an out, so I said, "Okay, but calm down with the macho act, all right?"

He said, "Sorry, man."

I went back into the kitchen and resumed cooking. At the end of the night, I went out to the dining room as they were about to order dessert.

He called me over and said, "Have a glass of wine with us so I know you're not still mad at me."

I said, "That's fine. I'm over it."

He said, "I ordered a special dessert wine for her."

"Oh yeah? What did you get?"

He said, "Dick-em."

I thought, "Here we go again," and said, "What!"

Then it hit me. He ordered the Château d'Yquem.

PENALTY CLAWS

One night a party of three sat down and proceeded with the incredibly complex task of ordering dinner. Some people can turn a simple lobster dinner into a Shakespearean tragedy.

"What's it come with?"

"What's in it?"

"How's it cooked?"

"How was it raised?"

"Did it go to college?"

"How was it killed?"

"Did the killer use any racial slurs?"

"Was the lobster profiled?"

"Does the fish monger practice diversity in hiring?"

Geez. It's food. Eat it.

My daughter, Courtney, was waiting on the table. Courtney has been in the business since she was born, and she's not only a great server, she's good with customers, has great tableside presence, knows the menu, and is very patient (a quality she got from her mother).

The lady, after exhausting every possible question pertaining to lobster, ordered the grilled Caribbean lobster with black Thai rice, snap peas, and mango rum butter. The other two had the sea bass. Out came dinner.

Courtney said, "Can I get you anything else?"

The woman said, "No, we're fine."

Twenty minutes later, Courtney walked to the table. All the plates were cleaned except for the lobster shell.

Courtney said, "How was your dinner?"

Here's the quote: "My lobster had no claws."

Courtney asked, "What?"

The woman said, "Where are the claws on my lobster? It had no claws."

Courtney said, "Ma'am, Caribbean lobsters are different from northern lobsters. They're a different species."

"Don't tell me they don't have claws. I'm a teacher and I've eaten lobster all over the world (except the Caribbean, apparently) and all lobsters have claws. I know what you did. You took my claws so you could eat them on your way home. And another thing, the two sea bass were only half portions. I'll bet the chef ate the other half or gave it to the dishwashers."

Conspiracy theorists make me a little nervous. This woman needs to pick up a summer school gig because she seems to have too much time to think about crustaceans.

Courtney decided to take the mature route and said, "They were full portions, but I'll get you another order if you'd like."

The woman said, "No thank you. What about the claws?"

"These lobsters don't have claws, ma'am."

"They do too."

"Do not."

"Do too."

"Not."

"Too."

"Not."

Courtney managed to get the last word in (a quality I also believe she got from her mother).

Courtney said, "Can I do anything else for you?"

"Get me the owner."

"He's not here."

"He is too."

"Not."

"Fine, I'll call him tomorrow."

"Fine."

The next day I got the call.

"My lobster had no claws and we got half a sea bass."

I said, "Caribbean lobsters don't have claws."

"They do too."

I said, "Do not."

"Do too."

I said, "Okay, how do we resolve this? Can I buy you dinner or something?"

She said, "That would be nice."

I said, "Great."

She asked, "Can I bring some friends?"

I said, "If it will make this problem go away, you can bring the Daughters of the American Revolution."

She said, "You're only saying that. You don't really mean it."

I said, "Do too."

She said, "You do not."

"Do too."

By the way, I have a question; are your school taxes as high as mine?

Lobster Risotto / Summer Corn / Tomato Basil Recipe

This recipe is much easier to make than the one in the story and much friendlier for the home cook. I love serving this for big groups and it's always a hit. The best thing about this recipe is that you can make it whether your lobsters have claws or not.

Ingredients:
4 cups lobster stock
4 tablespoons butter
1 cup onion, diced
1 cup Vialone Nano or aborio rice
Four 1 ¼ pound lobsters, steamed with meat removed from the shell
1 cup mixed heirloom tomatoes, peeled, seeded, and chopped
½ cup fresh corn, cut from the cob
2 tablespoons fresh basil, julienne

In a stockpot, bring lobster stock to a simmer and maintain throughout the preparation. In a large sauce pan, melt the butter and sauté the onion until translucent. Add the rice and stir for 1 minute until rice is coated with butter. Add ½ cup of stock and stir constantly until the stock is absorbed by the rice, repeating, adding a ½ cup of stock at a time until all the stock is absorbed by the rice. You must be constantly stirring the entire time the rice is cooking. Add the tomatoes and the corn. Continue to cook until the rice is tender but still slightly crunchy on the inside. Remove from heat, season with salt and pepper, stir in the basil, and serve in pasta bowls with the lobster on top. Garnish with fresh basil leaves.

Chef's tip: *If you don't happen to have any lobster stock hanging around, substitute 4 cups of clam juice with 2 tablespoons of tomato paste whisked in.*

Wine pairing: Waters Crest Chardonnay.

A Bad Case of Ammonia

You ever think you'd see me include myself in this book? Neither did I. But in the interest of consistency and fairness, and according to Michael Meehan's wife, Ronnie, I deserve it. And I wholeheartedly agree. So sit back and watch me scold myself.

Michael Meehan, who is an incredibly talented chef and a good friend of some twenty something years, had just opened a restaurant in Riverhead. The location is about ten minutes from my restaurant *Jedediah's* in Jamesport.

When he opened, I gave the edict to my employees to please go there to support my friend. For three weeks, no one on my staff was *allowed* to patronize any other restaurant. We all went there as often as we could in the first couple of weeks, which is when a restaurant needs the customers the most. I was stopping in as often as I could also, not out of obligation, but because I love Michael and his food.

One night, I stopped in with a friend for dinner. We sat down, ordered a bottle of wine, and looked over the menu. I decided on the local sea bass as an entrée. The waitress took our order and left. She returned a couple of minutes later to tell me that the kitchen had run out of sea bass, but they would make the dish with grouper instead. I love any fish so I didn't care. I was just happy that Michael, who was not there that night, was so busy that he ran out of the sea bass. I told the waitress that was fine and she left the table. She brought the appetizers and we began to eat.

The problem started with the delivery of the entrée. The waitress brought the grouper and set it down in front of me. I thanked her and off she went. I cut into the pure white flesh of the fish and as I brought it up to my mouth I got the distinct odor of ammonia.

Some background information: The ammonia smell is usually associated with shark and skate. Since they don't have bladders, they process uric acid through their flesh, so when the fish is old it can smell like a wet diaper.

Back to the grouper, I cut into the fish again on the other side and smelled it; same thing, ammonia. Now I had a dilemma. I can't send a piece of fish back to my friend's restaurant without feeling terrible, but if I don't, maybe some less forgiving customer will get a piece and as a result won't come back. I would have said something privately to Michael, but as I said before, he wasn't there. As I was wrestling with what to do, the waitress appeared.

She saw that I hadn't eaten any of the fish and said, "You're not enjoying the fish?"

I said sheepishly, "Not really."

She said, "Is there something wrong with it?"

Cringing, I said, "Yeah."

She then said the three words I'd been dreading: "What's the problem?"

I said quietly, "It smells like ammonia."

She said, "Excuse me."

I said a little louder, "It smells like ammonia."

"It smells like ammonia?"

I said, "I feel horrible about this. It's okay. We can keep this between us. I'll tell Michael when I see him."

She then proceeded to go and tell the kitchen, which is the correct thing to do. The kitchen told her that they got the fish in that afternoon and it was beautiful. Michael had checked out a couple of pieces and they appeared to be fine.

She came back to the table and recounted what the sous-chef told her. He thought the fish was great; I thought it smelled like Mr.

Clean. The problem was one hundred times worse because Michael was off. You can't imagine the series of phone calls that ensued.

When I talked to him the next day, he told me he got five phone calls about the incident. The sous-chef called, the GM called, the manager called, I think maybe *Michaels'* wife, Ronnie, called, and there was one homeless guy who got wind of it and weighed in. The sous-chef flipped out because Tom Schaudel, chef and lifelong friend of Michael Meehan, had sent his fish back. Michael explained to him that he knew that I would never do that unless there was a good reason. Maybe it was one bad piece in the batch, maybe it was stored against something rancid, or maybe an old piece got mixed in with the new at the warehouse. He calmed the sous-chef down and said that when he came in the following day, they would figure out what had happened.

The waitress took the fish off my bill and said, "We would like to buy you dessert for your trouble."

I normally don't do dessert since my induction into the "Fat Bastard Club," but this is Michael Meehan we're talking about. Shame and sugar are mutually exclusive. We ordered a key lime pie, maybe the best on the planet, and a banana cream concoction and finished both.

I got up to leave. As I was passing the open kitchen, the sous-chef called to me and said, "Hey, Tom. I'm really sorry about the grouper."

Just trying to slink out, I said, "Hey man, it's okay. That stuff happens."

He then hoisted up a grouper filet and said, "Look, it's beautiful; I don't know how it could have smelled like that."

Welcome to the theater of the absurd. The sous-chef felt terrible, and I was worried about *Michaels'* reaction upon finding out, but I was also trying to leave unnoticed, retaining what dignity I could, and the sous-chef was waving a piece of grouper out the kitchen window talking about shelf life and odors.

I said, "Don't worry, man; it happens," and I headed out the door.

For the rest of the night I felt awful. I woke up the next day knowing at some point Michael and I would be having an uncomfortable conversation. I decided to avoid it as long as possible.

The next morning, I went to my favorite bagel store in Jamesport and had the breakfast of champions: toasted poppy bagel with butter, a diet Snapple, and a *New York Post*. I sat down, cracked open the Snapple, opened the paper, and as I went to take a bite of the bagel, I realized it smelled like ammonia. (Huh?)

I asked the girl behind the counter, "Is there any grouper on this bagel?"

She said, "What?"

I said, "Nothing, just thinking out loud."

I smelled it again, and again it smelled like ammonia. I've never been so happy to smell ammonia in my whole life. It was like music to my nose.

I'd recently had a health episode and had been on some meds, so I started to suspect maybe that was throwing off some olfactory stuff. I called the doctor and asked if that was possible. She said she hadn't heard of it before, but couldn't rule it out. It would be just my luck to develop a brand-new side effect that would give new meaning to snorting cleaning products.

Anyway, I called *Michaels'* cell and left a message about the bagel. I didn't hear back from him all morning. I called the restaurant.

The hostess answered and said, *"Michaels' at the Boardwalk."*

I said, "Can I speak to Michael please?"

She asked, "Who's this?"

I said, "Tom Schaudel."

She asked, "He's in the middle of lunch. Is it important?"

I said, "Yes. I need to tell him that my entire olfactory system is screwed up and everything smells like ammonia. Isn't that wonderful!"

She hesitated and then asked, "Are you the guy from last night?"

I said, "Wow, word travels fast. Yeah that's me."

She said, "Hold on."

Michael came to the phone, and I asked him if he got my message. He told me his cell was broken and that he had not. I asked him if he might have gotten a phone call last night.

Michael said, "Yeah, at least five."

I told him the whole bagel-medication-doctor story, and he was happy for my new handicap. We laughed like hell about it and I'm sure I'll get some shit for it in the future, which I guess I deserve.

Update: The sous-chef and assistant manager have completed their therapy. Michael and I are still friends and although I'm still allowed to go to *Michaels'* for dinner, I have to pass a drug test to order fish.

It only took fifty-four years for me to turn into my worst Saturday night customer. The silver lining in this otherwise black cloud of a situation—and those of you who have read my previous writings will no doubt appreciate—is that I did not say, "I've eaten all over the world, and this grouper tastes like ammonia." Maybe there's some hope for me.

I'll Take Manhattan

What is it about Manhattan? Don't get me wrong, I love the place. Great night life, restaurants, art, theatre, culture, and—"citiots." Something strange happens to some people who live there. They become elite, forward-thinking geniuses, who know more, feel more, and are way more sophisticated, educated, and constipated, than the rest of us.

One of my closest friends in the world moved there seven years ago. Twenty minutes after moving her furniture into her apartment she was complaining about the bridge and tunnel crowd. I looked at my watch and said, "I think you just set a record."

It's true. Some Manhattanites just think they are better. I can't tell you how many times I've heard, "You know, we're from Manhattan, so we know good food."

"You know, we're from Manhattan, and the restaurants out here aren't any good."

"You know, we're from Manhattan, and we're used to better service."

No one ever says, "You know, we're from Manhattan, and your murder rate can't touch ours." This is the one I especially love, "You know, we're from Manhattan, and your restaurant is like a Manhattan restaurant." What does that mean?

I've got a bulletin. Zagat's NY is littered with restaurants that have low food ratings. There's no doubt that there are fabulous restaurants in Manhattan, but it's a function of the talent, not the zip code. And you can spot Manhattan dwellers a mile away. There's nothing like a Prada outfit at a farm stand if you want to blend in out in *the country*. I've had couples dripping in jewelry, Gucci, and attitude tell me, "You know, we're from Manhattan."

Apparently I look like a moron. Don't you just love to fake the surprise?

"You're from Manhattan? Wow—I would have guessed Brattleboro."

Come on, it's nothing but good clean fun and now that I have that off my chest, I feel a little better.

A woman and her husband walked into *Jedediah's*. The woman said to the hostess, "We have a five o'clock reservation under the name Jones. We're from Manhattan."

I'm not quite sure why she needed to tell us that, other than to elevate her status at the front desk. I have to try this next time I eat in New York. "Hello. I have an eight-thirty reservation under the name Schaudel, and I'm from Carle Place. Actually upper Carle Place, not that I like to brag."

I wonder if they would get it? I'll let you know.

So armed with the knowledge of her reservation time, her name, and her city of origin, the hostess proceeded to find her a "Manhattan-like" table.

The lady said, "No, not that one—um, no, I don't think so. Yeah, that looks a little better, but it's much too dark. That one looks good; I like that one."

It never fails. No one who does the table shopping routine is ever happy with a table unless someone else is sitting at it. It happens one hundred percent every time.

The hostess said, "There's someone sitting there."

The lady said, "Yeah, I know. Okay, well—."

The hostess said, "Surely we can find one you're happy with."

"Okay, we'll sit over there."

The hostess said excitedly, "You mean that one, the one with no one sitting there?"

The woman said, "Yes, that one. I'm sorry if I'm giving you a hard time, but it's just that, well—you know—we're from Manhattan, and—you know—."

The hostess said, "I know you're from Manhattan, I know."

The couple sat down and the lady said to the hostess, "Can I ask you a question?"

The hostess said, "Sure."

"Do you think an eighteen-hundred square foot, three bedroom, two bath home on the bay, is worth $1.5 million dollars?"

The hostess said, "Huh?"

"You know, we're from Manhattan and everything is so much more expensive there. I just don't have a grip on this market."

The hostess said, "You should probably check with a real estate agent."

The lady said, "Yeah, I know, but—we're from Manhattan—and we don't know anyone out here. Thanks anyway."

The waitress came for the drink order.

"Can I get you anything from the bar?"

The man said, "Do you have any decent wines by the glass? You know—we're from Manhattan and well—you know, we're used to good wine. I guess we'll have two glasses of the Paumanok Assemblage."

Tell me this isn't sweet. He's sitting in a restaurant, in a wine-producing region, surrounded by wineries, telling people who study, serve, and drink wine, that simply living in Manhattan makes you an expert on wine, and apparently every other subject. It turned out that the guy was just as nutty as his wife and a rabid Big Apple fan himself.

The waitress asked, "Are you ready to order?"

The lady said, "We would love to sample some of the local stuff you people make out here. Is any of it any good? You know, we're used to eating in Manhattan and, well—you know—is it good?"

"You people?" Is any of it any "good?" This is where I'd love to say, "Oh no, the food is awful here. We've been serving unadulterated garbage for five years now, and actually pride ourselves in getting worse every year. You know—we're not from Manhattan."

After ordering, she pulled the waitress back to the table by subtly waving her arms like an electrocution victim and screaming, "EXCUSE ME. WAITRESS!

This is a great technique for flagging down a taxi, but not a server, even if it's not a Manhattan server.
The waitress ran over to the table, hoping to quell the riot. The lady pulled the waitress' arm down so they were eye-to-eye, and then in her best let's-not-let-anyone-else-know tone, said, "I don't like the bread. You would never get bread like this in Manhattan."

The waitress said, "We bake our bread fresh every day; it's the only bread we have."

"I don't like it."

"What would you like me to do?"

The lady said, "I don't know, but you would never get bread like this in Manhattan. The bread is terrible."

Her dinner arrived. She had the duck. The lady, screaming and waving, said, "EXCUSE ME. WAITRESS!

The waitress ran over.

"My duck seems a little fatty. The ducks that I've had in the city are much leaner."

This is a piece of duck knowledge I must confess I never knew. The only possible explanation for this could be, and I'm only guessing here, is that it probably takes a duck about four hours to fly from Jamesport to Manhattan. I've got to believe that has to be at least a five to seven hundred calorie burn. The resulting buffed duck is way easier to render than the chubby little fellers we have out here. Therefore, it results in a much leaner bird; kind-of-like John Basedow. Oh wait, that couldn't be. He's from Long Island.

Gratefully, dessert was served without anyone getting hurt. They paid their check with a Manhattan credit card, left a Manhattan tip, and walked to the front desk.

The hostess said, "How was your dinner?"

The lady said, "It was fabulous. We tried some of the local wines and loved them. Dinner was great, although the duck was a little fatty. But all in all it was the best food I've had outside of Manhattan. We're from Manhattan, you know."

The hostess said, "That's great. Thanks for coming by and hopefully, we'll see you again soon."

The lady said, "Oh no, we would never come back here."

The hostess said, "I don't understand. Didn't you just tell me that dinner was great and you loved the wines? What's wrong?"

"Your bread sucks and your ducks are fatty."

Only in New York my friends, only in New York.

Seared Duck Breast/Citrus Sauce Recipe

T his recipe comes from Michael Ross, my partner in crime, chef de cuisine at *Jedediah's* and most importantly, an incredible friend. His inspired cooking keeps *Jedediah's* at the top of its game and his good sense and judgment have had a lasting effect on me (though his ducks can be a little *fatty*).

Ingredients:

4 Long Island duck breasts
2 tablespoons thyme, chopped
2 tablespoons marjoram
1 tablespoon olive oil
Salt and pepper to taste
½ cup sugar
2 tablespoons water
1 teaspoon light corn syrup
1 quart tangerine juice
¼ cup champagne vinegar
Arrowroot to thicken
Citrus segments

For the duck: Combine duck breasts, chopped herbs, and olive oil in a non-reactive bowl and toss to marinate for 2-3 hours. In a Teflon-coated pan, sear duck breasts, skin-side down, over a medium flame for 6-8 minutes until the skin has a crisp golden brown color. Turn the breasts over and place in a 350°F oven for an additional 5 minutes. Remove the breasts from the pan and let them rest at room temperature for 5 minutes before slicing.

For the sauce: Combine sugar, water, and corn syrup in a saucepot. Cook over low heat, stirring until sugar is dissolved. Cook until golden brown, without stirring. Remove from heat; add champagne vinegar and 1 quart of tangerine juice. Return to high heat. Let sugar dissolve again, add remaining tangerine juice. Reduce by 1/3. Thicken slightly with arrowroot, strain.

To serve: Slice duck breast, arrange on plate, spoon citrus sauce over duck, garnish with citrus segments.

Chef's tip: *You can substitute the tangerine juice to reflect different fruits if you wish. Berry juice would compliment blue or blackberries, for example, or cherry juice for cherries. You are only limited by your imagination, the disguises of your berries, and where you live.*

Wine pairing: Raphael Merlot.

Surprise Party

Off-premises catering is probably the most profitable part of our business. It's also the part that has the most potential for an all out disaster. It's the equivalent of taking your entire restaurant on the road for a day. I have friends who do just that for a living. They have companies that are specifically set up for off-premises catering, and they have the equipment and crews to do it well. I don't, but that fact has never once stopped me from trying to pull off the occasional miracle.

As I said before, the money is good, so that the temptation is there to do the party, regardless of the stress and pain involved. Every time I finish an off-premises event, I swear up and down that I'll never do another one. It's a little like childbirth. How many women do you think, while trying to push a baby out say, "I—can't—waaiit—to—*whew whew*—do—thiiisss—*whew*—again!" But then a few years go by, and you forget the pain because you have this wonderful little child, and it makes you want another.

It's exactly the same with the off-premises party; you forget. You forget the loading and unloading. You forget rinsing dishes until three in the morning. You forget running out of ice or not ordering enough glassware. I forget so much stuff that the first thing I do the day of the party is find a hardware store and a supermarket close to the location because I know I'm good for at least two trips that day. I don't know how those caterers remember it all.

The laws are different for off-premises catering also, and they're enforced by two dramatically opposed agencies: the Board of Health and Murphy's Law. One wants everything to be perfect; one insures that it's not. What's most amazing to me is that even though I'm armed with all this knowledge, have experienced catastrophe after catastrophe—and believe me, I'm on a first name basis with good ol' Mr. Murphy—I still say yes. Occasionally.

Consider this: I have had wedding cakes fall into the Long Island Sound, cooks who have forgotten to pack the entrées, trucks that have broken down, rental stoves that didn't work, a wait staff that was two hours late with *assistance* from MapQuest, bands who have showed up without drummers, grills that have blown up, and ice that was delivered to the wrong location. I have melted tennis racquets, set lawns on fire, forgotten the coffee, and on one occasion, I have threatened one visibly shaken road manager, of a very famous rock star, with an extended hospital stay. I have had employees walk through screen doors, step on bridal trains ripping the ass out, hit an elderly woman between the eyes with a champagne cork, plunged a wedding of two hundred and fifty people into total darkness with a coffee maker. There have been fist-fights, a stark-naked groom on a diving board waving hello to his blushing bride and her not-so-proud parents, and one waiter who plugged up a master bathroom toilet with what the plumber later announced, in front of the owner of the home, was a "world-class dooder." And I still say yes. Occasionally.

I got a call in my office one day from a woman inquiring about off-premises catering. I asked her how many people were coming and where she was planning on having it. The number matters because if you're going to get involved in one of these, it better be worth your while. You'll run just as much for a party of fifty as for a party of one hundred fifty. The place matters because I've never met anyone who believed that they couldn't squeeze one hundred fifty of their closest friends into a two-bedroom condo, with a band and a buffet.

She said that it was going to be between one hundred fifty

and two hundred people and that she was planning to have it at a vineyard on the North Fork, that just happens to be owned by a friend of mine.

I said, "Okay, I'll do it. Let's make an appointment to set the details."

She said, "Great, I can meet next week."

The next week we met as planned. She was a very nice woman, pleasant to talk to and more importantly, realistic in her ideas for the party. I say realistic because the only three things that are critical to a great party are the food, the music, and the free flow of alcohol.

The rest is just the product of an overactive imagination or, worse yet, an over-inflated ego. Having singing donkeys, a game of midget toss, or a Blue Angels flyover as the happy couple says, "I do," is ultimately a pointless exercise in vanity and will not affect the success or failure of the event. It's just stuff.

Years ago, I catered a birthday party in the backyard of a very large home. They hired a small plane to tow a flag overhead that said, "Happy Birthday Mildred." Mildred was about 117 years old, sitting in a lawn chair with a blanket over her knees, staring at the ground. Not to be harsh, but what was the point?

Anyway, the woman said, "I want this to be about the North Fork with local food and wine. I'm a big supporter."

Relieved, I said, "Great."

She went on, "I want all local ingredients, from the salad to the dessert. Use the local farms for all the vegetables. I want oysters, duck, striped bass or any other fish that's in season. The gentleman who owns the vineyard said that he could provide you with vine clippings to use for the grill."

I said, "This is great. I'm excited to do this party. I'll put a menu together for you and get you a price."

"Great," she said, and then added, "Oh, I almost forgot the most important part. In addition to dessert, we're going to need a birthday cake."

"Oh, it's a birthday party?"

"Yes."

"Whose birthday is it?"

"Mine. I'm turning fifty and I decided to celebrate in style."

I said, "You know, throwing your own party is very cool. You get to have it just the way you want it to be, and you don't have to invite anyone you don't like."

She said, "Exactly."

"What kind of cake do you want?"

"I'd like something big and whipped-creamy, with either lemon or raspberry filling."

"What would you like written on the cake?"

"I think just "Happy 50th Birthday Joanne."

"Done. I have a friend who's an amazing baker. His cake will blow you away."

"That's great. So you'll get back to me on a price this week?"

"Yeah, by Friday at the latest."

"Good, because I'll need to start thinking about sending out invitations."

"No problem, I'll have it to you by Friday."

"Thanks, Tom."

"Thank *you*, Joanne."

I sent her out a contract and she sent me a deposit and the now confirmed party was about two months away. It's never too early to stress about an off-premises event, so I began in earnest immediately. I recruited Diane right away to help with the floor staff and the set up of the bar and the alcohol. She's a tremendous asset when she's not driving me crazy. It runs about 50/50.

I called the rental company and ordered all the plate ware, silver, glasses, grills, napkins, tablecloths, tables, and chairs, and put up Post-it notes in the kitchen, my car, and my house reminding me not to forget the coffee. That's how I roll, as they say.

Party day started early. I was packing out at *CoolFish* and the vineyard was about sixty miles east, a good hour's ride. We got to the restaurant and began the loading process, carefully checking everything as it went on board, trying to make sure that I wouldn't be spending most of my day looking for stuff that we forgot. Two hours later, we were reasonably sure that we had ninety percent of what we intended to bring and off we went.

An hour and fifteen minutes later we arrived at the vineyard, and one of the critical issues of a catered party, the weather, was spectacular. I began to load out with the boys, while Diane and her merry pranksters set up the tables and chairs and the bar under the tent. We were three hours from start time.

Diane came over to me as I was setting up the tent kitchen and asked, "Do you want a separate table to display the cake, or are you just going to bring it out?"

I told her, "Yeah, let's do a table. Robert made a sick cake and fifty is a milestone, so let's display it. We can put the candles on right before they sing one more horrible rendition of "Happy Birthday."

Diane asked, "How big is it?"

"What, the cake?"

"Please, that's way too easy a set up, Chef; yeah, the cake."

"It's about—oh no—ahh!, oh shit!"

"What??"

"I forgot the 'effen cake! You didn't bring it did you?"

"Why would I bring the cake? You loaded the truck."

"It's in the walk-in back at *CoolFish*."

"Great. Now what?"

"We have to go get it."

"There's no *we* in this. I have a dining room to set up; *you* have a cake to get."

"Thanks for the help."

The problem stemmed from the fact that since she had a dessert on the menu, and then ordered the cake as almost an afterthought, the cake never made it to my checklist sheet. I'm straining for an excuse here. The truth is, I forgot to put it on the list and as a result forgot to put it on the truck.

One of the benefits of having several employees who do not speak English very well is that you can blame them for stuff they had nothing to do with, thereby making yourself look good without making them feel bad, because they don't know what you're talking about. If you smile while you're pointing at him telling the rest of your staff what a knucklehead Jose is for forgetting the cake, he assumes he's done something good. Which he did: he unknowingly accepted the blame for me being an idiot.

Shifting the blame is one thing, getting the cake is quite another. I had two hours until party time and the cake was, at sixty miles an hour, an hour away, and Saturday afternoon traffic was building. I called the restaurant and talked to Ann.

"I forgot the cake."

"How come I'm not surprised?"

"Do you have anyone who can bring it out here?"

"No, you took everyone for the party. We have a skeleton staff at best."

"I swear I'll never do another one of these again."

"Where have I heard that before?"

"I'm serious. If you hear me booking an off-premises event again, hit me in the head with something hard. I'm done."

"You're going to have to come and get it."

"I can't. Besides, with the traffic, I'll never make it."

"I don't know what to tell you."

I said, "Thanks for the help," and hung up.

I told Diane that there was no one available to bring the cake. She asked, "What are you going to do?"

I said, "I don't know, but we have to think of something."

As I'm agonizing over what to do about the cake, a limousine filled with eight over-served wine aficionados pulls into the parking lot to visit the vineyard's tasting room.

I thought, "There's my answer. I'll limo that sucker out here."

I called to Diane, "I've got the answer. I'll limo the cake out."

"You're going to what?"

"I'll limo it out. I'll call a limo service and have them bring the cake out."

"You don't happen to think that maybe they would be booked on a Saturday in September, now do you? They usually require more than five minutes notice," she said.

She was right. My two attempts at limo companies resulted in one, "Are you kidding?" and one fit of laughter. Not to be deterred, I dialed 411.

"City and state please."

"Syosset, New York."

"How can I help you in Syosset?"

"Syosset Taxi."

"Verizon wireless is connecting your call to...."

"Syosset Taxi."

"Hi, I'd like a pickup at *CoolFish* Restaurant."

"And where are you going?"

"Aquebogue."

"Where the hell is Aquebogue?"

"Out on the North Fork, one town past Riverhead."

"Past Riverhead?"

"Yeah, it's the next town."

"I have to check with my supervisor. I don't know if we can go that far."

"Okay, check."

He must have had his hand over the receiver because I could hear a muffled, back and forth conversation. A minute later he got back on the line.

He said, "Okay, we'll take you there, but it's going to be one hundred dollars and you have to pay a round-trip fare. One hundred dollars each way, two hundred total."

Truth be told, I would have paid five hundred, but I didn't want him getting any ideas, so I just said, "Wow, that's a lot of money. Okay. How soon can you be here?"

"Ten minutes. How many people are traveling?"

"None."

"What?"

"None. No people."

"No people?"

"No. Just a cake."

"A cake?"

"Yes."

"This is your idea of a joke?"

"No. I'm dead serious."

"Why would you call a taxi to deliver a cake?"

"Because there weren't any limos available. Look, I'm a caterer, and apparently not a very good one. I left the birthday cake at my restaurant, and I need it here in an hour. So, obviously I'm a little desperate."

"I don't believe this."

"Believe it, and there's a fifty-dollar tip in it if you can get it here in an hour."

"I guess it takes all kinds."

"Yeah, I know, I've fed almost all of 'em."

"Okay, we'll be there in ten minutes, and I want the money up front."

"Thanks, dude."

I filed a full report with the staff on the status of the cake and went back to getting ready for the party, which was about an hour and forty minutes from starting.

Now for the second debacle of yet another fun-filled off premises party: the grill. Joanne had gotten the owner of the vineyard to save grapevine clippings to cook on. In theory, that's great. They give good flavor, are very local, and have no big carbon footprint, but they are harder to control than gas. You have to worry about the clippings being green, not burning hot enough, you have to consider how long before you intend to cook you have to light the grill, and whether you have enough clippings to sustain the heat throughout the party.

Never having been a Boy Scout, I wasn't quite sure what to expect, and not having a Valium, I was a little edgy. I decided to light the grill a half-hour before the party started to give the embers time to develop that certain *glow*. Boy, did they glow. I piled grapevine cuttings about three feet high in the middle of the grill, doused them liberally with lighter fluid, struck a match, and became an eyewitness to Armageddon. When that baby got rolling, the flames were shooting five feet in the air. I'm assuming the grapevines were properly seasoned. I don't know what the actual temperature could have been, but you couldn't get within five feet of the grill.

The side of the kitchen tent was about four feet from the heat, so we had to act fast. We took two tablecloths, and crawling on our bellies to avoid the heat, looped them around the legs and pulled the grill away from the tent. As we were pulling the grill, some of the piled cuttings that were now the temperature of napalm fell onto the ground and ignited the grass. The vision of burning a friend's vineyard to the ground was close to becoming a reality.

That would be a tough one to explain, no? *"I used a few more vine clippings than I originally anticipated. You're not mad are you?"*

You had to be there. Five servers, two cooks, and one chef looking like a non-Irish cast of Riverdance trying desperately to stomp out the rapidly spreading brushfire. Just as we were getting the blaze under control—with eight pairs of slightly charred ankles, newly blackened socks, and about twenty minutes left to start time—the guests began to arrive.

One of them called Diane over and said, "It's very hot in the tent, and I'm not the only one who thinks so. Everyone is saying that it's hot in the tent."

Diane came over and said to me, "It's hot in the tent."

I said, "Of course it's hot in the tent. I have a three-alarm fire burning in the grill right behind it."

"Can't you do anything about it?"

"Not without a hook and ladder."

"Well, they're complaining."

"Don't worry, it'll cool down eventually."

"Yeah, maybe by February."

Ten minutes to start time, a car marked Syosset Taxi pulled into the parking lot. The cake had arrived with ten minutes to spare. As I was walking to the parking lot through the tent, I started to hear murmurs from the guests that Joanne was due any minute. I heard it a few more times as I walked into the parking lot, but I didn't think too much of it.

As I was unloading the cake from the taxi and coughing up

a fifty-dollar tip, a woman came running out of the tent, yelling, "She's right down the road! Joanne's right down the road! Hurry up and get back inside!"

I said, "Okay, relax, I'm coming."

"Come on, hurry!"

"What's the matter?" I asked.

She says, "You're going to spoil the surprise!"

"Surprise?"

"Yes, surprise. This is a surprise party for Joanne and she's almost here."

I looked at Diane, she looked at me, and at the same time we said, "Surprise?"

Diane said quietly to me, "How can it be a surprise when she booked the party?"

"Don't know. Maybe now that she's fifty, her memory's not what it used to be."

"That's insane."

"Yeah, throwing your own surprise party is kind of like birthday-party masturbation, no? And to be honest, I don't know how many more surprises I can take today."

Suddenly the tent went quiet and there were hushed whispers around the room.

"Shhh—she's here."

"She's getting out of the car."

"Shhhhh—she's coming—she's coming—quiet."

As Diane and I looked on in stunned disbelief, Joanne walked into the tent.

Everyone simultaneously yelled, "SURPRISE!!"

I swear to you, Joanne walked into a tent that she rented, at a party she planned, with a crew she hired, put both hands up to her chest and said, shortness of breath and all, "Oh my God—oh my

God—I don't—believe this. I don't—believe—you all did this."

They didn't.

Diane and I collapsed laughing. I didn't recover for an hour, which is when I could finally get near enough to the grill to cook anything. The rest of the night was relatively smooth, although every time Diane and I passed each other, she would do a dead-on imitation of Joanne's arrival and we would both crack up all over again.

At the end of the night after the guests left and we were cleaning up, Joanne came over to settle the bill. She thanked me, said we did a great job, and left us a very generous tip. Neither one of us mentioned the "surprise." There was no need to. It remains, to this day, my one and only self-thrown surprise party and is part of the history that makes off-premises catering such an interesting endeavor. The only thing more "surprising" than what happens at some of these affairs is the fact that I'm still willing to do them. Occasionally.

Desserts

Futile Negotiation

A gentleman called *CoolFish* one Thursday night and said, "I'm coming in with a large party, and I want to know what you can do for me." It was a reasonable enough question. I explained that we had catering packages that started at around forty dollars if you behaved yourself, got more expensive as you added different items, and that it didn't include tip, tax, or liquor.

He said, "No, that's not what I mean. I just want to know what you can do for me."

I said, "I don't understand the question."

He said, "I'm coming in tomorrow night with a party of eight people, and I want to know what you are going to do for me for bringing such a large group."

That's really what he said. I swear, I'm not kidding.

I said, "Oh my God, I didn't realize you were talking about that large of a group. We've never had a whole party of *eight* in the restaurant before. I'll tell you what we'll do. Tomorrow morning, we'll pick up your wife and take her for a day of beauty. We'll have them do her hair, nails, a facial, a massage, the works. While she's at the spa, we'll take you to Pete's Golf Shop and hook you up with a new set of Calloways. Then Saturday morning, after your dinner, we'll fly you to Miami for a weekend at Doral. The unlimited golf and spa package, of course. How's that? Is that okay?"

He said, "You're being sarcastic, right?"

I said, "Yes."

He said, "I don't get *anything* for bringing in all those people and having dinner there?"

I said, "Well dinner does come with a check. You can certainly get that."

He asked, "What if I pay you in cash? What then?"

Sometimes people can make you say things that make no sense at all. Like the following sentence.

I said, "What then what?"

He asked, "Well if I pay cash, will you charge me sales tax?"

I said, "I don't *charge* sales tax, I *collect* it."

He said, "You're splitting hairs."

I said, "No, I'm not. But if I were, I'd consider charging for that, too. There's the labor."

At that point I thought he was going to cancel the reservation, and I was kind of hoping he would, because I could see a bad moon risin', as they say. Of course, with my luck running true to form, he did not.

The next night he came in for dinner. My general manager and I were sitting in the office talking about how funny the guy was with the "What are you going to do for me" phone call. All of a sudden, she got really quiet and says, "Shhh—I think he's at the hostess desk."

The hostess desk is directly outside the office door. Sure enough, he was talking—begging really—with the hostess about his reservation. The hostess asked if his entire party, all eight of them, had arrived, and if so, if they would like to be seated or stay at the bar for a while.

He asked, "If we stay at the bar for a little while, can we have free drinks?"

The hostess said, "Why would you expect free drinks when you walk in?"

"Because I brought in eight people. That's a lot of people and you should show some gratitude."

At that point, I was rolling with laughter on the office floor, trying to picture the look on the hostess's face. It occurred to me that I should have gone out there to help her out, but I couldn't bring myself to do it. I was having way too much fun listening to the guy haggle and couldn't bear to bring it to a premature halt. After a while, he finally gave up and she brought them to their table. At a subsequent floor staff meeting, the hostess brought up the subject of combat pay for weekend shifts. I'm warming up to the idea.

STICKS AND STONES

For a short time, my girlfriend was helping me out, answering phones and taking reservations at one of the restaurants. I know this woman better than anyone, and I can unequivocally state that she doesn't have an angry bone in her body. She is educated and polite, calm and dignified, non-confrontational and accommodating, and has unlimited experience in dining out. Although she has forgiven me, part of me still feels bad for what she was subjected to. Reflecting on the situation, I probably should have prepared her better, but it really is next to impossible to anticipate the antics of some disturbed people.

One night a woman called and said, "I need to change a Saturday night reservation from seven-fifteen to eight o'clock."

My friend kindly explained, "We can't do that because there are reservations behind yours and that would not leave enough time for you to enjoy dinner."

The woman said, "We can't make it at seven-fifteen, but I'm not going to give up the reservation and I'm coming in at eight."

My friend said, "We can't push the reservation behind you back one hour, so if you can't make the seven-fifteen reservation, I could give you one at nine, or another reservation on another Saturday that would better fit your schedule."

The woman then said to my friend, "You know what, you're a dick!"

My friend said, "Excuse me?"

The woman repeated, "You are a dick, D-I-C-K, dick!" and slammed down the phone.

My friend came into the kitchen and with a very carefully

constructed, profanity laced tirade, told me what happened.

I said, "Okay, calm down, the woman is obviously crazy. Besides, why get upset? The dick thing doesn't even apply. It's like someone calling me a lousy electrician. Who cares? Don't let it bother you."

She was so upset that I kind-of had to get mad or risk getting in trouble. Knowing what was in my best interest, I got mad (kind-of). I actually thought it was pretty funny, but for the sake of my future domestic tranquility, I didn't let on. I dutifully called the woman back and told her what I thought of her behavior. She said that the hostess was nasty to her on the phone.

I said that I was sure that didn't happen and not only did I think she was rude, but a liar as well, so I was canceling her reservation.

She said, "Go ahead, cancel it. I could care less. You're a dick!" and slammed down the phone.

Eight minutes later, I got a call from the other couple who was to share the reservation with the lunatic. The woman said to me, "We're the other couple from the Johnson party. Please don't cancel our reservation! We didn't call anyone any names! We've waited a long time for this reservation. She does stuff like this all the time. She's crazy! We'll bring another couple; just please don't cancel it."

This was all very flattering.

I said, "I'd love for you to come, but you have to promise not to bring that woman."

She said, "I promise."

I said, "Thank you, see you Saturday."

Right after I hung up, my girlfriend and I blasted off for Venus and Mars.

She looked at me and asked, "Are you really going to let those people come here after all that?"

I said, "She wasn't the one who called you a dick, it was the other woman."

She said, "I know, but she's *friends* with her. Get it, birds of a feather and all that."

I said, "But she said some nice things about the restaurant, and she really wants to eat here. She told me that she would bring another couple and leave the crazy lady home."

She said, "What about me? What about my feelings?"

I said, "What about them?"

She said, "Her friend *insulted* me. You're just going to let them waltz in here like nothing happened?"

I said, "But they said nice things about the restaurant—and about the food and—they waited so long for a reservation—and—."

She said, "Does it always have to be about you? Does it always have to be about you? How many times do I have to ask you the same question?"

I said, "I don't know—seven…eight?"

They came in, were seated, and ate without incident. We're in relationship counseling.

PSYCHOTICS OF A FEATHER

Crazy people are few and far between, thank God, but sometimes they travel in packs. This one was brutal from beginning to end. A very large party came in on a Saturday night and started with drinks at the bar. After giving their order, sending most of the drinks back at least once, if not twice (mostly martinis), we decided we had to get them seated, fed, and out of the restaurant as soon as possible. (Yes, we do profile.)

We offered to seat them and they asked for the bar check. I'm always amazed at the personal risks people are willing to take for the shallow satisfaction associated with torturing a server. The servers are in total control of what you are about to consume. Beats me.

My brother, John, who was tending bar that night, is a big, strong guy. (I've seen him hit a golf ball four hundred yards.) He was adding up the check, but apparently not fast enough for one of the *gentleman* in the group.

The guy said to him, dripping with sarcasm, "Why don't you try carrying the one."

John said, "Excuse me?"

"Why don't you try carrying the one," and then added, "I'd like to eat sometime tonight."

John was incredulous, but also has a sense of humor. He said, "Now you made me forget where I was. I'll have to start over."

The guy was fuming. John ever so slowly added the check and said, "That'll be seventy dollars."

The guy then said, "Ever think of becoming an accountant? Can't you see yourself being good at it?"

251

For the sake of perspective, the guy was about 5'9" and built like Nicole Ritchie. John is 6'2" and about 230 pounds. There's a reason fighters are assigned a weight class. I do not pretend to know what this guy was thinking, at all.

John, muttering under his breath, said, "The only thing I see is the bridge of your nose." To his credit and my relief, John controlled himself. Frankly, I don't know how.

We got this bunch to sit down, but dinner was no better. They were just patently rude. Torturing the waitress, yelling at the busboy, asking for the manager—"the whole nine yams." We finally made it to dessert.

This was our first busy Saturday night, and we had run out of a couple desserts at about ten-thirty. This happens, and frankly folks, it's harder on us than it is on you. We don't get to sell what we don't have, but the way they were carrying on you'd have thought we did it intentionally to them.

They announced to the whole dining room, "These people are incompetent."

"They ran out of everything."

"They don't know how to run a restaurant."

"They're not going to make it."

"I think we should be compensated."

"Our table wobbles."

"The food sucked."

"The bartender is a moron."

And then on a brighter note, "We're never coming back here."

The guy who made the stink at the bar called for the manager. She came over and asked if they could lower the volume because other guests, who we actually did want to come back, were asking to be moved away from their table.

The guy went nuts. He screamed, "Are you kidding me?"

The manager said to the table, "These are the desserts we have left..." but before she could finish, the guy says, "Shut up!"
The manager, shaking with anger at this point said, "I'm just trying to do my job."

The guy then eloquently pointed out, "Your job is to stand there and shut your mouth."

The manager lost it, "Screw you!"

Then, with one of the most ridiculous statements ever made to a woman while maintaining a straight face, he said, "Do you want to step outside to settle this? Huh? Huh?"

Does it get any better than that? He literally called out a girl over a crème brûlée. Could you possibly put yourself in a worse position? If he were to beat up the manager, everyone would think he's an asshole and he may have gone to jail. If he lost the fight, as I suspect he would have, he would have had to cease telling all his tough guy stories and move out of state. Looking back on it, letting them go outside might have been the perfect solution. Seeing her kick his ass would have been very entertaining, and it would be very hard for him to come back to the restaurant from say, North Dakota.

By this time, the manager retreated to the office to breathe in a bag and the waitress is summoned to the table. She was hoping to present a check and get them out of there before the manager had time to recover. They weren't quite finished, though. It seemed they wanted coffee—and a favor.

One of the women said, "The least you can do is buy us coffee."

The waitress said, "I'll have to ask the manager."

The man, who I'm quite sure didn't know how funny he really was, said, "Yeah? You tell her my offer still stands."

The waitress came into the office and said to the manager and me, "They want free coffee and the man said that his offer still stands." I burst out laughing.

The manager's respiratory rate soared. She looked up from the bag like a woman possessed and said, "You tell that little shit I'm gonna kick his complaining ass all over the parking lot!"

God, I would have loved to have seen it, but someone had to act like we were in our forties. I said to the manager, "Calm down there, Rambo; you're scaring me." Showing my softer side, I told the waitress, "Get them the coffee. It's a small investment to get them out of here."

The waitress returned to the table. "How many want coffee?"

The woman at the table said, "Is it going on our bill?"

The waitress said, "Nope, tonight's your lucky night."

The woman said, "That's more like it. We'll all have cappuccinos."

"The boss didn't say anything about cappuccinos, just coffee."

"Cappuccino is coffee. What's the difference?"

The waitress said, "Two dollars a cup."

The woman said, "Oh, what, he can't afford it? I thought he was some big shot."

The waitress said, "I'll have to ask."

She came back into the office. "Now they want cappuccinos."

I thought I would have to duct tape the manager to the chair. I caught her as she was bolting to the table and had to hold her off the ground to keep her feet from bursting into flames. It was quite a struggle, because the harder she wiggled the funnier it became. She was scratching and screaming while running in thin air, and the waitress was standing there mute, waiting for an answer.

I managed to say, "Just give it to them and get them out of here before I have to use a straitjacket."

The waitress returned to the table and said, "I'm not sure why, but he said you can have the cappuccinos." They ordered them and the waitress brought them out.

Then, after three hours of the most piggish behavior exhibited by a table of six in recent memory, the woman said, "Excuse me. This has taken so long, and it's getting so late that four of us will have to switch these for decaf; otherwise we will be up all night."

We certainly wouldn't want that to happen, would we?

FLOUR POWER

ere's one that's just pure lunacy. I think that when I finally retire I would like to get a part-time job at the Center for Disease Control in Atlanta. I have first-hand experience with every allergy, phobia, and food neurosis known to man. I know the names of diseases I never even thought I'd be able to pronounce. I'm pretty sure I could contribute. I thought I'd heard them all. But, as I was to discover yet again, I was mistaken.

A woman came into *Starfish* for dinner. A miracle in itself considering she can eat *nothing.*

"Chicken makes me choke, fish makes me fart, meat makes me mean, vegetables are vulgar, and—oh yeah—I'm lactose intolerant."

This is where my imagination soars. *"Why don't you let me make you a Mixed Grill of chicken, meat, and fish and sauce it with reduced rosemary cream. That way you can go out in a blaze of glory, end it all, and if the multiple lives-karma thing is true, you can be reborn and get another shot at being sane."* Sparing you the gory details and a forty-minute dissertation on Candida, she made it to dessert. She wanted to have the flourless chocolate cake. The problem was that she has a fifteen-letter-allergic-to-flour disease, and she didn't trust the flourless part.

The woman said, "Is there any flour in the flourless chocolate cake?"

I said, "No."

She said, "Are you sure?"

"I'm positive. I make it. That's the reason it's called flourless chocolate cake." You would think some things would be self-

256

evident.

The woman then said, "I'm allergic to flour."

I said, "Of course you are."

"If there's any flour in the cake, I will get deathly ill."

"Why would I lie about flour?"

"Okay, I'll try it, but you better be telling me the truth and I better not get sick."

I was thinking, how much sicker could you get? We made the dessert and sent it out. It was garnished with an edible orchid, which as you may be aware, is a flower.

The woman said to the server, and I'm not kidding here, "I thought you said this was flourless."

The server said, "It is."

"There's a flower on it. I can't eat it." Right here I must confess that I thought she was kidding, and I was thinking that a friend of mine might have put her up to this as a practical joke. The server related to me what she said and we started laughing.

The woman saw us laughing and asked, "Is there something funny here? I specifically asked you if the cake was flourless and you lied to me."

Now realizing that she needed professional attention, I said, "I was under the impression you were allergic to the 'ou' flour, not the 'ow' flower."

The woman then said, "Flourless should be flourless! You get it? (Flowerless?) That means no flour! I'm allergic to both!"

I said, "I apologize. I had no idea."

Be forewarned brothers and sisters, this woman is walking around Long Island unmedicated.

Flourless Chocolate Cake Recipe

I'm glad her allergy was to flour, or flowers, or whatever the case may be, because to be allergic to chocolate would genuinely suck. I'm comforted to know that as that woman navigates her way through a minefield of itching, potential rashes, throat closings, and hospital stays that she can always take refuge in one of my favorite desserts.

Ingredients:

5 ounces bittersweet chocolate, preferably Valrhona
1 ounce decaffeinated espresso
¾ cup sugar
4 large eggs
½ cup unsweetened cocoa powder

Preheat oven to 375°F. Butter an 8-inch baking pan. Line the bottom with wax paper and butter the paper. Chop chocolate into small pieces. In a double boiler or metal bowl set over a sauce pan of simmering water, melt the chocolate and butter, stirring until smooth. Remove the bowl from heat and whisk the sugar into the chocolate mixture. Add the eggs one at a time and whisk in. Sift the unsweetened cocoa over the chocolate mixture and whisk in until just combined. Pour the batter into the pan and bake for 25 minutes in the middle of the oven, or until a thin crust forms on top. Cool cake for 15 minutes and invert onto a serving platter. Sprinkle with powdered sugar and serve.

Chef's tip: You can use buttered 4-ounce aluminum cups instead of the 8-inch baking pan to cook the cakes for individual servings.

Wine pairing: Pindar Blueberry Port.

EPIPHANY

I'm not a very religious person, but I do consider myself somewhat spiritual. It doesn't happen often but every once in a while, if you're paying attention, God will reveal His or Her existence. I saw evidence of this twice. The first time was when my daughter was born. The second was in *EVO* Restaurant on a Saturday night.

When you first enter *EVO*, there's a hostess station to the right. To the right of that is the dining room, and straight past the hostess desk is an aisle parallel to the open kitchen where we had the coat rack. That's the scene of the crime.

A party of four had finished dinner and was exiting the dining room past the hostess desk, when one of the women fainted. I believe someone mentioned a sale at Prada. She went down like she was shot. Boom—out. The manager rushed over and was attending to the woman.

This gets a little touchy. You wonder if she was taking any medication. Is she diabetic? Did she drink too much? Low blood sugar? Serial fainter? Should we call the EMTs? It's scary.

While all this was going on, a woman approached the manager, who is kneeling over this poor woman, and said, and I kid you not, "Can you get my coat?"

The manager was speechless. This happens very infrequently, if you happen to know the manager.

She looked up while gently smacking the fainted soul in the face, and said to this woman, who's face I'm sure she would much have preferred to be smacking, "Are you kidding me? Can't you see I have a situation here?"

"That's not my problem. I want my coat."

260

"Ma'am, you're just going to have to wait."

The woman was undeterred. "This is ridiculous, and I'm not waiting."

She then proceeded to step over the woman—who was mercifully still unconscious—and strode over to the coat rack.

I have to tell you that commercial coat racks just aren't that strong, and on any winter weekend, they support enough fur to piss off every animal lover in creation. The woman grabbed for her coat and as she pulled it off the hanger (this is where I saw God for the second time), the entire coat rack came crashing down on top of her, pinning her to the kitchen counter. It was one of the funniest sights I had ever seen.

She was stuck against the counter under five thousand pounds of fur, hands and feet flailing away, sweating, screaming, "Get this thing off of me! Get this thing off of me!"

Needless to say our response time was rather—casual. There is a God after all.

10,000 Reasons
TO BE GRATEFUL

I came to work early one morning and as I was walking though one of the dining rooms, I heard Jeff, my dear friend and manager, bitching and moaning about something. I asked him what was up.

He said, "Look in the booth over there."

There looked to be some small bags of garbage or something in the booth. He continued, "I can't believe people just leave their shit for everyone else to clean up."

We refer to Jeff as "Lurch" because he's tall, thin, extremely grumpy, and hasn't seen the positive side of a situation since the mid-fifties. In spite of his personal quirks, my partner Marty and I both love him and laugh at him when he goes off.

I went off to the office laughing. Five minutes later, Jeff walked into the office like he just saw the bright side of something. He was white as a sheet and stood there shaking his head.

I said, "What's up?"

He said, "You're not going to believe this."

He threw the brown paper bag he had taken out of the booth on the desk and said, "Check that out." Marty and I looked at it.

As I picked it up I realized it was pretty heavy. I looked inside and to my total disbelief, I saw stacks of rubber-banded hundred dollar bills—ten thousand dollars worth. We were looking at each other in shock. This was 1983 and ten thousand dollars was a lot more money back then than it obviously is today. This was temptation of the highest order, and it spoke volumes about Jeff's integrity because we were all struggling financially at the time. He could have taken it home and no one would have been the wiser.

We decided that we had to give the money back, but we had

no idea who it belonged to. We thought we would let the word out to some regular customers that we had found something of value and if they or anyone they knew lost something of value and could describe it, that we would be happy to give it back. Well, maybe not happy, but we would return it nonetheless.

A woman came in one day later and said excitedly, "My friend lost a lot of money and someone said you found it." Marty explained that he found *something of value* and that if her friend could describe it he would give it back to her.

She said, "Here's her number; give her a call."

I called and got her husband. I said, "Hi, I heard your wife may have lost something of value in my restaurant and I'm trying to locate her."

He said, "Oh, thank you. She's not here right now, but I'll tell her you called."

I said, " Thank you."

An hour later, the woman came roaring through the door, asking for Tom.

I said, "I'm Tom."

She said, "You know, you're a fucking asshole!"

I said, "Huh?"

She repeated, "You're an asshole!"

I'm looking all around the dining room for the asshole, but we're the only two there.

She said, "What kind of asshole calls someone's husband and tells him she lost ten thousand dollars! Now he thinks I'm a moron."

I knew this woman a total of ninety seconds, and I already had two "assholes" and one slightly more colorful version of the same under my belt, so I thought I was entitled to a little fun.

I said, "What are you talking about?"

She said, "You called my house and told my husband that I lost the money."

I said, "I called your house to say that I had found something of value. I didn't say a word about money. I found a watch."

Dead silence. She said, "I thought you found my money."

I said, "Sorry for the misunderstanding."

That was the only time I enjoyed watching the blood drain from someone's face.

She said, "My husband's going to kill me."

I told her, "Well, a good lawyer, a jury of his peers, a temporary insanity plea, and I think he's got a shot at beating it."

By this point, she was in tears so I figured enough was enough. I said, "Okay, stop crying. I have your money, but I have to tell you that I completely agree with your husband's conclusion on your intelligence. You're not only a moron, you're very rude, and you are the sworn enemy of common sense. The interesting thing is that as I'm giving you back this money, I'm beginning to believe you're right about me being a asshole." She just looked at me.

I gave her the money; she thanked me and turned to leave. As she walked to the door, she was fumbling in her pocketbook.

She turned around with a twenty-dollar bill in her hand and said, "Here, this is for you. You know as a reward."

I said, "You're much too generous. As tempting as that twenty is, why don't you keep it and apply it towards charm school."

FINGERED

Remember that soft spot I have for seniors? I'm over it. One Saturday night, a party of four women arrived at *Starfish* at eight o'clock. They were dressed to the nines. Hair, clothes, and makeup were all perfect and they looked great. The two daughters were in their twenties, Mom was in her fifties, and Grandma was somewhere between seventy-five and one hundred and twelve, depending upon who her plastic surgeon was.

One of the daughters said, "Table for four, please."

The hostess explained that it would be about an hour wait for a table of four. Grandma says, "That's ridiculous, we're not waiting an hour to eat here. There are plenty of restaurants we can go to."

The hostess said, "Okay, good luck and please come back another time."

Grandma said, "I don't think so."

Out the door they go, but before they get to the parking lot they have a little conference and they return.

Mom said, "We decided to wait for a table, but could you see about seating us sooner?"

You just know where this is going.

The hostess explained, "I don't want to get off on the wrong foot here. It probably won't happen, so if you're not happy with waiting an hour, we should probably do this another time." One of the daughters said, "No, we'll wait."

Eleven minutes later, Grandma went to the hostess station and said, very loudly, "We have been waiting for over an hour! Where's our table!"

The hostess, three of the wait staff, and anyone else who was within two miles of her voice started to giggle. The biggest problem with starting to giggle is stopping. They didn't. It degenerated down to suppressed hysteria.

Diane, the hostess, recovered momentarily and in that patronizing tone usually reserved for old people and children, said, "Come on now, you're fibbing. You haven't been here an hour yet. We're going to seat you as soon as we can. It's very busy, so try to be patient a little while longer."

Grandma was having none of it. She asked, "You're not going to seat us now?"

Diane explained again, "As soon as we have an open table, we will get you seated quickly."

Grandma said, "That's it! We're leaving!" and proceeds to stick her middle finger two inches from the hostess's nose. Yup, she flipped her the bird right there at the podium.

I didn't actually see the offending finger myself. It happened so fast and I wasn't really paying attention. It's a pretty traumatic moment to have been flipped off by an elderly woman and Diane was stunned. I don't think it was the emotion that bothered her as much as it was the finger itself. They tell me it was rather stumpy in an arthritic kind of way, withered with bumpy knuckles. It had a yellow nail from years of oxygen-starving polish, and it was blessed with a mole. You could probably hear someone giving you a finger like that.

As the finger was being described to me, I was as close to wetting my pants as I had been in more years than I care to remember. The humor was short-lived though, experiencing a nightmare of a bad finger dream after eating pizza late one night.

So now that Grandma had flipped the hostess the bird, she wheeled around on one foot and headed out the door. The two daughters followed her, mortified. As Mom passed the hostess desk, she let out a groan, looked straight up in the air, rolled her eyes, and said, "I don't believe this; she does this everywhere we go." How cool is that?

Nine and a Half Weeks

Table number eight is both a power table and the most romantic table *CoolFish* has to offer. It's located in the back left side corner of the dining room, on the banquet against the wall. If you're feeling romantic, that's the table. The lighting is low and you can sit next to one another at a right angle while you gaze out at the rest of the room.

A young couple—very much in love, as I was to discover—was camped out at table eight. They were having dinner on a reasonably busy weeknight. They had a couple of rounds of drinks, dinner, and dessert, and were relaxing and talking after they'd finished.

The night was winding down; the wait staff was beginning to clean up. There were a few tables left in both dining rooms, but most of the other diners had gone by ten o'clock. That's when we first noticed the goings-on. It started with a peck on the cheek followed by a light smooch, followed by a kiss, leading to the Stanley Cup of tonsil hockey. These two were going at it like they were in the Jungle Room at the *Commack Motor Inn*.

I've got to say something here: sex, unless you're one of the players, looks ridiculous in public. We were trying not to watch and laugh, but it was hard not to. These two were carrying on in the back of the restaurant like rabbits on crack for about an hour. Not a care in the world and no thought about who could be watching. We were growing impatient because we wanted to close the dining room, but the make-out session was so intense that no one was willing to go back to tell them to leave. We waited another half-hour, talking at the bar. I glanced back, fully expecting clothes to be flying off, and saw that there was no one at the table.

I asked the bartender, "Did they leave?"

He said, "I didn't see them leave."

I said, "They couldn't have left while we were talking, could they?"

The bartender said, "I don't think so."

I was just about to send the busboys in to clean up when a Manolo Blahnik comes flying up in the air from the banquet behind the table. A minute later, I see the other shoe, then an ankle, and finally a knee. Uh oh.

On one hand, I was very impressed with the degree of flexibility shown by both parties because there isn't much room back there. On the other hand, it needed to stop before it got totally out of control. I don't know if this is a Bill Clinton definition of sex because everyone still had their clothes on, but I'm sure old Willie would've been impressed.

Instead of ice water, an idea that was already on the table, we threw the lights up on them. I'm grateful that one of them noticed. They sat up and tried to straighten themselves out.

The man, who was completely disheveled with a noticeably elevated respiratory rate, looked at the busboy and asked, "Are you guys closing already?"

I'm betting they had the oysters.

Fried Oyster Bay Oysters/Avocado Relish/ Passion Fruit Fire Oil Recipe

My mom's sister, Aunt Pearl, owned three beach bungalows in Bayville, New York, and we spent many summer vacations and fall weekends there when I was growing up. It was only twenty minutes from where we lived, but it seemed like a different country. I would spend my days fishing from the pier or under the Bayville Bridge and picking berries in the woods. Speaking of berries, Aunt Pearl's husband, Uncle Berry (I swear that was his given name), decided to buy a boat. We graduated from fishing from the pier to the bay—Oyster Bay. I wouldn't trade those memories of the bay for anything. I still go there to stare at it when I get overloaded; it's very therapeutic. For many years, the oyster industry on Long Island was centered in Oyster Bay, hence the name. I remember seeing pictures of oyster shells piled into small mountains on the shore. As the bay became more and more polluted in the late fifties and early sixties, the oysters disappeared. The good news is that through conservation and farming the bay is clean again, and Flowers Oyster Farms have brought a dying industry back to this magnificent body of water. Anyone who has tasted a bluepoint oyster has probably had a Flowers oyster from Oyster Bay. This dish is a small tribute to those bay-men whose hard work and passion brought back a piece of history to Long Island.

Ingredients:

2 ripe avocados
2 plum tomatoes, blanched, peeled, seeded, and diced
¼ cup red onion, finely diced
1 serrano chile, seeded and minced

1 garlic clove, minced

1 tablespoon cilantro, chopped

Juice of two small limes

¼ cup passion fruit juice

¼ teaspoon cayenne pepper

¼ cup soy or canola oil

2 cups olive oil

1 cup Wondra flour

Kosher salt and black pepper to taste

1 dozen bluepoint oysters

Peel and pit the avocados. Place in nonreactive bowl and mash with a large fork. Fold in the diced tomato, red onion, serrano chile, and season with salt and pepper. Add one of the avocado pits to the mixture, cover with plastic wrap, and set aside. Place the passion fruit juice and the cayenne pepper into a blender and with the blade running, add the oil through the opening until emulsified and set aside. Heat the oil in a large heavy pan to 375°F. Whisk the flour together with the salt and pepper in a shallow dish. Toss the oysters in the flour mixture, shaking off any excess, and fry until golden brown, (2-3 minutes). Remove with slotted spoon and drain on a paper towel to absorb excess oil. Place a large teaspoon of the avocado relish in the center of the plate, arrange three oysters around the relish, and drizzle with the passion fruit fire oil.

Chef's tip: Pour a ½ inch layer of kosher salt on the plates. Wash and dry the oyster shells. Arrange three shells on each plate. Fill each shell with the avocado relish, top with an oyster, and drizzle the passion fruit fire oil on the oyster for a more dramatic presentation.

Wine pairing: Paumanok Semi Dry Riesling.

JUST DESSERTS

A couple arrived for dinner on a weeknight in September. They sat down and ordered cocktails: martinis actually. It's always the martinis. The server brought the drinks and took their dinner order. The appetizers were served and everything seemed okay. Then it happened.

The woman excused herself after half a Martini and half an appetizer, made her way unsteadily to the ladies' room, and proceeded to pass out cold on the floor. She was in there, out cold, five or ten minutes before another patron told us she was in trouble.

The manager and one of the waitresses went in there to try to rescue her. Now she was up off the floor, but she was kneeling in front of the bowl saying, "I think I'm going to be sick."

I'm glad I'm not allowed in the ladies' room. Ever been in there? It's scary. It's like a cross between the dressing room at Saks and your local landfill. She carried on for another half hour, praying to the porcelain, and then realizing that she'd been a little drained from the experience, decided to lie down and take a nap in the middle of the bathroom floor. Anyone trying to use the ladies' room now had to step over, on, or around this peacefully sleeping, heavily-soiled woman. We realized we had to get her out of there, but she was a dead weight disaster, a puddle.

My daughter, Courtney—who had a full station, by the way—was sitting on the floor with the woman's head in her lap, trying to revive her and clean her up. Another hour passed by. Now we were redirecting everyone to the ladies' room out in the office hallway, much to their annoyance, because of all the commotion. Every time we got her to sit up, she slumped back down. What do you do?

After waiting about one hour and fifteen minutes for her to come around with a full restaurant, and a very agitated line to the ladies' room, I decided to take over. Not that the girls weren't doing the best they could, but sometimes you just need the boss to take charge of the problem.

I asked what table she was sitting at. They told me table thirty-two. I went to table thirty-two, and frankly I was a little annoyed that the husband had been missing-in-action.

I walked up to the table, introduced myself, and said, "Did you know your wife is passed out in the bathroom?"

He said, "Yeah, I figured as much. She's been gone for some time. It happens occasionally when she drinks martinis before dinner."

"Oh, this has happened before?"

"Yeah, once in a while."

"Well, it's becoming a bit of a problem. She's been in there for over an hour. I'm down one waitress, one manager, one ladies' room, and I've been yelled at by about twenty people trying to get in there and use it."

He said, "What would you like me to do?"

Here's a brilliant thought. I said, "Maybe you could help us get her out of there and take her home."

The man looked me right in the eye, and I swear to God said, "I haven't had my dessert yet; it comes with the *Prix-Fixe* dinner." You couldn't make this stuff up.

My entire Friday night was spiraling into the tank, his wife was two sips away from an alcohol-induced coma, and his only worry was whether he should have the raspberry sorbet or the flaming pineapple shortcake.

He finished his dessert and *then* carried his wife to the car.

OTHER WORLDLY

I know, I know, I've said this before, but it always kills me when people preface their complaints with, "I've eaten all over the world." I guess it gives them some sort of worldly perspective on the sins of the restaurant business, and a continental flair for spotting and reporting shortcomings, mistakes, and the "little murders" that happen occasionally when dining out.

The other talent the "I've eaten all over the world" crowd seems to possess is, upon spotting a transgression and reporting said transgression to the proper authority, a world-class ability to negotiate a settlement. I don't know what part of the world these people have eaten in, but in most countries I've been to, the punishment fits the crime.

Not so much in the restaurant world. I once tried to buy dessert for a woman who had about a shot glass of water spilled on her. As the busboy was filling the water glasses, some of the condensation on the water pitcher dripped onto the woman's sweater.

She said, "That's it?"

I said, "That's what?"

She said, "That's all you are going to do for me?"

I said, "It was only a little water, but if it's a problem, I'll pick up your dry cleaning bill. We all know how stubborn those water stains can be."

She said, "You're a real big shot. That's all you intend to do? I've eaten all over the world and that's not how I'm usually treated when there's a problem. I think you should buy the entire table lunch. What kind of businessman are you?"

I said, "I'm sure you've experienced your share of problems in restaurants, but I honestly don't consider condensation to be in that category. And if I were any kind of businessman, I wouldn't be in the restaurant business, now would I? I'll tell you what I'll do though, I'll buy everyone lunch if you do me one favor."

She asked, "What's that?"

I said, "Let me make at least one mortgage payment for you. Now that I've thought about it, it's probably the right thing to do."

She said, "You think that's funny?"

I said, "I'm trying to illustrate an absurdity. We're talking a water spillage here, not battery acid."

She said, "You're an idiot."

I said, "Thank you."

I'm off on a tangent here, but I'm trying to illustrate how, in my world, there's no relevant value between the offense and the reward, and it's usually the same people involved over and over again, the people who "have eaten all over the world."

I eat out seven nights a week, three hundred and sixty-five nights a year. I can count on one hand how many times I, or anyone I was dining with, has sent back a dish. By contrast, my friend's mother, who eats out maybe five times a year, has sent back everything she has ever been served at least twice. There's a blossoming cottage industry of people who, "have eaten all over the world," who will try almost anything to get something for free, or something deducted from their check.

Here's the pattern. There needs to be a real or perceived problem. Once a problem, real or perceived, is established, one can then begin the negotiation process, establishing what amount of financial reward for the endured pain and suffering would be appropriate. The only glitch is when there is no problem, real or perceived, but this can be overcome by someone who "has eaten all over the world," by merely inventing one. If that's the only way you can get the discount, what the hell?

A couple of regular guests who eat out "all over the world," happened to be in *CoolFish*. It seems to be a regular stop on the World Culinary Tour. He's always happy, always grateful, and always pleasant. She is none of the above. She always has some kind of problem and never forgets to mention that she's eaten all over the world.

They finished their meal and on the way out, he saw me and called me over to tell me what a great night he had. He loved the food, had great service, and he even liked the music. She was not uttering a word, but the look on her face said it all. She looked like she was somewhere between miserable and angry, the perfect poster child for Preparation H. I don't know when I'll learn to just shut my mouth.

I turned to "Bubbles" and said, "How was your dinner?"

She said, "I didn't like it. In fact, I can't believe how you run this place, and I've eaten all over the world." This is the part where I want to put my head in a microwave and press number seven.

I said, "What happened? Your husband said he loved it. Were you at the same table?"

She said, "You know, you're really not as funny as you think you are." I was thinking, "*You could drain the funny out of anything,*" but I managed to keep the thought to myself.

I said, "Sorry, just trying to keep things light. Please, tell me what went wrong."

Are you ready for this?

She said, and I swear this is the God-honest truth, "My busboy didn't speak English."

I was stunned. "What?"

She repeated, "The busboy didn't speak English. I couldn't communicate with him. What kind of restaurant are you running here? Everywhere I've ever eaten the busboys generally speak the native language, why not here?"

I've honestly never considered a busboy's language skills when eating out. I just need him to bring the stuff I want and take away the stuff I don't. I can find other people to talk to, but hey, that's me.

I was wondering how far down on the restaurant-complaint manifesto do you have to travel to come up with, "The busboy doesn't speak English?" We've got to be on fire if that's your only bitch. That has to be a little further down than, "I was expecting Sprite and got 7 Up," "The chef is a little overweight," or "My waitress was too cheerful," all three of which I have heard before.

Still trying to digest that one, I said, "Tell me, what exactly was it that you wanted to chat with him about?"

She said, "I think your busboys should speak English."

Now feeling terribly sorry for her mortified husband, I said, "You know, you're right. It must have been horrible. Have a drink with me at the bar, while I go the office and peruse my seventeen hundred busboy resumes to see if I find one who's home from Harvard for the summer."

You would think someone who "has eaten all over the world" would be somewhat bilingual, no?

I've Got a Tip for You

'm amazed that after forty years of doing this that I can still be appalled by someone's behavior. I've literally seen and heard it all, right?

The coat check position is easy to fill in the dead of winter when everyone wears a coat. The job can be fairly lucrative. However, in the "shoulder" seasons when the weather is milder, the coat-check girls make less money. We do compensate them financially from the house, but we can't compensate them for their boredom. Subsequently, it's a hard job to fill.

We found our slow-season-coat-check savior, in the petite form of a sixteen-year-old, extremely intelligent, high school student. She was grateful for the money—a quality I rarely see from an employee, I might add—and she used all the down time to study. It was a perfect situation. So perfect, in fact, that you just knew something or someone would screw it up.

Restaurant patrons are a dependable lot. A couple finished their dinner and paid their check. They sashay through the dining room, past the bar, to the coat check room.

I have to describe this guy so you get the picture. The man was in his thirties, about 6'2" and about 250 pounds of steroid-assisted muscle. He wore black pants, duck-billed shoes, and a forty-dollar Marshalls shirt, with maybe two buttons buttoned. He had enough chest hair for the Syosset fire department to consider a controlled burn, and the very fashionable Mr. T starter set around his neck. Got to love the '70s.

This wrestle-mania wannabe walked up to the coat check room and squared off with Anna, who is sixteen-years-old, 5'0", and eighty-six pounds. He handed her a ticket for his imitation leather jacket, looked at her, and said, "This is how you dress?"

Anna had on designer jeans and a sweater; it's a coat check room.

Anna said sheepishly, "Excuse me?"

He said, "You ought to be ashamed of yourself. Look at you. You're a mess. Aren't you embarrassed to walk around like that? I can't believe your mother let you out of the house dressed that way."

Anna started to cry. She was scared, embarrassed, and intimidated.

Being a bully, he pressed on. He took two twenty-dollar bills from a very small wad, threw them in her tip cup, and said, "Here, buy yourself some decent clothes."

You can't even buy a gift certificate for forty dollars, let alone decent clothes. Memo to big spender: you seem to value exercise, so exercise your eighteen-point IQ and spell Bloomingdale's for me.

He left and Anna was still crying. A waitress saw her and asked, "What's wrong?"

She recounted the incident to one of the waitresses, who spreads it through the dining room like a wildfire. I'm always stunned at the speed of which *certain* information is passed around the dining room. If I tell one of my servers that I just ran out of tuna, I can guarantee you twenty minutes later, I will get seven orders for tuna from four servers who never got the memo. *"Nobody told me."* But if I tell one of my servers that I'm sleeping with one of the waiters and I'm pondering the advantages of a sex change operation, and then run as fast as I can to the hostess desk, I'm 100% sure I would hear, "I had no idea you were gay," upon arrival. Priorities, I guess.

Okay so all the employees were fuming. Diane, at 5'2", 110 pounds, well maybe 120 pounds, actually went outside to beat the guy up, but luckily he was gone. Since I'm almost always the last one to know anything around here, I got the story about a half hour later.

I walked over to Anna, who was still upset, and did my *Father Knows Best* routine. I said, "Listen, the guy's a jerk, probably drunk, and obviously obnoxious. You're beautiful, sweet, smart, and I love your jeans."

She was still crying and I was getting a little upset myself.

I said, "Don't cry; he's not worth the tears, and besides you'll ruin your makeup."

She said, "I'm not crying because of what he said."

I said, "Really? Why are you crying?"

She said, "I'm crying because his wife took the forty dollars back from my tip cup as they were leaving," and then burst out laughing. I told you she was smart. The kid gets it.

Having a Fling

We all know someone like this. He talks only about himself. *"Hey, that's enough about me, let's talk about you. What do you think of me?"*

You know the type. He knows the "hot" restaurants, all the "new" food trends, drives the "it" car, goes to all the "in" vacation spots, has the "best" house, and of course, the "trophy wife," who came in third. This guy sound familiar yet?

As insufferable as these guys are, somehow they get people to have dinner with them. A party of four arrived for dinner: Mr. "Hot Shot," his trophy wife, and another couple. The other couple must have been friends with the trophy wife, because the guy in the other couple looked like he was going to the dentist. You could tell he didn't want to spend two hours with Mr. Hot Shot. They sat down, ordered drinks, and Hot Shot starts his diatribe.

"We couldn't get into Per Se (hot restaurant) so we decided not to do the city and to bring you guys here."

"We took the Ferrari (hot car) because it was such a nice night."

"Hey, we just got back from Napa yesterday. We ate at the French Laundry." (Another "it" restaurant.)

"We had organic eggs from virgin chickens with tiny potatoes the size of your little finger." (Here's a finger for you.)

"Good to be home, though. The house is a mess. We're waiting for them to finish installing the indoor baseball field."

"Hey, doesn't Sonya look great? It cost me a fortune, but it was well worth it."

It was a full half hour of non-stop, run on, bullshit. By this time, the other guy's eyes were glazing over. You could tell he was just trying to survive it. Dinner came and went with pretty much the same routine. Hot Shot kept talking and everyone else was feigning interest.

Finally, it's time for dessert and coffee. It was the first glimmer of excitement you could detect in the eyes of the other couple at the table. The other guy ate a *Chocolate Bag* dessert in under a minute. For reference sake, I had a black Labrador that would take twice that long.

He drank his coffee so fast it had to scald him. Then came the check. I must tell you, I've seen and paid a lot of restaurant checks in my life; only people who pay them infrequently make a big show about paying the check. Charity is supposed to be a quiet affair. Not this time. Both guys take out their respective credit cards.

Hot Shot said, "I'll get this."

The other guy said, "No, please, let me."

Hot Shot said, "No, I insist."

The other guy, who would pay anything just to leave said, "No, please, let me."

Hot Shot insisted, "No, you paid the last thirty-seven times. It's my turn."

And with that statement, he grabbed the other guy's credit card and threw it across the dining room, flinging it like a gold card Frisbee, and it disappeared.

We looked high, we looked low. We had customers fan out two feet apart in one of the most well-dressed search parties in history. An APB went out shortly thereafter, and I'm told John Walsh was looking into it. We even searched the coffee station, all to no avail. Nothing. We felt horrible for the poor guy. After spending two and a half torturous hours with this moron, he was now down a gold card, and had to notify the bank and cancel the card.

He called us back after service and asked, "You find it yet?"

We said, "Nope."

Two days later the guy who lost the card called back, "Any luck finding my card?"

We said, "None whatsoever."

A week later, he called in one last attempt, "I guess no one found my card, huh?"

Our reply was, "Good guess."

I have no idea what happened to the card. I'm assuming someone picked it up because we never did find it. I guess no good deed goes unpunished.

Happy Birthday

This one comes from a friend, but it's too good not to tell. My friend manages a beautiful restaurant on the Long Island Sound with decking on the first and second floor. Fourteen women came in for lunch one afternoon, saying that they had a reservation. The manager couldn't find it. They said they had called to reserve a table for a birthday party and to see if they could bring in their own cake.

Reservations do occasionally get lost, but when it's a birthday party with a cake and balloons, the front of the house tends to pay attention. I know this may be hard to believe, but some customers screw up their own reservations. They forget to call. They get the date wrong. They make fifteen reservations in twelve different restaurants under nine different aliases, in three different states. So don't assume it's always us.

Anyway, the manager said she would get them seated. Some people, when they believe the restaurant has made a boo-boo, see an opportunity to use it to their advantage, like when a lioness sees a gazelle. The manager was marching these women from table to table, trying to find the perfect seat. The women felt that since the restaurant had screwed up their reservation, they were entitled to pretty much anything they wanted. That usually includes the requisite freebie and piles of abuse for the staff, but none of that can possibly start without parading around the dining room for forty-five minutes, trying to find the perfect table.

I've often wondered just what it is that these people are searching for. You're only going to be there for an hour or two. I've walked hundreds of people hundreds of miles around dining rooms just to find that special seat, only to have them change it five minutes later. It's patently ridiculous, but hilarious nonetheless. As I'm wandering aimlessly around the dining room I always think of the black Labrador I used to have. Ever walk a dog on a cold night? You know he has to go and he knows he has to go, but he will spend forty-five minutes sniffing every inch of turf to find the perfect spot. What the hell is the difference? Just go. It's the same thing. Just sit for God's sake.

I'll let you in on a little secret about the table-shopping game. Once we identify a table shopper we generally take those parties to the best table first, because we know there is no way they can bring themselves to sit at the first table offered. They just can't do it. They'd be thrown out of the club. We then bring them to the second and third-best tables and after two or three more refusals, we seat them where we had originally planned to. My therapist would call that immature, I call it fun.

Back to the story. They settled on a large table in the front room that had to be pushed out into part of the lobby, probably because it took a tremendous amount of chair and table moving, required the maximum amount of employee effort, and inconvenienced everyone in the dining room. (After all, you lost our reservation.) Fourteen ladies ordered fourteen salads, which just happened to come with fourteen problems. Go figure.

"Why is hers bigger than mine?"

"I asked for the dressing on the side."

"I wanted the dressing on the side also, but I wanted it on the left side not the right side."

"My tomatoes are hard."

"I ordered my tuna black and blue, and it's raw."

"My chicken isn't cooked enough."

"I didn't want eggs. What can I have instead?"

"Chick peas bother my stomach. Take them off."

"I want more lettuce and fewer vegetables."

"I want more vegetables and less lettuce."

"I don't like the way this looks."

"Can I get salmon instead of chicken?"

"Could you ask the chef to take off the chicken and give me sliced steak, and make sure the dressing is on the side, and chop the lettuce so I can eat it for God's sake?"

"Take mine back, it's disgusting. I can't eat it."

"Are you going to buy us a drink?"

"That's the least you can do for losing our reservation."

As they were finishing their lunch, a man walked into the upstairs bar from the outside deck with an infant in tow. He needed to change the diaper. He put the bag, which I'm guessing that his loving ex-wife packed for the day, with only about half of what he really needed, on the communal table by the mezzanine and gently laid the child down.

Downstairs the salad plates had been cleared and the ladies were ready for dessert. Out came a Fudgie-the-Whale cake with a twelve inch blaze on top, and fourteen mentally-ill women started on an off-key version of "Happy Birthday" at the top of their lungs.

Dad opened the diaper. The only living witness tells me that he could have used a fire hose and a beach towel to deal with the mess. Dad averted his eyes, held his breath and bravely went in armed with a handy wipe. He removed the soiled diaper, folded it up and placed it off to the side. The child was now squirming and Dad was wrestling for control, trying desperately not to get any on him. As Dad reached for another handy wipe, he knocked the diaper off the table and over the mezzanine ledge. Just as the fourteen women sang the last two off-key words, "To you," the diaper fell with the speed of a space shuttle landing and exploded all over the table.

Dead silence. I guarantee you it was the first time all fourteen of those women were quiet at the same time. Then the realization of what just transpired set in. You can only imagine what went on.

Ain't that some shit?

CHEAP WITH A CAPITAL "T"

For the life of me, I can't understand why people go to restaurants that they either can't afford or are unwilling to spend the money for. Why go and then expect the restaurant to discount and haggle like some street vendor in Acapulco? There are certainly enough restaurants around that offer more inexpensive fare. Choose one of them; that's cool. But torturing the rest of us about the price of a side of vegetables is not.

Inexplicably, some people are proud of being cheap. I'm not talking about being careful with money. I'm talking about cheap. We all know the difference. People who are careful with money never tip six percent; cheap people do. People who are careful with money never go to the bathroom when the check is presented; cheap people do. People who are careful with their money never drag another couple to a restaurant they don't like so they can use a gift certificate for their portion of the bill; cheap people do. Need I go on, because I could.

A table of five sat down for dinner at *Jedediah's*. There were two couples and one single guy. Guess who the cheap one was.

Single guy's opening statement to Eileen his waitress was, "We were thinking of staying in one of the rooms tonight, but you are *so expensive*. I can't believe anyone would spend that much for a room. Does it come with a woman?" *Ha, ha, ha.*

Take it easy there, Shecky. Most restaurant customers don't realize that we have heard every bad restaurant quip a thousand times. It gets old. Here's a great rule to live by: if you are not Chris Rock, don't do the comedy thing at the table. Been there, heard that.

The two couples started teasing the single guy about being

cheap, a fact he didn't even give a *head fake* towards hiding. He said, "I'm not cheap, I'm thrifty."

How's that for self-delusion? It's like those people who use the word "shoot" instead of "shit." "Oh shoot, I forgot our anniversary," really means, "Oh shit, I forgot our anniversary!" Shoot is just shit with two "Os." It's the same with thrifty. Thrifty is cheap with a "T."

As he was pondering his drink order, thrift overcame him.

"How much are your Martinis?"

Eileen, his waitress said, "Twelve dollars."

Single guy said to her, "Are you serious? How the hell do you get away with that? What, the owner's trying to get rich in one day? How about the wines by the glass, how much are they?"

Eileen said, "Eight to twenty dollars, depending on what you order."

Single guy said, "Twenty dollars? How big is the glass, forty ounces? What idiot would pay twenty dollars for a glass of wine?"

"I could hook you up with a Shirley Temple for say, two dollars."

Single guy laughed and says, "Two dollars for a soda? That's criminal."

All the while, the rest of the table was having fun, and I think even Eileen was enjoying it somewhat.

Single guy then said, "Okay. Bring me the eight-dollar glass of wine. Size is critical to cheap people. They really don't care what anything tastes like, there just has to be a lot of it and preferably for free. They judge restaurants by how many sandwiches they can make the next day with what they couldn't finish the night before.

"I love that place. They gave us so much food, I had calamari sandwiches for three days."

Do the division. Ten dollars worth of calamari, divided by four, adding the bread, equals about $2.75 per meal. You can eat like a king for seventeen dollars a week.

Appetizers and entrées pretty much get the same treatment. It's actually funny to see someone so uncomfortable with the price, forging ahead anyway, sweating as he's doing the math.

"How can you charge twelve dollars for a salad? Lettuce is lettuce."

"I can't believe you get thirty dollars for a half a chicken."

"I should at least get the other half to take home."

"What the hell is foie gras anyway?"

Eileen was amused and asked, "Anyone for dessert?"

Single guy said, "Do you have any under twenty dollars? You could at least buy us an after-dinner drink for all the money we've spent here."

Eileen quipped, "I'll suggest it to the owner."

They split some desserts and the whole time he was grumbling about the prices and how we would be out of business in less than a year. As the check was being presented, single guy's bladder gives out, and he does what cheap people do when the check comes—he checks out and disappears.

One of the other men paid the check. Single guy reappeared in time for the tip consultation. Isn't that always the way? Cheap people are always heavily involved in discussing the tip. Not the bill, just the tip. Twelve percent is considered extravagant in skinflint circles, and he was lobbying hard for that number. So hard, in fact, Eileen heard him. Being cheap with your money is one thing; being cheap with everyone else's is a whole new level. Thankfully sanity ruled and the tip was fine. The table got up to leave. Single guy hung back a little and flagged Eileen down.

Single guy said to her, "Hey, can I ask you something?"

"Does it have anything to do with price?"

"No, not at all."

Eileen said, "Okay, shoot."

"Would you consider going on a date with me?"

Eileen, happily married and very amused, asked, "Where would you like to go?"

Single guy said, "How about dinner?"

You can't make it up.

A Homeless "Bag Lady"

ell, here's another Martini story. It's the drink that keeps on giving. Drinking martinis has three possible outcomes. One is a starring role in a quick remake of the Dudley Moore movie *Arthur*. Two is a full-blown coma. And three, and the most interesting by far, is a combination of both. You know that dreamy state that flows in and out of consciousness, but allows you just enough brainpower to babble about stuff important to only you, in a language that no one has yet to translate? It's especially fun to watch on a date. I've heard a million reasons why people drink martinis.

"They get you where you want to go."

"It's the least caloric drink out there."

"They taste like watermelon."

But, by far the best one I ever heard was from a woman who said, "I drink a Martini when I go out on a date to break the ice."

Are ya' kidding? Breaking the ice on a date with a Martini is like trying to open a jammed window with a suitcase nuke. Same result. Bend down, place your head firmly between your knees, and kiss your ass goodbye. There should be no surprises here.

Two people on a date showed up at *CoolFish*. They each had a Martini at the bar. He was six feet tall, 210 pounds; she wasn't. They each ordered a second.

Halfway through their second drink, she decided to give a linguistics seminar at the bar. She started in English, I think, drifted into Russian with an Italian accent, and by the time she got to the table she was speaking fluent Chinese, Mandarin, I believe. Her date, not being from Shanghai, was trying desperately to make sense of what she was trying to say.

As Courtney went to the table to take a drink order, the woman passed out. Her forehead was on the table between the fork and knife and her arms were straight down.

Her date said (get this), "I think we're okay with drinks." How's that for a knee-slapper? I don't know about you, but I feel very strongly about this. When my forehead hits the table, it's absolutely time to stop. A guy's got to have some kind of self-control.

Her date said, "I'm going to have the crab cake and would you like the Asian Tuna Salad, honey?"

Without looking up, honey said, "Prstrq Hurmphor Frickin' Suna Taladal."

Courtney said, "Okay, one crab cake, and one Suna Taladel." I love that kid.

Courtney brought out the appetizers, and the man woke up his date to take a couple of bites. Martinis also do a major number on your motor skills, so she had a death grip on both utensils. She slowly cut a piece of the fish, and with her mouth half open, lifted the food, and placed a fork full of Asian tuna Salad squarely in her right eye, wonton and all.

Her date decided she needed a little help. To his credit, he hung in there and got some food both in and on her. Courtney took the entrée order.

Her date said, "I'm going to have the steak medium rare. Honey, would you like meat or fish?"

Honey said, "Yes."

Her date asked, "Honey, meat or fish. What are you in the mood for?"

Honey babbled, "Guess."

Her date patiently said, "Okay, give her the skate wing with the chili-lime vinaigrette."

Honey was starting to come alive with the arrival of the food.

She said, *"I love wait sking with the chili-stuff on it. You sake touch good care of be maby."*

Don't you just love the part where stone drunk people try to look sober?

He looked at her and said, "I love you."

She put on her best Martini sex-face. You know, the one where the eyes go in different directions, kind-of like Peter Falk. She then said, "Ahh live. Ahhh—Luv—All ives. I love olives. Ooofah!"

She had morphed into Al Pacino. Courtney cleared the table, called the clean-up crew, and prepared to take the dessert order.

We have a dessert at the restaurant called the *Chocolate Bag*. It's a banana split served in a bag made of chocolate, and apparently Honey had had it before.

Honey, now speaking in broken English at nine decibels said, "I want the chocolate house!"

Courtney said, "You mean the *Chocolate Bag?*"

"Noooo—I want the chocolate house!"

"We have a *Chocolate Bag* and a chocolate teepee. I guess you could consider the teepee a house in a Native American sort of way. I could bring you one of those."

Honey said, "No pee-pees or teepees. *Ha ha* Bring me a house!"

Courtney brought her a *Chocolate Bag*, which she managed to finish most of. Twenty percent went in her mouth, the rest in her ears, eyes, and on her clothes. I wish I had a picture of her walking out. She looked like a cross between the victim of a culinary drive-by and a drop cloth.

Someone once told me that if you saw a video of yourself when you were drunk, you would never drink again. Thankfully, I've never tried it. I'm sure one photograph would be all Honey would need to bring her Martini career to a screeching halt.

KLEPTOMANIAC
OCTOGENARIAN

fter all my bitching and moaning about bad restaurant behavior, and especially the stealing, it borders on hypocrisy that I should relate this story. Although I shouldn't think it's funny, I do; I make no apologies.

The greatest restaurant thief I've ever known was my friend's grandmother. She was absolutely the best. She was fearless, stealthy, clever, and inventive. She was as creative as MacGyver, but larcenous.

Something happens when you reach eighty. Your perceptions change and the lines between what's acceptable and what's unacceptable begin to blur. For example: If I slip and use profanity at the dinner table, everyone's horrified. If my mother does, they all crack up. You are given way more wiggle room as you age. The same is true for stealing. When you are young, it's a crime (unless, of course, you steal from a restaurant which is considered an entitlement); when you are over eighty, it's considered cute.

Anyway, my friend's grandmother was to restaurants what Willie Sutton was to banks. When she died I helped him clean out her house. I couldn't believe it. Restaurant Depot couldn't match her inventory. I could have opened two restaurants with what was in her basement. She had glasses, dishes, and silverware in all patterns and colors. Some were sets of six, which indicated to me multiple trips to the same establishment. Ashtrays were well represented. One even said "Swan Club" on it. There were hundreds of cases of Sweet'N Low, Equal, and Splenda, as well as enough tea bags to keep the good people of Boston partying for a month. I could swear I saw a 6' x 8' sign in the back of her garage that said "*Milleridge Inn,*" but I can't be sure.

When my friend first told me about her, I was skeptical. Although I've been the victim of some great restaurant thieves, one night I witnessed an event above and beyond anything I'd ever seen. Ever since that night, I've come to recognize her as the greatest, bar none.

I went to a dinner with my friend and his family. We were celebrating "Grandma's" one hundred and twenty-something birthday at her favorite restaurant. I didn't have an AARP card and the doorman gave me a hard time, but I did manage to talk my way in.

The restaurant looked like it was in a time warp. I don't know if I can use the word anachronism in a sentence, but I certainly know the meaning. My friend suggested that I sit next to Grandma. His logic was that since she knew that I'm in the business, she would behave. I was thrilled to have a front row seat to what potentially could be a very funny night, so I agreed. The ten of us were sitting around the table, talking, laughing, and reminiscing, with the smell of fried chicken and mothballs wafting through the dining room.

"Pass the bread please," someone said.

As the breadbasket was going around the table, I saw Grandma eyeing it like an eagle eyes a mouse.

She finally said, "Tom, isn't that a beautiful basket?"

I said, "You mean the breadbasket?"

Grandma said, "Yes, don't you just love it?"

It was a wire and wicker thing with birds hanging off it.

I said, "I guess it's nice, in a breadbasket kind-of-way."

Grandma then says, "I think it's beautiful actually. I'd love to have one like that."

My friend looked over at us and asked, "What are you and Grandma talking about?"

I told him, "Nothing, really. She was just saying how much she likes the breadbasket."

My friend said, "Oh shit, she's going for the basket. Don't let her take it. It's too big. I don't want her to get caught and be embarrassed."

I said, laughing, "Okay, I'll keep my eye on her."

He leaned across me and said to her, "Don't you even think about taking that basket. For once, just enjoy dinner and behave!"

She said to my friend, "Don't get all worked up. I don't need you telling me how to act for God's sake."

That seemed to be that, but as soon as my friend went back to the conversation at the table, Grandma turned to me, winked, and said, "It's as good as gone."

I was hysterical, but I was also trying to explain to her that the basket was too big, and it would be very embarrassing for her if she got caught. Hell, it would be embarrassing for all of us.

"Don't do it," I said to her.

She was resolute. She said, "Haven't been caught yet, young man, and I've dealt with better restaurant operators than you."

By this time I was laughing so hard I was crying. Who would suspect this regal lady with her flower print dress, the angelic face—although with a little too much lipstick—and the beauty parlor coiffed, sleeping-sitting-up-in-the-chair hairdo, to be the Princess of Darkness?

She was going on and on about the basket, my friend was getting more and more angry, and I couldn't stop laughing. I had to go to the bathroom, but I didn't want to miss any of the action.

My friend said, "You're encouraging her by laughing, you know. This is serious."

I said, "Serious? You're kidding, right? A heart attack is serious. This is funny. I can't believe that you would even think of denying me this entertainment."

Grandma said to the waitress, "Can we have more bread?"

Ten minutes later, the basket was on her lap under the tablecloth.

My friend said, "What if it was your grandmother?"

I said, "I'd be mortified."

My friend said, "So?"

I said, "So, it isn't my grandmother."

And so it went. He was pissed, she was hatching a plan, and I was on the floor with laughter. Out came the cake and candles. We all sang a god-awful "Happy Birthday." Grandma made a wish, which I'm sure had something to do with the basket, and proceeded to spit all over the cake while blowing out the candles. Coffee, cake, and saliva, who could ask for more?

My friend's father got the check, my bladder was screaming, and Grandma springs into action. As the check was being paid, everyone got up to leave. Grandma removed the bread and napkin from the basket, tapped out the crumbs, waited until everyone was about three steps ahead, placed the basket on her beauty parlor, sleep-sitting-up-in-the-chair head, and strutted out the front door sporting one of the best old lady hats I've seen since my Aunt Pauline was alive.

The look on my friend's face said it all. I literally wet my pants.

Reality Mint

I would like to spend fifteen minutes in a locked room with the first guy that decided that a free mint at the end of a dinner was a good idea. I wouldn't let up on him for one minute. Who doesn't like mints? Who doesn't like free? Throw in an aging boomer population and you have a recipe for disaster. Just for the record, before I recount this tale, the amount of mints a person is willing to steal is age related. You would think kids would be the most likely to steal them but you would be wrong. It's the greatest generation has the cleanest breath in America.

Here goes. I have a customer who religiously comes in once a week with her husband for dinner. I'm guessing late seventies, early eighties. They always arrive at five. This is roughly about half an hour after the hostess fills the mint bowl on the table in the foyer. I've come to believe that she comes early so that no one else grabs a mint before she plunders the thing. They know all my employees, so when they arrive, there are a lot of hello's and how are you's before catching up on the week. They are really, really nice people, except for the fact that, in any other business, with any other product, she would be considered, well—a criminal. But, hey, I'm in the restaurant business where stealing is considered an entitlement, remember.

Five o'clock is also the start of our *Prix-Fixe* dinners and they enjoy that. And that's cool because that's why we do it. I just don't remember the ad that says, "*CoolFish* Restaurant: *Prix-Fixe* 5:00-6:30, $26.95, includes three courses and thirty-seven pounds of individually wrapped mints."

The first time we became aware of the problem was about six

months after they started coming in. They had just left when one of the other customers asked the $65,000 question, "Hey do you guys have any after-dinner mints?"

The hostess said, "Sure, they're on the table in the foyer."

"I don't see them."

The hostess (annoyed), "They should be right there on the table sir, I just filled them up before dinner."

"Nope, don't see 'em."

The hostess (more annoyed) walked around the hostess desk and into the foyer saying, "Sir, they're right—" The two of them are staring at an empty bowl: one dumbfounded, one amused.

The man said, "Maybe you forgot to put them out."

The hostess said, "No I did not. I can't understand it. Only two people have finished dinner and left and—"

This is where Diane, the hostess, started to resemble Edith Bunker when she finally understands what Archie is trying to tell her.

The hostess said, "I'll bet the Mitchell's took them."

The man said, "How many mints could have been in the bowl?"

"Twelve hundred or so."

"Wow."

The hostess reloaded the bowl and began to form a plan to collar the alleged culprit. For the next few weeks, every time they came in, the hostess would try to catch them taking the mints. Not that we ultimately care all that much about the mints, it was just great fun. And let me tell you they were clever. They would talk at the hostess desk on the way out until a customer would have to be seated. As soon as Diane would bring someone to a table, they would break for the mint bowl, load up, and make for the car.

Then, one day, I lost my sense of humor. One of my employees left one of the drawers on the mint table open. This normally wouldn't get another thought, but this is where we store all the mints. Yup, you guessed it: one bowl and two drawers full of mints vanished. A whole case of mints was gone. They had to be working as a team; I'm sure he was the lookout. He had to be. I'm trying to picture him watching the dining room as she's stuffing mints in her bag, pockets, bra, girdle, socks, and shoes. Got any idea how many mints are in a case? I do, it's a shit-load. (That's metric.)

I've spent a lot of money on security cameras for the restaurant. I have a camera in the bar watching a bartender who would never steal. I have a camera in the office where there's no money. I have a camera in the kitchen where, by the end of the day, my crew doesn't even want to look at food. I have a camera in the storeroom in case someone tries to make off with one hundred pounds of Hi-Gluten flour, and a camera on the loading dock for whatever it is I'm supposed to be watching out there. The salesman told me that the money I saved with the security cameras would pay for them in under a year. How's that for a sales pitch?

Here's what the sales pitch ought to be, "I'll put a camera on your mint bowl and one on each pepper mill, and in one year you will be able to buy waterfront."

My bartender, Mark, had the best idea yet. He thinks we should set up a "mint cam" and have it hooked up to a flat screen and show it in the bar. Now that's reality entertainment. We never really were able to catch them in the act, and I never wanted to, honestly. As they got older they came in more infrequently, but the good news is that I was able to purchase new carpeting and chairs for the restaurant with the monies from my plunging mint budget.

ABUSE OF POWER

I need someone to explain to me why misery is a choice for some people. I mean, it's out there. Real misery exists. Manufacturing it is unnecessary. Happiness is so much easier. Oh, well.

Some people, when they walk though the doors of a restaurant, transform into angry, confrontational, unreasonable creatures that are just waiting, dying really, to be offended. (There's a problem here somewhere and I'll look until I find it. "Yup, my table wobbles, what are you going to do for me?") Get it?

Upon further investigation, you'll find most of these people aren't really mad, but they pretend to be because they think they'll get better service or better yet, a free *something*. It's like the Seinfeld episode where George pretends to be aggravated so everyone thinks he's working hard. The sad fact is that we in the business know this and view this behavior not with the fear that's intended, but in a more cartoon-like way with tongues planted firmly in cheeks. This tragic comedy plays itself out on the grand restaurant stage night after night.

The ironic point is that, for the most part, happiness is a choice also. If you're trying to enjoy yourself, you'll have a better shot at succeeding. But hey, what would all the therapists do?

Eight ladies came in for a dinner celebration. The word *celebration* needs an asterisk because it implies that you intend to enjoy yourself. I've come to believe that torturing restaurant workers provides the full party package for some, although it can't possibly be rewarding in the long-term.

I'll elaborate. The waitress was the beautiful, intelligent, sweet, witty, competent, and kindly, Courtney. Here's the opening onslaught with everyone talking at once:

"There's not enough light here."

"I don't like this table."

"Turn the AC up."

"Turn the AC down."

"Didn't I say there's not enough light?"

"Turn the lights down, it's too bright."

"There's nothing on the menu I can eat."

"I'm allergic to peas."

"I'm a vegetarian."

"I belong to PETA."

"Why are they serving swordfish?"

"I want that table. This one wobbles."

"I want a free something."

"Don't try and include the tip on the bill."

"I never liked this restaurant."

"Everything better be hot."

"The last time I was here my tomato salad was cold."

"I don't like ice in my soda."

"I'm allergic to everything."

"I'm lactose intolerant."

"I can't have anything with wheat."

"I can't eat eggs."

"Do you use MSG?"

"I can't have salt, dressing, sauce, pepper, spices, herbs, or flavor."

"Food makes me sick."

"Do you use trans fats?"

"I'm allergic to trans fats."

"Me too."

"Me too."

"Me too."

"Me too."

Courtney, amused, said, "So, can I get anyone something from the bar?"

One at a time, "I'll have a Cosmo, light on the cranberry."

"I'll have a Cosmo, heavy on the cranberry, light on Vodka."

"I'll have a diet coke, ice on the side and fill it to the top."

"I'll have a Watermelon Martini, but the last time I was here, it had too much watermelon. If he makes it like that again, I'm sending it back."

"I'll have an iced tea, but I want it made with Earl Grey Breakfast Tea, two NutraSweet, not Sweet'N Low, and bring me extra slices of lemon. Oh, and do you have any mint? Oh, and one slice of orange. Oh, and not too much ice. Oh, and bring some Sweet'N Low on the side. Oh, and can we get some bread? Oh, and she doesn't eat olives. Can you bring her something else?"

"I'll just have a diet coke." (I'm guessing she was from Ohio.)

"I'll have um—a Cosmo—no, a Watermelon Martini—no, a Watermelon Cosmo. Can he do that? You know what. Forget it. I'll have a Pineapple Cosmo with—do you think lime would be good in that? No—tell him to add some Coconut Vodka. That would be good. Kind of like a Piña Colada."

"Aren't you allergic to coconut?"

"Oh, you're right. I can't tolerate palm oil. Okay. I'll have an Absolut straight up, shaken not stirred, in a large glass with a little ice, a lemon wedge, and a piece of lime carved to look like the David."

"I'll have a glass of wine, but I don't know what I want. So just bring me a taste of every wine by the glass you have, so I can taste them all, tell you they suck, and order an Absolut on the rocks, water on the side, lemon on the side, lime carved like the David on the side, ice on the side, and the glass—on the side."

Courtney said, "Will that be all?"

The table, all at once, said, "Yes, and can you hurry up, we've been here for three minutes already."

"We're starving."

"It's cold in here."

"The service here sucks."

"I want a free something."

"We should get the drinks on the house."

"What's taking so long?"

"We should have gone to the Sagamore."

"What are the specials?"

Courtney, after the drinks were served, re-served and served again, said, "Do you know what you'd like to have for dinner?"

Everyone at once said, "How are we supposed to know? There's nothing on the menu."

"He never changes the specials."

"Is the fish fresh?"

"I'm allergic to fresh fish."

"How come you don't have more meat?"

"I can't eat crab."

"What's so special about skate?"

"What's skate?"

"I don't know, but I think I'm allergic to it."

"Me too."

"Me too."

"Me too."

"Can you split a Caesar salad eight ways?"

"This place is so inflexible."

"I'm not coming here anymore."

"I like Il Mulino much better."

"I'm allergic to Il Mulino."

"Does the sauce have cream?"

"Salt?"

"Herbs?"

"Flavor?"

"I can't have it."

"Could you make it with just lemon, with the lemon on the side?"

"Fennel makes me break out. There's no fennel in it, is there? If I break out, I'm not paying."

"This waitress is horrible."

"I've never had service this bad."

"She can't even get a simple drink order right."

"I can't wait to see how she screws up a simple dinner request."

Courtney, unflappable, said, "Ready ladies?"

Then one at a time, "Are there eggs in that?"

"Is it fresh?"

"Is it fattening?"

"Is it big enough?"

"Is it made with trans fats?"

"Am I allergic to it?"

Then, "I'll have the sea bass, no relish, sauce on the side."

"I'll have the sea bass, no spinach, with asparagus."

"I'll have the sea bass, no spinach, asparagus, and relish on the side."

"I'll have the sea bass, no relish, no sauce, corn, and sweet potatoes."

"I'll have the sea bass, no relish, no sauce, no asparagus, no corn, no sweet potatoes with wasabi on the side. Oh, and can I get soba noodles with that?"

"God, they never change the menu here."

"Soba noodles give me gas."

"Me too."

"Me too."

"Me too."

"She is the worst waitress we've ever had."

"Yeah, and nasty too."

"Not accommodating at all."

"What an attitude."

Then, I walked into the bar and one of the ladies spotted me. The ladies, all at once said, "Isn't that Tom?"

"Do you know him?"

"I think I met him once."

"I never met him, did you?"

"I think I'm allergic to him."

"Me too."

Courtney, very amused, said, "Would you like to meet him?"

The table said, "Oh yeah, like you really know him."

"Why would he bother with a waitress."

"I can't believe he keeps you here."

Then came the line of the night. "Besides, I don't think you have that kind of power." Courtney, finally having fun said, "Well, I've been working here since the beginning."

"That doesn't mean you know him."

"I would like to meet him, though."

"I hope you know him better than you know the menu, which he never changes by the way."

"He really needs to work on service here."

Courtney said, "Do you want to meet him or not?"

"Fine, let's go."

Courtney then led a very well-dressed conga line through the dining room and into the bar. She gathered the women around my bar stool and said, "Ladies, I'd like you to meet my dad, Tom Schaudel. Dad, meet table sixty-two."

Dead silence for second. They were all looking at each other, and as if on cue, everyone started talking at once.

"We love your restaurants."

"We go to them all the time."

"Your articles are so funny."

"We love your food."

"The service here is so good."

"I always feel welcome."

"Your daughter is the sweetest thing."

"The menu is so interesting."

"You guys are so accommodating."

"I have allergies, but there's always something for me to eat."

"I eat here twice a week."

And so it went. I was in the dark about everything that preceded meeting them and when Courtney told me the story, we were howling.

You Take the Cake

Some years back, a friend who I hadn't seen since high school, called me to ask if I would do a bat mitzvah party for her daughter. It was great to hear from her, and we did twenty minutes or so of catching up before discussing the event. When we finally got around to the details, she told me it would all be pretty standard stuff except for the cake. She told me her daughter was hell-bent on having a chocolate-covered cake with chocolate curls. Nothing less would do. She told me that she'd called several bakeries but none had given her that warm and fuzzy, confident feeling that would satisfy the out-of-control emotions of a thirteen-year-old girl.

This was the major concern, and if a chocolate cake with chocolate curls could not be pulled off, there would be no party and subsequently, no catering gig for yours truly. I told her that I had a friend who was a very talented baker, and he could make anything from a simple sheet cake to a multi-layered, power-sprayed, butter-creamed monstrosity in the likeness of Buddy Hackett.

Bored and obviously unimpressed, she said, "That's nice. Can he make a chocolate cake with chocolate curls?"

I said, "I believe he can."

My friend said, "You have no idea what my life will be like if the cake isn't what she wants. It has to be perfect."

I said, "I know, I had a thirteen-year-old once. Don't worry, Robert's the man. I'll call him just to make sure he's confident he can do it, and call you back."

I called my friend Robert Ellinger, who is as talented a baker as you will find on Long Island. His cakes are not only beautiful to look at, they taste great, and that's not always the case with other bakers. I told Robert that I had an emotional thirteen-year-old girl who has her heart set on a beautiful chocolate cake decorated with chocolate curls for her bat mitzvah, and did he think he could make it? It had to be perfect.

Robert said, "Yeah man, no problem."

I asked, "You're sure? I don't need the headaches."

Robert said, "I told you, no problem."

I said, "Thanks bro'. I'll get back to you."

I called my friend and told her that Robert was confident that he could handle the cake.

She remained skeptical. She asked, "Are you sure? Are you sure *he's* sure? You two have to be sure. I don't want to have to deal with this if you two screw up the cake."

I don't think there was this much anxiety involved in the Cuban Missile Crisis, but I was hanging in there.

I said. "Okay, how about this? I believe Robert's the man, but if for some reason, hormonal or otherwise, your daughter doesn't like the cake, I'll foot the therapy bill."

She said, "You're on."

I called Robert back and told him, "We're on." I told him the date and said goodbye.

Six months later, the day arrived, the place was decorated to the nines, and miraculously, all the employees showed up. We were prepping and getting ready to start the party when the cake arrived. You had to see it. It was about three-feet high with gorgeous chocolate fondant and covered in perfect, I mean *perfect* chocolate curls, from the widest part of the base to the tapered top tier. It was unbelievable. It looked like a Rastafarian version of Shirley Temple. Since it would have been impossible to write on the cake, Robert made a chocolate sign that said, "Mazel Tov Lisa" to be placed on top of the cake when it was served. It was the "dream cake," and although I was confident in Robert's talent, it was even better than I expected.

My friend arrived and I called her into the kitchen.

She asked, "How does the cake look?"

I said, "Better than I could have imagined."

She said, "Let me see it." We went downstairs to the walk-in refrigerator to see the cake. She looked and exclaimed, "Oh my God, it's beautiful!"

She told me that her daughter would absolutely love it and thanked me profusely.

I said, "Well, I'm happy that you're happy, and I'm glad I was able to avoid paying any psychiatric bills."

For about two-and-a-half hours, we had one big happy Bat Mitzvah. Then all the fun started. One of my crack (head) staff decided, for reasons that are still unclear, to bring the cake up to the kitchen to get ready to be served. I usually handle the delicate jobs myself, especially when the mental health of several people is riding on the outcome. I wouldn't have voluntarily given that task to anyone else so I don't know what he could have been thinking.

As he was about to place the chocolate sign that said, "Mazel Tov Lisa" into the top of the cake, it slipped out of his hand and landed on the floor, mazel tov-side down. Whatever Robert used to write the letters became the bonding agent that held the newly relocated sign fast to the floor. Although there was no discernable sucking noise, picking it up did nothing to improve its appearance. Logic and math would say that the dropped sign probably had a fifty-fifty chance of landing right side up, but the minute I'm involved the percentages plummet. I've come to accept it. That's why I bring the cakes up myself and stay out of Vegas.

So there we were: one enraged chef, one visibly shaken waiter, one unreadable chocolate mazel tov sign, eight kitchen employees giggling uncontrollably trying desperately not to get caught, two servers who dubiously prided themselves on being champions of the obvious, saying, "Chef, there's a problem with the cake," and a full dining room staff straining to look professional as thirty septuagenarians were slow-dancing to a horrible rendition of the song, "Feelings." Could there possibly be a better way to spend a Saturday afternoon?

I said to the two servers, "Oh, there's a problem with the cake? No shit!"

I was literally running in place trying to figure out what to do. Motion is anaesthetic for the clueless. We had wiped the ruined letters off the sign, but for the life of me I couldn't figure out what to use to replace them. I was going through the possibilities in my head thinking, whipped cream, white chocolate, powdered sugar and water, royal icing, when it hit me like a bolt from the cosmos: *Wite-Out!* Holy shit, *Wite-Out!*.

The dining room staff was now calling for the cake. I ran downstairs with the cake in a full-blown panic. I took the sign into the office, laid it on the desk and with my best imitation of my mother's handwriting, dipped the little *Wite-Out!* brush in the little *Wite-Out* bottle and wrote, "Mazel Tof Lisa." Yup, "tov," with an "f."

Not being Jewish and therefore never studying for my bar mitzvah is a perfectly legitimate excuse for weak Hebrew skills, but I had eighty people upstairs who knew "tov" ended with a "v," and as I have since learned, expected it to be spelled that way.

Still in the dark, I was elated. I had a perfectly repaired sign with a neatly written salutation, on a beautiful chocolate cake with chocolate curls that unbeknownst to me, was about five minutes away from making the bat mitzvah hall of fame.

I placed the sign in the cake, and, convinced that I'm a genius, grabbed the cake and went running up the stairs. Thank God that

Hal, who was the chef-de-cuisine at the time, was running down the stairs as I was running up. Hal, who is a talented, hard-working chef, a close friend, and one of the nicest human beings I know, also happens to be Jewish.

As I stopped to show him my brilliant repair job, I said, "Hal, check out the repair. The *Wite-Out* worked."

I was totally unprepared for his reaction. Hal burst into a convulsive, stomach-crunching fit of laughter, with small animal sounds emanating from somewhere deep within, tears flowing, and a runny nose.

I was incredulous. I asked, "What?!"

He couldn't speak. He was doubled over and kneeling on the stairs.

I asked him again, "Whaattt?!"

He was incapable of forming a word.

I said, "I don't have time for this, they need the cake upstairs."

Still unable to speak, Hal was violently shaking his head no and waving his hands. I was losing my patience, but it's impossible to see someone who has lost all control and not laugh. We were now both standing on the stairs laughing. Hal was struggling to get a grip on himself, and I was wondering what the hell was so funny.

Finally, Hal regained enough control to make a sound. As another wave of laughter began to subside, he exhaled and in a voice that sounded like air exiting from a balloon while the open end is pulled apart, he said, "It's a veeeee."

I said, "Huh?"

He said, gasping for air, "It's a veee, you idiot, a veeeeeeee!" and collapsed again.

I asked, "You kidding me?"

He started waving his hands and shaking his head again.

Finally, he says, "T, you have to re-do it. Mazel Tov is spelled with a "v."

Then he laid down on the stairs, threw his head back, and while holding his stomach, said, "Oh—oh—oh man. That may have been the funniest thing I've ever seen."

By then I was nuts. I went back down the stairs to the office. I was worried not only about fixing the sign, but I was also concerned about the cake holding up. It already had more mileage on it than my Explorer and it still had to survive the cutting ceremony and the serving. I changed the "F" to a "V" and back up the stairs I went.

Hal was still sitting there with his head between his knees, trying to compose himself. I don't know about you, but whenever I make a boo-boo of this magnitude it always makes me feel better to lash out at the people around me.

As I passed Hal on the stairs I said, giggling, "You're such a shit-head."

He said, "Lucky for you, I'm a shit-head who can spell," and lost it again. By the time I got to the kitchen, I was also hysterical.

Meanwhile, the wait staff was in a panic over the cake. "We need the cake. We need the cake."

I said, "All right, all right. I've got it."

We brought the cake out and everyone was blown away. They had a brief cutting ceremony and I went out to serve the cake. As I was standing behind the buffet, I could see Hal's face in the window of the kitchen door, still laughing and looking at me. Now that the stressful part was over, I was having trouble keeping a straight face myself and was giggling my way through the cake serving routine.

Ten minutes into the serving of the cake, a young boy about ten-years-old came up to me. He looked at the chocolate sign lying next to the cake and said to me, "Can I have the sign?"

Does it ever end? I'm not sure what the side effects of consuming

Wite-Out are, but I wasn't prepared to use a ten-year-old as a lab rat. I explained that it was Lisa's special day and that I was saving the sign for her.

He was unimpressed. He said, whining, "I want the sign."

I said, "I can't give you the sign, but I'll be happy to give you some extra cake."

The boy, now adamant, said, "I don't want extra cake, I want the sign."

I said, "Sorry. I can't do it. It's Lisa's sign."

The cake line at the buffet table was thinning out, and I was thinking about sneaking out and hitting the road. The party was under control and winding down. Just as I was about to get out of there, the boy returned to the buffet table with his grandmother.

He pointed to me, turned to his grandmother and said, "He won't give me the sign." I was thinking of giving him a sign all right, just not the one he was expecting.

Grandma asked me, "Why won't you give him the sign?"

Struggling, I told her, "Since its Lisa's special day, I was saving it for her in case she wanted it, you know, like a keepsake."

Grandma said, "What keepsake? Give the boy the sign."

I said, "I can't, it's Lisa's sign."

Grandma said, "Fine. Then we'll go and ask Lisa. You can't give the boy the sign, how ridiculous."

Grandma returns with Lisa, her mom, two servers, and most of the people who were dancing to "Feelings," and they all want to know why it is that I won't give the boy the sign. It was a chocolate posse with bad makeup.

I said sheepishly, "I was just saving it for Lisa."

Lisa asked, "What am I going to do with it?" It was actually a pretty good question.

The boy said, "Seeee, she doesn't want it."

This sign had already caused me way more than my share of pain and I admit that at that point, I was tempted to give it to him, if for no other reason than to watch him experience some of the fun that the sign brought me. I would have been rooting real hard for the *Wite-Out*. Knowing that germs and Grandmas are archenemies, I made a quick plan.

I said, "Okay son, you can have the sign."

I picked the sign up on the spatula and in a rather gaudy display of Badminton prowess, I let it fall off, batting it around like a chocolate shuttle-cock several times up in the air, only to whiff on the final attempt at a save, letting it hit the ground.

I said, looking at the boy contemptuously, "Oops. Do you still want it?"

He said, "You ruined it!"

Grandma said, "You can't eat it, now it has germs on it."

I said, "Sorry, I guess I'll just have to throw it away," and I did. Quite the day, wouldn't you agree?

A week later, Robert called to ask how everyone liked the cake. Somewhat healed I said, "They loved it. Thanks."

He said, "Hey T, how'd that sign work out for you? I tried to make something that was idiot proof."

I said, "Yeah, thanks man; that was pure genius."

)++))⌒)

GIFT CERTIFICATE

A table of four senior citizens came for dinner at *Jedediah's* one night this past winter. They were very nice, friendly, excited to be there, and excited about the *Prix-Fixe*. They thought it was a great deal. It is.

One of the couples was visiting the other from Europe and the *local* couple wanted to give them some *local* flavor, at a somewhat discounted price. The host couple had been showing their guests around the North Fork and the dinner was going to top off a great day of sightseeing and wine tasting.

They sat down and ordered a bottle of local wine and looked over the menu, discussing the difference between the flavor of local and European fish. They made their choices and handed the menus back to the server. The appetizers were served and eaten and they were complimenting the food, the décor, and the service. These four people seemed to be the epitome of your best kind of customer, low maintenance, happy, polite, grateful, and non-allergic.

The entrées were pure joy. They were oohing and ahhing, trying each other's choices, discussing the merits of the perfect roasted chicken and trying to decide whether Cabernet Franc or Merlot would be the grape that defines Long Island. You can't ask for anything more than a passionately interested customer. The plates were cleared and dessert was served, coffee included, inspiring a good chocolate-apple debate. Chocolate always wins by the way. The dinner was so very normal that you couldn't have possibly seen the storm clouds forming.

The host gentleman asked for the check. His server, Kate, made up his bill, placed it in the folder, brought it to the table, and placed

317

it down.

He said pleasantly, "Thank you."

Kate said, "You're welcome. I'll take that whenever you're ready."

He said, "Great. Oh, excuse me, miss. Are there any payment restrictions on the *Prix-Fixe* dinner?"

Kate asked, "What do you mean by restrictions?"

He asked her, "Can I use a gift certificate to pay for our dinner tonight even though it was ordered from the *Prix-Fixe* menu?"

Kate smiled and said, "Sure, no problem at all."

He thanked her and she left to attend to another table. Five minutes later, he caught Kate's eye and raised an index finger. Kate headed over to the table and when she arrived, he handed her the check folder.

Kate said, "Thank you. I'll be right back."

He said, "The gift certificate won't cover all of the check, so put the balance on my credit card."

She went back to the waitress station, fully expecting to find a gift certificate, but what she found instead was a place in this book. Inside the check folder where the gift certificate— provided they actually had one—would have been, was the equivalent of a mediocre fourth grade art project. I'll describe it for you. It was an 8 1/2" X 11" piece of white paper. Glued to the center of the paper was a quarter page ad for the *Jedediah Hawkins Inn*, which I had placed earlier in the week in *Dan's Paper*, advertising the weekday *Prix-Fixe* dinner. On the top of the page in big block letters, in a very soothing shade of aquamarine, was the word "GIFT." On the bottom of the page in big block letters, in an alarming shade of yellow, was the word "CERTIFICATE."

Down the sides of the page surrounding the *Dan's Paper* ad were "S" shaped squiggles and dots of various colors. Directly under the ad were the words "DINNER FOR TWO" in black. There you have it, my very first counterfeit gift certificate. I believe there's a law against that.

Kate, staring at this artistic monstrosity, started to laugh. What else can you do? She showed Michael the chef and Eileen the manager and asked what to do. It was a painfully rhetorical question. They told her to give it back and tell him, without laughing that is, that it was not valid. What else *could* you do? I guess you could always pay for their dinners yourself, frame the thing, hang it over your fireplace, and pray for it to go up in value after its creator passes away. Art's funny like that; it's collectable.

She brought it back to the table. This is a gigantically, if that's even a word, uncomfortable moment for a server, as you can probably imagine. He was as relaxed as he could be.

Kate said, "Sir, I'm not quite sure how to tell you this, but this isn't one of our gift certificates."

He asked, "What do you mean?"

Kate said, "Well, it's not valid. It's not one of our gift certificates. Ours look completely different."

He said, "But it says *Jedediah Hawkins Inn,* dinner for two, right on it."

Kate said, "That was one of our ads from *Dan's Paper.* There must be some kind of mistake."

The man's wife, who by this time was appalled, said, "It has to be good. We got it as a wedding gift from a friend. Could you please check your records? You do keep records, don't you?"

Kate said, "I'm sure we do. I'll check with the manager. When did you get it and what is the name of the person who gave it to you?"

The woman told her the date and name and said, "I'm sure it's in the records somewhere."

While we're on the subject of records, just for the record, they were either telling the truth or they were two world-class thespians. None of us believed they were trying to scam us, although I couldn't say the same about their friend, the wedding gift forger.

Kate went to the office with the name and date, and we checked all gift certificates back to three months before the date she gave us. This, of course, was an exercise in futility, but hey, you never know. I've seen some monumentally stupid stunts performed by some of my employees before, and we just wanted to make sure that someone hadn't gotten creative while believing us to be temporarily out of gift certificates. I have seen worse. It turned out no one did.

Kate returned to the table and realized by this point that everyone was uncomfortable. Trying to be as kind and understanding as she could, she said, "The manager checked back three months prior to the date you told us and there's no record for that name or the amount, *dinner for two*. We would have normally put a specific amount on the gift certificate."

What she should have said was, "With friends like yours, who needs a colonoscopy," but it's probably not the right thing to do under the circumstances and one of the main reasons I stay in the kitchen. I'm a slave to temptation.

Exasperated, the wife said, "That's impossible. That was a *wedding* gift given to us on our *wedding* day, by someone in my *book club!*"

Hmmm—don't those book club members have an unusually elevated interest in publishing? Just a thought.

Malpractice

eservations are the bane of my existence. As I may have mentioned before, three or four hundred times, taking reservations in a restaurant on Long Island is a fourteen-karat gold pain in the ass. The problems are the fault of both the restaurant and the customer for sure, but there's one distinct difference: we are sincere about taking the reservation. That's not to say we don't screw up; we do, but we screw up with the purest intentions. Sometimes reservations get lost or written on the wrong day and time, but the key here is that it's not done intentionally.

On the other hand reservations made in nine different restaurants, under five different names, for six different times, hoping to score the perfect slot and cuisine of choice, is the adult version of musical chairs. Trying to keep reservations on time and running smoothly is an inexact science, and hard enough by itself. Throw in a bunch of double bookings by the same party, no-shows, tardiness, and an inability to recall one's current alias, and you have what amounts to reservation chaos.

For this reason, everyone needs to understand that both sides should be given a fifteen-minute window of patience. If you have a nine o'clock reservation on a Saturday night, you probably have a better shot of being struck by lightning than being seated exactly at nine. What can we do if the table ahead of you at six-thirty decided to have a sixth cup of coffee? By contrast, if a customer had a flat, got stuck in traffic, or has a babysitter who failed geography, they would still expect to be seated when they finally arrived. So cut us a little slack on the weekends; we're trying. Everyone on Long Island wants to eat at eight on Saturday night, and as we all know, that's impossible.

I was sitting alone in my office one Sunday morning when the phone rang. Normally I avoid the phone the same way I avoid the proctologist, but hey, on Sunday you need all the reservations you can get. I picked up the phone. "Hello, *CoolFish*."

The caller said, "Can I speak to the manager?"

I said, "I'm the owner, how can I help you?"

The man said, "You're the owner?"

I said, "Yes."

"You should be ashamed of yourself," he told me.

I asked, "What did I do now?"

He said, "Let me ask you a question. Why do you take reservations if you don't plan to honor them?"

I asked him, "What are you talking about?"

"I'm talking about you not honoring your reservations. Did you ever see the *Seinfeld* episode where he was trying to rent a car? They didn't have his reservation so he said, 'You seem to be able to take the reservation, but you can't seem to hold the reservation.' That's apparently the problem with your restaurant. You take the reservation very well; you just don't seem to be able to honor it."

Since I've earned my PhD in all aspects of reservations, I find it monumentally irritating to be lectured on the subject by someone who's never walked a single mile in my clogs, and frankly, who uses the *Seinfeld* reference at 10:05 on Sunday morning?

Feeling a little like George Constanza, I said, "We do honor our reservations, or at least we try to," which is more than I can say about some of my customers, by the way.

He was unimpressed and said, "Well you certainly didn't honor them last night *my friend*, and I'm not sure we'll ever be returning."

This last part is a dead giveaway. Whenever somebody calls me *my friend*, all nice-like, then in the next breath threatens never to come back, it simply means he would love to come back, as long as his "friend" is picking up the tab.

He continued, "What are we going to do about this? I've eaten all over the world (here we go again), and no one has ever treated me that rudely."

I said, "You know, we're five or ten minutes into this conversation, and you haven't really told me what transpired, so how can we do anything?"

He said, "You didn't keep our reservation."

I said, "What do you mean we did didn't keep your reservation? You couldn't get in?"

He said, "Oh no, we did get in—eventually."

I asked, "So the dining room staff was late getting you *seated*?"

He answered, "Yes, and I think if you're going to take reservations, you should honor them."

This is usually where I get worn out, give in, and just buy them a new yacht or something. I mean, who's got the time or the tenacity to haggle over a blown reservation for a half an hour on a Sunday morning. Shouldn't you be watching *Meet the Press*, cutting the lawn, or sleeping late? Some sixth sense told me to hang out before buying this guy, who in my experience was clearly trolling for a freebie, anything as compensation.

I said, "Why don't you just tell me what happened and then I'll check with my staff to hear their side of it, and I'll get back to you."

Suspiciously, he asked, "You're going to get back to me?"

"Yeah."

"When?"

"As soon as I find out what happened and confirm it with my

staff."

"You know, if you don't call me back, I'll call you again."

"I believe you—with all my heart. What happened?"

He said, "We had a nine o'clock reservation last night. We got there at about ten minutes to nine. Your hostess told us that our table wasn't quite ready."

I asked, "Did you wait at the bar?"

He says, "No, I stayed right there by the hostess desk so she was sure to see us."

I said, "Good move. No sense buying a drink and relaxing when you can be annoying."

To his credit, he laughed and said, "Right, we had drinks at home before we came. So we stood there waiting and waiting and waiting until finally the hostess came and asked us to follow her to our table—at nine-fifteen."

I asked, "Nine-fifteen?"

He said, "Yeah, nine-fifteen. I was looking at my watch constantly while I was waiting, so I know that when she finally came to get us, it was nine-fifteen."

Again I asked, "Nine-fifteen?"

He said, "Nine-fifteen. Do you think its right to have a customer wait fifteen minutes for a reservation? What kind of service is that? I've eaten—"

"Yeah, yeah, I know, all over the world. You were seated at nine-fifteen?"

"Yeah, nine-fifteen."

"And you have me on the phone for half an hour on a Sunday morning to tell me that you were seated at nine-fifteen for a nine o'clock reservation on a Saturday night. If my staff got you seated at nine-fifteen for a nine o'clock reservation on a Saturday night, I'm going to high five them when they come in."

"I think it's inexcusable. I'm doing you a favor here by calling you. I could have just left and not said anything and not come back. Now you know there's a problem with your reservation system. The least you could do is buy us dinner."

I was ready to call the yacht broker and just make this maniac go away.

Finally I said, "Okay, give me your name and number, and I'll check with the staff to confirm what happened and maybe there's some small thing I could do to repay your generosity."

He says, "Okay, good. It's Doctor Jones, 867...5309." I almost fell down.

"Doctor?" I asked.

"Yes."

"No, I mean, Doctor?"

"Yes, Doctor Jones, 867..."

"Doctor!"

"Yes, Doctor."

I said, "Doc, you've got to be kidding."

Doc asked me, "What do you mean, kidding?"

Now laughing, I said, "Doctor, with all due respect, you have the balls of King Kong to tell me you waited fifteen minutes for a table. I can't believe this. Please tell me you're not a psychiatrist."

Doc said, "I wasn't kidding, and what's so funny?"

I said, "I'll make this really easy for you. I want you to impress me and tell me you've seen one, just one patient on time in your entire career; just one."

To his credit, we were both laughing when I hung up the phone, and he waived the free dinner. Touché.

MAKE A WISH

Years ago, a dear friend of mine came up with the term "unembarrassable." I don't know if it would fly in a competitive game of Scrabble, but you just can't beat it to describe the antics of some of my more memorable guests. In order to be considered "unembarrassable," we determined that one not only has to have a rather thick outer layer of skin and have absolutely no regard for how others see him, the person has to also achieve an act of Clintonian selfishness in the company of others and possess the ability to cleanse any peripheral thought that may dilute the fact that the rest of the world lives to serve him, not turn red in the process, and hopefully without the use of a cigar. It's quite a feat. That's why the term is usually reserved for ex-presidents, Peewee Herman, and a couple of my regulars; it takes a special cat.

I've said this a thousand times before, but here we go again. We do a *Prix-Fixe* dinner. It's served from Sunday through Friday, from five to six-thirty for $26.95. That's when we do it. Not five to eight or five to nine; five to six-thirty. What's so difficult to understand?

I've had people call me to ask if I could extend the *Prix-Fixe* to eight o'clock because they didn't get out of work early enough to make the six-thirty cut off. Hey, if the bargain is making you that sweaty, why not take a vacation day? Wouldn't you love to call your local appliance dealer on say, March fifth and ask, "I heard you guys had a crazy sale on President's Day. I've been on an extended vacation in the South of France, and I was wondering, would you lay a big old fatty flat screen on me for the same price as the sale?"

It's a reality show waiting to happen, with real reality, if you'll excuse the grammar. How many times, in *real* life, have you been

326

voted off an island? What kind of reality is that? But this, this *really* happens. I've even got a name: *Begging for Dollars*.

Seven o'clock on a weeknight, a table of three walked in for dinner: Dad, a son, and a daughter. Courtney went to the table and welcomed them.

She asked, "Can I get anyone something from the bar?"

Dad asked, "Can we get the *Prix-Fixe* menu?"

Courtney said, "I'm sorry sir, but *Prix-Fixe* ends at six-thirty."

"But we couldn't get here by six-thirty."

Courtney said, "I'm sorry, but it's after seven. If it was five or ten minutes, I could probably get the kitchen to make it for you, but not now. Not after seven."

The son chimed in, "We come here all the time for the *Prix-Fixe*, and we always make it on time, but we had to visit my mother in the hospital and there was a lot of traffic."

Courtney said, "You know what, it sounds like you've had a rough day. Let me see what I can do. Give me a minute."

Courtney is a very sensitive woman and this poor family got to her, so she went into the kitchen to talk to Lenny, the chef.

She said, "Lenny, don't kill me, all right, but I have a table out there that just asked for the *Prix-Fixe*."

Lenny said, "You're kidding right? It's like seven-fifteen."

Courtney said, "I know, but it's a man and his two children. They just told me they came from seeing their sick mother in the hospital, and the man said something about the doctor saying they think they got it all. I think maybe she has cancer."

Lenny, being a pretty sensitive guy himself, said, "Oh man, that sucks. You know, what the hell, give them the menus. They have enough problems."

Courtney went back out to the table and said, "The chef said he would make the *Prix-Fixe* menu for you."

Dad said, "Oh, that's great. Tell him thank you very much."

Courtney said, "I'll tell him."

Courtney took the order, placed it in the kitchen, and started talking to Lenny about Moms and how tough it must be to see your mother with a potentially fatal disease. They were both feeling good about giving them the *Prix-Fixe*, and for their sense of humanity, not to mention some possible future karmic reward. It was a short-lived euphoria.

Courtney served their food and it was a pretty routine dinner until dessert.

As they were finishing their coffee, Dad says to Courtney, "Can I order a *Prix-Fixe* dinner to go?"

Courtney said, "Sure, just make sure you call before six-thirty."

Dad said, "No. I'd like to order a *Prix-Fixe* to go tonight, for my wife, who is sick."

Courtney said, "Sir—it's after nine. We gave you the *Prix-Fixe* even though it had ended a half an hour before you came in. I don't know if the kitchen will do it again at ten after nine."

Dad said, "When we left the hospital, my wife said that she would like nothing more than a *Prix-Fixe* dinner from *CoolFish*, and I sort of promised I'd bring it back."

I have to ask a question here before we go on. If you were going to order what potentially could be your last meal, would you specify *Prix-Fixe*? Wouldn't you pull out all the stops? If it were me, it would take my waiter twenty minutes just to write down my order, and then a team of farmers a week to assemble the ingredients. But according to Dad she wanted a *Prix-Fixe* meal from *CoolFish*—amazing.

Courtney started to think she was being played, but it's a very hard call to make. Ordering a *Prix-Fixe* last supper is certainly suspect, but I've seen dumber decisions. The OJ jury comes to mind, as does the show *Jackass*. If you say something, and on the off-chance he's telling the truth, you would appear to be one heartless server. On the other hand, what are the chances?

Courtney chose to err on the side of safety and said, "Your wife said she wanted a *Prix-Fixe* dinner?"

Dad said, "Yeah, we come for the *Prix-Fixe* all the time, before she got sick that is, and she's craving a *Prix-Fixe* dinner." (Not a steak or a piece of fish, a *Prix-Fixe* dinner.) You must admit it's a rather unusual craving.

"Okay, let me go run it by the kitchen," Courtney said, surrendering.

She went back to the kitchen and told Lenny the story. Lenny said, "She's craving a *Prix-Fixe* dinner?!"

"Yep, it must be the medication. What tastes better than $26.95, especially when you're sick and haven't had it in a while?"

Lenny said, "Now I've heard it all."

What a naive statement. Lenny has been cooking for about ten years. I've been at it for over forty. There's a lot more of that coming his way, I respectfully submit.

Courtney asked, "So what do you want to do?"

Lenny said, "What can you do? Give him what he wants."

Courtney returned to the table and said, "I talked to the kitchen and although it's really not the house policy, they'll waive that if it's that important to your wife, and we hope she gets well really soon."

The daughter said, "Thanks a lot."

The son said, "We really appreciate it."

Dad said, "Okay, we'll take four crab cakes, two sea bass, one sliced sirloin, one pork chop, two apple tarts, and two flourless chocolate cakes."

GENERATION Y OH WHY?

We were catering a birthday party one afternoon at the restaurant. There were about 120 people milling about the bar area during the cocktail hour. Food was being passed, drinks were flowing, and a three-piece band was playing the hits you forgot to remember. It started out as a civilized affair until "Chucky" showed up. You remember Chucky, the deranged doll from the movie of the same name? I swear that's what this kid was like. If he had had access to a knife, thirty people might have died that day.

He came to the party about forty-five minutes late, with his mom and his sister. I'm assuming that Mom wasn't married because she came unescorted, and giving birth to a child like that is probably grounds for divorce in at least fourteen states.

Courtney saw them walk in and because there wasn't much time left in the cocktail hour, she rushed over to see if they wanted something from the bar. The woman was saying her hellos and the two, ehh, *children*, were hanging close by.

Courtney walked up to the woman and asked, "Excuse me, can I get anyone something from the bar?" Dead silence. The woman never acknowledged the question.

Courtney, thinking the woman may not have heard her, said, "Excuse me, would you like anything to drink?" The woman turned, gave Courtney an annoyed look, said not one word, and went back to her conversation without missing a beat.

Chucky chimed in, "I want pizza!"

Courtney told him, "The pizza is being passed around. A waitress will bring it to you."

Chucky said, "When?"

"When it's ready," she said.

"When is it going to be ready?"

"It'll be *ready* when it's *ready*."

"I don't like you!"

"I don't like you either," Courtney muttered as she walked away.

Courtney went back into the main dining room to help get it set up for the guests who were about to come in to be seated for dinner.

She was talking to another server and one of the runners and telling them, "Wow, I thought the mother was rude, but the little boy is the worst."

As Courtney is standing there talking and checking the table settings, Chucky came up behind her, and poking her in the back to get her attention, said, "When you're done *talking*, do you think you could finally take a drink order? Or is that too hard for you?"

It sounded a little too much like a coached line to me, coming from an eight-year-old, but coached or not, it's a show-stopper. Courtney, torn between laughter and murder said, "I'd *love* to get a sweet little child like *you* something from the bar. What would you like?"

"I want a Sprite, my sister wants orange juice, and my mother wants a Cosmic Politan."

Courtney explained, "Okay, everyone is coming in to find their seats, so get your sister and sit down and I'll bring the drinks to the table."

"Hurry up. I'm thirsty!"

"Are you familiar with the word please?"

"No!"

Courtney went to the bar, shaking her head. She said to the bartender, "I can't believe that little brat. He's horrible, but it still feels weird to hate a child you only know for ten minutes. I can't believe his mother puts up with him." They spent five minutes laughing and fantasizing about a shot of Tabasco in his Sprite, but ultimately one must take the high road, mustn't one?

In the time it took Courtney to bring the drinks back to the table, Chucky had bent two forks and a spoon, emptied two salt-shakers, unscrewed a pepper mill, and poked a hole in the banquet with a butter knife, with which he was now threatening his sister.

Courtney said, "What are you doing!"

"Nothing."

"Put the knife down!"

"You can't make me!"

Courtney said, "Give me that," and took the knife.

Meanwhile, Mom was nursing a Cosmo and catching up with family. Not a word was said.

Courtney said to her, "Excuse me. You have to get your child under control."

She turned and said, "Johnny, stop," striking fear into the heart of the possessed.

Bewildered, Courtney left the table after taking a drink order. As she was standing at the service bar giving Mark the order, Chucky came up behind her, poking her back to get her attention. Courtney said, "Oh, you again, huh? What can I do for you?"

"My mother said that you have to put my sister's juice in a sippy cup, because she can't drink out of a glass, and I want a goblet for my soda."

"Sorry there dude; we don't have goblets."

"Yes you do!"

"No we don't."

"I saw them on the table!"

"Let's go speak to your mom."

Courtney and Chucky went back into the dining room and as they neared the table, Chucky said, "Mom, she won't give me a goblet!"

Mom said, "Just give him a wine glass. That's what we give him at home. It makes him feel grown-up."

Courtney said, "Will he be able to hold it like a grown-up? They're quite large, expensive, and not made for drinking soda."

Mom said, "Just give it to him, please."

Chucky said, "Ha ha!"

Fuming, Courtney went to the service bar to get the wine glass. She told Mark, "No wonder this kid is a disaster, he gets anything he wants. I've just been kneecapped by an elementary school Napoleon with a clip-on tie."

Three minutes after transferring his soda into the wine glass, everything within ten square feet was soaked. Both tablecloths had to be changed along with bread plates, silverware, and the butter.

Mom took charge. "Johnny, try to be more careful."

Careful? This kid was to restaurants what Rambo was to bad guys. He shouldn't be careful, he should be caged. Why is it that some people assume restaurant employees to be some sort of babysitting service? It's like they come in, drop them off, and pick them up at the end of the affair. They need to get a bill.

The staff finally got the table back in shape when Chucky announced he had to go to the bathroom. He was in there only five minutes when it dawned on one of the busboys, "Uh oh." He dashed to the men's room in the nick of time. The sink was almost full with the water running full blast and half a roll of toilet paper was being soaked to—and I'm guessing here—ball up and try to stick it to the ceiling.

That was it. He brought Chucky back out to his seat, explained to Mom what had happened, and asked her to please get control of her son.

Mom finally lost her temper and said, "Johnny, you shouldn't do that."

It was truly unbelievable. The woman was sitting there like nothing had happened. The staff, meanwhile, was in the service station, plotting Chucky's demise. I think they finally agreed to try to lure him out the front door with a piece of pizza and then duct tape him to the awning post. I'm sure no one would have missed him, his mother would have never known, and it would have been an awful lot of fun to watch, but—well—you know.

It was time to take dinner orders and the servers went to their tables. They placed the dinner orders in the kitchen and service was pretty normal. Chucky was occupied with his dinner, which seemed to quell his need for attention.

Courtney went over to take a drink order from one of the guests and as she was writing down the words, "Absolut on the rocks with a twist," she was hit in the side of the face with a flying object. Surprised, she looked down, saw it was an onion ring, wiped her face, turned, and glared at Chucky.

Chucky looked right back at her and shouted, "Sprite! Now!" Mom kept right on chewing. It looks like I might have material for a very long time. Apple trees, as they say, make apples.

There's No Such Thing
As A Stupid Question

Throughout my entire life, my parents, my teachers, the clergy, my friends, my bosses, and my co-workers have all had one thing in common: I have heard from every group, at least once, that there is no such thing as a stupid question. Really? I certainly understand the emotion behind words. No one wants a child to be afraid or embarrassed to ask a question that would prevent them from learning important information. No one wants an employee or co-worker to not have the proper training to be able to perform their job. Who would ever want to prevent the acquisition of knowledge that is born from inquiry? But there's no such thing as a stupid question? You can't be serious. I hear them all the time and I'm sure I've asked my fair share of them.

The difference between someone asking a question that may be rhetorical or elementary, and someone that asks a question that causes your brain to momentarily cramp while trying to unscramble the patently ridiculous is, in my opinion, that which constitutes a stupid question. The reason I've decided to share with you some of the best stupid questions I've ever heard is because although you can choose to ignore them, quizzically raise one eyebrow, or respond sarcastically, you cannot deny their entertainment value. The criteria I have used for a thought to be transformed into a stupid question has had to satisfy the following five critical categories.

1. The thought had to pertain to some aspect of the restaurant business. I'm sure other types of businesses have their own litany of stupid questions, but I will leave those to their respective experts.

336

2. The thought had to be articulated and had to end with a question mark. This much should be obvious, so please, no questions.

3. The questioner had to be at least eighteen years of age with no previous evidence of diminished mental capacity.

4. The individual on the receiving end of the question had to have worn a look of stunned disbelief, while simultaneously evaluating the sanity of the person asking the question, and bravely riding the line between trying to formulate a response and realizing the ultimate futility.

5. Last and most importantly, the individual issuing the question had to have done so with a straight face, in the interest of expanding a somewhat suspect grasp of a subject that is taken for granted to be universally understood.

Please reserve any of your own questions until you have read the entire chapter and have thoroughly examined their content to consider the lasting effect they may have on the rest of us. I now give you the gift of my best *Stupid Restaurant Questions of All Time*, in order from bad to worse, or worse to best, or however it works out. You be the judge. Where it is deemed appropriate I will add a response that will best illustrate the absurdity of the question and hopefully cause the questioner to think things through in their future quests for answers. No names are necessary. You know who you are.

Sight for Sore Eyes

There are people in this world, who when given the most difficult of obstacles, rise to heights unknown to the rest of us. These truly special people accepted the challenges presented them, and have carved out successful lives in spite of their handicap. It's an amazing testament to the human condition when healthy people complain about inane things like being seated fifteen minutes late for a dinner reservation, or about the deterioration of their golf game. We seemed to have blurred the lines between inconvenience and catastrophe.

I have a close friend who was diagnosed with retinitis pigmentosa and has been steadily losing his eyesight for many years. He is now legally blind. It's a very difficult hand to be dealt, as you can imagine. I have never in our twenty-year friendship heard him complain, whine, or bitch about his condition, and believe me, if he did, I'd understand.

As limiting a handicap as Brian has, he has become a husband, a father, and a successful and brilliant guitar player. I'd kill for two percent of his musical talent. He has never once made or asked for concessions, and only wishes to be treated like everyone else. He's a very inspirational guy and one of my personal heroes. I find much to admire about people who make no excuses and just do it, whatever *it* is.

One night a woman called up for a reservation asking if we could accommodate her and her Seeing Eye dog. The hostess told her that it would not be a problem and that we'd had Seeing Eye dogs in the restaurant from time to time.

The woman made the reservation and came in the following

night. She and her friend, who was sighted, and the dog were seated at table eight in the corner. They each had a cocktail and then ordered dinner. If it weren't for the fact that she had the dog, you would have never suspected that she was blind.

As she and the dog got up to use the ladies' room, one of the servers, who I'll call "Mick," spotted her and said to another server, "That's Mrs. Eastman. I used to wait on her at the *West End Café* when I worked there."

The other server said, "You mean the woman with the dog?"

"Yeah."

"Is she blind?"

"No, she's an animal lover; of course she's blind. She also happens to be a very nice lady and a real pleasure to wait on; a good tipper, too."

"That's cool."

"Yeah, it's nice to see her out and about."

She returned to the table, and they finished their dinner, had coffee, and left.

The next day, the hostess got a phone call.

The hostess answered, "Hello, *CoolFish*."

The caller said, "Hi. I was in for dinner last night, and I enjoyed it so much that I would like to make reservations for tonight if you have the availability."

"Okay, what time were you interested in?"

"Between seven and seven-thirty?"

"And how many are in your party?"

"There are four of us and one dog. I was the woman with the Seeing Eye dog last night. It's my birthday today, and I wanted to bring some friends there tonight."

The hostess says, "No problem. I have you down for four people at seven-thirty tonight."

"Thank you very much."

That night the four of them and the dog arrived at seven-thirty. They were seated at the table and were given menus. One of the ladies excused herself to go to the ladies' room. On the way she flagged down her server and told her that it was her friend's birthday.

She asked, "Can you bring out a *Chocolate Bag* with a candle in it for dessert? It's my friend's birthday."

The server said, "Sure," and then asked her, "Which one is the birthday girl?"

"It's the lady with the blue sweater."

"Okay, no problem."

"Could you have a couple of people come over and sing 'Happy Birthday?'"

The server explained, "We really don't do that here. The boss doesn't like it, and we don't like to distract the other guests. We'll just put it in front of her with a candle."

Part of that is true. I'm not so concerned about the other guests because most people get into it and give a little applause at the end of the song. It's the song itself that I have a problem with. Have you ever heard one really good rendition of "Happy Birthday" in your whole life? I haven't. The *CoolFish Tabernacle Choir* usually consists of four or five heavily accented Spanish speaking busboys and a handful of American waiters who, if they could sing, wouldn't be waiting tables. Throw in the table that is having the party and ten-to-twenty people at the surrounding tables, all looking to lend their voices to the celebration, and you have the vocal equivalent of cats having sex. No one starts the song at the same time. Ever notice that? Not one "Happy Birthday" has ever started on cue.

"Ha—Hap—Happy—Happy Birth—Happy Birthday—Birth—day—to you…"

It always starts that way. Then once it's rolling, at least four of my staff are completely off key, five or six do not have the English skills required for the tune, three or four are always too loud, no one ever knows the name of the birthday person, and there's always one diva who inevitably feels the need to harmonize the last line. Why would I put my guests through it? Hell, why would I put myself through it?

The woman then explained to the server, "My friend is blind. She won't see the candle, but if you sing she'll know it's there."

The server said, "Oh, I'm sorry. I didn't realize that. No problem, I'll get some of the staff to sing. It'll be fine."

"Thank you."

After they finished dinner, the busboys cleared the table and the server returned to take the dessert order. As she was preparing the coffee and cappuccinos, she said to a few of the dining room staff, including Mick, "Hey, I'm going to need some of you to sing 'Happy Birthday' at a table."

Mick said, "I thought we weren't supposed to sing anymore."

The server said, "We're not. But the birthday girl is blind so she won't see the candle."

Mick said, "Oh, it's Mrs. Eastman? I used to wait on her at the *West End Café* when I worked there. She's great; I saw her come in before."

The server said, "Great, Mick; just be here in five minutes when we have to sing."

The desserts came out of the kitchen, the staff was assembled, the candle was lit, and my League of Nations Choir marched to the table. They set the *Chocolate Bag* with the lit candle down in front of the birthday girl. After three or four false starts, they completed a particularly poor version of my least favorite song. The woman made a wish, blew the candle out, and everyone applauded. The choir breaks up to get back to work; all except Mick.

He hung back for a moment and then said, "Happy Birthday, Mrs. Eastman."

Mrs. Eastman said, "Thank You."

Mick looked right at the woman who was wearing sunglasses and sitting next to a Seeing Eye dog and asked, "Do you remember me from the *West End Café?*"

Appropriate response: Yes, of course. I saw you as soon I walked in.

Altered Squid

One night, a woman came in for dinner with her husband and two friends. She had made the reservation, confirmed the reservation, suggested the restaurant, invited the friends, and had driven the car, I'm sure. You could see from the start that she was in charge of well—everything. She was very animated and somewhat dramatic, talking, laughing and having a great time. Her husband, probably as a result of not being able to get a word in for twenty years, was quiet, bordering on shy.

They had drinks at the bar and while standing there, the woman asked the bartender, "Do you have calamari on the menu?"

The bartender responded, "Yes, we do."

"How are they preparing it?"

"It's coated lightly with flour, fried in soy oil, and then tossed with pesto, tomatoes, and calamata olives."

"Oh that sounds great. I don't know what it is, but I am loving calamari lately. I can't seem to get enough of the stuff. I just worship calamari, worship it."

The bartender said, "That's nice."

They finished their drinks and headed to their table. Once seated, the waitress came over to explain the specials and take their drink order.

The woman took over, "I'll have another Cosmo and he'll have another beer. Jill, do you and Harry want the same thing or would you rather switch to wine?"

Jill said, "I think we'd rather do wine; Chardonnay."

The woman said, "Okay."

She turned to the waitress and said, "They'll have two

Chardonnays."

The waitress left and returned with drinks. The woman made a toast to whatever they were celebrating, then told the waitress they were ready to order. Jill and Harry gave their appetizer and main course orders to the waitress and since the woman's husband was not permitted to speak, she took charge.

"The bartender told us you have calamari on the menu tonight. How is it prepared again?"

The waitress said, "It's dusted lightly with flour, fried in soy oil, and then tossed with pesto, tomatoes, and calamata olives."
"That's right. That's what he told us. Now I remember. God, I just worship calamari. Okay, he'll have the calamari and the New York sirloin, medium rare. I'll have—let's see—I'm definitely having the calamari—and I'll have—okay, I'll have the tuna with the foie gras."

The waitress then said, "Great. I'll put your order in right away and I'll be back to check on you. Can I get anyone anything else in the meantime?"

The woman said to the waitress, "Excuse me, could you do me one big favor if it's not too much trouble?"

The waitress said, "Sure. What is it?"

The woman said, "Could I get my calamari without the testicles?"

Appropriate response: "Certainly, I'll have the kitchen give yours to your husband."

Fried Calamari/Pesto/Tomato/Olive Recipe

For years, calamari was thought of more as fluke bait than an appetizer in a restaurant. Thank God for the Italians; now we know why the fluke were so excited to eat it. These are flavors inspired by my trips to Italy that I believe work so well together. In the spirit of the story and for those who may be a little squeamish, I've left the testicles out of the recipe. Feel free to add them if you wish, or save them for someone who needs them.

Ingredients:

1 pound squid bodies, cleaned and cut into ½ inch rings
2 cups Wondra flour
Salt and pepper to taste
4 tablespoons pesto (see below)
½ cup cherry tomatoes, halved
¼ cup calamata olives, halved

Fill a heavy sauce pan with canola oil to a depth of 3 inches. Using a kitchen thermometer, heat the oil to 350°F. Mix the Wondra flour and the salt and pepper in a large bowl. Working in small batches, toss the squid in the flour to coat. Carefully add the squid to the oil and fry to a pale golden brown, about 1 minute per batch. Using a slotted spoon, transfer to a paper-towel-lined plate to drain. Place the squid in a large bowl and toss with pesto, tomatoes, and olives. Divide among 4 plates and serve.

Chef's tip: The calamari can be served with a simple tomato sauce for dipping, in case you can't (or don't) want to make pesto, or mess with the olives and tomatoes. Or, serve it like they do in Italy with lemons for squeezing. The pesto can be made in advance and stored in the refrigerator in an air-tight container. Place a thin layer of oil over the pesto in the container before sealing it. It will keep for three days.

Pesto:

1 cup cleaned basil leaves
2/3 cup grated pecorino romano cheese
1/3 cup extra virgin olive oil
1 teaspoon chopped garlic

Place basil leaves, pecorino, garlic, and the oil in a the bowl of a food processor. With the blade running add the oil in a thin stream and process until smooth.

Wine pairing: Channing Daughters Tocai.

EVERYONE CHOKED

This one was told to me by a friend who works in a very busy restaurant. It's in a resort area and as a result, the summers are insane.

This happened on a busy Saturday night. The 'joint was jumpin', as they say, and there was a huge waiting line jammed up at the front desk. The manager was trying her best to supervise the staff and attend to the diners, while trying to placate way too many impatient people waiting for a table.

The phenomenon of a restaurant with a seating capacity of one hundred, trying to feed three thousand people in forty-five minutes, is known in our industry as being "in the weeds." There is no worse feeling for a restaurant worker than being "in the weeds." It's like someone telling you to sail from New York to London and handing you a surfboard and a bed sheet. The level of stress when you are utterly overwhelmed is tremendous. You forget what you're doing, you're worrying about ten different things at the same time, and you can't think straight. All the while that's going on there are mobs of people threatening to leave, sue you, or beat you up if they're not seated immediately. I've been there a thousand times and I assure you that it's awful. I'm surprised more restaurant workers don't go postal. At least the mail doesn't call you names.

That night, the staff was stretched to the limits of human endurance and just when they thought it couldn't possibly get any worse, the unthinkable happened. Someone began to choke. Trust me if you've never experienced it, it's one of the most frightening things you could ever witness. Nothing that happens in a restaurant gets the staff's immediate and undivided attention faster than a

347

choking victim. The second you hear that it's happening, you start running to help. It's pure instinct.

The commotion started at the table and spread through the restaurant like a tsunami. The woman couldn't talk or breathe. Her family was flipping out, screaming for someone to do something. The other customers were watching the scene unfold. Some panicked, some yelled for a doctor, and some continued to chew.

The manager, still at the hostess desk getting clobbered, was told someone in the dining room was choking. She broke into a run while twenty people shouted, "Don't walk away while I'm talking to you!"

As she was fighting her way through the crowd to get to the victim, someone asked her, "Can I get more water here?" Someone else asked for cheese and another napkin. A third table said, "We've been waiting for an hour for our appetizers."

She ignored the requests and fought her way to the woman's side. She was now horrified to see that the woman was turning blue. She panicked and started to scream, "We need a Heimlich! We need a Heimlich!"

Not fully realizing that a Heimlich was a process and not a thing, two busboys dashed off to find one. Two waitresses were crying and two more stared in shocked silence. People were running every which way trying to find a doctor, a Heimlich, or a second glass of water.

Through all the pandemonium, a waiter ran in and said, "Get her off the floor, we need to Heimlich her! Get her up! Get her up! Hurry up, damn it!"

The manager struggled with the woman, who is now only semi-conscious and dead weight, and lifted her up with the waiter.

The waiter shouted, "Hold her so I can get behind and put my arms around her!" As he got into position and began the first series of successful Heimlich maneuvers, from which she made a quick and complete recovery, he shouted at the manager, "Call an ambulance!"

The manager was overwhelmed and in shock.

She said, "What?"

The waiter said, "Call an ambulance!"

She ran straight into the kitchen to the closest phone. Once she got there, all the stress and panic, combined with the noise level of an extremely busy kitchen, conspired to make her shout out at the top of her lungs, the question that she, and now the rest of us, will remember for the rest of her life, "What's the number for 911!"

Appropriate response: Call information. I'm sure they're listed.

Let's Have a Toast

Some years back I worked with a waiter who I'll call "John." John had an uncanny ability to drive everyone around him crazy. He didn't mean to, and he was really a very nice guy, but he could piss off Mother Teresa. He was like the kid in school who had to sit in the front row, wave his hand for every question the teacher asked, and then wash the blackboard after class. He could turn a simple pre-dinner menu meeting into a marathon of epic proportions, trying to comprehend the nuanced differences between flash fried and wok seared. He would have the entire dining room staff rolling their eyes as he asked question after question about specific Fahrenheit temperatures and the amount of oil involved in each process. What he planned to do with any of this knowledge was beyond my comprehension. I couldn't imagine a customer being the least bit interested in any of that so, like the proverbial kid in school, I think he did it just to be the teacher's pet; lucky me being the teacher.

He would come into the kitchen in the middle of a busy service for a clarification of the soil content of the various organic farms we were buying from. He would ask me things like: What types of clams were the blackfish and bass feeding on? What were the water temperatures of certain Central American shrimp-producing countries? And what was the vitamin content of what they fed to farm-raised salmon? Although I'm sure that somewhere in his altered thought process he believed that he was being a thorough and diligent employee, I thought he was flat out annoying.

Here's how it would unfold. He would come into the kitchen, usually at the worst possible time, and stand silently at attention two feet from where I was cooking. I had to speak first. I would acknowledge him and ask, "What is it John?"

He would always say the same thing. "Chef, may I ask you a question?"

Then I would always say the same thing. "Is it a stupid question, John?"

Then he always said, "There's really no such thing as a stupid question, Chef."

Then I always said, "Yeah, I've heard the rumor, but my experience has been quite different."

Then he'd say, "May I ask my question, Chef?"

Then I'd say, "Go ahead, we might as well get this over with," and he would ask me some inane thing like, "What are the biological differences between celery root and celeriac?"

It was painful. I lost my patience one day and snapped at him.

After another series of questions on the chemical breakdown of the tannins in red wine, I said, "John, you are the oracle of useless information! Do you understand that? Useless information! You ask questions that I have no prayer of knowing the answer to and no one gives a shit about. Ask me about *food* John, *food*! Ask me something easy like what animal beef comes from or what color peas are, instead of some ridiculous bullshit about the Brix levels at the time of harvest. Got it?"

He said, "Sorry, Chef. I was just trying to educate myself and learn as much as I can about this business."

I felt bad, but not that bad. I told him, "Then take a class because you're wearing me out." He looked dejected, so I then said, "Listen John, why don't we try this. Before you come in to ask me a question, consider these two points. Does my question have any bearing whatsoever on the ultimate satisfaction of my customer, and will the chef want to smash me in the face with a sauté pan for asking it? Oh and try to keep it related to food, John. Food. Okay? If your question passes the test, by all means ask it, if it doesn't, consider your health in jeopardy."

He agreed.

We had a wedding booked in the restaurant on a Saturday night. We were closed to the public, but we spent all day prepping for the big event. Weddings are especially stressful because they can be, in about half the cases, a once in a lifetime event. Everyone expects perfection because it's the bride's *special day.*

The restaurant business is a detail-oriented business, and there's nothing like a wedding to make you sweat the details. I've seen a bride in a complete meltdown because the color of the tablecloths didn't match her thong. Then throw in Mom, Grandma, and a couple dozen bridesmaids and the potential for a problem is enormous. So much more so than a regular dinner service.

About a half hour before the wedding was to start, I called a servers meeting. I told them, "Weddings are expected to be perfect. The bride and her mother have been looking forward to this day since she was born. I expect you to do everything possible to make sure she has everything she needs or wants. I don't care what it is, this is her day. I want you to pay attention to the details today. Details, details, details, that's what can make the difference between a nice wedding and a truly memorable one. Make sure you mark your tables, refill the water glasses, re-fold the used napkins, straighten your ties, and pay attention out there. Anticipate the needs of her guests. Keep your eyes open for any cocktail napkins on the floor or anything unsightly. Read the menu and if you have any questions, now's the time to ask them. Use your heads and get to it. Oh, and I want two servers on the bride's mother at all times. If she's happy, I know I'll get paid."

Off they went to their respective battle stations, everyone but

John. He was standing two feet from where I was cooking. We fell into our routine.

I said, "What is it, John?"

He said, "Chef, may I ask a question?"

In light of our previous conversation, I decided to change things up a bit.

Instead of asking him if it was a stupid question I asked, "Is it about food?"

He said, "Yes, Chef."

I asked, "Have you considered the ultimate satisfaction of the guests?"

He said, "I have, Chef."

I said, "Good. Is there any part of you that thinks you should be calling an ambulance?"

John said, "I don't believe so, Chef."

I said, "Well, that sounds like progress. Fire away."

He looked me right in the eye and asked, "What kind of bread are you using for the champagne toast?"

Appropriate response: Pumpernickel.

DRESSING DOWN

Any time you utter the four words, "Are there any questions," you expose yourself to stupidity of monumental proportions. We are constantly having meetings at the restaurants. We have meetings with the press, meetings with the partners, meetings with prospective employees, meetings with staff, meetings with purveyors, meetings with people selling wine, meetings, meetings, meetings. Of all the meetings I've attended—and there have been thousands—the ones that have the most potential for enlightenment are meetings about the menu. They are also the birthplace of some of the most hysterical questions I've ever heard.

In defense of my staff, I'll first tell you that the interest in the subject of food has exploded in the last twenty years, so the pressure on them to know every ingredient and cooking technique is huge. We are a food crazy nation evidenced by the popularity of restaurants, magazines, and especially the Food Channel. Chefs like Emeril Lagasse and Mario Batali have been teaching us how to cook and exposing their audiences to new and exotic ingredients. Air travel has also changed what we cook by making virtually any ingredient available within twenty-four hours. We've become global in our approach to how we cook and eat; some of us, anyway.

There are a few of us, though, who see a rash in every raspberry, a fever in a slice of fennel, and death in every doughnut. Thankfully for the rest of the nation, these people seem to be quarantined on Long Island. There are some who are so afraid of food that ordering dinner becomes an excruciating ordeal of the elimination process.

"I can't have that. Is it fattening? Can you leave out the butter? Can I have that on the side? Are you sure it's decaf? Is there any alcohol in it? I can't do carbs." The list goes on and on. Combine these folks with people who have allergies, both real and imagined, and you have to have a very well-informed wait staff. I say real or imagined because there are some very imagined allergies out there.

Need proof? I had a woman who told me she was allergic to parsley.

I asked her, "How would you even know that? Whose mother garnished plates with parsley when we were growing up, and who eats it as an adult? Maybe you're allergic to life." She just looked at me.

I'll go you one better. A woman once told a chef friend of mine, Michael Ross, that she was allergic to sauté. I kid you not. Could you just imagine how she found *that* out?

There I was watching Howdy Doody, coloring within the lines, and as my mother put the chicken breast in the pan, I broke out, stopped breathing, and was rushed to the hospital.

He asked her, "Sautéed what?"

She looked at him like *he* was nuts and said, "No, just sauté. Anything made sauté." So don't tell me there are no imagined allergies out there, I've experienced them.

Then on top of that, add the people who just like to see servers run back and forth from the dining room to the kitchen for their own personal entertainment, under the guise of an aversion to anything edible, and the need to school the staff is crucial. This phenomenon started in the sixties with the arrival, on Long Island, of a few Italian cruise-ship chefs who opened their restaurants out here. Tired of the pace of Manhattan, they came to the burbs to seek their fortunes. What they learned was that there weren't as many people out here and you had to fight for every customer. Consequently, they would go out of their way to coddle their clientele but unfortunately, they took it one small step too far.

Here's the line they all used that led to the extinction of the Long Island menu, as we know it today. The chef would come out of the kitchen and say something like this, "Bona sera senora, signore, you'ra back againa? Gooda to see you tonighta. Whadda you feel likea eata, hah. Pasta? Veal? You know what, forgetaboutit, don'ta evehlooka ata the mena-u, I gonna maka sometinga special justa for youa."

And that, my friends, started the slide into the customized neurosis of the Long Island restaurant customer. Everyone expects every dish to be altered to their exact specifications. I've eaten all over the country and believe me, nobody else behaves like this. No one orders dinner like we do here. If it's on the menu, we can't have it. If it's not on the menu, we want it. If it's hot, we want it cold; if it's cold, we need it heated. It's an alternate universe. We've even achieved the ultimate accolade. We have a dish named in our honor, or dishonor, depending upon your relationship with reality. You may have heard of it: the Long Island Chopped Salad. Where else would a person over the age of five have to have their salad chopped into plankton to be able to eat it?

Having had extensive experience with the menu murderers of the region, I always try to keep my servers informed on the menu, preparation, and cooking techniques on the *off-chance* someone has a special request.

We were opening a new restaurant, and I was meeting the service staff, explaining in detail each menu item, what was in it and how it was prepared. They were taking notes and asking questions and by opening night, I was fairly confident that they had a handle on it. The second night we were open, we got a little busy; I was in the kitchen trying to figure out where everything was. The dupes were coming in pretty fast and I was starting to get buried.

One of the waitresses came up to me nervously and said, "Are you busy?" I should have guessed what was coming because that in itself was a rather stupid question.

I chose not to comment on it and said, "A little. What's up?"

She said, "Can I ask you a question?"

I said, "Sure."

She asked, "Is there any sesame in the Sesame-Chili Vinaigrette?"

Appropriate Response: What could you possibly say?

SAKE TO ME

Since everyone in the United States became either a stockbroker or a real estate tycoon within the last ten years, the front of the house employee pool has dried up. Who wants to get up, shower, dress and go to a job when you can sit in front of your computer in your pajamas and day-trade or flip real estate? If it weren't for struggling actors and single moms, restaurants would go the way of the Studebaker. There used to be large number of talented servers spinning around the restaurant carousel, but now, not so much.

This has changed who we are able to hire, and as a result has drastically altered the interview process. In the past, when interviewing a prospective server, I would ask about their experience level, the chefs they worked with, the individual dishes that were served, where they ate on their nights off, and what trade magazines they read. It was always a very foodie interview.

Now, when I interview a server, I find myself asking things like, "How many children do you have in preschool? Have you ever eaten in a restaurant before? Could you spell brunch for me? Okay, just say *fish*. Great, could you start tomorrow?" The herd has been thinned to a dangerous level.

I really don't mind training green employees, largely because I don't have to do it, but it requires a lot of time, energy, and patience. The good part is that inexperienced employees have no previously formed bad habits, so you can train them to your way of doing things; the bad part is that they have no previously formed good habits, either. So you need to start from scratch and it takes that much longer to get them on the floor. Since the inexperienced server is trying to absorb so much information in such a short amount of time, the training always results in lots of questions, and usually they include a couple of real head scratchers.

I had placed an ad in the local paper for a lunch server. We had a very sweet single mom apply for the position. She wanted to get a part-time job since she was recently divorced and needed to make some money. She had no real restaurant experience, but when you are the only applicant for the job, your chances of getting that job skyrocket.

Since she was such a lovely person, we decided to give her a try. You can always train someone to wait tables; it's slightly easier than curing cancer. What you can't do is train someone to be pleasant or be a people person, so banking on that rationale, we hired her.

She started a few days later, *trailing* one of my regular servers. *Trailing* is basically following a regular server around for the entire shift to get a sense of how the restaurant operates, learn the point-of-sale system, and understand the policies of the kitchen and dining room. For an experienced server it doesn't take more than a few shifts. They've done it all before and they know how to wait on a customer, so it's just a matter of learning the computer and the house policy. For her, we opened up Dining Room 101.

I don't want to make it sound like she wasn't smart, because she was very smart, but if you don't know something, you don't know it, and you have to start at the beginning. We did.

She did so well and learned so fast that she got her first table a week later. She was very excited and did a great job. The party that she waited on called me over as they were leaving to tell me what great service they had and how nice she was. I was thrilled because I saw her as a diamond in the rough, and it looked like she had the potential to shine.

Her biggest obstacle was the menu. Not being someone who

had restaurant experience and not having eaten out much, she struggled with certain ingredients that were unfamiliar. Like most of us, she was raised on simple home-cooked meals and had spent the last several years raising her children, so the subject of esoteric food hadn't been a priority.

She was waiting on a table a few days after her debut, and one of the guests ordered an appetizer called *Tuna Three Ways*. This dish is served on a large square plate with four small plates inset. One plate is *Tuna Tartare*, one plate is a *Sesame Seared Tuna Loin*, one plate is a *Tuna Crudo*, and on the last plate we serve a shot of cold Sake. It's a fun presentation and it does get quite a bit of attention when it's served.

She brought it to the table with the rest of the appetizers and then returned to the kitchen.

She said, "Hey, Chef, can I ask you a question?"

I said, "Sure."

She said, "That tuna dish is pretty cool. What's actually on it again?"

I said, "You have *Tuna Tartare, Sesame Seared Tuna Loin, Tuna Crudo*, and a shot of Sake."

She said, "They're all raw, right?"

I said, "Correct."

She then said, "So it's sushi?"

I said, "No, sushi's different. It's served on rice, usually with wasabi, pickled ginger, and soy sauce."

She then said, "But it's *like* sushi, I mean, because it's raw."

I said, "Only in the sense that it's raw, but I don't want you to confuse yourself here. They are different."

She said, "Okay, I get it. What's that in the shot glass again?"

I said, "Sake."

She asked, "Don't they serve that with sushi?"

I said, "Yeah they do. I get the feeling that you're not going to be happy until we change the name of the appetizer. Do you want me to just stop all the bullshit and call it sushi?"

She laughed and asked, "No. What is Sake anyway?"

I answered her, "It's a *Japanese rice wine*. Think of it like this: Sake is to sushi what wine is to cheese."

She could have left it right there giving up her place in this book. Instead she looked at me quizzically and asked, "Sooo—is Sake made from fish?"

Appropriate response: Yeah, ricefish.

Yellowfin Tuna Tartare/Sesame Red Ginger/ Chilis Recipe

T his has become one of the signature appetizers at *CoolFish*. I've used it so often at fundraisers, it's become sort of an inside restaurant-industry joke. (I wonder what Schaudel is serving this year? Ha, ha, ha.) There are two reasons that I lean on this dish so much. The first is that I think it tastes great, and most of my customers agree. The second pertains to the fundraisers themselves. I like participating in fundraisers for all of the obvious reasons: It's very cool to be able to help, in some small way, people less fortunate than yourself. I love hanging with my bros, and it's fun to get out of the kitchen and interact with the public. But at the same time, they do take their toll. I realized some years ago that if you make something that is raw, you automatically eliminate a number of people from eating your dish. I further learned that if you make something spicy, that number went up as well. So, after doing the math, I realized I could work half as hard for essentially the same result. Results notwithstanding, this is a great start to a summer meal—and it's quick.

Ingredients:

1 pound sushi-grade yellowfin tuna, diced
2 tablespoons red and yellow peppers, finely minced
½ teaspoon red pepper flakes
2 tablespoons black and white sesame seeds
4 ounces Red Ginger Vinaigrette (see below)
Salt and pepper to taste

In a non-reactive bowl, toss the diced tuna, peppers, red pepper flakes, and the sesame seeds. Add the Red Ginger Vinaigrette and toss, coating evenly. season with salt and pepper.

Chef's tip: *Although I prefer yellowfin tuna, you may substitute bluefin, bigeye, or albacore. These are all fine fish from local waters. Salmon may be used as well, but I think the flavors work better with the richness of tuna. At CoolFish we serve this in a* Martini *glass, but for a more dramatic presentation, serve it in a halved coconut shell on crushed ice.*

Red Ginger Vinaigrette:

1 cup pickled ginger
½ teaspoon chopped garlic
¼ cup rice wine vinegar
½ cup soy or canola oil
4 tablespoons soy sauce
½ teaspoon sesame oil

Place ingredients in a blender at low speed for 2 minutes. season with more soy sauce, if necessary.

Wine pairing: *CoolFish* Riesling.

No Point in Squabbling

Even after spending most of my last forty years in a restaurant, going out to dinner is still my favorite pastime. There's something special about companionship and a leisurely meal that appeals to me, and it's the best way to get to know someone. A great meal can fuel a stalled conversation by the very nature of the fact that you have something in common to talk about, and wine is truth serum for those of us without a prescription. The combination of the two can make for a powerful and enlightening evening. You can tell a lot about a person by simply sharing a meal with them. If you pay careful attention, you will get a thumbnail sketch of who that person is by the time dessert is served.

You may have been to any number of dinners where you were turned off or on by your companion's behavior at the table. If you happen to be the proud owner of a serious character flaw, it will manifest itself somewhere between your first cocktail and your coffee. By contrast, if you're polite, well-mannered, and can negotiate a chicken breast without embarrassing yourself, that too will show.

Having been single most of my life, I've had the occasion to experience more than my share of these little fact-finding missions. These dinner dates have run from one end of the excitement spectrum to the other, from a woman who had two drinks, passed out cold, and had to be accompanied in the ambulance on the way to the hospital, undressed, and admitted—all before we sat down for dinner by the way—to a woman who was eating Belon oysters like she was going to the electric chair, and who I thought could have been my future ex-wife. It's been loads of fun, but believe me, I've learned a lot.

If you want to find out what someone is really like, take them to dinner and give them one too many glasses of wine. It can turn a wonderful, sensitive, caring human being into Vlad the Impaler. You might as well find out right away; at least you'll know what you're getting into.

Some months ago, I met a woman who, like me, worked in a restaurant. She was friendly and beautiful with a good sense of humor and had a smile that lit up the room. I was attracted. It took me several weeks to get up the courage to ask her out and when I finally did, she accepted. We made arrangements to go to dinner later that week.

I picked her up and when she got in the car, she said, "I have to tell you something."

I said, "What's that?"

She said, "I'm really intimidated going out to dinner with you. I grew up in a large family and we always ate very simply and here you are a chef, and all into food—and I don't know—I'm just a little nervous. I'm afraid I'm going to do or say something wrong. I was never all that into the going out to dinner thing like you are. I cook at home a lot."

I said, "We don't have to do dinner if you don't want to and besides, this isn't a test." That probably wasn't the most truthful statement I've ever made.

She said, "No, I want to. I'm just a little nervous."

I said, "No need to be nervous. Let's just have fun."

She said, "Okay."

We got to the restaurant and sat down. Whenever I walk through a restaurant door, I feel excited and energized; that night was no different. I suggested that if she could be a little adventurous, we should have the tasting menu. She said that although there were some things on it she had never tried before, she was willing to give it a shot. We had the tasting menu with accompanying wines, and she loved everything. She thanked me for turning her on to such great wines and such a wonderful dinner. I thanked her for not turning into Vlad.

We had such a good time we decided to do it again.

The following week, when I picked her up, I asked, "Are you nervous?"

She said, "No, not at all."

I said, "Good, let's go; I'm starving."

We arrived at the restaurant, I ordered a bottle of wine, and they gave us menus to look over. I asked her, "Want to do a tasting menu again?"

She said, "Normally I would say yes, because last week it was so good, but I'm not all that hungry and I don't want to feel stuffed. Let's just order something off the menu. Okay?"

I said, "Sure. We can always have a few appetizers if you want and split them so you don't have to eat as much."

She said, "That sounds better." We continued looking over the menus.

I said, "Do you know what you want?"

She said, "I think so."

The waitress came over to take our order. She asked us, "Are you ready to order?"

I said, "Yes." I then said to my date, who was still looking at her menu, "Are you ready or do you need a little more time?"

She said, "No, I think I'm ready."

Then she turned to me and asked, "What kind of fish is squab again?"

Appropriate response: Pigeon fish.

Cheffed Up

There are some people, and I'm sure this is true in every profession, who just don't possess the skills required for their chosen field. For example, if I were to get on the basketball court with the Knicks, how long do you think it would take me to make an ass of myself? How long do you think I would last in the ring with Mike Tyson? Can you picture Randy Moss shivering in his cleats if I were to line up against him?

Well damn it, not everyone can cook. Some people should just give up the dream of the bright lights and glitter of the restaurant business, take the civil service test, and do whatever it is that civil servants do when they actually show up for work. It would save us countless trips to the hospital, thousands of dollars in reimbursed meals, and it would translate into a windfall of *hanging chad voters* for our patrons of government who need as many people *suckling the public nipple* as possible.

Two major factors are contributing to the glut of people who can't cook but think they can. The popularity of cooking schools and Emeril, and they're related. The cooking schools have good intentions but they are now on financial level with a private college. So, if you graduate from a *chef* school with $50,000.00 in unpaid school loans, you kind-of need a *chef* salary to pay it off, and the first step to making a *chef* salary is applying for a *chef* job. Emeril's success has been so great that he has inspired legions of followers who dream of being the next Food TV star. So, by watching Emeril and then enrolling in cooking school, they begin a journey that, although eventually ending in a position with the county, will test the patience of every chef they come in contact with.

367

This is how I found out. I had a young man come to interview for a kitchen position. I was running a little late so when I arrived, I was feeling bad about making him wait. I apologized and offered him something to drink.

He said, "I'll have a Merlot." It was noon. I thought that was a little forward but said nothing.

I asked if he had a resume and he gave it to me. As I read, I saw that he had just graduated from C.I.A. about twelve minutes before the interview. I told him that I graduated in '73 and asked him who was still teaching there.

After reminiscing for a few minutes over an espresso and a Merlot I asked him, "So, what are you looking to do?"

He said, "Well, I really want to be a TV chef."

I said, "So why interview here? Why not go to Channel 12?"

He said, "I thought I would get some experience first before I tried to get on TV."

I said, "That's probably a good idea. What would you like to do here?"

He said, "Well, although I would prefer the chef's job, I would take either the sous-chef or executive sous-chef position if it's not available."

I'm rarely at a loss for words, but he had me. Recovering somewhat I said, "I'm personally not clear on just what an executive sous-chef is, but what makes you think you can handle a chef or sous-chef position, executive or otherwise, in a very busy three star restaurant, with no previous experience?"

He said, "My training. I just graduated from C.I.A."

I was dumbfounded. I said, "Okay, humor me. How long would you smoke an ostrich thigh and at what temperature to get it to medium rare?"

He said, "I'm not sure."

I said, "You're not sure? What ratio of sugar to water would you use to make lemon-thyme syrup?"

He said, " I don't really know."

I said, "Great. How long do you think it would take to bring thirty gallons of veal stock down to a glaze?" He just looked at me.

I said, "Listen, I mean no disrespect here, but if you're a sous-chef or an executive sous-chef, I'm an astronaut."

He said, "I guess I didn't get the job, huh."

I said, "I think you're probably overqualified. I'm looking for a line cook."

He said, "Okay, thank you for your time."

He finished his wine and got up to leave. I was trying to keep a straight face because, although I'm sure it wasn't his intention, this kid was downright funny.

As he was walking to the front door, he stopped and turned around. He called to me, "Chef, can I ask you a question?"

I said, "Sure, man. What's up?"

He said, "I'm thinking that this is the first interview I've been on and it didn't go very well. I have another interview for a sous-chef position at Fairway in an hour. Is there anything specific that you think I could do better when I interview there?"

Appropriate Response: Don't sell yourself short.

Licking Your Wounds

You meet the most interesting people in kitchens. Between the heat, the stress, and the long hours, it's bound to attract a certain breed of cat. I have worked with, and for, quite an assortment of characters in my day, but one of the top three was a cook who worked for me out east in Montauk. He was the complete cosmic lunatic. He came to me with little or no experience in the kitchen, from Colorado where he had just spent the winter skiing. His plan was to surf all summer but work enough to put a roof over his surfboard, which he slept with over his head. He told me he would work nights so he would be free to surf all day and was honest, or stupid, enough to tell me that he partied like a Viking every night, so would be useless until three o'clock anyway. I admire the truth.

He was in his early thirties, but had lived an endless party since high school. Right after graduating he enrolled in college and at age thirty-two he was on the verge of starting his sophomore year. According to him, he wanted to get in one more summer of surfing before he buckled down and started studying. The guy didn't know much about cooking but he had more energy than any five guys I knew. After smoking a ton of pot, drinking a quart of tequila, and dancing non-stop until four a.m., he would surf all day, come in at three and say, "What do you need me to do, Chef?"

I'd say, "Sleep?"

He'd say, "I'll sleep when I'm dead. Give me something to do."

I'd give him one or two things to do and he would say, "Chef, come on man. Give me more. I can do the work of ten men. Give me more." Which I would. The only problem was that he could never remember more than two things at a time. He was also a raging Deadhead, which meant he had total recall of every one of the five hundred and seventy-two Grateful Dead shows he had attended, but little of anything else.

We decided collectively that if we were going to keep him around, even if only for the entertainment factor, that we had to start making prep lists for him or he would never get anything done. It was difficult at first because you would make a prep list for him, explain it, and then he would forget where he put it.

Exasperated, I took him aside and said, "Look man, I understand that this is just a summer gig for you, but for the rest of us this is reality. This is what we do. I'm trying to hang with you here but you need to show me something. Too many people are depending on you to get your work done. You spend an hour a day yapping with the waitresses, you lose the damn prep lists, and every time "Sugar Magnolia" comes on the radio, we can't find you for a half an hour. It ain't working for me."

He said, "Dude, that's my favorite Dead tune."

I said, "Could you give me a break, please, and grow up?"

He said, "Man, I'm sorry. I'll pay attention more. You know I can do the work of ten men."

I said, "I don't need you to do the work of ten men, I need you to do *your* work."

He says, "All right man, tomorrow you'll see a new me. I promise."

He must have cut back on the tequila and been tucked in by three a.m. because for the next week and a half, I didn't recognize him. He was on it. He was ready for service on time. His station was immaculate. He was helping the other guys. I couldn't believe it. I told him that he was doing great, and he said, "I told you Chef-o. I love this place man. I'm thinking about bagging college and staying with you." I said, "You trying to make me cry?"

About three days later, his whole world fell apart. I heard the news as I was driving to work; Jerry Garcia died from an overdose.

When I pulled into the parking lot, he was standing there sobbing, looking up to the heavens asking, "Why? Why'd you leave Jerry, why?"

I didn't know whether to hug him or slap him but grief is grief so I went inside. An hour later, he's still out there, still crying, and still looking up.

I asked, "Are you gonna be okay?"

He said, "Look over there, Chef. You can see his face in the clouds." That was all I could take. I said, "I thought he was younger."

He looked at me like I was a heretic. I said, "Look man, you've been out here for an hour, crying and talking to the clouds. I never much cared for the band or his guitar playing, so you need to get your shit together and get ready for service. You've got five minutes."

He said, "Chef, he was the major influence in my life. His music touched me and is probably responsible for who I am today."

I asked, "And you admit that? He's probably responsible for why you're such a knucklehead at times. Fire up the bong, dude."

He asked, "You think the pot affected me?"

I said, "I do. Get back to work."

"I don't believe you, Chef-o."

He then set out to prove that pot had no effect on his short-term memory. He told everyone I thought that pot was affecting him but what did I know because I didn't smoke. Kitchens can be playful places and practical jokes are an occasional happening. I was standing with my sous-chef, who happened to be a woman, and we were making his prep list.

I got an idea. I said, "He's trying to prove that he's unaffected by twenty years of pot smoking, right. So, let's give him some fake prep thing to make to see how long it takes him to figure it out.

She said, "You mean like asking him to find a steam expander or the cheese straightener?"

I said, "Yeah, but more subtle."

Then it hit me. Right there in the middle of his prep list, between the caramelized fig vinaigrette and the roasted peppers, I wrote the word "cunnilingus."

She stared like I'd lost my mind. She said, "He'll know that."

I said, "I'm betting he doesn't."

The two of us collapsed laughing. This wasn't an easy one to keep the lid on. We had the whole kitchen involved, and everyone was on the verge of losing it all day. He was prepping his ass off but every time he looked at the list, this word was staring back at him and his face would twist up in hope of some cognitive awakening. Several of us had to go outside to laugh it off several times during the day, especially when he started asking some of the guys if they were familiar with cunnilingus. I told them to tell him that I had never shown them how to make it so he would eventually have to ask me, something he desperately wanted to avoid considering the point he was trying to prove.

As it got nearer and nearer to 5:00, he was panicking and you could see it on his face. At 4:55, I went into the pantry and asked, "Are you guys ready?"

He said nothing. The rest of the crew came over for a quick meeting.

I said to him, "Hey man, you ready for service?"

He looked at me dejectedly and at 4:59, with the entire kitchen staff present asked, "I know you probably showed me, but I just don't remember. How do you make the cunnilingus?"

Appropriate response: You laugh until it hurts.

YANKEE FANS

Sports fans are a trip. I understand that the word "fan" comes from the word "fanatic," but I don't think I was fully able to comprehend the level of fanaticism some fans are able to achieve, until I met "Bob."

Bob was a rabid Yankee fan, first and foremost. It was job number one. His second priority was his family, which I had to admire him for, and coming in a distant third was his job as a server in one of my restaurants. The job was somewhere between an inconvenience and an afterthought. He was really a very good waiter, in the off-season. In season, however, it was all Yankees all the time. He had season tickets, he watched them on TV, and he read every word of every column written about them. When they won, he was on cloud nine, a great worker, and a pleasure to be around, but when they lost, you had to talk him down off the ledge. It was a huge problem because, to my knowledge, no baseball team has ever finished the regular season undefeated. You almost couldn't schedule him to work on a night the Yankees were playing. He would be distracted to the point of uselessness. If he wasn't trying to sneak a peek at the TV in the bar, he was on his cell phone trying to get scoring updates every ten minutes. It was brutal.

One Saturday morning, I was in the kitchen and Bob came in. He was off that day because the Yankees were playing the Red Sox at home, and he was going to the game. I've since been informed that there is no greater thrill for a Yankee fan than seeing them beat the hated Red Sox at home, in person, when you should be working. What I also didn't know at the time was that a grown man could wear a particularly ridiculous outfit and apparently not feel the slightest bit of shame. I guess once you get to the stadium, you blend in.

Bob walked into the kitchen, nodded to me, and headed straight for the ice machine and started filling a cooler. You had to see the get up. He had on a Yankee hat, Yankee sunglasses, a Yankee shirt with the name Jeter emblazoned across the back, Yankee sneakers with Yankee shoelaces, and I suspect a Yankee Speedo, although I couldn't bring myself to ask.

Instead, I asked, "What are you doing?"

He said, "I'm borrowing some ice. I'm going to the game."

I asked, "What time is the game?"

He said, "Eight p.m."

I said, "It's only eleven in the morning. Won't the ice melt by the time you leave for the stadium?"

He said, "No. I'm leaving now."

I asked, "What the hell are you going to do there for eight hours?"

He said, "We tailgate. You know, cook some stuff, talk about the game, maybe have a catch and some beers."

I asked, "For eight hours, and you don't get bored?"

He said, "Chef, we're talking about the Yankees here."

I said, "Yeah, I got that part." I couldn't help myself. I asked, "Who's playing?"

He said, "You're kidding me, right? Yankees versus Red Sox, Chef. We're gonna kick their asses."

I asked, "We?" Then I said, "Let me ask you a question. Don't you feel even mildly ridiculous dressed like that?"

He looked at me like *I* was the one who was unbalanced and said, "No, why?"

I said, "It just seems a little odd to me that a grown man would take a night off work, dress up in a Halloween costume, eat, drink, and fart in a parking lot for eight hours, then pay hundreds of dollars for the privilege of watching twenty-two guys run in a circle more times than twenty-two other guys."

Bob said, "I guess you're not a sports fan, huh."

I said, "I guess not, but can I ask you another question, just for the sake of perspective? If I came into work one day and I had on a chef's jacket with the name Wolfgang Puck written right there above the pocket, wouldn't you think I was a dick?"

Annoyed, he asked, "What's your point?"

I said, "My point is that I'm much closer to being Wolfgang Puck than you are to being Derek Jeter. At least I can cook."

Blissfully undeterred, he said, "Hey Chef, to each his own; I gotta go," and left.

Six months later, I opened a new restaurant. One of my partners happened to know Yogi Berra. Aside from being a Yankee icon, Yogi's rumpled, grandfatherly demeanor, and his complete annihilation of the English language, have made him one of the most beloved ex-athletes of all time. I mentioned to Bob that my partner knew Yogi and he flipped out. He recited his statistics, called him the greatest Yankee catcher ever, and told me that if I didn't let him know when Yogi was coming to dinner, that he would seriously consider ending my life.

A couple of weeks later, I got the word that Yogi was thinking of coming to dinner on that Friday night. Not quite ready to die, I called Bob and told him. He got all excited and told me he was going to take the night off and come to the restaurant and hopefully meet him. The day arrived, and Bob showed up, waiting patiently in the bar for Yogi. The bar was pretty full and he was chatting excitedly about Yogi to some of the customers.

Then the unthinkable happened. My partner came into the kitchen and informed me that Yogi wasn't coming. It seemed that when Yogi had called for a reservation earlier in the week, one of my hostesses, not knowing who he was, told him that we were completely booked for the night, and since it was the only night that he could make it, he said that he would have to try again another time. Even though I don't get the whole sports thing, just knowing how much it meant to Bob made it difficult to tell him what had happened. He was devastated. There were several other people who he had been talking to who were also disappointed.

He said, "Show me the hostess."

I started laughing.

He said, "No, I'm serious. Which one was it?"

He almost needed to be restrained, so of course, I felt the need to egg him on.

I said, "Maybe he'll come another time; and then quoting Yogi, "Maybe he'll see the fork in the road and take it." He said, "Come on, Chef, this isn't funny."

As all this was going back and forth, a young couple had come into the bar and ordered drinks. It's not a big space, so they could hear most of what was going on.

The guy asked, "Yogi was supposed to be here tonight?"

The bartender said, "Yeah, but there was a mix-up with his reservation."

The guy said, "Oh man, that's too bad. I'm a big Yankee fan. I would have loved to have met him."

He turned to his girlfriend and said, "I can't believe it. Yogi Berra was supposed to be here tonight."

She happened to be blonde and I swear to you, this is what she said, "Yogi the Bear was supposed to eat here tonight?"

Appropriate response: Yeah, but we couldn't let him in. He doesn't wear pants.

LITTLE LOBSTERS

Years ago on the East End, I once saw a two-hundred-year-old contract between a farmer and his day laborers that stated that he couldn't serve them lobster for dinner more than three times a week. I'm assuming they were so plentiful that they were thought of as being garbage seafood. It was pretty amusing considering what we know today.

Lobsters are one of my all time favorite foods to cook and to eat. The only thing better than eating a lobster in the summer with the juices running down your arms, on the beach, is having it served to you in a restaurant already removed from the shell. It's way more elegant and you don't need a fire hose and three rolls of Bounty to clean yourself up afterwards. Don't get me wrong, I enjoy it both ways, but as I get older, I'm trying to avoid any extra work.

Believing some people must feel like I do, I've been serving it out of the shell in some of the restaurants to a mixed degree of success. I say mixed because, although everyone enjoys the flavor, it's the size that matters most. Some people cannot grasp the fact that when a lobster is removed from the shell that the lobster doesn't weigh as much as it did when it was wearing the shell. I'm not so sure what's so difficult to understand, but that concept has managed to bewilder an awful lot of people. I can't tell you how many times I've heard, "This isn't a one and one-half pound lobster. Take it back."

Once the meat is removed, the weight of the lobster becomes irrelevant, unless of course, you plan on eating the shell. But some people can't get past it. There's a completely different set of rules for meat. Ever hear someone who is eating a sixteen ounce steak say, "That doesn't look like no twenty-seven hundred pound steer to me,

George." You have to get it through your head that you are eating *part* of the lobster, not the lobster itself.

One night back in my Montauk days, I was running a lobster dish that I thought was the essence of the East End in summer. We were doing a grilled BBQ one and one-half pound lobster with purple potatoes, a local corn sauté, and basil oil, and serving it out of the shell. I had a female dishwasher named Lucy who nearly wore her fingerprints off de-shelling lobsters that summer. It was far and away the most popular dish on the menu, and the most troublesome.

For every four or five that I served, one came back because someone complained about the size. We had to go to 2 lb. lobsters and that calmed it down somewhat, but we still had the occasional complaint even with the bigger lobsters.

That summer, I had a woman working as a server who was a complete disaster. She was very sweet and very motivated, but she was clueless in the dining room and had no ability to organize her thought processes to be able to do more than one task at a time. She would be running around like a chicken without a head with just two tables, and though it was a strain on the other servers, it usually resulted in some awfully funny scenes. By the end of her shift she always looked like she had run a marathon, but I guess if you run in circles long enough you do eventually get in the twenty-six miles. It was very hard to get seasonal help in Montauk, and she was a warm body, so we thought if we watched her carefully and didn't give her too many tables, that she had a slight chance of surviving the season.

One night a table of four people came in and sat in her station. They told her that they were on vacation and couldn't wait to have a lobster dinner.

They asked, "Do you have lobster on the menu tonight?"

She told them about the special. Three of them said that it sounded great, one gentleman was not so sure.

He asked, "It's served out of the shell?"

She said, "Yes."

Another table sat in her section and since she was now at her full capacity, her anxiety level began to rise.

He asked, "It comes with corn and potatoes also, correct?"

She said, "Yes."

Her right foot was beginning to tap and she was growing impatient waiting for him to make up his mind. Eyeing the new table she asked him, "Would you like the lobster, sir?"

He said, "I'm not sure. How big is it?"

She said, "It's a two-pound lobster."

He said, "I know that, but it's out of the shell and I just want to make sure that it's going to be enough food for me. Give me another minute."

She excused herself and headed to the new table to take a drink order. She served the drinks and the table asked if there were any specials.

Completely scrambled she said, "I'll be right back to tell you the specials as soon as I finish taking that table's dinner order."

She ran back to the first table and asked, "Are you going to have the lobster?"

The guy said, "I can't make up my mind. I want to have it but I'm very hungry and I'm torn between the lobster and the sirloin. I'm afraid it won't be enough to eat. How much lobster meat do you get?" The other table was looking at her trying to get her attention, and she was becoming more and more stressed.

She said, "I don't know, maybe this much," touching her thumbs and middle fingers together in a circle. He says, "That doesn't help me much. Could you ask the chef how much lobster meat is in the dish?"

She said, "Fine, good idea. I'll go ask the chef."

As she headed for the kitchen, the other table flagged her down and asked, "Can you tell us about those specials now?"

Hanging on to her composure by her fingernails she said, "I'm very busy but I promise I'll be right back." She made a mad dash for the kitchen, ran up to the cooking line, and in a panic, looked at me and asked, "Chef, how much do the two-pound lobsters weigh!"

Appropriate response: I'm guessing—about two pounds.

Toupee or Not Toupee?

That is the question. I'll spare you the "whether it is nobler" part of the quote but the question begs an answer. Do you, or don't you wear a toupee? I don't mean is he or isn't he wearing a toupee; I can spot one of those babies one hundred yards away. I mean should you or should you not wear one. I'm lucky enough to have plenty of hair for my age so maybe I'm not the best one to address the subject, and I can sympathize with men who are prematurely bald. But something cool happened to bald in the nineties: it became very hip, and continues to be. I sort of understood toupees in the seventies when everyone had hair down to their knees, but now the only people left with long hair are musicians, one or two chefs, me, and Professor Irwin Corey.

It's a great time to be bald. I even know some younger guys who have full heads of hair that shave them in *order* to be bald. So why, why, would anyone glue something that is the visual equivalent of road-kill on a perfectly cool bald head, and then have the audacity to look the rest of us in the eye, which is exactly where I have to look because if I look up at the toupee, I giggle.

"Hey, that's quite a head of hair you have there."
"Thanks."

Can't help it, call me immature. It's like talking to someone who has just had plastic surgery and has a huge bandage across the bridge of their nose. I can't do it. I can't have a serious conversation with someone whose nose is mummified. Come back when you heal, then we'll talk.

If passing counterfeit money is illegal, how come toupees are not? If you knew someone was flat out lying to you, you'd call him on it, no? Well? I just don't get it. And another thing: if you insist on wearing someone else's hair, or worse yet, Berber carpet, you can't go to the one-size-fits-all rack. Spend some money for Pete's sake. How can you justify $250,000.00 dollars for a Ferrari, a convertible no less, and $25.00 on a toupee that looks like an osprey's nest when you pull up to a steakhouse for the Thursday night singles scene—single being the operative word. $250,000.00 for a toupee and $25.00 for a car sounds like the better plan for singles night, but hey, that's me. Not to belabor the point, but bald is the new hair; it's cool, wear it! Maybe it's a generational thing.

One of my follically-challenged customers is an elderly gentleman who chooses to wear a toupee. It's actually a pretty good "piece" because I didn't know he had one on until he was *ninety* feet away. He likes to come around and try to pick up some of the younger sixty-something chicks that work in the office building and frequent the bar.

One night he pulled into the parking lot and as he got out of his car, he dropped his keys on the ground and accidentally kicked them under the car. He's somewhere in his eighties so he's not quite as limber as when he was younger. He bent down and lowered one knee to the ground followed by the other and while on his hands and knees, searched in vain for the keys. He then spotted them directly in the middle, under the car, which is where all the keys usually end up, so he slid on his stomach under the car to try to retrieve them.

Funny thing about toupees: they get caught on shit. He hooks the top of his toupee on the catalytic converter, or whatever the hell is under there, and was hanging, under the car, by a thread: a carpet thread. Realizing that, he panicked. It seems to me, if you insist on wearing a toupee, the time to panic is when you're approaching a mirror. The fact that it's caught on something and may rip off your head would, in almost all cases, be an improvement.

The situation called for calm. As he twisted and turned, contorting his body into positions it had no hope of recovering from, his worst nightmare walked out into the parking lot: Diane. Diane has a birth defect. She was born without a filter between her brain and her mouth.

Diane saw him writhing under the car, trying to make sure that the only carpet attached *to* the car is actually on the *inside*, and asks the obvious question, "What are you doing?"

I'm not exactly sure of the response she was expecting, but what she got was, "I'm trying to unhook my hair from the car."

You can't say something like that to Diane and expect anything good to happen. She completely lost it. Laughing uncontrollably for about ten minutes as this poor guy is desperately trying to salvage his evening, his dignity and his...ehh...hair, she finally said, "Hair, let me help you," and lost it all over again.

Ten minutes later, Diane helped him out from under the car with most of his toupee. He's a regular in Diane's station and knows her well.

Finally standing, he had about forty percent of his toupee still attached and the rest of it in a bunch on top of his head, grease marks all over his face and clothes, and parking lot dirt on his knees. He looked like Braveheart with a bad wig.

He said to Diane, "Do I look okay to go in and have a drink?"

"You're kidding, right?"

"No, I'll wash my face first. But is my hair all right?"

"John, I'm not quite sure how to break this to you, but...you don't have hair."

"Could you please not break my chops and just answer the question."

"Well, you may want to stick it down a little; it looks like it's alive."

"Thanks for your help."

To compound the problem, it happened to be very windy. John and Diane walked back through the parking lot and up to the front door.

John walked in first, before Diane had a chance to warn anyone. He stepped up to the hostess desk. Looking like his own personal Hurricane Katrina had hit him in the forehead, with his toupee literally on upside down, looked right at Ali, who subsequently had to be physically removed after the question, and asked, with a straight face mind you, "Do you think I need a little more glue?"

Appropriate response: Nah, you're good.

Passing Thoughts

This is an open letter to all bathroom users from all restaurant owners. I'll consider myself the spokesman. No pun intended, but there's something about bathrooms that bring out the worst in people. Although the techniques employed are different, the resulting destruction is the same for both sets of bathrooms.

First, I'll deal with the men. I don't know what it is that triggers the response, but there's something about the relationship between alcohol and a fully tiled room with a toilet that sends some men into a jihadist rage. Drunken guys are to bathrooms what Al Qaeda is to buildings. I never met a drunken guy that couldn't kick a bathroom's ass, and kick it good. Assaults of this type have to be taken more seriously. We lose hundreds of thousands of dollars industry-wide every year repairing bathrooms. The bathroom jihadists must be severely dealt with. How long will our lawmakers continue to ignore their crimes against "the vanity"? And some of these incidents are hateful. I've personally witnessed a drunken guy referring to gender saying, "This don't look like no fucking men's room to me," while kicking a bathroom's ass. Knowingly or unknowingly, that's a bias crime.

A friend of mine was a witness to a full-blown hate crime. He told me he was in the men's room returning a quart of beer he had just rented, when this guy starts trashing the place yelling, "I hate white tile. It looks like a sanitarium in here. I hate white fucking tile." In our politically correct world, you have to leave color out of it. Kick the bathroom's ass if you must, but refer to color and you're really asking for trouble. The fact that he knew what a sanitarium looked like would have concerned me the most.

Women, on the other hand, have a different method of bathroom destruction. Although I have seen some female potty pugilists, women, for the most part, when drunk and confronted with a bathroom, tend to redecorate. One of the more popular techniques is toilet paper. On any given Saturday, after three women have used the ladies' room, it looks like a white replica of "The Gates" in Central Park. How do they get it to stick to the ceiling? If I had a nickel for every roll of paper that passed through the ladies' room, I'd be living in an oceanfront home.

Paper towels are another medium used in the ladies' rooms. Remember paper mâché in kindergarten? Substitute hand soap for plaster of Paris and you have sculpting material. I once thought I saw the ghost of Telly Savalas on the ladies' room floor, but it was just three hundred hand towels and two quarts of soap shaped into a ball.

Rearranging furniture is another female bathroom pastime. I guess while waiting for a booth, one can become bored. Rarely is the bathroom furniture in the same place as when we opened. Women also become lighting engineers when combing their hair or applying makeup. Too much light? Unscrew the bulb—oh, and take it with you. Too many candles? Blow some out—and take them with you. Between the toilet paper, hand towels, soap, light bulbs, and candles, it's like Bed, Bath and Bankrupt in there.

The other question I have is why do ladies' rooms have toilets? I always thought that the bathrooms in Europe that are basically rooms with holes in the floor were primitive. Now I get it. It's pointless to have toilets when no one uses them. Whatever they need to do is everywhere *but* the toilet. I've seen 'em hit the walls, ceiling, sink, just about everywhere but the bowl.

My porter, Antonio, has said only two words to me in the three years that I've known him. When I walk in the kitchen with that look on my face, he says, "Bano?" I shake my head yes. He says, "Mujeres." I shake my head yes. That's our entire relationship.

Oprah needs to do a show on the dysfunctional relationship between women and toilets because we need a national discussion on healthy public bathroom habits for ladies. It seems to me like they go into the booth, lock the door, pull eleven miles of toilet paper off the roll and then shrink-wrap the seat. Once the seat has been artfully wrapped in six inches of Charmin, they don't sit on it. No, that would be way too effective. There's not a woman that I know who will let her behind touch a public toilet seat. So, why wrap it? You would think after all that work you would need to sit down and rest. What they do, it seems, since I've never actually witnessed it, is hover twelve inches over the seat like a UFO, or in some extreme cases stand on the seat, and while doing the Tarantella, they let it fly.

Can we give just a passing thought to the next person in line or to the guy who has to clean up? Someone should build a practice range like golf courses have, although I can't imagine what the stalls would look like at the end of the day, but we really need a place for the ladies to go to sharpen their skills. A couple of buckets after work every day couldn't hurt the aim. Maybe we could paint the toilet bowls like archery targets with points for a bull's-eye, and maybe one or two of the outer rings. It would be incentive to concentrate on what you're doing. Hit *something*, for God's sake. I'll even be willing to give prizes like stuffed animals. Outer ring: stuffed flounder; inner ring: stuffed quail; bull's-eye: stuffed lobster.

This really needs to be addressed because I'm on the verge of tears. Please, all you bathroom Bin Ladens out there, let's work harder for a lot less violence and better aim. Thank you.

The Hall of Fame

Every sport has its Hall of Fame, that hallowed place where only the truly special reside. The jerseys hanging on their walls are rayon reminders of talent that soared above talented competition. Men and women whose feats were never matched by their peers are recognized as giants in their fields, and as a result deserve special recognition for the contributions they have made, and for so raising the standard of their chosen endeavors that they set new goals for all who came after them. The names Muhammad Ali, Jack Nicklaus, Billie Jean King, Michael Jordan, and Mickey Mantle define the term excellence and are synonymous with their sport. Their individual achievements were so profound that a special category needed to be created to honor them: the Hall of Fame.

I have decided to open a Restaurant Customer's Hall of Fame. After forty years in the business and much consideration, I believe there are individuals out there whose behavior rises to a level unprecedented in the annals of the human experiment. Performances that are so outrageous that special recognition is the only fair reward, granting them the attention that they so sorely crave. There are three requirements to gain entry into the Hall of Fame:

1. A contestant's performance had to rise to the level of appalling that leaves even the most cynical among us (me) utterly speechless, suppressing waves of nausea that can only be relieved through the use of medical marijuana.
2. A contestant must possess a Machiavellian lust to satisfy

his or her desires while exhibiting a wanton disregard for anyone or anything that may stand in the way of said satisfaction; not unlike a certain ex-governor of New York.

3. A contestant must raise the simple act of deceit to an art form, weaving lie upon lie into a blanket of bullshit that seduces the susceptible, cons the conniving, and usurps the unprepared, while observing a sense of entitlement combined with a profound dose of righteous indignation.

Any one of the previous requirements qualifies a contestant for *consideration* into the Hall of Fame; it does not guarantee entry. Each event is judged on a case-by-case basis and evaluated on the merits of the individual performance. Hall of Fame entry is bestowed by a jury of peers (me), reviewed by a distinguished panel (me), and voted on by the board of directors (me). No plastic statues or proclamations are given to the winners; entry is its own reward. I will be happy to provide proof of entry to any entrant who feels the need to display it proudly in their office or home. Send me your name and address, and I'm sure I will get plenty of volunteers willing to *deliver the goods*. Without further ado I announce (drum roll): the Hall of Fame.

SOPRANOS FAN

One Sunday afternoon, two women checked into the *Inn* for an overnight stay. It happened to be the Sunday when the last *Sopranos* episode was to air. The ladies were a couple and like most couples, one was dominant and one more passive, and just like with most men, the smaller of the two was the problem. She was kind of demanding in an entitled way and had no problem letting you know who was in charge. She handled the check-in. Her partner waited demurely in the wings and said nothing.

"We're here to check in," she said to Debbie, the reservations manager.

Debbie said, "Okay, we have you booked for the Sage room for one night. Will you be joining us for dinner tonight?"

The woman asked, "What time do you start serving dinner? We are planning to watch the ending of *The Sopranos* and I don't want to miss it."

Debbie said, "We have an opening for two at six if you would like that."

The lady then said, "*The Sopranos* starts at nine. That should give us enough time. I don't want to be rushed, but I do not want to miss any of the show. We have to be back in our room by 8:45."

Debbie said, "That shouldn't be a problem."

The woman said, "Are you sure, because I've been looking forward to this all week. I don't want to miss any of it."

Debbie said, "You'll be done in plenty of time. Don't worry; I'll take you to your room so you can relax before dinner."

Debbie gave the ladies a tour of the *Inn*, explaining the history, the amenities, things they could do on the North Fork, and then led them upstairs to their room.

Debbie said, "If there's anything at all you need, please don't hesitate to call the front desk." The woman thanked Debbie and the two women retired to their room.

Fifteen minutes later, this 5'1" ball of fury with slightly frizzy hair came ripping down the staircase, two stairs at a time. She was moving so fast, she took the corner a foot and a half up on the wall. She ran up to Debbie in the office and screamed, "You don't have HBO! I've tried every channel and you don't have fucking HBO!"

Debbie, taken by surprise, said, "I know. We can't get it for commercial use. Is that a problem?"

The woman said, "How am I supposed to watch *The Sopranos* with no HBO?"

Debbie said, "I don't know, but maybe calming down would be a good first step."

The woman said, "We're out of here. Find me another hotel," and ran back upstairs, presumably to pack. Debbie decided to go up to try to calm her down.

She knocked on the door.

"What!" the woman yells.

Debbie asked, "Can I talk to you for a minute?"

"Come in. What do you want," she said.

"I just want to see if there was anything I could do. I feel terrible."

"You should. I was lied to. I was told by someone on the phone that you have HBO."

This, of course, was not true because we never had HBO in the rooms, so why would anyone tell her that? It didn't really matter; the woman was way beyond the point of reason. She was slamming doors, throwing her clothes around, and talking herself into a full-blown tantrum. Her partner was locked in the bathroom.

Giving up, Debbie said, "I'll make some calls and see if I can find you a room with HBO."

The woman said, "No, you *will* find us a room with HBO."

Debbie went back downstairs to the office. She called three or four places and compiled a short list of rooms with HBO. The two women came back downstairs with their luggage and approached Debbie at the desk. As Debbie was telling them about their choices, the phone rang.

Debbie asked, "Will you excuse me a moment?"

The lady muttered under her breath, "I guess we'll have to, won't we?" Her partner looked like she was going to cry.

On the phone was a friend of Debbie's who was looking for one of the *Inn's* partners.

The friend said, "Hey Deb, is Jeff around?"

Debbie said, "No, but I can't talk now. I have a problem with one of the guests."

The friend asked, "How bad a problem? Should I hold?"

Debbie said, "No, they wanted to watch *The Sopranos* and we don't have HBO, so I'm trying to find them other accommodations."

The friend, thinking he was being funny said, "Hey, we're watching it tonight; tell them to come over here. Ha, ha, ha." Debbie, trying desperately to lighten the mood said to the women, "My friend says you can come over and watch it at his house."

To Debbie's horror, the woman looked at her and said, "Okay. I'll go over and watch it there, but I'm going to need a ride to and from. We came out on the Jitney and I don't have a car. And, I don't want to socialize or have to talk to anybody. I just want to watch the show and leave."

Debbie was speechless. Momentarily recovering she told her friend, "She just accepted your offer, but she doesn't want to have to talk to you. Is that okay?" Suddenly he couldn't talk either.

The woman said, "We're going back up to our room. Have a car in time to get us to his house at 8:45, so we're sure not to miss the beginning."

Back to the room they went. Debbie called her friend back and said, "I think they're really coming. She told me to get her there by 8:45."

Her friend Dave, who has a great sense of humor said, "What the hell, bring her over, it should make for quite a night." Debbie punched out at three and went home.

She returned at eight-thirty and the woman was waiting by herself in the parlor.

Debbie asked, "Are we waiting for your partner?"

The woman said, "No, she's too embarrassed to come."

Debbie said, "Okay, then let's go."

Off they went, like driving Miss Crazy. They got to the house by 8:45 and rang the bell. Dave answered the door said, "Hi," to Debbie, and while keeping a straight face, deadpanned, "Listen, I don't want to hear any talking when the show starts. There's no food or drinks being served and no bathroom breaks. Got it?" The woman, I swear to you, walked right past him into the living room, sat on the couch and said not one word. The friend's entire family, two daughters, a son, and his wife were all in the living room, as was Debbie, and not a word was spoken.

At the end of the show, the woman got up and walked out the door to Debbie's car without as much as a thank you. Debbie said she could hear her friend's family laughing all the way to the car. Debbie drove her back to the *Inn* and dropped her off. The woman got out of the car and went up to bed. No thanks, no nothing.

The next day, while they were checking out, Debbie asked them if they enjoyed their stay. The woman's partner said that she thought the *Inn* was, "quite lovely," and her dinner was "delicious." The woman looked at Debbie and said, "I thought the ending sucked."

Lack of Prozac

Here's the move, go to the restaurant an hour before your reservation time, and when your reservation is due, scream at the hostess that you have been waiting an hour for your reservation. (None of us have ever seen that one before.) In she walked at eight on a Saturday night. I'll be kind and call her "The Beast." She seemed ordinary enough. She had a nine o'clock reservation. There were about 150 people in the bar waiting to be seated. At approximately 9:02, The Beast walked up to the hostess stand. Let the games begin.

The Beast turned to the hostess and asked, "Is our table ready yet?"

The hostess said, "I'm sorry, it will be just a couple more minutes."

The Beast screamed (and I do know the difference between an elevated voice level and screaming), "I've been waiting an hour! This is bullshit! Who the fuck do you people think you are! Do you think you are some kind of Manhattan fucking restaurant! Nobody does this to me! Do you know who I am? I know Peter Giannotti! You're not going to do this to me. I don't care how many people you have waiting, I don't WAIT!"

Whoa. The hostess was dumbfounded and made a feeble attempt to calm her down. The hostess said, "Could you please calm down. We're very busy here and it won't be more than a minute or two and could you watch the language."

The Beast continued, "You people will be fucking sorry! I'm telling all my friends! Nobody will come here anymore! I'm going to fucking *close* you! Do you hear me? *Close* you!" And then in one final magnificent display of insanity, she took the reservation sheet off the hostess stand, ripped it to shreds, threw the pieces up in the air and said, "Fuck all of you!" She then turned around and walked out of the restaurant. Wow! I wonder if the attendants realized that she had escaped.

But it wasn't over. The Beast proceeded to another restaurant down the block, owned by a friend of mine. When she arrived, she announced to anyone who would listen, that she was just at *CoolFish* and the hostess was nasty and rude so she put her in her place, ripped up the reservation sheet, and left. This is just what a wait staff wants to hear.

My friend called me to confirm the story. All this is going on while we are trying to get through Saturday night service. I confirmed that yes, it was true.

He said, "What do you want me to do?"

I said, "Kill her."

He said, giggling, "I can't!"

I said, giggling, "Why not?"

He said, laughing, "I have a family and I can't afford to go to jail."

I said, laughing at that point myself, "It'd be worth it to me. Besides it would probably take the police at least three months to narrow the suspect list down to somewhere around fifteen hundred people. I don't think they'll figure it out."

By that time we were both howling. He said, "I love you, but I can't take the risk."

I said, "Okay, I understand. You're a *wuss*." Hey, I tried.

DEAD WRONG

A couple of years ago on New Year's Eve, in a very fine North Shore Restaurant, a waiter collapsed on the floor. The man had suffered a heart attack. It was horrible. The manager asked if there was a doctor in the house. There were twelve. The doctors were attending to the waiter as the manager called an ambulance, and it was chaos as you might well expect. The EMTs arrived and started treatment while preparing to rush the waiter to the hospital. One of the doctors accompanied the man in the ambulance in a touching display of the Hippocratic oath.

You can imagine the effect this sort of event will have on a New Year's Eve party. The employees were all worried about their co-worker and the diners were feeling terrible. After the ambulance left for the hospital, the manager was running around, trying as best he could to put out the "fires," rally the staff, and insure that the patrons were as back to normal as they could possibly be, considering what had happened.

Most people can identify with this poor waiter, his family, and the staff. Others see an opportunity. A man approached the manager and said, "Are you the manager?"

The manager said, "Yes, what can I do for you?"

The man said, "That's exactly what I wanted to talk to you about. What are you going to do for me?"

Confused, the manager said, "I don't understand what you mean."

The man then said, "I witnessed something here tonight that was very upsetting to both my wife and me."

The manager said, "Yes, I know. It was terrible. We are all just hoping he is going to be okay."

The man then said, and you may want to sit down for this, the words that got him into the Hall of Fame. "This is not what I had envisioned when I made my reservation, and it's certainly not how we planned to spend our New Year's Eve, so I think you should consider taking something off my bill."

The horrified manager said, "What!"

The man went on, "You heard me. I want something off the bill. The waiter dropped right in front of our table. My wife is upset and this is not how I planned to spend my New Year's Eve. It looked to me like he died."

The manager said, "If I take something off your bill and he survives, will you come back in and reimburse us?"

The man said, "Why would I do that," and returned to his table. The manager was so angry that he decided to try to embarrass the man, like that was even possible given what he'd just heard.

He walked up to the table, looked at the man, his wife, and their two guests and said, "Let me just make sure I have this right. You want me to discount your dinner check because the waiter had the gall to have a heart attack in front of your table, ruining *your* New Year's Eve. Have I got that right?" All three of the other guests looked at him and said, "HAARRRYYY!!"

I think we owe it to all the Harry's out there, and hopefully there aren't too many, to set up some rules for discounting restaurant checks so that we can all be consistent, and a poor soul like Harry doesn't have to humiliate himself at the expense of a comatose server. Here's what I propose, and I do welcome input from my restaurant brethren:

Forgetting your drink order or somehow screwing up the cocktails: I think a ten percent discount is fair.

If your entrée is late coming to the table, cold, cooked wrong, or otherwise inedible: I think a twenty percent discount should do the trick.

But if your waiter faints, goes into a coma, or has the *audacity* to die at your table, I don't think anything under a seventy-five percent discount could makeup for the inconvenience.

I'm as dumbfounded now as I was when I first heard the story. The rest of the details are somewhat foggy, but I believe the waiter survived. Every time you think you've heard it all, someone reaches deep down inside and comes up with something so bizarre it just can't go unrecognized.

A Rather Strange
Point of View

This story was told to me by an amateur cook and restaurant worker. He was a fan of my magazine articles and wrote me a letter to relate what happened. It was too good not to get into the Hall of Fame.

A friend of the man who told me this story was in charge of catering at a popular restaurant in Brooklyn. In the early summer of 2000, he had booked a wedding to be held in December 2001. They settled on a price and made the contract. The woman who booked the party was to come back two months before the wedding to firm up the menu and attend to any last minute details or requests.

She came in the weekend after September 11th and told the receptionist that she had an appointment with the manager. The manager took her into the office and asked if she had chosen her menu and if she had decided on a choice of appetizers and the cake filling. She told him that she had and gave him her selections. He dutifully wrote them in the contract and was about to wind up their appointment when she said, "We have to talk about one other little detail."

The manager said, "Sure, what is it?"

She said, "I think we have to renegotiate my contract."

The manager asked, "How come? I thought everything was settled."

The woman, "Well, it was but there's a little problem that has since come up, and I think you're going to have to lower the original price."

The manager asked, "Why would I do that?"

She said, "Because, obviously, the view has changed, and the

401

view is the main reason we chose to have our wedding here. With the towers gone, it's not as dramatic as it once was."

To credit the manager, who is French with a Frenchman's temper, he told her to get lost, as in *excuse my French*. I think that pretty much says it all. There's no sense in letting three thousand dead people and a couple of buildings get in the way of a discount, now is there?

We Come Here
Religiously

Matt Hisiger of *Panama Hatties* called me as I was writing this book to tell me this doosey. Matt got an e-mail from a guest on a Monday night, and it went pretty much like this. (They all start the same way.)

"I am one of your best and most loyal customers. (As soon as I hear that, I'm also pretty sure they have eaten all over the world.) In fact, *Panama Hatties* is my favorite restaurant, and we've eaten all over the world. (See, I told you.) But I'm afraid we will never come back again. Last night we attempted to eat at your establishment, and it was a total disaster. We waited twenty minutes in the front dining room before a hostess came to greet us. When she finally sat us, we waited an additional half hour for a waitress to come to our table.

Finally out of frustration, we flagged a waitress down. She informed us, quite rudely, that she was not our waitress but she would find out who was. Twenty more minutes passed before our real waitress arrived and took our drink orders. When she brought the drinks to us, both of them were wrong and had to be reordered. She then took our food order, and we waited another half hour before our appetizers came out, one of which was ice cold.

We sent my wife's appetizer back to be reheated, but our server didn't have the brains to keep mine warm while they were heating hers, so we had to send them both back to be reheated again. Then the entrées came out and we wished they hadn't. Both were terrible so we sent them back and changed our order. Running true to form, our second entrées took an excruciatingly long time to come out. They were terrible also, but we were so hungry, we ate them anyway.

Dessert was as horrible as the rest of the meal. At that point, we just wanted to leave, so we asked for a doggie bag and paid our check. Just when we thought this miserable evening was over, we discovered, to our mutual disgust, that the food in the doggie bag was not ours. I was sick. I'm informing you of these problems so you can correct them, although we'll try you again if you are willing to compensate us for our trouble."

It always floors me when people say they have had the most horrid experience in your restaurant, and then start talking about coming back for more, but at a somewhat reduced rate. At this point I would be wondering how *Panama Hatties* got fifteen stars from the *New York Times*, but I know better.

Let's continue. Matt e-mails him back to say that because of the late hour, he will call him the following day. Everyone goes to sleep. The next day, Matt called but got the man's wife instead. He said that he was terribly sorry for what happened and could she please explain it again so he could fully understand what he needed to correct. The wife went through the whole litany again, word for painful word, about the hostess, the waitress, the appetizers, the entrées, (all four of them), the desserts, and the doggie bag. And she thought the least he could do was to buy her and her husband dinner.

Matt, now smiling, said, "You were here Sunday night, correct?"

She said, "Yes."

Matt said, "Boy, that must have been a dreadful experience."

The woman said, "The worst I've had in a restaurant, and I've eaten all over the world."

Matt, looking at the number seven button on the microwave, said, "I've been at this a long time, and obviously we did nothing to live up to our reputation. When things like this happen, we like to invite the guests back to have dinner on us, to show them it was an aberration."

The woman, "Well, that's the least you can do for that terrible performance of your staff on Sunday night."

Matt, smiling broadly, asked again, "Are you sure it was Sunday night?"

The woman, "I'm positive. It was Sunday night, the day before yesterday, seven-thirty at *Panama Hatties*. Can I be any clearer?"

Matt said, "That's funny, we were closed Sunday night for Passover." Click.

About the Author

Born in Queens, NY and raised on Long Island, Tom began his career as a dishwasher at the age of fifteen, and continued to cook in various restaurants throughout high school. That fall, he enrolled in the *Culinary Institute of America*, graduating in 1973, and after six years of working insane hours, in numerous restaurants, under various chefs, Tom landed his first head position in 1979.

Four years later, with the help of two friends, he opened his first restaurant, *Panama Hatties*. Tom has been the driving force behind numerous restaurants on Long Island.

Writing this book has been an awful lot of fun for me in spite of being the most difficult challenge I've ever undertaken. Dealing with difficult customers is "way easier" than writing about them. As I said before, they make up a miniscule part of my customer base, but I can't imagine how much time and effort it would take to write about all the wonderful people I've met and the friends I've made through my restaurants during the course of the last forty years. All I can do is say a very humble and sincere thank you to all the great people of Long Island and beyond who continue to make it such a great place to work and live. I promise to continue to feed you to the best of my ability and to keep a sharp eye on my dining rooms. Who knows what's next? Sometimes you just have to have a SECOND HELPING.

PLAYING WITH FIRE

For more information regarding Tom Schaudel
and his work, visit his Web site: www.tomschaudel.com.

Further copies of this book may be purchased online,
via the author's Web site, www.tomschaudel.com;
LegworkTeam.com; Amazon.com;
BarnesandNoble.com; or Borders.com.

You can also obtain a copy by ordering it
from your favorite bookstore.

Contrary to the stories in this book, if you really want to
experience a great meal served at one of Tom's restaurants,
select a location listed below to begin your adventure.

a Mano Osteria & Wine Bar
13550 Main Road, Mattituck, NY 11952

CoolFish Grille & Wine Bar
6800 Jericho Turnpike, Syosset, NY 11791

Jedediah Hawkins Inn
400 South Jamesport Avenue, Jamesport, NY 11947

Gabrielle's Brasserie & Wine Bar
22 North Park Avenue, Rockville Centre, NY 11570